Bounds on Prayer & Spiritual Warfare

Bounds on Prayer & Spiritual Warfare

E. M. BOUNDS

Whitaker House

Unless otherwise indicated, all Scripture quotations are taken from the *King James Version Easy Read Bible*, KJVER®, © 2001, 2007, 2010, 2015 by Whitaker House. Used by permission. All rights reserved. Unless otherwise indicated, all Scripture quotations are taken from the King James Version (KJV) of the Holy Bible. Unless otherwise indicated, Scripture quotations are taken from the *New King James Version* (NKJV), © 1979, 1980, 1982, 1984 by Thomas Nelson, Inc. Used by permission. Scripture quotations marked (RV) are taken from the *Revised Version* of the Holy Bible.

Publisher's note:
The text of this new book from Whitaker House has been updated for the modern reader. Words, expressions, and sentence structure have been revised for clarity and readability. The author's selection of Bible versions has been retained whenever possible, including the *Revised Version* when it was originally cited.

BOUNDS ON PRAYER & SPIRITUAL WARFARE
Five Books in One

ISBN: 979-8-88769-387-3
eBook ISBN: 979-8-88769-388-0
Printed in the United States of America
© 2025 by Whitaker House

Titles included in this anthology:
The Reality of Prayer
ISBN: 978-1-60374-557-4
© 2000 by Whitaker House

Equipped: The Weapon of Prayer
ISBN: 978-1-64123-025-4
© 1996, 2018 by Whitaker House

Power Through Prayer
ISBN: 978-0-88368-811-3
© 1982 by Whitaker House

Prayer and Spiritual Warfare
ISBN: 978-0-88368-361-3
© 1984 by Whitaker House

Guide to Spiritual Warfare
ISBN: 978-0-88368-643-0
© 1984 by Whitaker House

Whitaker House
1030 Hunt Valley Circle
New Kensington, PA 15068
www.whitakerhouse.com

Library of Congress Control Number: 2025933944

No part of this book may be reproduced or transmitted in any form or by any means, electronic or mechanical—including photocopying, recording, or by any information storage and retrieval system—without permission in writing from the publisher. Please direct your inquiries to permissionseditor@whitakerhouse.com.

1 2 3 4 5 6 7 8 9 10 11 ⨄ 32 31 30 29 28 27 26 25

CONTENTS

BOOK ONE: *THE REALITY OF PRAYER*

1. A Sacred Privilege 11
2. Man's Poverty and God's Riches 18
3. The Essence of Earthly Worship 25
4. God's Part in Prayer 30
5. The Divine Teacher of Prayer 39
6. The Lesson of Prayer 47
7. Jesus, Our Example in Prayer 56
8. Insights from Prayers of Our Lord 64
9. Learning from the Prayers of Jesus 70
10. Our Lord's Model Prayer 78
11. Our Lord's High Priestly Prayer 82
12. The Gethsemane Prayer 89
13. The Holy Spirit and Prayer 97
14. The Holy Spirit, Our Helper in Prayer 105

15. The Two Comforters and Two Advocates 113

16. Prayer and the Holy Spirit Dispensation...................................... 117

BOOK TWO: *EQUIPPED: THE WEAPON OF PRAYER*

1. Why Prayer is Important to God 125

2. Putting God to Work 134

3. The Necessity for Praying People.. 146

4. God's Need for People Who Pray.. 153

5. Prayerless Christians 159

6. Praying for Others 166

7. Preachers and Prayer 173

8. Prayerlessness in the Pulpit.. 185

9. Equipped by Prayer 194

10. The Preacher's Cry: "Pray for Us!"..204

11. Modern Examples of Prayer 212

12. More Modern Examples of Prayer...224

BOOK THREE: *POWER THROUGH PRAYER*

1. The Divine Channel of Power 237

2. Our Sufficiency Is of God 242

3. Man's Most Noble Exercise 246

4. Talking to God for Men.. 250

5. How to Get Results for God 254

6. Great Men of Prayer 258

7. "Early Will I Seek Thee" 266

8. The Secret of Power 269

9. Power through Prayers 276

10. Under the Dew of Heaven 281

11. The Example of the Apostles 289

12. What God Would Have 291

BOOK FOUR: *PRAYER AND SPIRITUAL WARFARE*

1. Prayer and Faith 305

2. Prayer That Gets Results 312

3. Prayer and Trusting God 321

4. Prayer and Desire 328

5. Prayer and Enthusiasm... 336

6. Prayer That Is Persistent 341

7. Prayer That Motivates God 347

8. Prayer and Christian Conduct 353

9. Prayer and Obedience... 360

10. Prayer and Full Surrender... 368

11. Prayer and Spiritual Warfare 373

12. Prayer and God's Promises 380

13. Prayer and the Word of God 387

14. Prayer and the House of God.................................... 392

BOOK FIVE: *GUIDE TO SPIRITUAL WARFARE*

Foreword.. 399

1. Who Is the Invisible Enemy?.................................... 401

2. Identifying the Devil's Personality............................ 406

3. Recognizing the Prince of This World 415

4. What Is the Devil's Business?.................................... 418

5. Satan's Main Target 425

6. Satan's Subversion of the Church............................. 433

7. Overcoming the Enemy of God................................ 441

8. Satan's Mobilizing of the World's Forces 448

9. How Powerful Is the Devil? 453

10. Exposing the Rulers of Darkness 459

11. The Devil's Battleground 465

12. Satan's Clever Strategies 472

13. Our Most Vulnerable Areas 477

14. Where Does Satan Attack? 487

15. Using Our Defenses 496

16. Weapons That Work 504

About the Author 511

BOOK ONE:

THE REALITY OF PRAYER

ONE:

A SACRED PRIVILEGE

I am the creature of a day, passing through life as an arrow through the air. I am a spirit come from God and returning to God, just hovering over the great gulf, until a few moments hence I am seen no more; I drop into an unchangeable eternity! I want to know one thing: the way to heaven—how to land safe on that happy shore. God Himself has condescended to teach the way; for this end He came from heaven. He has written it down in a book. O give me that book! At any price, give me the Book of God! Lord, is it not Your word, *"If any of you lacks wisdom, let him ask of God, who gives to all liberally and without reproach, and it will be given to him"* (James 1:5)? You give liberally, and do not rebuke. You have said, if any are willing to do Your will, he will know it. I am willing to do; let me know Your will.
— John Wesley

The word *prayer* expresses the largest and most comprehensive approach to God. It gives prominence to the element of devotion. It is communion and communication with God. It is enjoyment of God and access to God.

SUPPLICATION

Supplication is a more restricted and more intense form of prayer, accompanied by a sense of personal need and limited to the urgent seeking of an answer to a pressing need. Supplication is the very soul of prayer in regard to an intense pleading for something that is greatly needed.

INTERCESSION

Intercession is an enlargement in prayer, a going out in broadness and fullness from self to others. Primarily, it does not center on praying for others, but refers to the freeness, boldness, and childlike confidence of the praying. It is characterized by a complete comfort in the soul's approach to God, unlimited and unhesitating in its access and its demands. This influence and confident trust is to be used for others.

CONFIDING IN THE FATHER

Prayer always, and everywhere, is an immediate confiding approach to, and a request of, God the Father. In the universal and perfect prayer, we see the pattern for all praying: *"Our Father in heaven"* (Matthew 6:9). At the grave of Lazarus, Jesus lifted up His eyes and said, *"Father"* (John 11:41). In His High Priestly Prayer, Jesus again lifted up His eyes to heaven and said, *"Father"* (John 17:1). His praying was personal, familiar, and paternal. It was also strong, touching, and tearful. Read these words of Paul written about Jesus:

> *Who, in the days of His flesh, when He had offered up prayers and supplications, with vehement cries and tears to Him who was able to save Him from death, and was heard because of His godly fear, though He was a Son, yet He learned obedience by the things which He suffered.* (Hebrews 5:7–8)

ASKING

In addition, we have asking set forth as prayer: *"If any of you lacks wisdom, let him ask of God, who gives to all liberally and without reproach, and it will be given to him"* (James 1:5). Asking God and receiving from the

Lord—direct application to God, immediate connection with God—that is prayer. In 1 John 5:14–15, we have this statement about prayer:

> *Now this is the confidence that we have in Him, that if we ask anything according to His will, He hears us. And if we know that He hears us, whatever we ask, we know that we have the petitions that we have asked of Him.*

In Philippians 4:6 we find these words about prayer: *"Be anxious for nothing, but in everything by prayer and supplication, with thanksgiving, let your requests be made known to God."*

WHAT IS GOD'S WILL ABOUT PRAYER?

First, it is God's will that we pray. Jesus Christ *"spoke a parable to them, that men always ought to pray and not lose heart"* (Luke 18:1). Paul wrote to young Timothy about the things that God's people are to do, and first among them, he listed prayer: *"I exhort first of all that supplications, prayers, intercessions, and giving of thanks be made for all men"* (1 Timothy 2:1).

In connection with these words Paul declared that the will of God and the redemption and mediation of Jesus Christ for the salvation of all men are all vitally concerned in this matter of prayer. His apostolic authority and solicitude of soul act in harmony with God's will and Christ's intercession to will that *"men pray everywhere"* (v. 8).

Note how frequently prayer is brought forward in the New Testament: *"Continuing steadfastly in prayer"* (Romans 12:12). *"Pray without ceasing"* (1 Thessalonians 5:17). *"Continue earnestly in prayer, being vigilant in it with thanksgiving"* (Colossians 4:2). *"Be serious and watchful in your prayers"* (1 Peter 4:7). Christ's clarion call was *"watch and pray"* (Matthew 26:41). What significance do these verses and others have if it is not the will of God that men should pray?

Prayer complements, makes efficient, and cooperates with God's will, whose sovereign sway is to run parallel in extent and power with the atonement of Jesus Christ. Christ, through the eternal Spirit, by the grace of God, *"taste[d] death for everyone"* (Hebrews 2:9). We, through the eternal Spirit, by the grace of God, pray for every man.

HOW CAN WE KNOW THAT WE ARE PRAYING IN THE WILL OF GOD?

Every true attempt to pray is in response to the will of God. Prayer may be awkward and inarticulate, but it is acceptable to God, because it is offered in obedience to His will. If I will give myself up to the inspiration of the Spirit of God, who commands me to pray, the details and the petitions of that praying will all fall into harmony with the will of Him who wills that I should pray.

WHAT CAN PRAYER ACCOMPLISH

Prayer is no little thing, no selfish and small matter. It does not concern the petty interests of the person. The littlest prayer expands by the will of God until it touches all words, conserves all interests, and enhances man's greatest wealth and God's greatest good. God is so concerned that men pray that He has promised to answer prayer. He has not promised to do something general if we pray, but He has promised to do the very thing for which we pray.

Prayer, as taught by Jesus in its essential features, enters into all the relations of life. It sanctifies brotherliness. To the Jew, the altar was the symbol and place of prayer. The Jew devoted the altar to the worship of God. Jesus Christ takes the altar of prayer and devotes it to the honor of the brotherhood. How Christ purifies the altar and enlarges it! How He takes it out of the sphere of a mere performance and makes its virtue to consist, not in the mere act of praying, but in the spirit that inspires good actions toward men. Our spirit toward others is affected by a life of prayer. We must be at peace with men (see Romans 12:18), and, if possible, have them at peace with us, before we can be at peace with God. Reconciliation with men is the forerunner of reconciliation with God. (See Matthew 5:22–24.) Our spirit and words must embrace men before they can embrace God. Unity with the brotherhood goes before unity with God.

Therefore if you bring your gift to the altar, and there remember that your brother has something against you, leave your gift there before the altar, and go your way. First be reconciled to your brother, and then come and offer your gift. (Matthew 5:23–24)

Not praying results in lawlessness, discord, and anarchy. Prayer, in the moral government of God, is as strong and far-reaching as the law of gravitation in the material world, and it is as necessary as gravitation to hold things in their proper sphere and in life.

WHAT IS THE VALUE OF PRAYER

The space occupied by prayer in the Sermon on the Mount indicates its value to Christ and the importance it holds in His system. Many important principles are discussed in a few verses. The Sermon consists of one hundred and eleven verses, and eighteen are about prayer directly, and others indirectly.

Prayer was one of the chief principles of piety in every dispensation and to every child of God. It did not pertain to the business of Christ to originate duties, but to recover, recast, spiritualize, and reinforce those duties that are essential and original.

With Moses, the great features of prayer were prominent. He never beat the air or fought a false battle. The most serious and strenuous business of his serious and strenuous life was prayer. He prayed often and with intense earnestness of his soul. Intimate as he was with God, his intimacy did not lessen the necessity of prayer. This intimacy only brought clearer insight into the nature and necessity of prayer. It led him to see the greater obligations to pray, and to discover the larger results of praying. In reviewing one of the crises through which Israel passed, when the very existence of the nation was endangered, he wrote: *"I prostrated myself before the Lord; forty days and forty nights I kept prostrating myself"* (Deuteronomy 9:25). Wonderful praying brought wonderful results! Moses knew how to do wonderful praying, and God knew how to give wonderful results.

CAN PRAYER CHANGE GOD'S MIND?

The collective force of the truths in the Bible are to increase our faith in the doctrine that prayer affects God. It secures favors from God that can be secured in no other way, and which will not be bestowed by God if we do not pray. The whole canon of Bible teaching is to illustrate the great truth that God hears and answers prayer. One of the great purposes of

God in His book is to impress upon us indelibly the great importance, the priceless value, and the absolute necessity of asking God for the things that we need. He urges us by every consideration and presses and warns us by every interest. He points us to His own Son as His pledge that prayer will be answered. He teaches us that God is our Father, able to do all things for us and to give all things to us, much more than earthly parents can do or are willing to do for their children. (See Matthew 7:11; Luke 11:13.)

HOW CAN WE PRAY WELL?

Let us thoroughly understand ourselves and this great business of prayer. Our one great business is prayer, and we will never do it well unless we fasten to it all binding force and arrange the best conditions for doing it well. Satan has suffered so much from good praying that all his wily, shrewd, and ensnaring devices will be used to cripple its performance. We must, by all means, securely attach ourselves to prayer. To be careless in setting a time and place of prayer is to open the door to Satan. To be exact, prompt, unswerving, and careful in even the little things is to buttress ourselves against the Evil One.

PRAYER ADVANCES GOD'S CAUSE

Prayer, by God's own oath (see Isaiah 56:7), is put in the stones of God's foundations, as eternal as its companion, *"Men always ought to pray"* (Luke 18:1). This is the eternal condition that advances His cause and makes it powerfully aggressive. Men are always to pray for the advance of God's plan. Its strength, beauty, and aggression lie in their prayers. Its power lies simply in the Christian's power to pray. No power is found elsewhere but in the ability to pray. *"My house shall be called a house of prayer for all nations"* (Isaiah 56:7). The advance of His kingdom is based on prayer and carried on by the same means.

PRAYER IS MORE THAN A PRIVILEGE

Prayer is a privilege, a sacred, princely privilege. Prayer is a duty, an obligation most binding and most imperative, which should hold us to it. But prayer is more than a privilege, more than a duty. It is a means, an instrument, a condition. Not to pray is to lose much more than to fail in the exercise and enjoyment of a high, sweet privilege. Not to pray is to fail along lines far more important than even the violation of an obligation.

PRAYER ACCESSES GOD'S HELP

Prayer is the appointed condition of receiving God's aid. This aid is as manifold and infinite as God's ability; it is as varied and inexhaustible as man's need. Prayer is the avenue through which God supplies man's needs. Prayer is the channel through which all good flows from God to man, and from men to men. God is the Christian's Father. Asking and giving are found in that relationship.

PRAYER ENNOBLES THE ONE WHO PRAYS

Man is the one more immediately concerned in this great work of praying. It ennobles man's reason to employ it in prayer. The office and work of prayer is the divinest engagement of man's reason. Prayer makes man's reason to shine. Intelligence of the highest order approves prayer. He is the wisest man who prays the most and the best. Prayer is the school of wisdom as well as of piety.

Prayer is not a picture to handle, to admire, to look at. It is not beauty, coloring, shape, attitude, imagination, or genius. These things do not pertain to its character or conduct. It is not poetry or music. Its inspiration and melody come from heaven. Prayer belongs to the spirit, and at times it possesses the spirit and stirs the spirit with high and holy purposes and resolves.

TWO:

MAN'S POVERTY AND GOD'S RICHES

For two hours I struggled on, forsaken of God, and met neither God nor man, all one chilly afternoon. When at last, standing still and looking at Schiehallion[1] clothed in white from top to bottom, these words of David shot up into my heart: *"Wash me, and I shall be whiter than snow"* (Psalm 51:7). In a moment I was with God, or rather God was with me. I walked home with my heart in a flame of fire.
—Alexander Whyte

We have much fine writing and learned talk about the subjective benefits of prayer—how prayer secures its full measure of results, not by affecting God, but by affecting us, by becoming a training school for those who pray. We are taught by such teachers that the province of prayer is not to get, but to train. Prayer thus becomes a mere performance, a drill sergeant, a school in which patience, tranquility, and dependence are taught. In this school, denial of petitions is the most valuable teacher. However well all

---

1. Schiehallion, with an elevation of 3,553 feet, is a mountain in Central Scotland.

this may look, and however reasonable it may seem, there is nothing of it in the Bible. The clear and often repeated language of the Bible is that prayer is to be answered by God, that God occupies the relation of a father to us, and that as our Father He gives to us the things for which we ask. The best praying, therefore, is the praying that receives an answer.

THE SIGNIFICANCE OF PRAYER

The possibilities and necessity of prayer are carved on the eternal foundations of the Gospel. The relationship that is established between the Father and the Son and the decreed covenant between the two, have prayer as the base of their existence. Prayer is the condition of the advance and success of the Gospel. Prayer is the condition by which all foes are to be overcome and all the inheritance is to be possessed.

These are self-evident truths, though they may be very familiar ones. But these are the times when biblical principles need to be stressed, pressed, and reiterated. The very air is rife with influences, practices, and theories that sap foundations, and the most veritable truths and the most self-evident axioms go down by insidious and invisible attacks.

THE WORK OF PRAYER

Additionally, the tendency of these times is to an ostentatious parade of doing what enfeebles the life and dissipates the spirit of praying. There may be kneeling, and there may be standing in prayerful attitude. There may be much bowing of the head, and yet there may be no serious, real praying. Prayer is real work. Praying is vital work. Prayer has in its keeping the very heart of worship. There may be the exhibit, the circumstance, and the pomp of praying, and yet no real praying. There may be much attitude, gesture, and verbiage, but no praying.

THE SCHOOL OF PRAYER

Who can come into God's presence in prayer? Who can come before the great God, *"Maker of all things"* (Jeremiah 10:16), *"the God and Father of our Lord Jesus Christ"* (Colossians 1:3), who holds in His hands all good, and who is all-powerful and able to do all things? For man to approach this great God, what lowliness, truth, cleanness of hands, and purity of heart are needed and demanded!

Throughout the Bible, we are impressed that it is more important and urgent that men pray than that they be skilled in the sermonizing teachings about prayer. (See, for example, Matthew 6:6–7; Luke 18:10–14.) Prayer is a thing of the heart, not of the schools. It is more about feeling than about words. Praying is the best school in which to learn to pray; prayer is the best dictionary to define the art and nature of praying.

I repeat: Prayer is not a mere habit, riveted by custom and memory, something that must be gone through with, its value depending upon the decency and perfection of the performance. Prayer is not a duty that must be performed to ease obligation and to quiet conscience. Prayer is not a mere privilege, a sacred indulgence to be taken advantage of at leisure, at pleasure, or at will, with no serious loss attending its omission.

THE RESULTS OF PRAYER

Prayer is a solemn service due to God, an adoration, a worship, an approach to God for some request, the presenting of some desire, the expression of some need to Him, who supplies all need, and who satisfies all desires; who, as a Father, finds His greatest pleasure in relieving the needs and granting the desires of His children. Prayer is the child's request, not to the winds or to the world, but to the Father. Prayer is the outstretched arms of the child for the Father's help. Prayer is the child's cry calling to the Father's ear, the Father's heart, and the Father's ability. Prayer is the cry that the Father is to hear, the Father is to feel, and the Father is to relieve. Prayer is the seeking of God's great and greatest good that will not come if we do not pray.

Prayer is an ardent and believing cry to God for some specific thing. God's rule is to answer by giving the specific thing asked for. With it may come much of other gifts and graces. Strength, serenity, sweetness, and faith may come as the bearers of the gifts. But even they come because God hears and answers prayer.

We are following the plain letter and spirit of the Bible when we affirm that God answers prayer, and answers by giving us the very things we desire, and that the withholding of what we desire and the giving of something else is not the rule, but rare and exceptional. When His children cry for bread, He gives them bread. (See Matthew 7:9–11; Luke 11:3, 11–13.)

THE DEFINITION OF PRAYER

Revelation does not deal in philosophical subtleties, verbal niceties, or hairsplitting distinctions. It unfolds relationships, declares principles, and enforces duties. The heart must define; the experience must realize. Paul came on the stage too late to define prayer. What had been so well done by patriarchs and prophets needed no return to dictionaries. Christ is Himself the illustration and definition of prayer. He prayed as man had never prayed. He put prayer on a higher basis, with grander results and simpler being than it had ever known. He taught Paul how to pray by the revelation of Himself, which is the first call to prayer, and the first lesson in praying. Prayer, like love, is too ethereal and too heavenly to be held in the coarse arms of cold definitions. It belongs to heaven, and to the heart, not to words and ideas only.

Prayer is no petty invention of man, a contrived relief for imagined ills. Prayer is no dreary performance, dead and death-dealing, but is God's enabling act for man, living and life-giving, joy and joy-giving. Prayer is the contact of a living soul with God. In prayer, God stoops to kiss man, to bless man, and to assist man in everything that God can devise or man can need. Prayer fills man's emptiness with God's fullness. It fills man's poverty with God's riches. It replaces man's weakness with God's strength. It banishes man's littleness with God's greatness. Prayer is God's plan to supply man's great and continuous need with God's great and continuous abundance.

THE POWER OF PRAYER

What is this prayer to which men are called? It is not a mere form, a child's play. It is serious, difficult work, the manliest, the mightiest, the most divine work that man can do. Prayer lifts men out of the earthly and links them with the heavenly. Men are never nearer heaven, nearer God, never more Godlike, never in deeper sympathy and truer partnership with

Jesus Christ, than when praying. Love, philanthropy, holy confidences—all of them helpful and tender for men—are born and perfected by prayer.

Prayer is not merely a question of duty, but of salvation. Are men saved who are not men of prayer? Is not the gift, the inclination, the habit of prayer one of the elements or characteristics of salvation? Can it be possible to be in affinity with Jesus Christ and not be prayerful? Is it possible to have the Holy Spirit and not have the spirit of prayer? Can one have the new birth and not be born to prayer? Are not the life of the Spirit and the life of prayer coordinate and consistent? Can brotherly love be in the heart that is unschooled in prayer?

THE FORMS OF PRAYER

We have two kinds of prayer named in the New Testament: prayer and supplication. Prayer denotes prayer in general. Supplication is a more intense and special form of prayer. These two should be combined. Then we would have devotion in its widest and sweetest form, and supplication with its most earnest and personal sense of need.

In Paul's Prayer Directory, found in the sixth chapter of Ephesians, we are taught to be always in prayer, as we are always in the battle. (See verses 10–18.) The Holy Spirit is to be sought by intense supplication, and our supplications are to be charged by His vitalizing, illuminating, and ennobling energy. Watchfulness is to fit us for this intense praying and intense fighting. Perseverance is an essential element in successful praying, as in every other realm of conflict. The saints universal are to be helped on to victory by the aid of our prayers. Apostolic courage, ability, and success are to be gained by the prayers of the soldier-saints everywhere.

THE INTELLIGENCE OF PRAYER

It is only those of deep and true vision who can administer prayer. In Revelation 4:6, 8, the *"living creatures"* are described as *"full of eyes in front and in back"* and *"full of eyes around and within."* Eyes are for seeing. Clearness, intensity, and perfection of sight are in prayer. Vigilance and profound insight are in it, the faculty of knowing. It is by prayer that the eyes of our hearts are opened. (See Ephesians 1:15–19.) Clear, profound knowledge of the mysteries of grace is secured by prayer. These *"living creatures"* had eyes *"around and within."* They were *"full of eyes."* The highest form of life is intelligent. Ignorance is degrading and low, in the spiritual realm as it is in other realms. Prayer gives us eyes to see God. Prayer is seeing God. The prayer life is knowledge without and within. All vigilance without, all vigilance within. There can be no intelligent prayer without knowledge within. Our inner condition and our inner needs must be felt and known.

It takes prayer to minister. It takes the highest form of life to minister. Prayer is the highest intelligence; the profoundest wisdom; the most vital, the most joyous, the most efficacious, the most powerful of all vocations. It is life, radiant, transporting, eternal life. Away with dry forms, with dead, cold habits of prayer! Away with sterile routine and with senseless performances in prayer! Let us get at the serious work, the chief business, of men, that of prayer. Let us work at it skillfully. Let us seek to be adept in this great work of praying. Let us be master workmen in this high art of praying. Let us be in the habit of prayer, so devoted to prayer, so filled with its rich spices, so ardent by its holy flame, that all heaven and earth will be perfumed by its aroma, and nations will be blessed by our prayers. Heaven will be fuller and brighter in glorious inhabitants, earth will be better prepared for its bridal day, and hell robbed of many of its victims, because we have lived to pray.

THE STANDARD OF PRAYER

There is not only a sad and ruinous neglect of any attempt to pray, but also an immense waste in the apparent praying that is done, such as formal prayers or repetitive prayers. Men cleave to the form and semblance of a thing after the heart and reality have gone out of it. This truth finds illustrations in many who seem to pray. Formal praying has a strong hold and a strong following.

For example, Eli thought that Hannah was not really praying because he saw her lips moving but could not hear any sound (1 Samuel 1:12–13). He urged her, *"Put your wine away!"* (v. 14). He thought she was guilty of hypocrisy. Her prayer, though, was sincere, and she answered Eli's accusations by saying, *"I have drunk neither wine nor intoxicating drink, but have poured out my soul before the Lord"* (v. 15). God's serious promise to the Jews was, *"Then you will call upon Me and go and pray to Me, and I will listen to you. And you will seek Me and find Me, when you search for Me with all your heart"* (Jeremiah 29:12–13).

Let all present-day praying be measured by these standards: pouring out our souls before God and seeking Him with all our hearts. How much prayer will be found to be mere form, waste, and worthless in light of these standards? James said of Elijah that he *"prayed earnestly"* (James 5:17).

In Paul's directions to Timothy about prayer (1 Timothy 2:1–2), we have a comprehensive description of prayer in its different types or manifestations. They are all in the plural form: *"supplications, prayers, intercessions"* (v. 1). They reveal the many-sidedness, the endless diversity, and the necessity of going beyond the formal simplicity of a single prayer. They show the need to deliberately add prayer upon prayer, supplication to supplication, and intercession to intercession, until the combined force of prayers in their most excellent forms unite their power to our praying. Unlimited excellence and continuous accumulation of prayer in its various forms are the only measures of prayer. The term *prayer* is the common and comprehensive description for the act, the duty, the spirit, and the service of our various interactions with God. It is our condensed word for worship. The element of prayer is not as conspicuous in heavenly worship; prayer is the conspicuous, all-important essence, and all-coloring ingredient of earthly worship, while praise is the preeminent, comprehensive, all-coloring, and all-inspiring element of heavenly worship.

> *Then you will call upon Me and go and pray to Me, and I will listen to you. And you will seek Me and find Me, when you search for Me with all your heart.* —Jeremiah 29:12–13

> *Be anxious for nothing, but in everything by prayer and supplication, with thanksgiving, let your requests be made known to God.* —Philippians 4:6

THREE:

THE ESSENCE OF EARTHLY WORSHIP

> Where the spiritual consciousness is concerned— the department that asks the question and demands the evidence—no evidence is competent or relevant except such as is spiritual. Only that which is above matter and above logic can be heard, because the very question at issue is the existence and personality of a spiritual and supernatural God. Only *the Spirit Himself bears witness with our spirit*" (Romans 8:16). This must be done in a spiritual or supernatural way, or it cannot be done at all. —C. L. Chilton

The Jewish law and the prophets knew something of God as a Father. They had comforting glimpses, although occasional and imperfect, of the great truth of God's Fatherhood and our sonship. Christ lays the foundation of prayer deep and strong with this basic principle: the law of prayer, the right to pray, rests on sonship. Saying *Our Father*" (Matthew 6:9) brings us into the closest relationship to God. Prayer is the child's approach, the child's plea, the child's right. The law of prayer involves looking up; we must lift our eyes to *"our Father in heaven"* (v. 9). Our Father's house is our home in heaven. Both heavenly citizenship and heavenly homesickness are found in prayer. Prayer is an appeal from the lowness, the emptiness, the need of earth to the highness, the fullness, and the all-sufficiency of heaven. Prayer turns the eye and the heart heavenward with a child's longings, a child's trust, and a child's expectancy. To hallow God's name, to speak it with bated breath, to hold it sacredly—this also belongs to prayer.

THE WAY TO SALVATION

It is requisite to dictate to children the necessity of prayer in order to secure their salvation. Unhappily, it is thought sufficient to tell them there is a heaven and a hell, that they must avoid the latter place and seek to reach the former. Yet they are not taught the easiest way to arrive at salvation. The only way to heaven is by the route of prayer. Everyone is capable of such prayers of the heart. Prayer that leads to heaven is not reasonings that are the fruit of study or exercises of the imagination that fill the mind with puzzling thoughts but that fail to settle salvation. The simple, confidential prayer of the child to his Father is the way to heaven.

THE ATTITUDE OF PRAYER

Poverty of spirit enters into true praying. *"Blessed are the poor in spirit, for theirs is the kingdom of heaven"* (Matthew 5:3). *"The poor"* means paupers or beggars, those who live on the bounties of others. Christ's people live by asking. Prayer is the Christian's vital breath. It is his affluent inheritance, his daily annuity.

THE NEED FOR PRAYER

By His own example, Christ illustrated the nature and necessity of prayer. Everywhere He declared that he who is on God's mission in this world will pray. He is an illustrious example of the principle that the more devoted the man is to God, the more prayerful he will be. The more of the Spirit of the Father and of the Son a man has, the more prayerful he will be. Conversely, it is true that the more prayerful he is, the more of the Spirit of the Father and of the Son he will receive.

At the great events and crowning periods of the life of Jesus, we find Him in prayer—at the beginning of His ministry (see John 2:1–11); at the fords of the Jordan, when the Holy Spirit descended upon Him (see Luke 3:21–22); just prior to the Transfiguration (see Luke 9:28–36); and in the Garden of Gethsemane (see Matthew 26:36–46). The words of Peter apply here well: *"Christ also suffered for us, leaving us an example, that* [we] *should follow His steps"* (1 Peter 2:21).

THE PROGRESSIVE NATURE OF PRAYER

There is an important principle of prayer found in some of the miracles of Christ. It is the progressive nature of the answer to prayer. God does not always give the full answer to prayer at once, but rather progressively, step by step. Mark described a case that illustrates this important truth that is too often overlooked:

> *Then* [Jesus] *came to Bethsaida; and they brought a blind man to Him, and begged Him to touch him. So He took the blind man by the hand and led him out of the town. And when He had spit on his eyes and put His hands on him, He asked him if he saw anything. And He looked up and said, "I see men like trees, walking." Then He put His hands on his eyes again and made him look up. And he was restored and saw everyone clearly.* (Mark 8:22–25)

At times, He has to take us aside from the world, where He can have us all to Himself, and there speak to and deal with us.

GOD WORKS IN HIS OWN WAY

Three cures for blindness demonstrated in the ministry of our Lord illustrate the nature of God's working in answering prayer and show the inexhaustible variety and omnipotence of His working.

In the first case Christ came incidentally on a blind man at Jerusalem. (See John 9:1.) Jesus made clay, softened it with saliva, and smeared it on the eyes of the blind man (v. 6). Then He commanded the man, *"Go, wash in the pool of Siloam"* (v. 7). The gracious results lay at the end of his obedient washing. The failure to go and wash would have been fatal to the cure.

No one, not even the blind man, in this instance, requested the cure. (See John 9:1–38.)

In the second case the parties who bring the blind man to Jesus back their bringing with earnest prayer for his cure; they beseech Christ to simply touch him, as though their faith would relieve the burden of a heavy operation (Mark 8:22). But Jesus *"took the blind man by the hand and led him out of the town"* (v. 23). Alone, in secret, apart from the crowd, this work was to be done. Jesus spat *"on his eyes and put His hands on him"* (v. 23). The response was not complete; there was a dawning of light, a partial recovery (see v. 24.) The first gracious communication gave him a disordered vision, but the second stroke perfected the cure (see v. 25.) The man's submissive faith in giving himself up to Christ to be led away alone to a private spot was a prominent feature of his cure, as were the gradual reception of sight, and the necessity of a second touch to finish the work.

The third was the case of blind Bartimaeus. (See Mark 10:46–52.) His healing demonstrated the urgency of his faith. He declared his need in clamorous utterances that were rebuked by those who were following Christ. The warnings to be quiet only intensified the man's efforts and emboldened him. Despite the opposition, *"he cried out all the more, 'Son of David, have mercy on me!'"* (Mark 10:48). Jesus restored Bartimaeus' sight and told him, *"Your faith has made you well"* (v. 52).

The first case came on Christ unawares; the second was brought with specific intent to Him. The last went after Christ with irresistible urgency and was met by the resistance of the multitude and the seeming indifference of Christ. The cure, though, was without the interposition of any agent—no taking by the hand, no gentle or severe touch, no spittle or clay or washing—a word only and his sight, full-orbed, came instantly. Each one experienced the same divine power, the same blessed results, but with marked diversity in the expression of their faith and the mode of their cure. Suppose the first had set up the particulars and process of his cure—the spittle, the clay, the washing in Siloam—as the only divine process, as the only genuine credentials of a divine work. How far from the truth, how narrow and misleading, would such a standard of decision have been! Not methods, but results, are the tests of the divine work.

Each one could say, *"One thing I know: that though I was blind, now I see"* (John 9:25). The results were conscious results. They knew that Christ did the work. Faith was the instrument, but it was exercised in different ways. The method of Christ's working was different; the various steps that brought them to the gracious end on their parts and on His part were strikingly dissimilar at many points.

QUESTIONS FOR CONSIDERATION

What are the limitations of prayer? How far do its benefits and possibilities reach? What part of God's dealing with man, and with man's world, is unaffected by prayer? Do the possibilities of prayer cover all temporal and spiritual good? The answers to these questions are of transcendental importance. The answers will gauge the effort and results of our praying. The answers will greatly enhance the value of prayer, or will greatly depress prayer. The answers to these important questions are fully covered by Paul's words on prayer: *"Be anxious for nothing, but in everything by prayer and supplication, with thanksgiving, let your requests be made known to God"* (Philippians 4:6).

> *When you pray, go into your room, and when you have shut your door, pray to your Father who is in the secret place; and your Father who sees in secret will reward you openly.* —Matthew 6:6

> *If you then, being evil, know how to give good gifts to your children, how much more will your Father who is in heaven give good things to those who ask Him!* —Matthew 7:11

> *If you ask anything in My name, I will do it.* —John 14:14

FOUR:

GOD'S PART IN PRAYER

Christ is all. We are complete in Him. He is the answer to every need, the perfect Savior. He needs no decoration to heighten His beauty, no prop to increase His stability, no girding to perfect His strength. Who can gild refined gold, whiten the snow, perfume the rose, or heighten the colors of the summer sunset? Who will prop the mountains or help the great deep? It is not Christ and philosophy or Christ and money or civilization or diplomacy or science or organization. It is Christ alone. He trod *the winepress alone*" (Isaiah 63:3). "*His own arm brought salvation*" (Isaiah 59:16). He is enough. He is the comfort, the strength, the wisdom, the righteousness, the sanctification of all men.   —C. L. Chilton

Prayer is God's business to which men can attend. Prayer is God's necessary business that only men can do, and that men must do. Men who belong to God are obliged to pray. They are not obliged to grow rich or to make money. They are not obliged to have large success in business. These activities are incidental, occasional, merely nominal, as far as integrity to heaven and loyalty to God are concerned. Material successes are immaterial to

God. Men are neither better nor worse with those things or without them. They are not sources of reputation or elements of character in the heavenly estimates. But to pray, to really pray, is the source of revenue, the basis of reputation, and the element of character in the estimation of God. Men are obliged to pray as they are obliged to be Christlike. Prayer is loyalty to God. Not to pray is to reject Christ and to abandon heaven. A life of prayer is the only life that heaven counts.

PRAYER RELEASES GOD'S PROMISES

God is vitally concerned that men should pray. Men are bettered by praying, and the world is bettered by prayer. God does His best work for the world through prayer. God's greatest glory and man's highest good are secured by prayer. Prayer forms the godliest men and the godliest world.

God's promises lie like giant corpses without life, headed for decay and dust, unless people appropriate and give life to these promises through earnest and prevailing prayer.

Promise is like the unsown seed, the germ of life in it, but the soil and culture of prayer are necessary to germinate and culture the seed. Prayer is God's life-giving breath. God's purposes move along the pathway made by prayer to their glorious designs. God's purposes are always moving to their high and gracious ends, but the movement is along the way marked by unceasing prayer. The breath of prayer in man is from God.

PRAYER CHANGES THE ONE WHO PRAYS

God has everything to do with prayer, as well as everything to do with the one who prays. To him who prays, and as he prays, the hour is sacred because it is God's hour. The experience is sacred because it is the soul's approach to God, and a time of dealing with God. No hour is more hallowed, because it is the occasion of the soul's mightiest approach to God and brings the fullest revelation from God. Men are Godlike and men are blessed, inasmuch as the hour of prayer has the most of God in it. Prayer makes and measures the approach to God. He knows not God who knows not how to pray. He has never seen God whose eye has not been seeking for God in the prayer closet. God can be seen in the private place of prayer. His dwelling place is in secret. *"He who dwells in the secret place of the Most High shall abide under the shadow of the Almighty"* (Psalm 91:1).

He has never studied God who has not had his intellect broadened, strengthened, clarified, and uplifted by prayer. Almighty God commands prayer. God waits on prayer to order His ways, and God delights in prayer. To God, prayer is what incense was to the Jewish temple. It impregnates everything, perfumes everything, and sweetens everything.

PRAYER ACCOMPLISHES GOD'S PURPOSES

The possibilities of prayer cover the whole purposes of God through Christ. God conditions all gifts in all dispensations to His Son. *"Ask of Me,"* God the Father said to the Son, as that Son was moving earthward on the stupendous enterprise for a world's salvation, *"and I will give You the nations for Your inheritance, and the ends of the earth for Your possession"* (Psalm 2:8). Hinging on prayer were all the means, results, and successes of that wonderful and divine movement for man's salvation. Broad and profound, mysterious and wonderful, was the scheme.

PRAYER DRAWS US CLOSER TO GOD

The answer to prayer is assured not only by the promises of God, but also by God's relation to us as a Father.

> *But you, when you pray, go into your room, and when you have shut your door, pray to your Father who is in the secret place; and your Father who sees in secret will reward you openly.*   (Matthew 6:6)

Again, we have these words:

> *If you then, being evil, know how to give good gifts to your children, how much more will your Father who is in heaven give good things to those who ask Him!*   (Matthew 7:11)

PRAYER INCREASES CONFIDENCE IN ASKING

God encourages us to pray, not only by the certainty of the answer, but also by the generosity of the promise, and the bounty of the Giver.

How princely the promise! *"And whatever things you ask in prayer, believing, you will receive"* (Matthew 21:22). Then add to that *"whatever"* this promise: *"If you ask **anything** in My name, I will do it"* (John 14:14, emphasis added). That verse covers all things, without qualification, exception, or limitation. The word *"anything"* expands and makes specific the promise. The challenge of God to us is, *"Call to Me, and I will answer you, and show you great and mighty things, which you do not know"* (Jeremiah 33:3). This includes, like the answer to Solomon's prayer (see 1 Kings 3:5–14), what was specifically prayed for, but embraces vastly more of great value and of great necessity.

Almighty God seems to fear we will hesitate to ask largely, apprehensive that we will strain His ability. He declares that He is *"able to do exceedingly abundantly above all that we ask or think"* (Ephesians 3:20). He almost paralyzes us by giving us a carte blanche, *"Ask Me of things to come concerning My sons; and concerning the work of My hands, you command Me"* (Isaiah 45:11). How He charges, commands, and urges us to pray! He goes beyond promise and says, *"God so loved the world that He gave His only begotten Son"* (John 3:16). *"He who did not spare His own Son, but delivered Him up for us all, how shall He not with Him also freely give us all things?"* (Romans 8:32).

God gave us *"all things"* in prayer by promise because He had given us "all things" in His Son. What an amazing gift—His Son! Prayer is as immeasurable as His own blessed Son. There is nothing on earth or in heaven, for time or eternity, that God's Son did not secure for us. By prayer, God gives us the vast and matchless inheritance that is ours by virtue of His Son. God charges us to *"come boldly to the throne of grace"* (Hebrews 4:16). God is glorified and Christ is honored by large asking.

PRAYER IS A PART OF GOD'S PLAN

What is true of the promises of God is equally true of the purposes of God. We might say that God does nothing without prayer. His most gracious purposes are conditioned on prayer. His marvelous promises in the thirty-sixth chapter of Ezekiel are subject to this qualification and condition. *"Thus says the Lord God: 'I will also let the house of Israel inquire of Me to do this for them'"* (v. 37).

34 E. M. Bounds on Prayer & Spiritual Warfare

In Psalm 2 the purposes of God to His enthroned Christ are enjoined by prayer. The decree that promises to Him the nations for His inheritance relies on prayer for its fulfillment: *"Ask of Me"* (v. 8). We see how sadly the decree has failed in its operation, not because of the weakness of God's purpose, but by the weakness of man's praying. It takes God's mighty decree and man's mighty praying to bring to pass these glorious results.

In the Seventy-second Psalm we have an insight into the mighty power of prayer as the force that God moves on the conquest of Christ: *"Prayer also will be made for Him continually"* (v. 15). In this statement Christ's movements are put into the hands of prayer.

When Christ, with a sad and sympathizing heart, looked upon the ripened fields of humanity and saw the great need for laborers, His purposes were for more laborers, and so He charged His disciples, *"Pray the Lord of the harvest to send out laborers into His harvest"* (Matthew 9:38).

Paul reminded the believers of the eternal purposes of God, and how he bowed his knees to God in order that His eternal purpose might be accomplished (Ephesians 2:8–3:19), and that they might *"be filled with all the fullness of God"* (v. 19).

We see in Job how God made His purposes for Job's three friends conditional on Job's praying, and God's purposes in regard to Job were brought about by the same means. (See Job 42:8–13.)

The relationship and necessity of saintly prayers to God's plans and operations in executing the salvation of men are set forth in rich, expressive symbol, wherein the angels are involved in the prayers of the saints (Revelation 8:3–4).

Prayer gives efficiency and utility to the promises. The mighty ongoing of God's purposes rests on prayer. The representatives of the church in heaven and of all creation before the throne of God have *"golden bowls full of incense, which are the prayers of the saints"* (Revelation 5:8).

PRAYER IS BASED ON A RELATIONSHIP

We have said before that prayer is based not simply on a promise, but on a relationship. The returning, penitent sinner's prayer is based on a promise. The child of God's prayer is founded on his relationship to his heavenly Father. What the earthly father has belongs to the child for present and prospective uses. The child asks; the father gives. The relationship is one of asking and answering, of giving and receiving. The child is dependent on the father, must look to the father, must ask of the father, and must receive of the father.

We know how with earthly parents asking and giving are inherent in the parent-child relationship, and how in the very act of asking and giving, the relationship of parent and child is cemented, sweetened, and enriched. The parent finds his wealth of pleasure and satisfaction in giving to an obedient child, and the child finds his wealth in the father's loving and continuous giving.

It must be kept in mind that there is no test of our being in the family of God that is surer than this thing of prayer. God's children pray. They rest in Him for all things. They ask Him for all things—for everything. The faith of the child in the father is evinced by the child's asking. It is the answer to prayer that convinces men not only that there is a God, but also that He is a God who concerns Himself about men and about the affairs of this world. Answered prayer brings God near and assures men of His being. Answered prayers are the credentials of our relationship to, and our representation of, Him. Men cannot represent God who do not receive answers to prayer from Him.

The possibilities of prayer are found in the unlimited promise, the willingness, and the power of God to answer prayer, to answer all prayer, to answer every prayer, and to supply fully the immeasurable needs of man. None is so needy as man, none is so able and anxious to supply every need and any need as God.

PRAYER IS POWERFUL

Prayer affects God more powerfully than His own purposes. God's will, words, and purposes are all subject to review when the mighty power of prayer comes in. How mighty prayer is with God may be seen as He readily sets aside His own fixed and declared purposes in answer to prayer. The whole plan of salvation would have been blocked had Jesus Christ prayed for the twelve legions of angels to carry dismay and ruin to His enemies. (See Matthew 26:53.)

The fasting and prayers of the Ninevites changed God's purpose to destroy that wicked city (see Jonah 3:1–10), after Jonah had gone there and cried unto the people, *"Yet forty days, and Nineveh shall be overthrown!"* (v. 4).

JESUS SETS THE EXAMPLE IN PRAYER

Almighty God is concerned in our praying. He wills it, He commands it, He inspires it. Jesus Christ in heaven is always praying for us. (See Hebrews 7:25.) Prayer is His law and His life. The Holy Spirit teaches us how to pray. He prays for us *"with groanings which cannot be uttered"* (Romans 8:26). All these examples show the deep concern of God in prayer. They reveal very clearly how vital prayer is to His work in this world, and how far-reaching are its possibilities. Prayer is at the very center of the heart and will of God concerning men. *"Rejoice always, pray without ceasing, in everything give thanks; for this is the will of God in Christ Jesus for you"* (1 Thessalonians 5:16–18). Prayer is the polestar around which rejoicing and thanksgiving revolve. Prayer is the heart sending its full and happy pulsations up to God through the glad currents of joy and thanksgiving.

PRAYER BRINGS AMAZING RESULTS

By prayer God's name is hallowed. By prayer God's kingdom comes. By prayer is His kingdom established in power and made to move with conquering force swifter than light. By prayer God's will is done until earth rivals heaven in harmony and beauty. By prayer daily labor is sanctified and enriched; pardon is secured, and Satan is defeated. Prayer concerns God and concerns man in every way.

God has nothing too good to give in answer to prayer. There is no vengeance pronounced by God so dire that does not yield to prayer. There is no justice so flaming that is not quenched by prayer.

Take the record and attitude of heaven concerning Saul of Tarsus. That attitude is changed and that record is erased when the astonishing condition is announced, *"Behold, he is praying"* (Acts 9:11).

The cowardly Jonah was alive, and on dry ground, with scarcely the taste of the sea or the smell of its weeds about him, when he prayed:

Out of the belly of Sheol I cried, and You heard my voice....The waters surrounded me, even to my soul; the deep closed around me; weeds were wrapped around my head. I went down to the moorings of the mountains; the earth with its bars closed behind me forever; yet You have brought up my life from the pit, O Lord, my God. When my soul fainted within me, I remembered the Lord; and my prayer went up to You, into Your holy temple.... So the Lord spoke to the fish, and it vomited Jonah onto dry land. (Jonah 2:2, 5–7, 10)

Prayer has all the force of God in it. Prayer can get anything that God has. Thus prayer has all of its plea and its claim in the name of Jesus Christ, and there is nothing too good or great for God to give that name.

THE SALVATION OF SOULS RELIES ON PRAYER

Preaching should no more fully declare and fulfill the will of God for the salvation of all men, than should the prayers of God's saints declare the same great truth, as they wrestle in their prayer closets for this sublime end. God's heart is set on the salvation of all men. This concerns God. He has declared this truth in the death of His Son by an unspeakable voice, and every movement on earth for this end pleases God. And so He declares that our prayers for the salvation of all men are well pleasing in His sight. The sublime and holy inspiration of pleasing God should ever move us to pray for all men. God eyes the prayer closet, and nothing we can do pleases Him better than our sympathetic, ardent praying for all men. It is the embodiment and test of our devotion to God's will and of our sympathetic loyalty to God.

The apostle Paul did not descend to a weak argument, but pressed the necessity of prayer by the most forceful facts. Jesus Christ, the God-man, the highest illustration of manhood, is the *"Mediator between God and men"* (1 Timothy 2:5). Jesus died for all men. His life is an intercession for all men. His death is a prayer for all men. On earth, Jesus Christ knew no higher law, no holier business, no diviner life, than to plead for men. In heaven He knows no more royal estate, no higher theme, than to intercede for men. On earth He lived and prayed and died for men. His life, His death, and His exaltation in heaven all plead for men.

Is there any work, any higher work, for the disciple to do than His Lord did? Is there any loftier employment, more honorable, more divine, than to pray for men? Is there anything more important than to take their woes, their sins, and their perils before God—to be one with Christ? Can we neglect to pray when prayer can break the chains that bind them and the hell that holds them, and lift them to immortality and eternal life?

FIVE:

THE DIVINE TEACHER
OF PRAYER

[A man knocks on the door of his neighbor's house and says,] "A friend of mine in his journey has come to me, and I have nothing to set before him!" He knocks again. "Friend! lend me three loaves." He waits a while and then knocks again. "Friend! I must have three loaves!" "Trouble me not: the door is now shut; I cannot rise and give thee!" He stands still. He turns to go home; He comes back. He knocks again. "Friend!" he cries. He puts his ear to the door. There is a sound inside, and then the light of a candle shines through the hole of the door. The bars of the door are drawn back, and he gets not three loaves only, but as many as he needs. *"So I say to you, ask, and it will be given to you; seek, and you will find; knock, and it will be opened to you"* (Luke 11:9).   —Alexander Whyte

Jesus Christ was the divine Teacher of prayer. Its power and nature had been illustrated by many saints and prophets in olden times, but modern sainthood and modern teachers of prayer had lost their inspiration and life. Religiously dead, teachers and superficial ecclesiastics had forgotten what it was to pray. They recited many prayers on state occasions, in public meetings, with much ostentation and parade, but they did not pray. To them it was almost a lost practice. In the multiplicity of "saying prayers," they had lost the art of praying.

THE SERIOUS EFFECTS OF NEGLECTING PRAYER

The history of the disciples during the earthly life of our Lord was not marked by much devotion. They were enamored by their personal association with Christ. They were charmed by His words, excited by His miracles, and entertained and concerned by the hopes that a selfish interest aroused in His person and mission. Taken up with superficial and worldly views of His character, they neglected and overlooked the deeper and weightier things that belonged to Him and His mission. The neglect of the most obligatory and ordinary duties by them was a noticeable feature in their actions. So evident and singular was their conduct in this regard that it became a matter of grave inquiry on one occasion and severe chiding on another.

The scribes and Pharisees said to Jesus:

"Why do the disciples of John fast often and make prayers, and likewise those of the Pharisees, but Yours eat and drink?" And He said to them, "Can you make the friends of the bridegroom fast while the bridegroom is with them? But the days will come when the bridegroom will be taken away from them; then they will fast in those days."

(Luke 5:33–35)

JESUS TEACHES THE IMPORTANCE OF PRAYER

In the example and teaching of Jesus Christ, prayer assumes its proper relationship to God's person, God's movements, and God's Son. Jesus Christ was essentially the Teacher of prayer by precept and example. We have glimpses of His praying that, like indices, tell how full of prayer the pages, chapters, and volumes of His life were. The summation that covers not just one segment, but the whole circle of His life and character, is preeminently that of prayer! *"In the days of His flesh,"* the divine Record reads, *"...He...offered up prayers and supplications, with vehement cries and tears"* (Hebrews 5:7). He was the most earnest of all who have prayed or will pray, the Intercessor of all intercessors. He approached God with humility, and He supplicated with strongest pleas.

Jesus Christ taught the importance of prayer when He urged His disciples to pray. But He shows us more than that. He shows how far prayer enters into the purposes of God. We must always keep in mind that the relationship of Jesus Christ to God is the relationship of asking and giving, the Son ever asking, the Father ever giving. We must never forget that God has put the conquering, inheriting, and expanding forces of Christ's cause into prayer. *"Ask of Me, and I will give You the nations for Your inheritance, and the ends of the earth for Your possession"* (Psalm 2:8).

"Ask of Me" embodied the royal proclamation and the universal condition when the Son was enthroned as the world's Mediator, and when He was sent on His mission of receiving grace and power. We very naturally learn from these examples how Jesus stressed praying as the sole condition of His receiving His possession and inheritance.

PRAYER HAS NO BOUNDARIES

Necessarily in this study on prayer, lines of thought will cross each other, and the same Scripture passage or incident will be mentioned more than once, simply because a passage may teach one or more truths. This is the case when we speak of the vast comprehensiveness of prayer. How all-inclusive Jesus Christ makes prayer! It has no limitations in extent or things! The promises to prayer are Godlike in their magnificence, wideness, and universality. In their nature these promises, inspiration, creation, and results have to do with God. Who but Jesus could say, *"Whatever things you ask in prayer, believing, you will receive"* (Matthew 21:22)? Who can command and direct *"whatever things"* but God? Neither man nor chance nor the law of results are so far lifted above change, limitations, or condition, or have in them mighty forces that can direct and cause all things, as to promise the bestowment and direction of all things.

Parables and incidents from life were used by Christ to emphasize the necessity and importance of prayer. His miracles are but parables of prayer.

In nearly all of them prayer figures distinctly, and some features of it are illustrated. The Syro-Phoenician woman is a preeminent illustration of the ability and the success of perseverance in prayer. (See Mark 7:25–30.) The case of blind Bartimaeus makes the same point. (See Mark 10:46–52.) Jairus (see Mark 5:22–24, 35–43) and the centurion (see Matthew 8:5–13) illustrate and emphasize other aspects of prayer. The parable of the Pharisee and the tax collector urge humility in prayer, declare the wondrous results of praying, and show the vanity and worthlessness of wrong praying. (See Luke 18:10–14.) The failure to enforce church discipline and the readiness to violate the brotherhood are both used as examples of the far-reaching results of agreeing in prayer. Matthew recorded these words of Jesus:

> *If your brother sins against you, go and tell him his fault between you and him alone. If he hears you, you have gained your brother. But if he will not hear, take with you one or two more, that "by the mouth of two or three witnesses every word may be established." And if he refuses to hear them, tell it to the church. But if he refuses even to hear the church, let him be to you like a heathen and a tax collector. Assuredly, I say to you, whatever you bind on earth will be bound in heaven, and whatever you loose on earth will be loosed in heaven. Again I say to you that if two of you agree on earth concerning anything that they ask, it will be done for them by My Father in heaven. For where two or three are gathered together in My name, I am there in the midst of them.*
>
> (Matthew 18:15–20)

AGREEMENT IN PRAYER

It is of prayer in concert—two agreed ones, two whose hearts have been keyed into perfect symphony by the Holy Spirit—that Christ is speaking. Anything that they will ask, it will be done. Christ had been speaking of discipline in the church, how things were to be kept in unity, and how the fellowship of the brethren was to be maintained by the restoration of the offender or by his exclusion. Members who had been true to the brotherhood of Christ, and who were laboring to preserve that brotherhood unbroken, would be the ones in agreement to make appeals to God in united prayer.

PRAYER IS A SPIRITUAL DIRECTIVE

In the Sermon on the Mount, Christ lays down constitutional principles. Types and shadows are retired, and the law of spiritual life is declared. In this foundational law of the Christian system, prayer assumes a conspicuous, if not a paramount, position. It is not only wide, all commanding, and comprehensive in its own sphere of action and relief, but it is also ancillary to all duties. Both the teaching that demands kindly and discriminating judgment toward others, as well as the royal injunction, the Golden Rule of action, owe their being to prayer. Christ puts prayer among the statutory promises. He does not leave it to natural law. The law of need, of supply and demand, of helplessness, of natural instincts, or the law of sweet, high, attractive privilege—these, however strong as motives of action, are not the basis of praying. Christ puts it as spiritual law. Men must pray. Not to pray is not simply a privation, an omission, but a positive violation of law, of spiritual life, a crime, bringing disorder and ruin. Prayer is law worldwide; it reaches throughout eternity.

THE NECESSITY OF PRIVATE PRAYER

In the Sermon on the Mount many important utterances are dismissed with a line or a verse, while the subject of prayer occupies a large space. Christ returns to it again and again. He bases the possibilities and necessities of prayer on the relationship of father and child, the child crying for bread, and the father giving that for which the child asks. Prayer and its answer are in the relationship of a father to his child. The teaching of Jesus Christ on the nature and necessity of prayer as recorded in His life is remarkable. He sends men to their prayer closets. Prayer must be a holy exercise, untainted by vanity or pride. It must be in secret. The disciple must live in secret. God lives there, is sought there, and is found there. The command of Christ as to prayer is that pride and publicity should be shunned. Prayer is to be in private.

> But you, when you pray, go into your room, and when you have shut your door, pray to your Father who is in the secret place; and your Father who sees in secret will reward you openly.   (Matthew 6:6)

PRAYER REQUIRES A RIGHT SPIRIT

The Beatitudes are not only to enrich and adorn, but they are also the material out of which spiritual character is built. The very first one of these fixes prayer in the very foundation of spiritual character, not simply to adorn, but to compose. *"Blessed are the poor in spirit"* (Matthew 5:3). Again, the word *"poor"* here in the Greek means a pauper, one who lives by begging. The real Christian lives on the bounties of Another, whose bounties he gets by asking. Prayer then becomes the basis of Christian character, the Christian's business, his life and his living. This is Christ's law of prayer, putting it into the very being of the Christian. It is his first step, and his first breath, which is to color and to form the rest of his life. Blessed are the poor ones, for only they can pray.

> Prayer is the Christian's vital breath,
> The Christian's native air;
> His watchword at the gates of death,
> He enters heaven with prayer.

From praying Christ eliminates all self-sufficiency and all pride. The poor in spirit are the praying ones. Beggars are God's princes. They are God's heirs. Christ removes the rubbish of Jewish traditions and interpretations of the law from the regulations of the prayer altar.

> *You have heard that it was said to those of old, "You shall not murder, and whoever murders will be in danger of the judgment." But I say to you that whoever is angry with his brother without a cause shall be in danger of the judgment. And whoever says to his brother, "Raca!" shall be in danger of the council. But whoever says, "You fool!" shall be in danger of hell fire. Therefore if you bring your gift to the altar, and there remember that your brother has something against you, leave your gift there before the altar, and go your way. First be reconciled to your brother, and then come and offer your gift.* (Matthew 5:21–24)

He who tries to pray to God with an angry spirit, with loose and irreverent lips, with an irreconcilable heart, and with unsettled neighborly scores, spends his labor for what is worse than nothing, violates the law of prayer, and adds to his sin.

How rigidly exacting is Christ's law of prayer. It goes to the heart and demands that love be enthroned there, love for the brotherhood. The sacrifice of prayer must be seasoned and perfumed with love, by love in the inward parts. The law of prayer, its creator and inspirer, is love.

PRAYING BRINGS RESULTS

Praying must be done. God wants it done. He commands it. Man needs it and man must do it. Something must surely come of praying, for God promises that something will come out of it, if men are in earnest and are persevering in prayer.

After Jesus taught, *"Ask, and it will be given to you"* (Matthew 7:7), He encouraged real praying, and more praying. He repeated and asserted with redoubled assurance, *"For everyone who asks receives"* (v. 8). He left no room for exception when He said, *"Everyone."*

"He who seeks finds" (v. 8). Here it is again, measured and stamped with infinite truth. It is closed and signed, as well as sealed, with divine attestation: *"To him who knocks it will be opened"* (v. 8).

Note how we are encouraged to pray because of our relationship with God:

If you then, being evil, know how to give good gifts to your children, how much more will your Father who is in heaven give good things to those who ask Him! (Matthew 7:11)

CHRISTIANS MUST PRAY

The relation of prayer to God's work and God's rule in this world is most fully illustrated by Jesus Christ in both His teaching and His practice. He is first in every way and in everything. Among the rulers of the church He is primary in a preeminent way. He has the throne. The golden crown is His in eminent preciousness. The white garments enrobe Him in incomparable whiteness and beauty. In the ministry of prayer He is a divine example as well as the divine Teacher. His examples and His teaching on prayer abound. How imperative the teaching of our Lord when He affirms that *"men always ought to pray and not lose heart"* (Luke 18:1). Then

He presents a striking parable of an unjust judge and a poor widow to illustrate and reinforce His teaching. (See Luke 18:2–8.) It is a necessity to pray. It is exacting and binding for men always to be in prayer. Courage, endurance, and perseverance are demanded so that men may never become discouraged in prayer.

"And shall God not avenge His own elect who cry day and night to Him?" (v. 7). This is His strong and indignant questioning and affirmation. Men must pray according to Christ's teaching. They must not become tired or grow weary in praying. God's character is the assurance that much will come of the persistent praying of true men.

Doubtless, the praying of our Lord had much to do with the revelation made to Peter and the confession he made to Christ, *"You are the Christ, the Son of the living God"* (Matthew 16:16). Prayer mightily affects and molds the circle of our associates. Christ made disciples and kept them disciples by praying. His twelve disciples were impressed by His praying. No man ever prayed like He did. How different His praying was from the cold, proud, self-righteous praying that they heard and saw on the streets, in the synagogue, and in the temple.

> *Until now you have asked nothing in My name. Ask, and you will receive, that your joy may be full.* —John 16:24

> *Confess your trespasses to one another, and pray for one another, that you may be healed. The effective, fervent prayer of a righteous man avails much.* —James 5:16

> *And I will give you the keys of the kingdom of heaven, and whatever you bind on earth will be bound in heaven, and whatever you loose on earth will be loosed in heaven.* —Matthew 16:19

SIX:

THE LESSON OF PRAYER

Luke tells us that as Jesus was praying in a certain place, when He ceased, one of His disciples said to Him, *"Lord, teach us to pray"* (Luke 11:1). This disciple had heard Jesus preach, but did not feel like saying, "Lord, teach us to preach." He could learn to preach by studying the methods of the Master. But there was something about the praying of Jesus that made the disciple feel that he did not know how to pray, that he had never prayed, and that he could not learn even by listening to the Master as He prayed. There is a profound something about prayer that never lies on the surface. To learn it, one must go to the depths of the soul, and climb to the heights of God.

—A. C. Dixon

Let it not be forgotten that prayer was one of the great truths that Jesus came into the world to teach and illustrate. It was worth a trip from heaven to earth to teach men this great lesson of prayer. It was a great lesson, a very difficult lesson, for men to learn. Men are naturally averse to learning this lesson of prayer. The lesson is a very lowly one. Only God can teach it. It is a despised poverty, a sublime and heavenly vocation. The disciples were very slow-witted students, but were quickened to prayer by hearing Jesus pray and talk about prayer.

THE NEED TO BE TAUGHT

The state of Christ's personality was not and could not be displayed in its fullest and highest sense of need and dependence, yet Christ did try to impress on His disciples not only the deep need for prayer in general, but also the importance of prayer for their personal and spiritual needs. And there were moments when they felt the need of a deeper and more thorough schooling in prayer and of their grave neglect in this regard. One of these hours of deep conviction on their part, as well as of eager inquiry, was when He was praying at a certain place and time, and they saw Him and said to Him, "*Lord, teach us to pray, as John also taught his disciples*" (Luke 11:1).

As they had listened to Him praying, they had felt very keenly their ignorance and deficiency in praying. Who has not felt the same deficiency and ignorance? Who has not longed for a teacher in the divine art of praying?

The conviction that these twelve men had of their shortcomings in prayer arose from hearing their Lord and Master pray, but likewise from their sense of serious deficiency even when they compared their training with John the Baptist's training of his disciples in prayer. As they listened to their Lord pray—for unquestionably He must have been seen and heard by them as He prayed with marvelous simplicity and power, so human and so divine—such praying had a stimulating charm for them. In the presence and hearing of His praying, they felt their ignorance and deficiency in prayer very keenly. Who has not felt the same ignorance and deficiency?

We do not regret the schooling our Lord gave these twelve men, for in schooling them, He schools us. The lesson is one already learned in the law of Christ. But they were so dull that repeated, patient instruction was required to teach them this divine art of prayer. Likewise, we are so dull and inept that many patient repetitions must be taught to us before we will learn any important lesson in the all-important school of prayer.

THE CONNECTION BETWEEN FAITH AND PRAYER

This divine Teacher of prayer lays Himself out to make it clear and strong that God answers prayer, assuredly, certainly, inevitably; that it is the duty of the child to ask and to press; and that the Father is obliged to answer and to give as a result of the asking. In Christ's teaching, prayer is no sterile, vain performance, not a mere rite or a form, but a request for an answer, a plea to gain, the seeking of a great good from God. It is a lesson of getting that for which we ask, of finding that for which we seek, and of entering the door at which we knock. (See Matthew 7:7; Luke 11:9.)

We have a notable example of this as Jesus comes down from the Mount of Transfiguration. He finds His disciples defeated, humiliated, and confused in the presence of their enemies. A father has brought his child possessed with a demon to have the demon cast out. They tried to do it, but failed. They had been commissioned by Jesus and sent to do that very work, but had signally failed.

> *And when He had come into the house, His disciples asked Him privately, "Why could we not cast it out?" So He said to them, "This kind can come out by nothing but prayer and fasting."* (Mark 9:28–29)

Their faith had not been cultured by prayer. They failed in prayer before they failed in ability to do their work. They failed in faith because they had failed in prayer. The one thing that was necessary to do God's work was prayer. The work that God sends us to do cannot be done without prayer.

In Christ's teaching on prayer we have another pertinent statement. It was in connection with the cursing of the barren fig tree.

> *Jesus answered and said to them, "Assuredly, I say to you, if you have faith and do not doubt, you will not only do what was done to the fig tree, but also if you say to this mountain, 'Be removed and be cast into the sea,' it will be done. And whatever things you ask in prayer, believing, you will receive."* (Matthew 21:21–22)

In this passage we have faith and prayer, their possibilities and powers joined. A fig tree had been blasted to the roots by the words of the Lord Jesus. The power and quickness of the result surprised the disciples. Jesus

50 *E. M. Bounds on Prayer & Spiritual Warfare*

said to them that it should be no surprise to them that such a difficult work was done. *"If you have faith"* (Matthew 21:21), then faith's possibilities in affecting change will not be confined to the little fig tree, but will also apply to the gigantic, rocky mountains—uprooting and moving them into the sea. Prayer is the leverage behind this great power of faith.

PRAYER SECURES WORKERS

It is well to refer again to the occasion when the heart of our Lord was so deeply moved with compassion as He gazed at the multitudes, *"because they were weary and scattered, like sheep having no shepherd"* (Matthew 9:36). Then He urged this injunction upon His disciples, *"Pray the Lord of the harvest to send out laborers into His harvest"* (v. 38), clearly teaching them that it belonged to God to call into the ministry men whom He will call, and that in answer to prayer the Holy Spirit does this very work.

Prayer is as necessary now as it was then to secure the needed laborers to reap earthly harvests for the heavenly granaries. Has the church of God ever learned this lesson of so vital and exacting import? God alone can choose the laborers and thrust them out, and this choosing He does not delegate to man, church, convocation, synod, association, or conference. God is moved by prayer to this great work of calling men into the ministry. Earthly fields are rotting. They are untilled because prayer is silent. The laborers are few. Fields are unworked because prayer to God has not been exercised.

ABIDING IN CHRIST IS NECESSARY FOR TRUE PRAYER

We have the prayer promise and the prayer ability put in a distinct form in the higher teachings of prayer by our Lord: *"If you abide in Me, and My words abide in you, you will ask what you desire, and it shall be done for you"* (John 15:7).

Here we have a fixed attitude of life as the condition of answered prayer—not simply a fixed attitude of life toward some great principles or purposes, but the fixed attitude and unity of life with Jesus Christ. To live in Him, to dwell there, to be one with Him, to draw all life from Him, to let all life from Him flow through us—this is the attitude of prayer and the ability to pray. No abiding in Him can be separated from His Word abiding in us. It must live in us to give birth to and food for prayer. The attitude of the person of Christ is the condition of prayer.

The Old Testament saints had been taught that God has *"magnified [His] word above all [His] name"* (Psalm 138:2). New Testament saints must learn fully how to exalt by perfect obedience that Word issuing from the lips of Him who is the Word. Praying ones under Christ must learn what praying ones under Moses had already learned: *"Man shall not live by bread alone, but by every word that proceeds from the mouth of God"* (Matthew 4:4). The life of Christ flowing through us and the words of Christ living in us give potency to prayer. They breathe the spirit of prayer, and make the body, blood, and bones of prayer. Then it is Christ praying in me and through me, and all things that I will are the will of God. My will becomes the law and the answer, for it is written, *"You will ask what you desire, and it shall be done for you"* (John 15:7).

FRUIT-BEARING IS A CONDITION OF PRAYER

Our Lord puts fruit-bearing at the forefront of our praying:

You did not choose Me, but I chose you and appointed you that you should go and bear fruit, and that your fruit should remain, that whatever you ask the Father in My name He may give you. (John 15:16)

Barrenness cannot pray, but fruit-bearing capacity and reality can pray. Jesus does not talk about fruitfulness in the past but in the present. He says, *"That your fruit should remain."* Fruit, the product of life, is a condition of praying. A life vigorous enough to bear fruit, much fruit, is the condition and the source of prayer.

And in that day you will ask Me nothing. Most assuredly, I say to you, whatever you ask the Father in My name He will give you. Until now you have asked nothing in My name. Ask, and you will receive, that your joy may be full. (John 16:23–24)

"In that day you will ask Me nothing." Our business is not about solving riddles, revealing mysteries, or curious questionings. This is not our attitude, not our business under the dispensation of the Spirit; instead, we

are to pray, and to pray largely. Much true praying increases man's joy and God's glory.

ASK IN HIS NAME

"*Whatever you ask the Father in My name* [I] *will give you*," says Christ, and the Father will give. Both Father and Son are pledged to give the very things for which we ask. But the condition is "*in* [His] *name*." This does not mean that His name is a talisman to ward off evil and bring good. It does not mean that His name in beautiful settings of pearl will give value to prayer. It is not that His name perfumed with sentiment and mixed with our prayers and actions will do the deed. How fearful the statement,

> *Many will say to Me in that day, "Lord, Lord, have we not prophesied in Your name, cast out demons in Your name, and done many wonders in Your name?" And then I will declare to them, "I never knew you; depart from Me, you who practice lawlessness!"* (Matthew 7:22–23)

How blasting the doom of these great workers and doers who claim to work in His name!

Following Christ means far more than sentiment, verbiage, and nomenclature. It means to stand in His stead, to bear His nature, to stand for all for which He stood: righteousness, truth, holiness, and zeal. It means to be one with God as He was, one in spirit, in will, and in purpose. It means that our praying is singly and solely for God's glory through His Son. It means that we abide in Him, that Christ prays through us, lives in us, and shines out of us; that we pray by the Holy Spirit according to the will of God.

As Christ nears the close of His earthly mission, nearer to the greater and more powerful dispensation of the Spirit, His teaching about prayer takes on a more absorbing and higher form. It has now become a graduate school. His connection with prayer becomes more intimate and more absolute. He becomes in prayer what He is in all else pertaining to salvation, "*the Beginning and the End, the First and the Last*" (Revelation 22:13). His name becomes all potent. Mighty works are to be done by the faith that can pray in His name. Like His nature, His name covers all needs, embraces all worlds, and gets all good.

> Do you not believe that I am in the Father, and the Father in Me? The words that I speak to you I do not speak on My own authority; but the Father who dwells in Me does the works. Believe Me that I am in the Father and the Father in Me, or else believe Me for the sake of the works themselves. Most assuredly, I say to you, he who believes in Me, the works that I do he will do also; and greater works than these he will do, because I go to My Father. And whatever you ask in My name, that I will do, that the Father may be glorified in the Son. If you ask anything in My name, I will do it. (John 14:10–14)

The Father, the Son, and the praying one are all bound up together. All things are in Christ, and all things are in prayer in His name. *"If you ask anything in My name."* The key that unlocks the vast storehouse of God is prayer. The power to do greater works than Christ did lies in the faith that can grasp His name truly and in true praying.

PRAYER'S PROTECTIVE POWER

At the end of His earthly life, note how He urges prayer as a protection against the many evils to which His disciples were exposed. In view of the temporal and fearful terrors of the destruction of Jerusalem, He charges them to this effect: *"Pray that your flight may not be in winter"* (Matthew 24:20).

How many evils in this life can be escaped by prayer! How many fearful earthly calamities can be mitigated, if not wholly relieved, by prayer! Notice how, amid the excesses and stupefying influences to which we are exposed in this world, Christ charges us to pray:

> But take heed to yourselves, lest your hearts be weighed down with carousing, drunkenness, and cares of this life, and that Day come on you unexpectedly. For it will come as a snare on all those who dwell on the face of the whole earth. Watch therefore, and pray always that you may be counted worthy to escape all these things that will come to pass, and to stand before the Son of Man. (Luke 21:34–36)

WATCH AND PRAY

Even amid the darkness of Gethsemane, with the stupor that had settled upon the disciples, we have the sharp warning from Christ to His sluggish disciples, *"Watch and pray, lest you enter into temptation. The spirit indeed is willing, but the flesh is weak"* (Matthew 26:41). How necessary it is for us to hear such a warning to awaken all our powers, not simply for the great crises of our lives, but as the inseparable and constant attendants of a life marked with perils and dangers on every hand.

In view of the uncertainty of the timing of Christ's coming in judgment, and the uncertainty of the day of our going out of this world, He says:

> But of that day and hour no one knows, not even the angels in heaven, nor the Son, but only the Father. Take heed, watch and pray; for you do not know when the time is. (Mark 13:32)

PRAYER EQUIPS FOR SERVICE

We have the words of Jesus as given in His last interview with His twelve disciples, found in the gospel of John, chapters fourteen to seventeen. These are true, solemn parting words. The disciples were to move out into the regions of toil and peril, bereft of the personal presence of their Lord and Master. They were to be impressed that prayer would serve them in everything, and its use and unlimited possibilities would in some measure supply their loss. By it they would be able to command all the possibilities of Jesus Christ and God the Father.

It was the occasion of momentous interest to Jesus Christ. His work was to receive its climax and crown in His death and His resurrection. His glory and the success of His work and its execution under the mastery and direction of the Holy Spirit were to be committed to His apostles. To them it was an hour of strange wonderment and of peculiar, mysterious sorrow. They were only too well assured of the fact that Jesus was to leave them; all else was dark and impalpable.

He was to give them His parting words and pray His parting prayer. Solemn, vital truths were to be the weight and counsel of that hour. He spoke to them of heaven. These young men, strong though they were, could not meet the duties of their preaching life and their apostolic life, without the fact, the thought, the hope, and the relish of heaven. These things were to be present constantly in all sweetness, in all their vigor, in all freshness, and in all brightness. He spoke to them about their spiritual and conscious connection with Himself, an abiding indwelling, so close and continuous that His own life would flow into them, as the life of the vine flows into the branches. (See John 15:1–8.) Their lives and their fruitfulness were dependent upon this connection. Then praying was urged upon them as one of the vital, essential forces. This was the one thing upon which all the divine force depended, and this was the avenue and agency through which the divine life and power were to be secured and continued in their ministry.

He spoke to them about prayer. He had taught them many lessons about this all-important subject as they had been together. He seizes this solemn hour to perfect His teaching. They must be made to realize that they have a limitless and inexhaustible storehouse of good in God, and that they can draw on Him at all times and for all things without limitation. As Paul said in later years to the Philippians, *"My God shall supply all your need according to His riches in glory by Christ Jesus"* (Philippians 4:19).

Having risen a long while before daylight, He went out and departed to a solitary place; and there He prayed. —Mark 1:35

When you pray, say: Our Father in heaven, hallowed be Your name. Your kingdom come. Your will be done on earth as it is in heaven. Give us day by day our daily bread. And forgive us our sins, for we also forgive everyone who is indebted to us. And do not lead us into temptation, but deliver us from the evil one. —Luke 11:2–4

Father, if it is Your will, take this cup away from Me; nevertheless not My will, but Yours, be done. —Luke 22:42

SEVEN:

JESUS, OUR EXAMPLE IN PRAYER

Christ, when He saw that He must die, and that now His time was come, wore His body out. He did not care, as it were, what became of Himself. He wholly spent Himself in preaching all day, in praying all night, in preaching in the temple those terrible parables and praying in the Garden such prayers as the High Priestly Prayer (John 17) and *"Your will be done"* (Matthew 26:42), praying so earnestly that *"His sweat became like great drops of blood"* (Luke 22:44).
                                                        —Thomas Goodwin

The Bible record of the life of Jesus Christ gives but a glance at His busy days, a small selection of His many words, and only a brief record of His great works. But even in this record we see Him as being much in prayer. Even though He was busy and exhausted by the severe strain and toils of His life, *"in the morning, having risen a long while before daylight, He went out and departed to a solitary place; and there He prayed"* (Mark 1:35). Alone in the desert and in the darkness with God!

TO BE LIKE JESUS IS TO PRAY

Prayer filled the life of our Lord while He was on earth. His life was a constant stream of incense, sweet and perfumed by prayer. When we see how the life of Jesus was but one of prayer, then we must conclude that to be like Jesus is to pray like Jesus and is to live like Jesus. It is a serious life to pray as Jesus prayed.

JESUS'S LIFE WAS MARKED BY PRAYER

We cannot follow any chronological order in the praying of Jesus Christ. We do not know what His steps of advance and skill in the divine art of praying were. He is in the act of prayer when we find Him at the fords of the Jordan, when, at the hands of John the Baptist, the waters of baptism are upon Him. Passing over the three years of His ministry, when closing the drama of His life in that terrible baptism of fear, pain, suffering, and shame, we find Him in the spirit, and also in the very act, of praying. The baptism of the Cross, as well as the baptism of the Jordan, are sanctified by prayer. With the breath of prayer in His last sigh, He commits His spirit to God. (See Luke 23:46.) In His first recorded utterances, as well as His first acts, we find Him teaching His disciples how to pray as His first lesson and as their first duty. (See Luke 11:1–4.) Under the shadow of the Cross, in the urgency and importance of His last interview with His chosen disciples, He is at the same all-important business, teaching the world's teachers how to pray, trying to make prayerful those lips and hearts out of which were to flow the divine deposits of truth. (See Luke 22:40.)

The great eras of His life were created and crowned with prayer. What His habits of prayer during His stay at home and His work as a carpenter in Nazareth were, we have no means of knowing. God has veiled them, and guess and speculation are not only vain and misleading, but also proud and unwholesome. It would be presumptuous searching into what God has hidden, which would make us seek to be wise above that which was written, trying to lift up the veil with which God has covered His own revelation.

At this point, we find Christ in the presence of John the Baptist, the famed prophet and preacher. He has left His Nazareth home and His carpenter shop by God's call. He is now at a transitional point. He has moved out to His great work. John's baptism and the baptism of the Holy Spirit are prefatory and are to qualify Him for that work. This epochal and transitional period is marked by prayer.

> *When all the people were baptized, it came to pass that Jesus also was baptized; and while He prayed, the heaven was opened. And the Holy Spirit descended in bodily form like a dove upon Him, and a voice came from heaven which said, "You are My beloved Son; in You I am well pleased."* (Luke 3:21–22)

This supreme hour in Jesus's history is different from and in striking contrast with, but not in opposition to, His past. The descent and abiding of the Holy Spirit in all His fullness, the opening heavens, and the attesting voice that involved God's recognition of His only Son—all these are the result of, if not the direct creation of and response to, His praying on that occasion.

IMITATE CHRIST IN HIS SPIRIT OF PRAYER

"As He was praying" (Luke 11:1), so we are to be praying. If we would pray as Christ prayed, we must be as Christ was, and must live as Christ lived. The character of Christ, the life of Christ, and the spirit of Christ must be ours if we would pray as Christ prayed and would have our prayers answered as He had His prayers answered. The business of Christ even now in heaven at His Father's right hand is to pray for us. (See Romans 8:34.) Certainly if we are His, if we love Him, if we live for Him, and if we live close to Him, we will catch the contagion of His praying life, both on earth and in heaven. We will learn His trade and carry on His business on earth.

Jesus Christ loved all men, He tasted death for all men, and He intercedes for all men. Let us ask, then, are we the imitators, the representatives, and the executors of Jesus Christ? Then we must in our prayers run parallel with His atonement in its extent. The atoning blood of Jesus Christ gives sanctity and efficiency to our prayers. As worldwide, as broad, and as human as the Man Christ Jesus was, so must be our prayers. The intercessions of Christ's people must give currency and expedition to the work of Christ, carry the atoning blood to its gracious ends, and help to strike off the chains of sin from every ransomed soul. We must be as praying, as tearful, and as compassionate as was Christ.

PRAYER MUST BE PRIMARY

Prayer affects all things. God blesses the person who prays. He who prays goes out on a long voyage for God and is enriched himself while enriching others, is blessed himself while the world is blessed by his praying. To *"lead a quiet and peaceable life in all godliness and reverence"* (1 Timothy 2:2) is the richest wealth.

The praying of Christ was real. No man prayed as He prayed. Prayer pressed upon Him as a solemn, all-imperative, all-commanding duty, as well as a royal privilege in which all sweetness was condensed, alluring, and absorbing. Prayer was the secret of His power, the law of His life, the inspiration of His work, and the source of His wealth, His joy, His communion, and His strength.

To Christ Jesus, prayer occupied no secondary place but was exacting and paramount, a necessity, a life, the satisfying of a restless yearning, and a preparation for heavy responsibilities.

Closeting with His Father in counsel and fellowship, with vigor and in deep joy—all this was His praying. Present trials, future glory, the history of His church, and the struggles and perils of His disciples in all times and to the very end of time—all these things were born and shaped by His praying.

Nothing is more conspicuous in the life of our Lord than prayer. His campaigns were arranged, and His victories were gained in the struggles and communion of His all-night praying. By prayer He rent the heavens. Moses and Elijah and the glory of the Transfiguration waited on His praying. His miracles and teaching had their power from the same source. Gethsemane's praying crimsoned Calvary with serenity and glory. His High Priestly Prayer made the history and hastens the triumph of His church on earth. What an inspiration and command to pray is the prayer life of Jesus Christ while he was in this world! What a comment it is on the value, the nature, and the necessity of prayer!

The dispensation of the person of Jesus Christ was a dispensation of prayer. A synopsis of His teaching and practice of prayer was that *"men always ought to pray and not lose heart"* (Luke 18:1).

PRAY IN JESUS'S NAME

The Jews prayed in the name of their patriarchs and invoked the privileges granted to them by covenant with God. We have a new name and a new covenant, more privileged, more powerful, more comprehensive, more authoritative, and more divine; and as far as the Son of God is lifted above the patriarchs in divinity, glory, and power, by so much should our praying exceed theirs in range of largeness, glory, and power of results.

Jesus Christ prayed to God as Father. Simply and directly, He approached God in the charmed and revered circle of the Father. The awful, repelling fear was entirely absent, lost in the supreme confidence of a child.

Jesus Christ crowned His life, His works, and His teaching with prayer. How His Father attested to His relationship with Him and put on Him the glory of answered prayer at His baptism and transfiguration, when all other glories were growing dim in the night that was settling on Him! What almighty power is in prayer when we are charged and surcharged with but one inspiration and aim! *"Father, glorify Your name"* (John 12:28). This attitude sweetens all, brightens all, conquers all, and gets all. *"Father, glorify Your name."* That guiding star will illumine the darkest night and calm the wildest storm; it will make us brave and true. It is an imperial principle. It will make an imperial Christian. The range and power of prayer, so clearly shown by Jesus in His life and teaching, reveal the great purposes of God. They not only show the Son in the reality and fullness of His humanity, but also reveal the Father.

PRAY AS A CHILD

Christ prayed as a child. The spirit of a child was found in Him. At the grave of Lazarus, *"Jesus lifted up His eyes and said, 'Father'"* (John 11:41). Again we hear Him begin His prayer after this fashion: *"In that hour Jesus rejoiced in the Spirit and said, 'I thank You, Father'"* (Luke 10:21).

So also on other occasions we find Him in prayer addressing God as His Father, assuming the attitude of the child asking something of his father. What confidence, simplicity, and guilelessness! What readiness, freeness, and fullness of approach are all involved in the spirit of a child! What confiding trust, what assurance, what tender interest! What profound concern and tender sympathy on the Father's part! What respect deepening into reverence! What loving obedience and grateful emotions glow in the child's heart! What divine fellowship and royal intimacy! What sacred and sweet emotions! All these meet in the hour of prayer when the child of God meets His Father in heaven and when the Father meets His child! We must live as children if we would ask as children. We must act as children if we would pray as children. The spirit of prayer is born of a childlike spirit.

The profound reverence in this relationship of paternity must forever exclude all lightness, frivolity, and pertness, as well as all undue familiarity. Solemnity and gravity become the hour of prayer. It has been well said:

> The worshipper who invokes God under the name of Father and realizes the gracious and beneficent love of God must at the same time remember and recognize God's glorious majesty, which is neither annulled nor impaired, but rather supremely intensified through His fatherly love. An appeal to God as Father, if not associated with reverence and homage before the Divine Majesty, would betray a lack of understanding of the character of God.

And, we might add, would show a lack of the attributes of a child.

Patriarchs and prophets knew something of the doctrine of the Fatherhood of God to God's family. They *"all died in faith, not having received the promises, but having seen them afar off were assured of them,* [and] *embraced them"* (Hebrews 11:13), even though they did not understand them in all their fullness.

> *And all these, having obtained a good testimony through faith, did not receive the promise, God having provided something better for us, that they should not be made perfect apart from us.* (Hebrews 11:39–40)

PRAY EARNESTLY

"*Behold, he is praying*" (Acts 9:11) was God's statement of wonder and surprise to the timid Ananias in regard to Saul of Tarsus. "Behold, He is praying" applied to Christ has in it far more wonder, mystery, and surprise. He, the Maker of all worlds; the Lord of angels and of men; coequal and coeternal with the everlasting God; "*the brightness of His glory and the express image of His person*" (Hebrews 1:3); fresh from His Father's glory and from His Father's throne—"*Behold, He is praying.*" To find Him in a lowly, dependent attitude of prayer, the Suppliant of all suppliants, His richest legacy and His royal privilege to pray—this is the mystery of all mysteries, the wonder of all wonders.

The writer of Hebrews gave a brief but comprehensive statement regarding the habit of our Lord in prayer:

> *Who, in the days of His flesh, when He had offered up prayers and supplications, with vehement cries and tears to Him who was able to save Him from death, and was heard because of His godly fear.*
>
> (Hebrews 5:7)

We have in this description of our Lord's praying the outgoing of great spiritual forces. He prayed with "*prayers and supplications.*" It was no formal, tentative effort. He was intense, personal, and real. He was a pleader for God's good. He was in great need, and He had to cry with "*vehement cries*" made stronger still by His tears. In agony, the Son of God wrestled. His praying was no playing a mere part. His soul was engaged, and all His powers were taxed. Let us pause and look at Him and learn how to pray in earnest. Let us learn how to win in an agony of prayer what seems to be withheld from us. "*Godly fear*"—what a beautiful phrase that is! It occurs only two other times in the New Testament. (See Hebrews 11:7; 12:28.)

NEVER TOO BUSY TO PRAY

Jesus Christ was always a busy man with His work, but He was never too busy to pray. Divine business filled His heart and His hands, consumed His time, and exhausted His nerves. But with Him even God's work must not crowd out God's praying. Saving people from sin or suffering must not, even with Christ, be substituted for praying, or lessen in the least the time or the intensity of these holiest of seasons. He filled the day with working for God; He employed the night with praying to God. The work of the day made the prayers of the night a necessity. The praying sanctified and made successful the working. Too busy to pray gives religion a Christian burial; it is true, but kills it nevertheless.

In many cases, only the bare fact, yet the important and suggestive fact, is stated that He prayed. In other cases, the very words that came out of His heart and fell from His lips are recorded. The man of prayer, by preeminence, was Jesus Christ. The epochs of His life were created by prayer, and all the minor details of His life were inspired, colored, and impregnated by prayer.

The prayer words of Jesus are sacred words. By them, God speaks to God, and by them, God is revealed, and prayer is illustrated and reinforced. Here is prayer in its purest form and in its mightiest power. It would seem that earth and heaven would open their ears wide to catch the words of His praying who was truest God and truest man, divinest of suppliants, who prayed as no man has ever prayed. His prayers are our inspiration and pattern to pray.

Ask, and it will be given to you; seek, and you will find; knock, and it will be opened to you. For everyone who asks receives, and he who seeks finds, and to him who knocks it will be opened. —Matthew 7:7–8

Likewise the Spirit also helps in our weaknesses. For we do not know what we should pray for as we ought, but the Spirit Himself makes intercession for us with groanings which cannot be uttered.
—Romans 8:26

Now to Him who is able to do exceedingly abundantly above all that we ask or think, according to the power that works in us, to Him be glory in the church by Christ Jesus to all generations, forever and ever.
—Ephesians 3:20–21

EIGHT:

INSIGHTS FROM PRAYERS OF OUR LORD

There was a great cape at the south of Africa and so many storms and so much loss of life until it was called the Cape of Death. One day in 1789 a bold navigator shoved the prow of his vessel into the storms that thundered around it and found a calm sea. He then named it the Cape of Good Hope. So there is a cape that jutted out from earth into the sea of eternity called death. All were afraid of it. All navigators, sooner or later, must contend with these murky waters. But once upon a time, nearly two thousand years ago, a brave Navigator from heaven came and drove the prow of His frail humanity bark down into the gloomy waters of this cape and lay under its awful power for three days. Emerging from it, He found it to be the door to endless calm and joy, and now we call it Good Hope.

—John W. Baker

One of Christ's most impassioned and sublime hymns of prayer and praise is found recorded by both Matthew and Luke, with a few verbal contrasts and some diversity of detail and conditions. (See Matthew 11:25–30 and Luke 10:21–22.) In this context, Jesus is reviewing the results of His ministry and remarking upon the feeble responses of man to God's vast outlay of love and mercy. He is rebuking men for their ingratitude to God, and is showing the fearfully destructive results of their indifference, considering their increased opportunities, favors, and responsibilities.

TRUTH IS REVEALED TO BABES

In the midst of these charges, denunciations, and woes, the seventy disciples return to report the results of their mission. They are full of exhilaration at their success and show it with no little self-congratulation. The spirit of Jesus is diverted, relieved, and refreshed by their animation, catching somewhat the contagion of their joy, and sharing in their triumph. He rejoices, gives thanks, and prays a prayer wonderful in its brevity, its inspiration, and its revelation.

In that hour Jesus rejoiced in the Spirit and said, "I thank You, Father, Lord of heaven and earth, that You have hidden these things from the wise and prudent and revealed them to babes. Even so, Father, for so it seemed good in Your sight. All things have been delivered to Me by My Father, and no one knows who the Son is except the Father, and who the Father is except the Son, and the one to whom the Son wills to reveal Him." (Luke 10:21–22)

GOD'S WILL COMES FIRST

Christ's life was lived in the image of His Father. He was the *"express image of His person"* (Hebrews 1:3). And so, for Christ, the spirit of prayer with Christ was to do God's will. His constant affirmation was that He came to do His Father's will, and not His own will. (See, for example, Matthew 26:39, 42; Luke 11:2; John 5:30.) When the fearful crisis came in His life in Gethsemane, along with all its darkness, direness, and dread, with the crushing weight of man's sins and sorrows pressing down upon Him, His spirit and frame crushed and almost expiring, He cried for relief, yet it was not His will that was to be followed. (See Matthew 26:39.) His cry was only an appeal out of weakness and death for God's relief in God's way. God's will was to be the law and the rule of His relief, if relief came.

CHARACTER INFLUENCES PRAYING; PRAYING INFLUENCES CHARACTER

So he who follows Christ in prayer must have God's will as his law, his rule, and his inspiration. In all praying, it is the man who prays. Man's life and character flow into the prayer closet. There is a mutual action and reaction. The place of prayer has much to do with making the character, while the character has much to do with making the place of prayer. It is *"the effective, fervent prayer of a righteous man* [that] *avails much"* (James 5:16). It is *"with those who call on the Lord out of a pure heart"* (2 Timothy 2:22) that we are to associate. Christ was the greatest of prayers because He was the holiest of men. His character is the praying character. His spirit is the life and power of prayer. The best prayer is not the one who has the greatest fluency, the most brilliant imagination, the richest gifts, or the most fiery ardor, but the one who has absorbed the most of the spirit of Christ.

It is he whose character is the nearest to a facsimile of Christ. Christ's prayer recorded in Matthew and Luke sets forth the characters of those on whom God's power is bestowed and to whom God's person and will are revealed. Jesus said that God has *"hidden these things from the wise and prudent"* (Matthew 11:25)—those, for instance, who are *"wise"* in their own eyes, scholars, cultured, philosophers, doctors, rabbis, and those who are *"prudent,"* who can put things together, have insight, comprehension, and eloquence.

God's revelation of Himself and His will cannot be sought out and understood by reason, intelligence, or great learning. Great men and great minds are neither the channels nor the depositories of God's revelation by virtue of their culture, intelligence, or wisdom. God's system of redemption and providence is not to be thought out; it is not open only to the learned and the wise. Those who follow their own learning and wisdom have always sadly and darkly missed God's thoughts and God's ways.

GOD REVEALS HIMSELF TO THE CHILDLIKE

The condition of receiving God's revelation and of holding God's truth is one of the heart, not one of the head. The ability to receive and search out is like that of a child, a babe, the synonym of teachability, innocence, and simplicity. These are the conditions on which God reveals Himself to men. The world by wisdom cannot know God. The world by wisdom can never receive or understand God, because God reveals Himself to men's hearts, not to their heads. Only hearts can ever know God, can feel God, can see God, and can read God in His Book of Books. God is not grasped by thought but by feeling. The world receives God by revelation, not by philosophy. It is not apprehension, the mental ability to grasp God, but plasticity, the ability to be molded, that men need. It is not by hard, strong, stern, great reasoning that the world finds God or takes hold of God, but by big, soft, pure hearts. Men do not need light to see God as much as they need hearts to feel God.

Human wisdom, great natural talents, and the culture of the schools, however good they may be, can neither be the repositories nor conservators of God's revealed truth. The tree of knowledge has been the bane of faith, ever trying to reduce revelation to a philosophy and to measure God by man. In its pride, it removes God and puts man into God's truth. To become babes again, on our mother's bosom, quieted, weaned, without clamor or protest, is the only position in which to know God. A calmness on the surface and in the depths of the soul, in which God can mirror His will, His Word, and Himself is the attitude toward Him through which He can reveal Himself, and this attitude is the right attitude of prayer.

PRAYER PRECEDES MINISTRY

Our Lord taught us the lesson of prayer by putting into practice in His life what He taught by His lips. Here is a simple but important statement, full of meaning:

And when He had sent the multitudes away, He went up on the mountain by Himself to pray. Now when evening came, He was alone there. (Matthew 14:23)

The multitudes had been fed and were dismissed by our Lord. The divine work of healing and teaching must be stayed awhile in order that time, place, and opportunity for prayer might be secured. Prayer is the most divine of all labor, the most important of all ministries. Away from the eager, anxious, seeking multitudes, He went, while the day was still bright, to be alone with God. The multitudes had taxed and exhausted Him. The disciples were being tossed on the sea (see verses 22, 24), but calmness reigned on the mountaintop where our Lord knelt in secret prayer— where prayer rules.

He must be alone in that moment with God. Temptation was in that hour. The multitude had feasted on the five loaves and two fish. Filled with food and excited beyond measure, they had desired to make Him king. *"When Jesus perceived that they were about to come and take Him by force to make Him king, He departed again to the mountain by Himself alone"* (John 6:15). He flees from the temptation to secret prayer, for it is the source of His strength to resist evil. What a refuge was secret prayer even to Him! What a refuge to us from the world's dazzling and deceptive crowns! What safety there is to be alone with God when the world tempts us, allures us, attracts us! The prayers of our Lord were prophetic and illustrative of the great truth that the greatest measure of the Holy Spirit, the attesting voice and opening heavens, is secured only by prayer. This is suggested by Christ's baptism by John the Baptist, when He prayed as He was baptized and immediately the Holy Spirit descended upon Him *"like a dove"* (Luke 3:22). More than prophetic and illustrative was this hour to Him. This critical hour was real and personal, consecrating and qualifying Him for God's highest purposes. Prayer to Him, just as it is to us, was a necessity— an absolute, invariable condition of securing God's fullest, consecrating, and qualifying power. The Holy Spirit came upon Him in fullness of measure and power in the very act of prayer.

SONSHIP IS CONFIRMED THROUGH PRAYER

And so the Holy Spirit comes upon us in fullness of measure and power only in answer to ardent and intense praying. The heavens were opened to Christ, and access and communion established and enlarged, by prayer. Freedom and fullness of access and closeness of communion are secured to us as the heritage of prayer. The voice attesting His Sonship came to Christ in prayer. The witness of our sonship, clear and indubitable, is secured only by praying. The constant witness of sonship can be retained only by those who *"pray without ceasing"* (1 Thessalonians 5:17). When the stream of prayer is shallow and arrested, the evidence of our sonship becomes faint and inaudible.

NINE:

LEARNING FROM THE PRAYERS OF JESUS

Sin is so unspeakably awful in its evil that it struck down, as to death and hell, the very Son of God Himself. He had been amazed enough at sin before. He had seen sin making angels of heaven into devils of hell. Death and all its terrors did not much move or disconcert our Lord. No, it was not death. It was sin. It was hellfire in His soul. It was the coal and the oil and the rosin and the juniper and the turpentine of the fire that is not quenched (Mark 9:43–48).
—Alexander Whyte

We note that from the revelation and inspiration of a transporting prayer-hour of Christ, as its natural sequence, there sounds out that gracious, encouraging proclamation for heavyhearted, restless, weary souls of earth. Christ's words have so impressed, arrested, and drawn humanity as they have fallen on the ears of burdened souls. These words have so sweetened and relieved men of their strenuous work and burdens:

Come to Me, all you who labor and are heavy laden, and I will give you rest. Take My yoke upon you and learn from Me, for I am gentle and lowly in heart, and you will find rest for your souls. For My yoke is easy and My burden is light. (Matthew 11:28–30)

JESUS'S CONFIDENCE IN PRAYER

At the grave of Lazarus and as preparatory to and as a condition of calling him back to life, we have our Lord calling on His Father in heaven. *"Father, I thank You that You have heard Me. And I know that You always hear Me"* (John 11:41–42). *"Jesus lifted up His eyes"* (v. 41)—how much was in that heavenly look! How much confidence and plea were in that look to heaven! His very look, the lifting of His eyes, carried His whole being heavenward and caused a pause in that world. His look drew attention and help. All heaven was engaged, pledged, and moved when the Son of God looked up from this grave. Oh, for a people with a Christlike eye, heaven-lifted and heaven arresting! As it was with Christ, so should we be so perfected in faith, so skilled in praying, that we could lift our eyes to heaven and say with Him, with deepest humility and with commanding confidence, *"Father, I thank You that You have heard Me."*

JESUS'S DIRECTIVE TO PRAY

Once more we have a very touching, beautiful, and instructive incident in Christ's praying, which is parabolic as well as historical. This time it had to do with infants in their mothers' arms:

Then they brought little children to Him, that He might touch them; but the disciples rebuked those who brought them. But when Jesus saw it, He was greatly displeased and said to them, "Let the little children come to Me, and do not forbid them; for of such is the kingdom of God. Assuredly, I say to you, whoever does not receive the kingdom of God as a little child will by no means enter it." And He took them up in His arms, put His hands on them, and blessed them. (Mark 10:13–16)

This was one of the few times when ignorance and unspiritual views aroused His indignation and displeasure. Vital principles were involved.

Foundations were being destroyed, and worldly views influencing the actions of the disciples. Their temper and their words in rebuking those who brought their children to Christ were exceedingly wrong. The very principles that He came to illustrate and propagate were being violated.

Christ received the little ones. The big ones must become little ones. The old ones must become young ones before Christ will receive them. Prayer helps the little ones. The cradle must be invested with prayer. We are to pray for our little ones. Children are now to be brought to Jesus Christ by prayer, as He is in heaven and not on earth. They are to be brought to Him early for His blessing, even when they are infants. His blessing descends on these little ones in answer to the prayers of those who bring them. With untiring importunity they are to be brought to Christ in earnest, persevering prayer by their fathers and mothers. Before they themselves know anything about coming of their own accord, parents are to present them to God in prayer, seeking His blessing on their offspring. At the same time, parents should ask for wisdom, grace, and divine help to rear their children so that they may come to Christ when they arrive at the years of accountability.

Holy hands and holy praying have much to do with guarding and training young lives and in forming young characters for righteousness and heaven. What simplicity, kindness, spirituality, humility, and meekness, linked with prayerfulness, are in this act of the divine Teacher!

THE PERSONAL ASPECT IN JESUS'S PRAYERS

It was as Jesus was praying that Peter made that wonderful confession of his faith that Jesus was the Son of God. *"And it happened, as He was alone praying, that His disciples joined Him, and He asked them, saying, 'Who do the crowds say that I am?'"* (Luke 9:18). The disciples answered,

> *"Some say John the Baptist, some Elijah, and others Jeremiah or one of the prophets." He said to them, "But who do you say that I am?" Simon Peter answered and said, "You are the Christ, the Son of the living God." Jesus answered and said to him, "Blessed are you, Simon Bar-Jonah, for flesh and blood has not revealed this to you, but My Father who is in heaven. And I also say to you that you are Peter, and on this*

rock I will build My church, and the gates of Hades shall not prevail against it. And I will give you the keys of the kingdom of heaven, and whatever you bind on earth will be bound in heaven, and whatever you loose on earth will be loosed in heaven." (Matthew 16:14–19)

It was after our Lord had made large promises to His disciples, appointing to each of them a kingdom, that they should sit at His table in His kingdom and sit on thrones judging the twelve tribes of Israel (see Luke 22:29–30), that He gave these words of warning to Simon Peter, telling him that He had prayed for him.

And the Lord said, "Simon, Simon! Indeed, Satan has asked for you, that he may sift you as wheat. But I have prayed for you, that your faith should not fail; and when you have returned to Me, strengthen your brethren." (Luke 22:31–32)

Happy Peter, to have the Son of God pray for him! Unhappy Peter, to be so in the toils of Satan as to demand so much of Christ's concern! How intense are the demands upon our prayers for some specific cases! Prayer must be personal in order to be, to the fullest extent, beneficial. Peter drew on Christ's praying more than any other disciple because of his exposure to greater perils. Pray for the most impulsive, the most endangered ones, by name. Our love and their danger give frequency, inspiration, intensity, and personality to praying.

THE POWER IN JESUS'S PRAYERS

We have seen how Christ had to flee from the multitude after the magnificent miracle of feeding the five thousand as they sought to make Him king. Then prayer was His escape and His refuge from this strong worldly temptation. He returned from that night of prayer with strength and calmness, and with a power to perform that other remarkable miracle of walking on the sea.

Even the loaves and fish were sanctified by prayer before He served them to the multitude. *"And when He had taken the five loaves and the two fish, He looked up to heaven, blessed and broke the loaves"* (Mark 6:41). Prayer should sanctify our daily bread and multiply our seed sown.

He looked up to heaven and heaved a sigh when He touched the tongue of the deaf man who had an impediment in his speech. This sigh was similar to that groaning in spirit that He evinced at the grave of Lazarus. *"Then Jesus, again groaning in Himself, came to the tomb"* (John 11:38). Here was the sigh of the Son of God over a human wreck, groaning that sin and hell had such a mastery over man, troubled that such a desolation and ruin were man's sad inheritance. This is a lesson to be constantly learned by us. Here is a fact always to be kept in mind and heart, and that must ever, in some measure, weigh upon the inner spirits of God's children. We who have received the *"firstfruits of the Spirit...groan within ourselves"* (Romans 8:23) at sin's waste and death, and are filled with longings for the coming of a better day.

CHARACTER AND PRAYER ARE INTERCONNECTED

Present in all great praying, making, and marking it is the man. It is impossible to separate the praying from the man. The elements of the man are the constituents of his praying. The man flows through his praying. Only the fiery Elijah could do Elijah's fiery praying. We can get holy praying only from a holy man. Holy being can never exist without holy doing. Being is first; doing comes afterward. What we are gives being, force, and inspiration to what we do. Character, that which is graven deeply, indelibly, imperishably within us, colors all we do.

The praying of Christ, then, is not to be separated from the character of Christ. If He prayed more unweariedly, more self-denyingly, more holily, more simply, and directly than other men, it was because these elements entered more largely into His character than into that of others.

PRAYER AFFECTS THE ONE WHO PRAYS

The Transfiguration marks another epoch in Christ's life, one that was preeminently a prayer epoch. Luke gives an account of this event along with its intention and purpose:

> *Now it came to pass, about eight days after these sayings, that He took Peter, John, and James and went up on the mountain to pray. As He prayed, the appearance of His face was altered, and His robe became*

white and glistening. And behold, two men talked with Him, who were Moses and Elijah, who appeared in glory and spoke of His decease which He was about to accomplish at Jerusalem. (Luke 9:28–31)

The selection was made of three of His disciples for an inner circle of associates in prayer. Few have the spiritual tastes or aptitude for this inner circle. Even these three favored ones could scarcely stand the strain of that long night of praying. We know that He went up on that mountain to pray, not to be transfigured. But it was as He prayed that His appearance was altered and His clothing became white and glistening. There is nothing like prayer to change character and whiten conduct. There is nothing like prayer to bring heavenly visitants and to gild with heavenly glory earth's dull and drear mountain. Peter calls it the *"holy mountain"* (2 Peter 1:18), made so by prayer.

JESUS WAS A MAN OF PRAYER

Three times the voice of God bore witness to the presence and person of His Son, Jesus Christ. First, at His baptism by John the Baptist, and then at His transfiguration, where the approving, consoling, and witnessing voice of His Father was heard. Jesus was found in prayer both of these times. The third time the attesting voice came, it was not on the heights of His transfigured glory, nor was it as He was girding Himself to begin His conflict and to enter upon His ministry, but it was when He was hastening to the awful end. He was entering the dark mystery of His last agony, and looking ahead to it. The shadows were deepening, a dire calamity was approaching, and an unknown and untried dread was before Him. As He pondered His approaching death, prophesying about it, and forecasting the glory that would follow—in the midst of His high and mysterious discourse—the shadows came like a dread eclipse, and He burst out in an agony of prayer.

"Now My soul is troubled, and what shall I say? 'Father, save Me from this hour'? But for this purpose I came to this hour. Father, glorify Your name." Then a voice came from heaven, saying, "I have both glorified it and will glorify it again." Therefore the people who stood by and heard it said that it had thundered. Others said, "An angel has spoken

to Him." Jesus answered and said, "This voice did not come because of Me, but for your sake." (John 12:27–30)

But let it be noted that Christ is meeting and illuminating this fateful and distressing hour with prayer. Even then, the flesh reluctantly shrank from the contemplated end!

How fully does His prayer on the cross for His enemies synchronize with all He taught about love to our enemies, and mercy and forgiveness to those who have trespassed against us! *"Then Jesus said, 'Father, forgive them, for they do not know what they do'"* (Luke 23:34). Apologizing for His murderers, and praying for them while they were jeering and mocking Him at His death pains, and their hands were reeking with His blood—what amazing generosity, pity, and love!

JESUS REVEALED HIS HEART IN PRAYER

Again, take another one of the prayers on the cross. How touching the prayer and how bitter the cup! How dark and desolate the hour as He exclaims, *"My God, My God, why have You forsaken Me?"* (Matthew 27:46). This is the last stroke that tears His heart in two, more exquisite in its bitterness and its anguish and more heart-piercing than the kiss of Judas. All else was looked for, all else was put in His book of sorrows. How excruciating to have His Father's face withdrawn, to be forsaken by His Father during the hour when these distressing words escaped the lips of the dying Son of God! And yet how truthful He is! How childlike we find Him! And so when the end really comes, we hear Him again speaking to His Father: *"'Father, "into Your hands I commit My spirit."' Having said this, He breathed His last"* (Luke 23:46).

Pray without ceasing. —1 Thessalonians 5:17

I do not pray for these alone, but also for those who will believe in Me through their word; that they all may be one, as You, Father, are in Me, and I in You; that they also may be one in Us, that the world may believe that You sent Me. —John 17:20–21

Watch and pray, lest you enter into temptation. The spirit indeed is willing, but the flesh is weak. —Mark 14:38

TEN:

OUR LORD'S MODEL PRAYER

What satisfaction must it be to learn from God Himself with what words and in what manner He would have us pray to Him so as not to pray in vain! We do not sufficiently consider the value of this prayer, the respect and attention that it requires, the preference to be given to it, its fulness and perfections, the frequent use we should make of it, and the spirit that we should bring with it. *"Lord, teach us [how] to pray"* (Luke 11:1).   —Adam Clark

Jesus gives us the pattern of prayer in what is commonly known as the Lord's Prayer. In this model, perfect prayer, He gives us a form to be followed, and yet one to be filled in and enlarged as we may decide when we pray. The outlines and form are complete, yet it is but an outline, with many blanks that our needs and convictions are to fill in.

PRAYER NEEDS WORDS

Christ puts words on our lips, words that are to be uttered by holy lives. Words belong to the life of prayer. Wordless prayers are like human spirits; they may be pure and high, but are too ethereal and intangible for earthly conflicts and earthly needs and uses. We must have spirits clothed in flesh and blood, and our prayers must be likewise clothed in words to give them point and power, a local habitation, and a name.

PRAYER HONORS GOD'S NAME

This lesson of the Lord's Prayer, elicited by the request of the disciples, *"Lord, teach us to pray"* (Luke 11:1), has something in form and verbiage like the prayer sections of the Sermon on the Mount. It is the same great lesson of praying to *"our Father in heaven"* (v. 2), and is one of insistent importunity. No prayer lesson would be complete without it. It belongs to the first and last lessons in prayer. God's Fatherhood gives shape, value, and confidence to all our praying.

Christ teaches us that to hallow God's name is the first and the greatest of prayers. A desire for the coming and the establishment of God's glorious kingdom follows in value and in sequence the hallowing of God's name. He who really hallows God's name will hail the coming of the kingdom of God, and will labor and pray to bring that kingdom to pass and to establish it. Christ's pupils in the school of prayer are to be taught diligently to hallow God's name; to work for God's kingdom; and to do God's will perfectly, completely, and gladly, *"as it is in heaven"* (v. 2).

PRAYER ESTABLISHES GOD'S WILL ON EARTH

Prayer engages the highest interests and secures the highest glory of God. God's name, God's kingdom, and God's will are all in it. Without prayer His name is profaned, His kingdom fails, and His will is devalued and opposed. God's will can be done on earth as it is done in heaven. God's will done on earth makes earth like heaven. Persevering prayer is the mighty energy that establishes God's will on earth as it is established in heaven.

PRAYER PROVIDES BREAD, FORGIVENESS, AND PROTECTION FROM EVIL

Christ is still teaching us that prayer sanctifies and makes hopeful and sweet our daily work for daily bread. Forgiveness of sins is to be sought by prayer, and the great prayer plea we are to make for our forgiveness is that we have forgiven all those who have sinned against us (Matthew 6:12). It involves love for our enemies so far as to pray for them, to bless them and not curse them, and to pardon their offences against us whatever those offences may be (Luke 6:27–29).

We are to pray, *"Do not lead us into temptation"* (Matthew 6:13), that is, while we thus pray, the Tempter and the temptation are to be watched against, resisted, and prayed against.

PRAYER IS FOR ALL STAGES OF LIFE

Jesus lays down all these things in this law of prayer, but He teaches many simple lessons through the comments and expressions He adds to expand and explain His model prayer.

In this prayer Jesus teaches His disciples to pray words that have become so familiar to thousands in this day who learned it at their mothers' knees in childhood. These words are so childlike that children find their instruction, edification, and comfort in them as they kneel and pray. The most glowing mystic and the most careful thinker each finds his own language in these simple words of prayer. Beautiful and revered as these words are, they are our words for solace, help, and learning.

Christ led the way in prayer so that we might follow His footsteps. Matchless Leader in matchless praying! Lord, teach us to pray as You Yourself pray!

How marked the contrast is between the High Priestly Prayer and this Lord's Prayer, the model for praying that He gave to His disciples as the first elements of prayer. How simple and childlike! No one has ever approached in composition a prayer so simple in its petitions and yet so comprehensive in all of its requests.

How these simple elements of prayer as given by our Lord commend themselves to us! This prayer is for us as well as for those to whom it was first given. It is for the child in the ABCs of prayer, and it is for the graduate of the highest institutions of learning. It is a personal prayer, reaching to all our needs and covering all our sins. It is the highest form of prayer for others. As the student can never in all his studies or learning dispense with his ABCs, and as the alphabet gives form, color, and expression to everything that is learned after it, impregnating and grounding everything, so the learner in Christ can never dispense with the Lord's Prayer. But he may make it form the basis of his higher praying, such as intercession for others as is seen in Christ's High Priestly Prayer.

The Lord's Prayer becomes ours at our mother's knee and fits us in all the stages of a joyous Christian life. The High Priestly Prayer is ours also in the stages and office of our royal priesthood as intercessors before God. Here we have oneness with God, deep, spiritual unity and unswerving loyalty to God. We live and pray to glorify God.

ELEVEN:

OUR LORD'S HIGH PRIESTLY PRAYER

Jesus closes His life with inimitable calmness, confidence, and sublimity. *"I have glorified You on the earth. I have finished the work which You have given Me to do"* (John 17:4). The annals of earth have nothing comparable to it in real serenity and sublimity. May we come to our end thus, in supreme loyalty to Christ.

—E. M. Bounds

We come now to consider our Lord's High Priestly Prayer, as found recorded in the seventeenth chapter of John's gospel. Obedience to the Father and abiding in the Father belong to the Son and belong to us, as partners with Christ in His divine work of intercession. How tenderly, how compassionately, and how fully He prays for His disciples! *"I pray for them. I do not pray for the world"* (John 17:9). What a pattern of prayerfulness for God's people! For God's people are God's cause, God's church, and God's kingdom. Pray for God's people, for their unity, their sanctification, and their glorification. How the subject of their unity pressed upon

Him! These walls of separation, these alienations, these fractured circles of God's family, and these warring tribes of ecclesiastics—how He is torn and bleeds and suffers afresh at the sight of these divisions! Unity—that is the great burden of the remarkable High Priestly Prayer. *"That they may be one as We are"* (John 17:11, see also, v. 22). The spiritual oneness of God's people is the heritage of God's glory to them, transmitted by Christ to His church.

JESUS PRAYS FOR HIMSELF

First of all, in this prayer, Jesus prays for Himself. He does not petition, as in Gethsemane, out of weakness, but in strength. Now there is not the pressure of darkness and hell, but passing for the time over the fearful interim, He asks that He may be glorified, and that His exalted glory may secure glory to His Father. His sublime loyalty and fidelity to God are declared, that fidelity to God that is the very essence of prayer. Our devoted lives pray. Our unswerving loyalty to God are eloquent pleas to Him, and give access and confidence in our advocacy. This prayer is gemmed, but its walls are unshakable. What profound and granite truths! What fathomless mysteries! What deep and rich experiences such statements as these involve:

> *And this is eternal life, that they may know You, the only true God, and Jesus Christ whom You have sent....And all Mine are Yours, and Yours are Mine, and I am glorified in them....And I have declared to them Your name, and will declare it, that the love with which You loved Me may be in them, and I in them....And now, O Father, glorify Me together with Yourself, with the glory which I had with You before the world was.* (John 17:3, 10, 26, 5)

Let us stop and ask, do we have eternal life? Do we know God experientially, consciously, really, and personally? Do we know Jesus Christ as a person, and as a personal Savior? Do we know Him by a heart acquaintance, and know Him well? This, this only, is eternal life. And is Jesus glorified in us? Let us continue this personal inquiry. Do our lives prove His divinity? Does Jesus shine brighter because of us? Are we opaque or transparent bodies, and do we darken or reflect His pure light? Once more let us ask: Do we seek God's glory? Do we seek glory where Christ sought it? *"Glorify Me together with Yourself"* (John 17:5). Do we esteem the presence and the possession of God as our most excellent glory and our supreme good?

How closely does He bind Himself and His Father to His people! His heart centers on them in this high hour of holy communion with His Father.

> *I have manifested Your name to the men whom You have given Me out of the world. They were Yours, You gave them to Me, and they have kept Your word. Now they have known that all things which You have given Me are from You. For I have given to them the words which You have given Me; and they have received them, and have known surely that I came forth from You; and they have believed that You sent Me. I pray for them. I do not pray for the world but for those whom You have given Me, for they are Yours. And all Mine are Yours, and Yours are Mine, and I am glorified in them.* (John 17:6–10)

JESUS PRAYS FOR HIS FOLLOWERS

He prays also for keeping for His disciples. Not only were they to be chosen, elected, and possessed, but also kept by the Father's watchful eyes and by the Father's omnipotent hand.

> *Now I am no longer in the world, but these are in the world, and I come to You. Holy Father, keep through Your name those whom You have given Me, that they may be one as We are.* (John 17:11)

He prays that they might be kept by the Holy Father in all holiness by the power of His Name. He asks that His people may be kept from sin, from all sin, from sin in the concrete and sin in the abstract, from sin in all its shapes of evil, from all sin in this world. He prays that they might not only be fit and ready for heaven, but also ready and fit for earth, for its sweetest privileges, its sternest duties, its deepest sorrows, and its richest joys. He prays that they might be ready for all of its trials, consolations, and triumphs. *"I do not pray that You should take them out of the world, but that You should keep them from the evil one"* (John 17:15).

He prays that they might be kept from the world's greatest evil: sin. He desires that they may be kept from the guilt, the power, the pollution, and the punishment of sin. He prays that they might be kept from the Devil, so that he might not touch them, find them, or have a place in them; that they all might be owned, possessed, filled, and guarded by God. *"Kept by the power of God through faith for salvation"* (1 Peter 1:5).

JESUS ENTRUSTS HIS FOLLOWERS TO THE FATHER'S CARE

He places us in the arms of His Father, on the bosom of His Father, and in the heart of His Father. He calls God into service and places us under His Father's closest keeping, under His Father's shadow, and under the shelter of His Father's wing. The Father's rod and staff are for our security, our comfort, our refuge, our strength, and our guidance.

These disciples were not to be taken out of the world, but kept from its evil, its monstrous evil, which is itself. *"Deliver us from this present evil age"* (Galatians 1:4).

How the world seduces, dazzles, and deludes the children of men! His disciples are chosen out of the world, out of the world's bustle and worldliness, out of its all-devouring greed of gain, out of its money-desire, money-love, and money-toil. Earth draws and holds as if it were made out of gold and not out of dirt, as though it were covered with diamonds and not with graves.

"They are not of the world, just as I am not of the world" (John 17:14). They were to be kept not only from sin and Satan, but also from the soil, stain, and the taint of worldliness, as Christ was free from it. Their relationship to Christ was to free them from the world's defiling taint, its unhallowed love, and its criminal friendships. The world's hatred would inevitably follow their Christlikeness. No result so necessarily and universally follows its cause as this: *"The world has hated them because they are not of the world, just as I am not of the world"* (v. 14).

How solemn and almost terrifying the repetition of the declaration, *"They are not of the world, just as I am not of the world"* (v. 16). How pronounced, radical, and eternal was our Lord Christ's divorce from the world! How pronounced, radical, and eternal is our Lord's true followers' separation from the world! The world hates the disciples as it hated their Lord, and will crucify the disciples just as it crucified their Lord. How pertinent are these questions: Are we Christlike in our detachment from this world? Does the world hate us as it hated our Lord? Are His words fulfilled in us?

> *If the world hates you, you know that it hated Me before it hated you. If you were of the world, the world would love its own. Yet because you are not of the world, but I chose you out of the world, therefore the world hates you.* (John 15:18–19)

He presents Himself to us as a true portrait of an unworldly Christian. Here is our changeless pattern. *"They are not of the world, just as I am not of the world"* (John 17:14, 16). We must be modeled after this pattern.

JESUS PRAYS FOR UNITY

The subject of His followers' unity pressed upon Him. Note how He called His Father's attention to it, and see how He pleaded for their unity:

> *Now I am no longer in the world, but these are in the world, and I come to You. Holy Father, keep through Your name those whom You have given Me, that they may be one as We are.* (John 17:11)

Again He returns to this subject as He foresees the great crowds flocking to His standard as the ages pass on:

> *That they all may be one, as You, Father, are in Me, and I in You; that they also may be one in Us, that the world may believe that You sent Me. And the glory which You gave Me I have given them, that they may be one just as We are one: I in them, and You in Me; that they may be made perfect in one, and that the world may know that You have sent Me, and have loved them as You have loved Me.*
> (John 17:21–23)

Notice how intently His heart was set on this unity. What shameful and bloody history has this lack of unity written for God's church! These walls of separations, these alienations, these divided circles of God's family, these warring tribes of men, and these deadly battles among brothers!

Christ looks ahead and sees how He is torn, how He bleeds and suffers afresh in all these sad events of the future. The unity of God's people was to be the heritage of God's glory promised to them. Division and strife are the Devil's bequest to the church, a heritage of failure, weakness, shame, and woe.

The oneness of God's people was to be the one credential to the world of the divine nature of Christ's mission on earth. Let us ask in all candor, Are we praying for this unity as Christ prayed for it? Are we seeking the peace, the welfare, the glory, the might, and the divine nature of God's cause as it is found in the unity of God's people?

Note how He puts Himself as the champion and the pattern of this unworldliness that He prays may possess His disciples. He sends them into the world just as His Father sent Him into the world. He expects them to be and do just as He was and as He did for His Father. He sought the sanctification of His disciples so that they might be wholly devoted to God and purified from all sin. He desired in them a holy life and a holy work for God. He devoted Himself to death in order that they might be devoted in life to God. He prayed For a true sanctification, a real, whole, and thorough sanctification, embracing soul, body, and mind, for time and eternity. With Him the Word itself had much to do with their true sanctification. "*Sanctify them by Your truth. Your word is truth....And for their sakes I sanctify Myself, that they also may be sanctified by the truth*" (John 17:17, 19).

Entire devotedness was to be the type of their sanctification. His prayer for their sanctification marks the pathway to full sanctification. Prayer is that pathway. All the ascending steps to that lofty position of entire sanctification are steps of prayer, increasing prayerfulness in spirit and increasing prayerfulness in fact. "*Pray without ceasing*" (1 Thessalonians 5:17) is the imperative prelude to "*May the God of peace Himself sanctify you completely*" (v. 23). And prayer is but the continued interlude and doxology of this rich grace in the heart: "*May your whole spirit, soul, and body be preserved blameless at the coming of our Lord Jesus Christ. He who calls you is faithful, who also will do it*" (vv. 23–24).

We can only meet our full responsibilities and fulfill our high mission when we go forth sanctified as Christ our Lord was sanctified. He sends us into the world just as His Father sent Him into the world. He expects us to be as He was, to do as He did, and to glorify the Father just as He glorified the Father. What longings He had to have us with Him in heaven: "*Father, I desire that they also whom You gave Me may be with Me where I am, that they may behold My glory which You have given Me*" (John 17:24). What response do our truant hearts make to this earliest, loving longing of Christ? Are we as eager for heaven as He is to have us there? How calm, how majestic, and how authoritative is His "*I desire.*"

He closes His life with inimitable calmness, confidence, and sublimity. "*I have glorified You on the earth. I have finished the work which You have given Me to do*" (John 17:4).

The annals of earth have nothing comparable to it in real serenity and sublimity. May we come to our end thus in supreme loyalty to Christ.

TWELVE:

THE GETHSEMANE PRAYER

The cup, the cup, the cup! Our Lord did not use many words, but He used His few words again and again—*"this cup"* and *"Your will"* (Luke 22:42). *"Your will be done"* (Matthew 26:42), and *"Let this cup pass"* (v. 39) were His prayer. "The cup, the cup, the cup!" cried Christ—first on His feet, then on His knees, and then on His face. *"Lord, teach us to pray"* (Luke 11:1).

—Alexander Whyte

We come to Gethsemane. What a contrast to His High Priestly Prayer, which was a prayer of intense feelings, of universal grasp, and of worldwide and infinite sympathy and concern for His church. Perfect calmness and perfect poise reigned in His High Priestly Prayer. He was majestic, simple, and free from passion or disquiet. As royal Intercessor and Advocate for others, His petitions were like princely edicts, judicial and authoritative. How changed now! In Gethsemane He seems to have entered another region and become another man. His Priestly Prayer, so exquisite in its tranquil flow, so unruffled in its strong, deep current, is like the sun, moving in its orbit with unsullied glory as it brightens, vitalizes, ennobles, and blesses everything. The Gethsemane Prayer is that same sun declining in the West, plunged into an ocean of storm and cloud, storm-covered, storm-eclipsed, with gloom, darkness, and terror on every side.

JESUS PRAYED WITH GREAT SORROW

The prayer in Gethsemane is exceptional in every way. The oppressive load of the world's sin is upon Him. The lowest point of His depression has been reached. The bitterest cup of all, His bitter cup, is being pressed to His lips. The weakness of all His weaknesses, the sorrow of all His sorrows, the agony of all His agonies are now upon Him. The flesh is giving out with its fainting and trembling pulsations, like the trickling of His heart's blood. His enemies have thus far triumphed. Hell is in a jubilee, and bad men are joining in the hellish carnival.

Gethsemane was Satan's hour, Satan's power, and Satan's darkness. It was the hour of massing all of Satan's forces for a final, last conflict. Jesus had said, *"The ruler of this world is coming, and he has nothing in Me"* (John 14:30). The conflict for earth's mastery is before Him. The Spirit led and drove Him into the stern conflict and severe temptation of the wilderness. But His Comforter, His leadership, His inspiration through His matchless history seems to have left Him now. *"He began to be sorrowful and deeply distressed"* (Matthew 26:37), and we hear Him under this great pressure exclaiming, *"My soul is exceedingly sorrowful, even to death"* (v. 38). The depression, conflict, and agony had gone to the very core of His spirit, and had sunk Him to the very verge of death. He was *"deeply distressed."*

Surprise and awe depressed His soul. *"Deeply distressed"* was the hour of hell's midnight that fell upon His spirit. He was *"exceedingly sorrowful"* this hour when the sins of all the world, of every man, of all men, with all their stain and all their guilt, fell upon His immaculate soul.

He cannot abide the presence of His chosen friends. They cannot enter into the depths and demands of this fearful hour. His trusted and set watchers are asleep. His Father's face is hidden. His Father's approving voice is silent. The Holy Spirit, who had been with Him in all the trying hours of His life, seems to have withdrawn from the scene. Alone He must drink the cup, alone He must tread the winepress of God's fierce wrath and of Satan's power and darkness, and of man's envy, cruelty, and vindictiveness. The scene is well described by Luke:

> *Coming out, He went to the Mount of Olives, as He was accustomed, and His disciples also followed Him. When He came to the place, He said to them, "Pray that you may not enter into temptation." And He was withdrawn from them about a stone's throw, and He knelt down and prayed, saying, "Father, if it is Your will, take this cup away from Me; nevertheless not My will, but Yours, be done." Then an angel appeared to Him from heaven, strengthening Him. And being in agony, He prayed more earnestly. Then His sweat became like great drops of blood falling down to the ground. When He rose up from prayer, and had come to His disciples, He found them sleeping from sorrow. Then He said to them, "Why do you sleep? Rise and pray, lest you enter into temptation."* (Luke 22:39–46)

JESUS PRAYED FOR RELIEF

The prayer agony of Gethsemane crowns Calvary with glory, and while the prayers offered by Christ on the cross are the union of weakness and strength, of deepest agony and desolation, here they are accompanied by sweetest calm, divine submission, and implicit confidence.

Nowhere in prophet or priest, king or ruler, synagogue or church, does the ministry of prayer assume such marvels of variety, power, and fragrance as in the life of Jesus Christ. It is the aroma of God's sweetest spices, aflame with God's glory and consumed by God's will.

We find in this Gethsemane Prayer what we find nowhere else in the praying of Christ. *"O My Father, if it is possible, let this cup pass from Me; nevertheless, not as I will, but as You will"* (Matthew 26:39). This is different from the whole tenor and trend of His praying and doing. How different from His High Priestly Prayer! *"Father, I desire"* (John 17:24) is the law and life of that prayer. In His last directions for prayer, He makes our will the measure and condition of prayer. *"If you abide in Me, and My words abide in you, you will ask what you desire, and it shall be done for you"* (John 15:7). He

92 E. M. Bounds on Prayer & Spiritual Warfare

said to the Syro- Phoenician woman, *"Great is your faith! Let it be to you as you desire"* (Matthew 15:28).

But in Gethsemane His praying was against the declared will of God. The pressure was so heavy upon Him, the cup was so bitter, the burden was so strange and intolerable, that the flesh cried out for relief. Prostrate, sinking, *"exceedingly sorrowful, even to death"* (Mark 14:34), He sought to be relieved from what seemed too heavy to bear. He prayed, however, not in revolt against God's will, but in submission to that will, and yet He prayed to change God's plan and to alter God's purposes. Pressed by the weakness of the flesh and by the powers of hell in all their dire, hellish malignity and might, Jesus was on this single occasion constrained to pray against the will of God. He did it, though, with great wariness and pious caution. He did it with declared and inviolable submission to God's will. But this was exceptional.

CONFORMITY IS MORE THAN SUBMISSION

Simple submission to God's will is not the highest attitude of the soul to God. Submission may be seeming, induced by conditions, nothing but an enforced surrender, not cheerful but grudging, only a temporary convenience, an intermittent resolve. When the occasion or calamity that called it forth is removed, the will returns to its old ways and to its old self.

With this one exception, Jesus Christ always prayed in conformity with the will of God. He was one with God's plan, one with God's will. To pray in conformity with God's will was the life and law of Christ. Conformity, to live in oneness with God, is a far higher and diviner life than to live simply in submission to God. To pray in conformity— together with God—is a far higher and diviner way to pray than mere submission. At its best state, submission is non-rebellion, an acquiescence, which is good, but not the highest. The most powerful form of praying is positive, aggressive, mightily outgoing and creative. It molds things, changes things, and brings things to pass.

Conformity means to *"stand perfect and complete in all the will of God"* (Colossians 4:12). It means to delight to do God's will, to run with eagerness and ardor to carry out His plans. Conformity to God's will involves submission— patient, loving, sweet submission. But submission in itself falls short of and does not include conformity. We may be submissive but not conformed. We may accept results against which we have warred and even be resigned to them.

Conformity means to be one with God, both in result and in processes. Submission may be one with God in the end. Conformity is one with God in the beginning and the end. Jesus had conformity, absolute and perfect, to God's will, and by that He prayed. This was the single point where there was a drawing back from God's processes, extorted by insupportable pain, fear, and weariness. His submission was abject, loyal, and confiding, as His conformity had been constant and perfect. Conformity is the only true submission, the most loyal, the sweetest, and the fullest.

SUFFERING YIELDS TO PERFECTION

Gethsemane has its lessons of humble supplications, as Jesus knelt alone in the Garden; lessons of burdened prostration, as He fell on His face; of intense agony; of distressing dread; of hesitancy and shrinking back; of crying out for relief—yet amid it all, of cordial submission to God, accompanied with a singleness of purpose for His glory.

Satan will have for each of us his hour and power of darkness (see Luke 22:53) and for each of us the bitter cup and the fearful spirit of gloom.

We can act against God's will as Moses did when he struck the rock and was denied entrance to the Promised Land (see Numbers 20:2–12), or pray against God's will as Paul did three times about the thorn in the flesh (see 2 Corinthians 12:7–9); as David did for his doomed child (see 2 Samuel 12:15–23); as Hezekiah did to live (see 2 Kings 20:1–19). We may pray against God's will three times when the stroke is the heaviest, the sorrow is the keenest, and the grief is the deepest. We may lie prostrate all night, as David did, through the hours of darkness. We may pray for hours, as Jesus did, and in the darkness of many nights, not measuring the hours by the clock or the nights by the calendar. It must all be, however, the prayer of submission.

When the sorrow and desolation of Gethsemane fall in heaviest gloom upon us, we ought to submit patiently and tearfully, if need be, but sweetly and resignedly, without tremor or doubt, to the cup pressed by a Father's hand to our lips. *"Not My will, but Yours, be done"* (Luke 22:42), our broken hearts will say. In God's own way, mysterious to us, that cup has in its bitterest dregs, as it had for Christ, the gem and gold of perfection. We are to be put into the crucible to be refined. Christ was made perfect in Gethsemane, not by the prayer, but by the suffering. *"For it was fitting for Him...to make the captain of their salvation perfect through sufferings"* (Hebrews 2:10). The cup could not pass because the suffering had to go on and yield its fruit of perfection. Through many hours of darkness and of hell's power, through many sore conflicts with the prince of this world, by drinking many bitter cups, we are to be made perfect. To cry out against the fearful and searching flame of the crucible of the Father's painful processes is natural and is no sin, if there is perfect acquiescence in the answer to our prayer, perfect submission to God's will, and perfect devotion to His glory.

THE HIGHEST PRAYING OVERCOMES OBSTACLES TO PRAYER

If our hearts are true to God, we may plead with Him about His way and seek relief from His painful processes. But the fierce fire of the crucible and the agonizing victim with His agonizing and submissive prayer is not the normal and highest form of majestic and all-commanding prayer. We can cry out in the crucible and can cry out against the flame that purifies and perfects us. God allows this, hears this, and answers this, not by taking us out of the crucible or by mitigating the fierceness of the flame, but by sending more than an angel to strengthen us. And yet crying out thus, with full submission, does not satisfy the real, high, worldwide, royal, and eternity-reaching urgent requests of prayer.

The prayer of submission must not be used so as to impair or substitute for the higher and mightier prayer of faith. Nor must it be stressed so as to break down importunate, prevailing prayer, which would be to disarm prayer of its efficiency and de-crown its glorious results, and would be to encourage listless, sentimental, feeble praying.

We are ever ready to excuse our lack of earnest and arduous praying, by an imagined and delusive view of submission. We often end praying just where we ought to begin. We quit praying when God waits and is waiting for us to really pray. We are deterred by obstacles from praying, or we succumb to difficulties, and call it submission to God's will. A world of beggarly faith, spiritual laziness, and halfheartedness in prayer is covered under the high and pious name of submission. To have no plan but to seek God's plan and carry it out is the essence and inspiration of Christlike praying. This is far more than putting in a clause of submission. Jesus did this once in seeking to change the purpose of God, but all His other praying was the output of being perfectly at one with the plans and purposes of God. It is after this order that we pray when we abide in Him and when His word abides in us. Then we ask what we will and it is done (John 15:7). It is then that our prayers fashion and create things. Our wills then become God's will and His will becomes ours. The two become one, and there is not a note of discord.

> *Now this is the confidence that we have in Him, that if we ask anything according to His will, He hears us. And if we know that He hears us, whatever we ask, we know that we have the petitions that we have asked of Him.* (1 John 5:14–15)

And then it proves true that *"whatever we ask we receive from Him, because we keep His commandments and do those things that are pleasing in His sight"* (1 John 3:22).

What restraint, forbearance, self-denial, and loyalty to duty to God, and what deference to the Old Testament Scriptures, are in this statement of our Lord:

> *Do you think that I cannot now pray to My Father, and He will provide Me with more than twelve legions of angels? How then could the Scriptures be fulfilled, that it must happen thus?* (Matthew 26:53)

> *I say to you who hear: Love your enemies, do good to those who hate you, bless those who curse you, and pray for those who spitefully use you.* —Luke 6:27–28

> *The harvest truly is great, but the laborers are few; therefore pray the Lord of the harvest to send out laborers into His harvest.* —Luke 10:2

Watch therefore, and pray always that you may be counted worthy to escape all these things that will come to pass, and to stand before the Son of Man. —Luke 21:36

THIRTEEN:

THE HOLY SPIRIT AND PRAYER

During the great Welsh Revival a minister was said to be very successful in winning souls. By one sermon that he preached, hundreds were converted. Far away in a valley news reached a brother minister of the marvelous success of this sermon. He desired to find out the secret of the man's great success. He walked the long way and came to the minister's poor cottage, and the first thing he said was, "Brother, where did you get that sermon?" He was taken into a poorly furnished room, and the minister pointed to a spot where the carpet was worn threadbare, near a window that looked out upon the everlasting hills and solemn mountains, and said, "Brother, there is where I got that sermon. My heart was heavy for men. One night I knelt there—and cried for power as I never preached before. The hours passed until midnight struck, and the stars looked down on a sleeping world, but the answer did not come. I prayed on until I saw a faint streak of gray shoot up, then it was silver—silver became purple and gold. Then the sermon came and the power came and men fell under the influence of the Holy Spirit."

—G. H. Morgan

The Gospel without the Holy Spirit would be vain and inconsequential. The gift of the Holy Spirit was vital to the work of Jesus Christ in the Atonement. As Jesus did not begin His work on earth until He was anointed by the Holy Spirit, so the same Holy Spirit is necessary to carry forward and make effective the atoning work of the Son of God. As His anointing by the Holy Spirit at His baptism was an era in His life, so also is the coming of the Holy Spirit at Pentecost a great era in the work of redemption in making effective the work of Christ's church.

THE HOLY SPIRIT BRINGS DIVINE HELP

The Holy Spirit is not only the bright lamp of the Christian era, its Teacher and Guide, but also the divine Helper.

He is the enabling Agent in God's new dispensation of doing. As the pilot takes his stand at the wheel to guide the vessel, so the Holy Spirit takes up His abode in the heart to guide and empower all its efforts. The Holy Spirit executes the whole Gospel through the man by His presence and control of the spirit of the man.

In the execution of the atoning work of Jesus Christ, in its general and more comprehensive operation, or in its minute and personal application, the Holy Spirit is the one efficient Agent, absolute and indispensable.

The Gospel cannot be executed except by the Holy Spirit. He only has the regal authority to do this royal work. Intellect cannot execute it, neither can learning, eloquence, nor truth; not even the revealed truth can execute the Gospel. The marvelous facts of Christ's life told by hearts unanointed by the Holy Spirit will be dry and sterile, or like a "tale told by an idiot, full of sound and fury, signifying nothing" (*Macbeth*, 5.5.26–28). Not even the precious blood can execute the Gospel. Not any, or all of these, though spoken with angelic wisdom and angelic eloquence can execute the Gospel with saving power. Only tongues set on fire by the Holy Spirit can witness to the saving power of Christ with power to save others.

No one dared move about Jerusalem to proclaim the message to the dying multitudes until the Holy Spirit came in baptismal power. John could not utter a word, though he had pillowed his head on Christ's bosom and caught the pulsations of Christ's heart, and though his brain was full of the wondrous facts of that life and of the wondrous words that fell from His lips. John had to wait until a fuller and richer endowment than all of these came on him. Moreover, though she had nurtured Christ and stored her heart and mind full of holy and motherly memories, even Mary needed to be empowered by the Holy Spirit.

THE HOLY SPIRIT COMES THROUGH PRAYER

The coming of the Holy Spirit is dependent upon prayer, for only prayer can surround, with its authority and demands, the realm where this person of the Godhead has His abode. With Christ, it is, ever has been, and ever will be, *"Ask, and it will be given to you; seek, and you will find; knock, and it will be opened to you"* (Matthew 7:7; Luke 11:9). To His disconsolate disciples, He said, *"I will pray the Father, and He will give you another Helper"* (John 14:16). This law of prayer for the Holy Spirit presses on the disciples and on the Master as well, for even Christ was subject to this law. Of so many of God's children it may truly be said, *"You do not have because you do not ask"* (James 4:2). And of many others it might be said, "You have Him in weak measure because you pray for Him in weak measure."

The Holy Spirit is the spirit of all grace and of each grace as well. Purity, power, holiness, faith, love, joy, and all grace are brought into being and perfected by Him. Would we grow in grace in particular? Would we be perfect in all graces? We must seek the Holy Spirit by prayer.

I urge the seeking of the Holy Spirit. We need Him, and we need to stir ourselves up to seek Him. The measure we receive of Him will be gauged by the fervor of faith and prayer with which we seek Him. Our ability to work for God, to pray to God, to live for God, and to affect others for God will be dependent on the measure of the Holy Spirit received by us, dwelling in us, and working through us.

THE HOLY SPIRIT BRINGS CONVICTION

Christ lays down the clear and explicit law of prayer in this regard for all of God's children. The world needs the Holy Spirit to convict it *"of sin, and of righteousness, and judgment"* (John 16:8), and to make it feel its guiltiness in God's sight. And this spirit of conviction on sinners comes in answer to the prayers of God's people. Moreover, God's children need Him more and more, need His life, His more abundant life, His superabundant life. But that life begins and ever increases as the child of God prays for the Holy Spirit.

> *If you then, being evil, know how to give good gifts to your children, how much more will your heavenly Father give the Holy Spirit to those who ask Him!* (Luke 11:13)

This is the law, a condition brightened by a promise and sweetened by a relationship.

THE HOLY SPIRIT MUST BE SOUGHT

The gift of the Holy Spirit is one of the benefits flowing to us from the glorious presence of Christ at the right hand of God; and this gift of the Holy Spirit, together with all the other gifts of the enthroned Christ, are secured to us by prayer. The Bible by express statement, as well as by its general principles and clear and constant intimations, teaches us that the gift of the Holy Spirit is connected with and conditional on prayer. That the Holy Spirit is in the world as God is in the world is true. That the Holy Spirit is in the world as Christ is in the world is also true. It is additionally true that there is nothing declared of Him being in us and in the world that is not declared of God and Christ being in us and in the world. The Holy Spirit was in the world in a measure before Pentecost, and in the measure of His operation then, He was prayed for and sought for, and the principles are unchanged. The truth is, if we cannot pray for the Holy Spirit, we cannot pray for any good thing from God, for He is the sum of all good to us. We seek after the Holy Spirit just as we seek after God, and just as we seek after Christ, with strong cries and tears, and we are to seek always for more and more of His gifts, power, and grace. The presence and power of the Holy Spirit at any given meeting is conditional on praying faith.

Christ lays down the doctrine that the reception of the Holy Spirit is conditional on prayer, and He Himself illustrated this universal law, for when the Holy Spirit came upon Him at His baptism, He was praying. The apostolic church in action illustrated the same great truth.

A few days after Pentecost the disciples were in an agony of prayer. *"And when they had prayed, the place where they were assembled together was shaken; and they were all filled with the Holy Spirit"* (Acts 4:31). This incident destroys every theory that denies prayer as the condition of the coming and re-coming of the Holy Spirit after Pentecost; it confirms the view that the pouring out of the Spirit at Pentecost as the result of a long struggle of prayer illustrates and affirms that God's great and most precious gifts are conditional on asking, seeking, knocking, and praying ardently and persistently.

The same truth comes to the front very prominently in Philip's revival at Samaria. Though filled with joy by believing in Christ, and though received into the church by water baptism, the new believers did not receive the Holy Spirit until Peter and John went down there and prayed with and for them. (See Acts 8:5–17.)

Paul's praying was God's proof to Ananias that Paul was in a state that conditioned him to receive the Holy Spirit. (See Acts 9:10–18.)

THE HOLY SPIRIT EMPOWERS PRAYER

The Holy Spirit is our Teacher, our Inspirer, and our Revealer in prayer. The power of our praying in degree and force is measured by the Spirit's power working in us, as the will and work of God, according to God's *"good pleasure"* (Philippians 2:13). In the third chapter of Ephesians, after the marvelous prayer of Paul for the church, he seemed to be apprehensive that the Ephesians would think he had gone beyond the ability of God in his large asking. And so he closed his appeal for them with the words, "[God] *is able to do exceedingly abundantly above all that we ask or think"* (Ephesians 3:20). The power of God to act for us is measured by the power of God in us. *"According to,"* said the Apostle to the Gentiles, that is, after the measure of, *"the power that works in us"* (v. 20). The effectiveness of our prayers is directly related to the effective working of God in us. A feeble operation of God in us brings feeble praying. The mightiest operation of God in us brings the mightiest praying. The secret of prayerlessness is the absence of the work of the Holy Spirit in us. The secret of feeble praying wherever it occurs is the lack of God's Spirit in His mightiness.

The ability of God to answer and work through our prayers is measured by the divine energy that God has been enabled to put in us by the Holy Spirit. The effectiveness of our praying is the measure of the Holy Spirit in us. The statement of James speaks to this effect: *"The effective, fervent prayer of a righteous man avails much"* (James 5:16). The prayer forged in the heart by the almighty energy of the Holy Spirit works mightily in its results just as Elijah's prayer did (verses 17–18).

Would we pray efficiently and mightily? Then the Holy Spirit must work in us efficiently and mightily. Paul made the principle of universal application. *"To this end I also labor, striving according to His working which works in me mightily"* (Colossians 1:29). All labor for Christ that does not spring from the Holy Spirit working in us is inconsequential and vain. Our prayers and activities are so feeble and lacking in results because He has not worked in us His glorious work. Would you pray with mighty results? Seek the mighty workings of the Holy Spirit in your own spirit.

THE HOLY SPIRIT IS A GIFT

We have the initial lesson in prayer for the gift of the Holy Spirit, which was to enlarge to its full harvest in Pentecost. In John 14:16, Jesus promises to ask the Father to send another Comforter who will dwell with His disciples and be in them. Note that this is not a prayer that the Holy Spirit might do His work in making us children of God by regeneration, but for that fuller grace and power and person of the Holy Spirit that we can claim by virtue of our relationship to God as His children. His work in us to *make* us the children of God, and His person abiding with us and in us, as children of God, are entirely different stages of the same Spirit's relationship to us. In this latter work, His gifts and works are greater, and His presence, even Himself, is greater than His works or gifts. His work in us prepares us for Himself. His gifts are the provisions of His presence. He places and makes us members of the body of Christ by His work. He keeps us in that body by His presence and person. He enables us to discharge our functions as members of that body by His gifts.

The whole lesson culminates in asking for the Holy Spirit as the great objective of all praying. In the direction in the Sermon on the Mount, we have the very plain and definite promise:

If you then, being evil, know how to give good gifts to your children, how much more will your Father who is in heaven give good things to those who ask him! (Matthew 7:11)

In Luke's version of this verse, *"good things"* is substituted by *"the Holy Spirit"* (Luke 11:13). All good is comprehended in the Holy Spirit, and He is the sum and climax of all good things.

How complex, confusing, and involved are many human directions about obtaining the gift of the Holy Spirit as the abiding Comforter, our Sanctifier, and the One who empowers us! How simple and plain is our Lord's direction—Ask! Ask with urgency, ask without fainting. Ask, seek, knock, until He comes. Your heavenly Father will surely send Him if you ask for Him. Wait in the Lord for the Holy Spirit. It is the child waiting, asking, urging, and praying perseveringly for the Father's greatest gift and for the child's greatest need, the Holy Spirit.

THE HOLY SPIRIT IS FOR THOSE WHO ASK

How are we to obtain the Holy Spirit so freely promised to those who seek Him believingly? Wait, press, and persevere with all the calmness and all the ardor of a faith that knows no fear, that allows no doubt, that does *"not waver at the promise of God through unbelief"* (Romans 4:20), that in its darkest and most depressed hours believes in hope, that is brightened and strengthened by hope, and that is saved by hope.

Wait and pray: here are the keys that unlock every castle of despair and that open every treasure-house of God. This is the simplicity of the child's asking of the Father, who gives with a largeness, liberality, and cheerfulness infinitely above everything ever known to earthly parents. Ask for the Holy Spirit; seek for the Holy Spirit; knock for the Holy Spirit. He is the Father's greatest gift for the child's greatest need.

In these three words, *"ask,"* *"seek,"* and *"knock"* (Matthew 7:7), given to us by Christ, we have the repetition of the advancing steps of insistence and effort. He is laying Himself out in command and promise in the strongest way, showing us that if we will lay ourselves out in prayer and will persevere, rising to higher and stronger attitudes and sinking to deeper depths of intensity and effort, the answer must inevitably come. The stars would fail to shine before the asking, the seeking, and the knocking would fail to obtain what is needed and desired.

There is no elect company here, only the election of undismayed, importunate, never-fainting effort in prayer: *"To him who knocks it will be opened"* (Matthew 7:8; Luke 11:10). Nothing can be stronger than this declaration assuring us of the answer unless it is the promise on which it is based, *"So I say to you, ask, and it will be given to you"* (Luke 11:9).

> *And I will pray the Father, and He will give you another Helper, that He may abide with you forever.* —John 14:16

> *I will pray with the spirit, and I will also pray with the understanding.* —1 Corinthians 14:15

> *Is anyone among you suffering? Let him pray. Is anyone cheerful? Let him sing psalms. Is anyone among you sick? Let him call for the elders of the church, and let them pray over him, anointing him with oil in the name of the Lord. And the prayer of faith will save the sick, and the Lord will raise him up. And if he has committed sins, he will be forgiven.* —James 5:13–15

FOURTEEN:

THE HOLY SPIRIT, OUR HELPER IN PRAYER

We must pray in the Spirit, in the Holy Spirit, if we would pray at all. Lay this, I beseech you, to heart. Do not address yourselves to prayer as to a work to be accomplished in your own natural strength. It is a work of God, of God the Holy Spirit, a work of His in you and by you, and in which you must be fellow workers with Him— but His work notwithstanding.

—Archbishop Trench

One of the revelations of the New Testament concerning the Holy Spirit is that He is our Helper in prayer. So we see in the following incident in our Lord's life the close connection between the Holy Spirit's work and prayer:

In that hour Jesus rejoiced in the Spirit and said, "I thank You, Father, Lord of heaven and earth, that You have hidden these things from the wise and prudent and revealed them to babes. Even so, Father, for so it seemed good in Your sight." (Luke 10:21)

PRAYER CONNECTS THE FATHER TO THE CHILD

In this passage we have revelations of what God is to us. Only the child's heart can know the Father, and only the child's heart can reveal the Father. It is only by prayer that all things are delivered to us by the Father through the Son. It is only by prayer that all things are revealed to us by the Father and by the Son. It is only in prayer that the Father gives Himself to us, which is much more in every way than all other things whatsoever.

THE HOLY SPIRIT IS OUR HELPER

The Revised Version reads, *"In that same hour he rejoiced in the Holy Spirit."* This sets forth that great truth not generally known, or if known, ignored, that Jesus Christ was generally led by the Holy Spirit, and that His joy and His praying, as well as His working and His life, were under the inspiration, law, and guidance of the Holy Spirit.

Turn to and read this passage: *"Likewise the Spirit also helps in our weaknesses. For we do not know what we should pray for as we ought"* (Romans 8:26).

This text is most pregnant and vital, and needs to be quoted. Patience, hope, and waiting help us in prayer. But the greatest and the divinest of all helpers is the Holy Spirit. He takes hold of things for us. We are dark and confused, ignorant and weak in many things, in fact in everything pertaining to the heavenly life, especially in the simple service of prayer. There is an "ought" on us, an obligation, a necessity to pray, a spiritual necessity upon us of the most absolute and imperative kind. But we do not feel the obligation and have no ability to meet it. The Holy Spirit helps us in our weaknesses, gives wisdom to our ignorance, turns ignorance into wisdom, and changes our weakness into strength. The Spirit Himself does this.

He helps and takes hold with us as we tug and toil. He adds His wisdom to our ignorance, gives His strength to our weakness. He pleads for us and in us. He quickens, illumines, and inspires our prayers. He composes and elevates the subject of our prayers and inspires the words and feelings of our prayers. He works mightily in us so that we can pray mightily. He enables us to pray always and ever according to the will of God.

PRAY ACCORDING TO THE WILL OF GOD

In 1 John 5 we have these words:

Now this is the confidence that we have in Him, that if we ask anything according to His will, He hears us. And if we know that He hears us, whatever we ask, we know that we have the petitions that we have asked of Him. (1 John 5:14–15)

What gives us boldness and so much freedom and fullness of approach toward God, the fact and basis of that boldness and liberty of approach, is that we are asking *"according to His will."* This does not mean submission, but conformity. *"According to"* means after the standard, conformity, agreement. We have boldness and all freedom of access to God because we are praying in conformity to His will. God records His general will in His Word, but He has this special work in praying for us to do.

How can we know the will of God in our praying? What are the things that God designs specially for us to do and pray? The Holy Spirit reveals them to us perpetually.

The Spirit Himself makes intercession for us with groanings which cannot be uttered. Now He who searches the hearts knows what the mind of the Spirit is, because He makes intercession for the saints according to the will of God. (Romans 8:26–27)

Combine this text with these words of Paul in First Corinthians:

But as it is written: "Eye has not seen, nor ear heard, nor have entered into the heart of man the things which God has prepared for those who love Him." But God has revealed them to us through His Spirit. For the Spirit searches all things, yes, the deep things of God. For what man knows the things of a man except the spirit of the man which is in him? Even so no one knows the things of God except the Spirit of God. Now we have received, not the spirit of the world, but the Spirit who is from God, that we might know the things that have been freely given to us by God. These things we also speak, not in words which man's wisdom teaches but which the Holy Spirit teaches, comparing spiritual things with spiritual. But the natural man does not receive the things of the

Spirit of God, for they are foolishness to him; nor can he know them, because they are spiritually discerned. But he who is spiritual judges all things, yet he himself is rightly judged by no one. For "who has known the mind of the Lord that he may instruct Him?" But we have the mind of Christ. (1 Corinthians 2:9–16)

"*Revealed them to us through His Spirit*" (v. 10). Note these words. God searches the heart where the Spirit dwells and knows the mind of the Spirit. The Spirit who dwells in our hearts searches the deep purposes and the will of God for us, and reveals those purposes and that will of God, "*that we might know the things that have been freely given to us by God*" (v. 12). Our spirits are so fully indwelt by the Spirit of God, so responsive and obedient to His illumination and to His will, that we ask with holy boldness and freedom the things that the Spirit of God has shown us as the will of God, and faith is assured. Then "*we know that we have the petitions that we have asked of Him*" (1 John 5:15).

THE SPIRIT HELPS US TO INTERCEDE

The natural man prays, but prays according to his own will, imagination, and desire. If he has ardent desires and groanings, they are merely the fire and agony of nature, and not of the Spirit. What a world of natural praying there is, which is selfish, self-centered, self-inspired! The Spirit, when He prays through us, or helps us to meet the mighty "oughtness" of right praying, trims our praying down to the will of God, and then we give heart and expression to His unutterable groanings. Then "*we have the mind of Christ*" (1 Corinthians 2:16), and pray as He would pray. His thoughts, purposes, and desires are our thoughts, purposes, and desires.

This revelation of the Spirit is not a new and different Bible from what we already have, but it is the Bible we have, applied personally by the Spirit. It is not new texts, but rather the Spirit's elevating of certain texts for us at the time.

It is the unfolding of the Word by the Spirit's light, guidance, and teaching, enabling us to perform the great office of intercessors on earth, in harmony with the great intercessions of Jesus Christ at the Father's right hand in heaven. (See Romans 8:34.)

We have in the Holy Spirit an illustration and an enabler of what this intercession is and ought to be. We are charged to supplicate in the Spirit and to pray in the Holy Spirit. We are reminded that the Holy Spirit *"helps in our weaknesses"* (v. 26), and that while intercession is an art of so divine and so high a nature that *"we do not know what we should pray for as we ought"* (v. 26), yet the Spirit teaches us this heavenly science, by making *"intercession for us with groanings which cannot be uttered"* (v. 26). How burdened are these intercessions of the Holy Spirit! How profoundly He feels the world's sin, the world's woe, and the world's loss, and how deeply He sympathizes with the dire conditions, are seen in His groanings that are too deep for utterance and too sacred to be voiced by Him. He inspires us to this most divine work of intercession, and His strength enables us to sigh unto God for the oppressed, the burdened, and the distressed creation. The Holy Spirit helps us in many ways.

How intense will be the intercessions of the saints who make their requests in the Spirit! How vain and delusive and how utterly fruitless and inefficient are prayers without the Spirit! Official prayers they may be, appropriate for state occasions, beautiful and courtly, but worth less than nothing as God values prayer.

PERSEVERE IN PRAYER

It is our persevering prayers that will help the Holy Spirit to His mightiest work in us; and, at the same time, He helps us to these strenuous and exalted efforts in prayer.

We can and do pray by many inspirations and in many ways that are not of God. Many prayers are stereotyped in manner and in matter, in part, if not as a whole. Many prayers are hearty and vehement, but it is natural heartiness and a fleshly vehemence. Much praying is done out of habit and through form. Habit is a second nature and holds to the good, when so directed, as well as to the bad. The habit of praying is a good habit, and should be early and strongly formed, but to pray by habit alone is to destroy the life of prayer and allow it to degenerate into a hollow and false form. Habit may form the banks for the river of prayer, but there must be a strong, deep, pure current, crystal and life-giving, flowing between these two banks. Hannah multiplied her praying; she *"poured out [her] soul before the* LORD*"* (1 Samuel 1:15). We cannot make our prayer habits too marked and controlled if the life-waters are full and overflow the banks.

PRAY IN THE SPIRIT

Our divine example in praying is the Son of God. Our divine Helper in praying is the Holy Spirit. He quickens us to pray and helps us in praying. Acceptable prayer must be begun and carried on by His presence and inspiration. We are charged in the Holy Scriptures to pray in the Holy Spirit: *"Praying always with all prayer and supplication in the Spirit"* (Ephesians 6:18). We are also encouraged with these words:

> *Likewise the Spirit also helps in our weaknesses. For we do not know what we should pray for as we ought, but the Spirit Himself makes intercession for us with groanings which cannot be uttered. Now He who searches the hearts knows what the mind of the Spirit is, because He makes intercession for the saints according to the will of God.*
> (Romans 8:26–27)

So ignorant are we in this matter of prayer, so impotent are all other teachers to impart its lessons to our understanding and heart, that the Holy Spirit comes as the infallible and all-wise Teacher to instruct us in this divine art. As someone has said, "To pray with all your heart and all your strength, with the reason and the will, this is the greatest achievement of the Christian warfare on earth." This is what we are taught to do and enabled to do by the Holy Spirit. If no man can say that Jesus is the Christ except by the Spirit's help (1 Corinthians 12:3), for a much greater reason, no man can pray except with the help of God's Spirit. Our mother's lips, perhaps now sealed by death, taught us many sweet lessons of prayer— prayers that have bound and held our hearts like golden threads; but these prayers, flowing through the natural channel of a mother's love, cannot serve the challenges and storms of our adult life. These maternal lessons are but the ABCs of praying. For the higher and graduate lessons in prayer, we must have the Holy Spirit. He only can unfold to us the mysteries of the prayer life, its duty and its service.

THE HOLY SPIRIT ABIDES WITHIN US

To pray by the Holy Spirit we must have Him, always. He does not, like earthly teachers, teach us the lesson and then withdraw. He stays to help us practice the lessons He has taught. We do not pray by the precepts and lessons He has taught, but we pray by Him. He is both Teacher and Lesson.

We can know the lesson only because He is ever with us, to inspire, to illumine, to explain, to help us to do. We do not pray by the truth the Holy Spirit reveals to us, but we pray by the actual presence of the Holy Spirit. He puts the desire in our hearts and kindles that desire by His own flame. We simply give lip and voice and heart to His unutterable groanings. Our prayers are taken up by Him and energized and sanctified by His intercession. He prays for us, through us, and in us. We pray by Him, through Him, and in Him. He puts the prayer in us, and we give it utterance and heart.

We always pray *"according to the will of God"* (Romans 8:27) when the Holy Spirit helps our praying. He prays through us only *"according to the will of God."* If our prayers are not *"according to the will of God,"* they die in the presence of the Holy Spirit. He gives such prayers no approval, no help. Disclaimed and unhelped by Him, prayers that are not according to God's will soon die out of every heart where the Holy Spirit dwells.

We must, as Jude said, "[Pray] *in the Holy Spirit"* (Jude 20). As Paul said, we should always pray *"with all prayer and supplication in the Spirit"* (Ephesians 6:18). Never forget that

> *the Spirit also helps in our weaknesses. For we do not know what we should pray for as we ought, but the Spirit Himself makes intercession for us with groanings which cannot be uttered.* (Romans 8:26)

Above all, over all, and through all, our praying must be in the name of Christ, which includes the power of His blood, the energy of His intercession, and the fullness of His royal authority. *"Whatever you ask in My name, that I will do"* (John 14:13).

And whenever you stand praying, if you have anything against anyone, forgive him, that your Father in heaven may also forgive you your trespasses. —Mark 11:25

But you, beloved, building yourselves up on your most holy faith, praying in the Holy Spirit, keep yourselves in the love of God, looking for the mercy of our Lord Jesus Christ unto eternal life. —Jude 20–21

Give ear, O Lord, to my prayer; and attend to the voice of my supplications. —Psalm 86:6

FIFTEEN:

THE TWO COMFORTERS AND TWO ADVOCATES

If we were asked whose Comforter the Holy Spirit was, the answer would be: Ours. The answer is not so ready when we are asked whose Advocate He is. The Spirit is Christ's Advocate, not ours. It is Christ's place He takes, Christ's cause He pleads, Christ's name He vindicates, Christ's kingdom He administers.

—Samuel Chadwick

The fact that man has two divine Comforters, Advocates, and Helpers declares the affluence of God's provisions in the Gospel, and also the settled purpose of God to execute His work of salvation with efficacy and final success. Many-sided are the infirmities and needs of man in his pilgrimage and warfare for heaven. These two Christs—Jesus and the Holy Spirit— can join together with manifold wisdom.

GOD'S RESOURCES ARE BOUNDLESS

The affluence of God's provision of two Intercessors in executing the plan of salvation finds its counterpart in the following prayer promise in its unlimited nature, encompassing all things, great and small. *"Whatever things you ask in prayer, believing, you will receive"* (Matthew 21:22). We have all things in Christ, all things in the Holy Spirit, and all things in prayer.

THE TWO CHRISTS

How much is ours in God's plan and purposes in these two Christs, the One ascended to heaven and enthroned there to intercede for our benefit, the Other, His Representative, and better Substitute (see John 14:12), on earth, to work in us and make intercessions for us!

The first Christ was a person who came in human flesh (John 1:14). The other Christ is a person, but not clothed in physical form or subject to human limitations as the first Christ necessarily was. Transient and local was the first Christ. The other Christ is not limited to locality; not transient, but abiding. He does not deal with the material, the fleshly, but enters personally into the mysterious and imperial domain of the spirit, to emancipate and transform into more than Eden-beauty that desolate and dark realm. The first Christ left His novitiates that they might enter into higher regions of spiritual knowledge. The man-Christ withdrew so that the Spirit-Christ might train and school into the deeper mysteries of God, so that all the historical and physical might be transmuted into the pure gold of the spiritual. The first Christ brought to us a picture of what we must be. The other Christ mirrored this perfect and fadeless image on our hearts. The first Christ, like David, gathered and furnished the material for the temple. The other Christ forms God's glorious temple out of this material.

THE TWO INTERCESSORS

The possibilities of prayer, then, are the possibilities of these two divine Intercessors. Where are the limitations to results when the Holy Spirit intercedes *"for us with groanings which cannot be uttered"* (Romans 8:26), when He so helps us that our prayers run parallel to the will of God, and we pray for the very things and in the very manner in which we ought to pray, schooled in and pressed to these prayers by the urgency of the Holy Spirit! How measureless are the possibilities of prayer when we are *"filled with all the fullness of God"* (Ephesians 3:19), when we *"stand perfect and complete in all the will of God"* (Colossians 4:12)!

If the intercession of Moses so wondrously preserved the being and safety of Israel throughout its marvelous history and destiny, what may we not secure through our Intercessor, who is so much greater than Moses? All that God has lies open to Christ through prayer. All that Christ has lies open to us through prayer.

THE HOLY SPIRIT MAKES CHRIST KNOWN

If we have the two Christs covering the whole realm of goodness, power, purity, and glory, in heaven and on earth—if we have the better Christ with us here in this world—why is it that we sigh to know the Christ in the flesh as the disciples knew Him? (See 2 Corinthians 5:16.) Why is it that the mighty work of these two almighty Intercessors finds us so barren of heavenly fruit, so feeble in all Christlike principles, so low in the Christlike life, and so marred in the Christlike image? Is it not because our prayers for the Holy Spirit have been so faint and few? The heavenly Christ can come to us in full beauty and power only when we have received the fullness of the present earthly Christ, even the Holy Spirit.

Living always the life of prayer, breathing always the spirit of prayer, being always in the fact of prayer, *"praying always...in the Spirit"* (Ephesians 6:18), the heavenly Christ would become ours by a clearer vision, a deeper love, and a more intimate fellowship than He was to His disciples in the days of His flesh.

We would not disguise or lessen the fact that there is a loss to us by our absent Christ as we will see and know Him in heaven. But in our earthly work to be done by us, and above all to be done in us, we will know Christ and the Father better, and can better utilize them by the ministry of the Holy Spirit than would have been possible under the personal, human presence of the Son. So to the loving and obedient one who is filled with the Spirit, both the Father and the Son *"will come to him and make [Their] home with him"* (John 14:23). In the day of the fullness of the indwelling Spirit, *"You will know that I am in My Father, and you in Me, and I in you"* (John 14:20). Amazing oneness and harmony, wrought by the almighty power of the other Christ!

THE HOLY SPIRIT BRINGS THE FULLNESS OF GOD

There is not a note in the archangel's song with which the Holy Spirit does not attune man into sympathy, not a pulsation in the heart of God to which the Holy Spiritfilled heart does not respond with loud amens and joyful hallelujahs. Even more than this, by the other Christ, the Holy Spirit, we *"know the love of Christ which passes knowledge"* (Ephesians 3:19). More than this, by the Holy Spirit we are *"filled with all the fullness of God"* (v. 19). More than this, God *"is able to do exceedingly abundantly above all that we ask or think, according to the power that works in us"* (v. 20).

The presence and power of the other Christ more than compensated the disciples for the loss of the first Christ. His going away had filled their hearts with a strange sorrow. A loneliness and desolation like an orphan's woe had swept over their hearts and stunned and bewildered them; but He comforted them by telling them that the coming of the Holy Spirit would be like the rapture of a travailing mother who has just given birth—all the pain is forgotten in the joy that a man-child has been born into the world.

The Lord is far from the wicked, but He hears the prayer of the righteous.
                                                      —Proverbs 15:29

Assuredly, I say to you, if you have faith and do not doubt, you will not only do what was done to the fig tree, but also if you say to this mountain, "Be removed and be cast into the sea," it will be done. And whatever things you ask in prayer, believing, you will receive.
                                                      —Matthew 21:21–22

We will give ourselves continually to prayer and to the ministry of the word.
                                                      —Acts 6:4

SIXTEEN:

PRAYER AND THE HOLY SPIRIT DISPENSATION

How God needs, how the world needs, how the church needs the flow of the mighty river more blessed than the Nile, deeper, broader, and more overflowing than the Amazon's mighty current! And yet what mere little brooks we are! We need, the age needs, the church needs memorials of God's mighty power, which will silence the Enemy and the Avenger, dumbfound God's foes, strengthen weak saints, and fill strong ones with triumphant raptures.

—E. M. Bounds

The dispensation of the Holy Spirit was ushered in by prayer. Read these words from Acts:

When they had entered, they went up into the upper room where they were staying: Peter, James, John, and Andrew; Philip and Thomas; Bartholomew and Matthew; James the son of Alphaeus and Simon the Zealot; and Judas the son of James. These all continued with one accord

*in prayer and supplication, with the women and Mary the mother of
Jesus, and with His brothers.* (Acts 1:13–14)

This oneness of accord in prayer was the attitude that the disciples
assumed after Jesus had ascended to heaven. Their meeting for prayer ushered in the dispensation of the Holy Spirit, to which prophets had looked
forward with entranced vision. And to prayer, in a marked way, has this
dispensation, which holds in its keeping the fortune of the Gospel, been
committed.

PUT PRAYER FIRST

Apostolic men knew well the worth of prayer and were jealous of the
most sacred offices that infringed on their time and strength and hindered
them from giving themselves *continually to prayer and to the ministry of the
word"* (Acts 6:4). They put prayer first. The Word depends on prayer so
that it *"may run swiftly and be glorified"* (2 Thessalonians 3:1). Praying apostles make preaching apostles. Prayer gives edge, entrance, and weight to the
Word. Sermons conceived by prayer and saturated with prayer are weighty
sermons. Sermons may be ponderous with thought, sparkle with the gems
of genius and of taste, pleasing and popular, but unless they have their birth
and life in prayer, for God's uses, they are of little value, dull and dead.

The Lord of the harvest sends out laborers, full in number and perfect
in kind, in answer to prayer. (See Matthew 9:38.) No prophetic vision is
needed to declare that if the church had used prayer force to its utmost, the
light of the Gospel would have long since encircled the world.

God's Gospel has always waited more on prayer than on anything else
for its successes. A praying church is strong, though poor in all besides. A
prayerless church is weak, though rich in all besides. Only praying hearts
will build God's kingdom. Only praying hands will put the crown on the
Savior's head.

BE FILLED WITH THE SPIRIT

The Holy Spirit is the divinely appointed Substitute for and
Representative of the personal and humanized Christ. How much He is

to us! And how we are to be filled by Him, live in Him, walk in Him, and be led by Him! How we are to conserve and kindle to a brighter and more consuming glow the holy flame! How careful should we be never to quench that pure flame! How watchful, tender, and loving ought we to be so as not to grieve His sensitive, loving nature! How attentive, meek, and obedient we should be, never resisting His divine impulses, always listening for His voice, and always ready to do His divine will. How can all this be done without much and continuous prayer?

The importunate widow had a great case to win against helpless, hopeless despair, but she did it by persevering prayer. (See Luke 18: 1–8.) We have this great treasure to preserve and enhance, but we have a divine Person who will maintain and help us. We can be enabled to meet our duties only by much prayer.

Prayer is the only element in which the Holy Spirit can live and work. Prayer is the golden chain that happily enslaves Him to His happy work in us.

Everything depends upon our having this Second Christ and retaining Him in the fullness of His power. With the disciples, Pentecost was made by prayer. With them, Pentecost was continued by their giving themselves to continued prayer. Persistent and unwearied prayer is the price we will have to pay for our Pentecost, by immediate and continued prayer. Abiding in the fact and in the spirit of prayer is the only surety of our abiding in Pentecostal power and purity.

THE HOLY SPIRIT ENLARGES OUR PRAYER

Not only should the many-sided operation of the Holy Spirit in us and for us teach us the necessity of prayer for Him, but also His condition with our praying assumes another attitude, the attitude of mutual dependence, that of action and reaction. The more we pray, the more He helps us to pray, and the larger the measure of Himself He gives to us. We are not only to pray and press and wait for His coming to us, but after we have received Him in His fullness, we are also to pray for a fuller and still larger bestowment of Himself to us. We are to pray for the largest, ever increasing, and constant fullness of capacity. Paul prayed this prayer for the Spirit-baptized Ephesian church:

That He would grant you, according to the riches of His glory, to be strengthened with might through His Spirit in the inner man, that Christ may dwell in your hearts through faith; that you, being rooted and grounded in love, may be able to comprehend with all the saints what is the width and length and depth and height; to know the love of Christ which passes knowledge; that you may be filled with all the fullness of God. (Ephesians 3:16–19)

In that wonderful prayer for those Christians, Paul laid himself out to pray to God, and by prayer he sought to fathom the fathomless depths and to measure the measureless purposes and benefits of God's plan of salvation for immortal souls by the presence and work of the Holy Spirit. Only importunate and invincible prayer can bring the Holy Spirit to us and secure for us these indescribable, gracious results. *"Always laboring fervently for you in prayers, that you may stand perfect and complete in all the will of God"* (Colossians 4:12).

THE HOLY SPIRIT BRINGS POWER

The Word of God provides for a mighty, consciously realized faith in His saints, into whose happy, shining spirits God has been brought as a Dweller, and whose heaven-toned lives have been attuned to God's melody by His own hand.

Then will it prove true: *"He who believes in Me, as the Scripture has said, out of his heart will flow rivers of living water"* (John 7:38). This Scripture is a promise concerning the indwelling and outflowing of the Holy Spirit in us—life-giving, fruitful, irresistible, a ceaseless outflow of the river of God in us.

How God needs, how the world needs, how the church needs the flow of this mighty river; again, it is more blessed than the Nile, deeper, broader, and more overflowing than the Amazon's broad and mighty current! And yet what mere little brooks we are and have!

Oh, that the church, by the infilling and outflowing of Holy Spirit, might be able to raise up everywhere memorials of the Holy Spirit's power, which might fix the eye as well as engage the heart! We need, the age needs, the church needs, memorials of God's mighty power, which will silence the

Enemy and the Avenger, dumbfound God's foes, strengthen weak saints, and fill strong ones with triumphant raptures.

THE HOLY SPIRIT BRINGS ASSURANCE OF SALVATION

A glance at more of the divine promises concerning this vital question of the Holy Spirit working in us would show us how these promises need to be projected into the experiential and the actual. Jesus said, *"If anyone wants do His will, he shall know concerning the doctrine, whether it is from God or whether I speak on My own authority"* (John 7:17). How we need a conscious faith, personal and vital, unspeakable in its joy, and full of glory (1 Peter 1:8)! The need is for a conscious faith, made so by the Spirit bearing *"witness with our spirit that we are children of God"* (Romans 8:16). A faith of "I know" is the only powerful, vital, and aggressive religion. *"One thing I know: that though I was blind, now I see"* (John 9:25). We need men and women in these loose days who can verify the abovementioned promise of Christ in their inner consciousnesses. And yet how many untold thousands of people in all of our churches have only a dim, impalpable, "I hope so, maybe so, I trust so," kind of religion, all dubious, intangible, and unstable.

In these days, there is certainly a great need in the church, first, for Christians to see and seek and obtain the high privilege in the Gospel of a heaven-born, clearcut, and happy religious experience, born of the presence of the Holy Spirit, giving an undoubted assurance of sins forgiven, and of adoption into the family of God.

THE HOLY SPIRIT BRINGS PURITY AND POWER

Second, there is a need in believers' lives, subsequent to this conscious realization of divine favor in the forgiveness of sins, and added to it, for the reception of the Holy Spirit in His fullness. He will purify their hearts by faith, perfecting them in love, helping them to overcome the world; bestow a divine, inward power over all sin, both inward and outward; give boldness to bear witness; and qualify them for real service in the church and in the world.

There is a fearfully prevailing agnosticism in the church at this time. I greatly fear that a vast majority of our church members are now in this school of spiritual agnosticism, and really deem it to be a virtue to be there. God's Word gives no encouragement whatever to a shadowy religion and a vague religious experience. It calls us definitely into the realm of knowledge. It crowns religion with the crown of "I know." It passes us from the darkness of sin, doubt, and inward misgivings into the marvelous light, where we see clearly and know fully our personal relationship to God.

The things unknown to feeble sense, Unseen by reason's glimmering ray, With strong, commanding confidence, Their heavenly origin display.

Two things may be said in conclusion: First, this sort of Bible religion comes directly through the office of the Holy Spirit dealing personally with each soul; second, the Holy Spirit in all of His offices pertaining to spiritual life and religious experience is secured by earnest, definite, prevailing prayer.

BOOK TWO:

EQUIPPED:
THE WEAPON OF
PRAYER

ONE:

WHY PRAYER IS IMPORTANT TO GOD

Then shall you call, and the LORD shall answer; you shall cry, and He shall say, Here I am.... Then shall you delight yourself in the LORD; and I will cause you to ride upon the high places of the earth, and feed you with the heritage of Jacob your father: for the mouth of the LORD has spoken it. —Isaiah 58:9, 14

It must never be forgotten that almighty God rules this world. He is not an absentee God. His hand is always on the controls of human affairs. He is present everywhere in the concerns of time. *"His eyes behold, His eyelids try, the children of men"* (Psalm 11:4). He rules the world just as He rules the church—through prayer. This lesson needs to be taught and taught again to men and women. Then this lesson will affect the consciences of those whose eyes have no vision for eternal things, whose ears are deaf toward God.

In dealing with mankind, nothing is more important to God than prayer. Prayer is likewise of great importance to people. Failure to pray is failure in all of life. It is failure of duty, service, and spiritual progress. It is only by prayer that God can help people. He who does not pray, therefore, robs himself of God's help and places God where He cannot help people.

We must pray to God if love for God is to exist. Faith and hope and patience and all the strong, beautiful, vital forces of piety are withered and dead in a prayerless life. An individual believer's life, his personal salvation, and his personal Christian graces have their being, bloom, and fruit in prayer.

All this and much more can be said about how prayer is necessary to the life and piety of the individual. But prayer has a larger sphere, a loftier inspiration, a higher duty. Prayer concerns God, whose purposes and plans are conditioned on prayer. His will and His glory are bound up in praying. The days of God's splendor and renown have always been the great days of prayer. God's great movements in this world have been conditioned on, continued by, and fashioned by prayer. God has put Himself in these great movements just as men and women have prayed. Present, prevailing, conspicuous, and overcoming prayer has always brought God's presence. The real and obvious test of a genuine work of God is the prevalence of the spirit of prayer. God's mightiest forces fill and permeate a movement when prayer's mightiest forces are there.

> We must pray to God if love for God is to exist. Faith and hope and patience and all the strong, beautiful, vital forces of piety are withered and dead in a prayerless life. An individual believer's life, his personal salvation, and his personal Christian graces have their being, bloom, and fruit in prayer.

God's movement to bring Israel from Egyptian bondage had its inception in prayer. (See Exodus 2:23–25; 3:9.) Thus, it was early in history when God made prayer one of the granite forces upon which His world movements would be based.

Hannah's petition for a son (see 1 Samuel 1:11) began a great prayer movement for God in Israel. Praying women, like Hannah, whose prayers can give men like Samuel to the cause of God, do more for the church and the world than all the politicians on earth. People born of prayer are the saviors of the state, and people saturated with prayer give life and impetus to the church. Under God they are saviors and helpers of both church and state.

We must believe that the divine record about prayer and God is given in order that we might be constantly reminded of Him. And we are ever refreshed by the knowledge that God holds His church and that God's purpose will be fulfilled. His plans concerning the church will most assuredly and inevitably be carried out. That record of God has been given without doubt; therefore, we may be deeply impressed that the prayers of God's saints are a great factor, a supreme factor, in carrying forward God's work with ease and in time. When the church is in the condition of prayer, God's cause always flourishes, and His kingdom on earth always triumphs. When the church fails to pray, God's cause decays, and evil of every kind prevails.

In other words, God works through the prayers of His people, and when they fail Him at this point, decline and deadness follow. It is according to the divine plan that spiritual prosperity comes through the prayer channel. Praying saints are God's agents for carrying on His saving and providential work on earth. If His agents fail Him, neglecting to pray, then His work fails. Praying agents of the Most High are always forerunners of spiritual prosperity.

In all ages, those who have led the church of God have had a full and rich ministry of prayer. In the Bible, the rulers of the church had preeminence in prayer. They may have been eminent in culture, intellect, and all human abilities, or they may have been lowly in physical attainments and natural gifts. Yet, in each case, prayer was the all-powerful force in the leadership of the church. This was so because God was with them in what they did, for prayer always carries us back to God. It recognizes God and brings God into the world to work and to save and to bless. The most effective agents in spreading the knowledge of God, in performing His work on the earth, and in standing as a barrier against the billows of evil, have been praying church leaders. God depends on them, employs them, and blesses them.

Prayer cannot be retired as a secondary force in this world. To do so is to retire God from moving in our lives. It is to make God secondary. The prayer ministry is an all-engaging force; it must be all-engaging to be a force at all. Prayer is the sense of a need for God and the call for God's help to supply that need. How we estimate and place prayer is how we estimate and place God. To give prayer a secondary place is to make God secondary in life's affairs. To substitute other forces for prayer excludes God and materializes the whole movement.

Prayer is absolutely necessary if we want to carry on God's work properly. God has intended it to be so. The Twelve in the early church knew the importance of prayer. In fact, when they heard the complaint that certain widows had been neglected in the daily distribution, they did not handle it all by themselves. (See Acts 6:1–2.) The Twelve called all the disciples together and told them to select seven men, *"full of the Holy Ghost and wisdom"* (v. 3), whom they would appoint over that benevolent work. They added this important statement: *"But we will give ourselves continually to prayer, and to the ministry of the word"* (v. 4). They surely realized that the success of the Word and the progress of the church were dependent in a preeminent sense on their giving themselves to prayer. God could effectively work through them in proportion to how much they gave themselves to prayer.

The apostles were as dependent on prayer as everyone else. Sacred work, or church activities, may make us so busy that they hinder praying; and when this is the case, evil always results. It is better to let the work go by default than to let the praying go by neglect. Whatever affects the intensity of our praying affects the value of our work. "Too busy to pray" is not only the keynote to backsliding, but it mars even the work that is done.

Nothing is done well without prayer for the simple reason that it leaves God out of the work. It is so easy to be seduced by the good to the neglect of the best, until both the good and the best perish. How easily believers, even leaders of the church, are led by the deceptive wiles of Satan to cut short their praying in the interests of the work! How easy it is to neglect prayer or abbreviate our praying simply by the excuse that we have church work on our hands. When he can keep us too busy to stop and pray, Satan has effectively disarmed us.

"We will give ourselves continually to prayer, and to the ministry of the word" (Acts 6:4). The Revised Version states, *"We will continue stedfastly in prayer."* The implication of the word *"continue"* is to be strong, steadfast, to be devoted to, to keep at it with constant care, to make a business out of it. We find the same word in Colossians 4:2, which reads, *"Continue in prayer, and watch in the same with thanksgiving."* We also find it in Romans 12:12, which is translated, *"Continuing instant in prayer."*

The apostles were under the law of prayer. This law recognizes God as God, and it depends on Him to do what He would not do without prayer. They were under the necessity of prayer, just as all believers are, in every age and in every place. They had to be devoted to prayer in order to make their ministry of the Word effective. The business of preaching is worth very little unless it is in direct partnership with the business of praying.

Apostolic preaching cannot be carried on unless there is apostolic praying. Alas, this plain truth has been easily forgotten by those who minister in holy things! Without in any way passing a criticism on the ministry, I feel it is high time that somebody declared to ministers that effective preaching cannot take place without effective praying. The preaching that is most successful comes from a ministry that prays much. Perhaps one might go so far as to say that such a ministry is the only kind that is successful. God can mightily use the preacher who prays. He is God's chosen messenger for good, and the Holy Spirit delights to honor him. A praying preacher is God's effective agent in saving sinners and in edifying saints.

In Acts 6:1–8, we have the record of how, long ago, the apostles felt that they were losing—indeed, had lost—apostolic power because they were involved in certain duties that prevented them from praying more. So they called everything to a halt. They had discovered, to their regret, that they were too deficient in praying. Doubtless, they had kept up the form of praying, but it was seriously lacking in intensity and in the amount of time given to it. Their minds were too preoccupied with the finances of the church.

Likewise, even in the church today, we find both laymen and ministers so busily engaged in "serving" that they are glaringly deficient in praying.

In fact, in present-day church affairs, people are considered religious if they give largely of their money to the church; and people are chosen for official positions, not because they are people of prayer, but because they have the ability to run church finances and to get money for the church.

Now, when these apostles looked into this matter, they determined to put aside these hindrances resulting from church finances, and they resolved to give themselves to prayer. Not that these finances were to be ignored or set aside, but ordinary laymen, "*full of faith and of the Holy Ghost*" (Acts 6:5), could work with the finances. These men were to be truly religious men who could easily attend to these financial matters without it affecting their piety or their praying in the least. They would thus have something to do in the church, and at the same time, they could take the burden off of the apostles. In turn, the apostles would be able to pray more. Praying more, they themselves would be blessed in soul, and they would be more effective in the work to which they had been called.

The apostles realized, too, as they had not realized before, that they were being so pressured by attention to material things, things right in themselves, that they could not pray fully. They could not give to prayer that strength, zeal, and time that its nature and importance demand.

Likewise, we will discover, under close scrutiny of ourselves sometimes, that legitimate and commendable things may so engross our attention that prayer is omitted, or at least very little time is given to it.

How easy to slip away from the prayer closet! Even the apostles had to guard themselves at that point. How closely we need to watch ourselves at the same place! Things legitimate and right may become wrong when they take the place of prayer. Things right in themselves may become wrong things when they are allowed to fasten themselves excessively upon our hearts. It is not only the sinful things that hurt prayer. It is not only questionable things that are to be guarded against, but it is also things that are right in their places but that are allowed to sidetrack prayer and shut the door of the prayer closet, often with the self-comforting plea that "we are too busy to pray."

Possibly, busyness has had as much to do with the breaking down of family prayer in this age as any other cause. Busyness has caused family religion to decay, and busyness is one cause of the decline of the prayer meeting. Men and women are too busy with legitimate things to give themselves to prayer. Other things are given the right-of-way. Prayer is set aside. Business comes first. And this does not always mean that prayer is second, but oftentimes, prayer is left out entirely.

> *Busyness has caused family religion to decay, and busyness is one cause of the decline of the prayer meeting. Men and women are too busy with legitimate things to give themselves to prayer. Other things are given the right-of-way. Prayer is set aside. Business comes first. And this does not always mean that prayer is second, but oftentimes, prayer is left out entirely.*

The apostles tackled this problem, and they determined that not even church business would affect their praying habits. Prayer had to come first; then they would be God's real agents in His world, in deed and truth. God could work effectively through them because they prayed and thereby put themselves directly in line with His plans and purposes. And His plan and purpose is to work through people who pray.

When the complaint about the daily distribution came to the apostles' ears, they discovered that their work had not been accomplishing fully the divine ends of peace, gratitude, and unity. On the contrary, discontent, complaining, and division were the result of their work, which had far too little prayer in it. So, they promptly restored prayer to its rightful prominence.

Praying men and women are a necessity in carrying out God's plan for saving sinners. God has made it so. God established prayer as a divine ordinance, and therefore we are to pray. The fact that God has so often employed men and women of prayer to accomplish His plans clearly proves we are to pray. It is unnecessary to name all the instances in which God used the prayers of righteous men and women to carry out His gracious designs. Time and space are too limited for the list. However, I will name one or two cases.

In the case of the golden calf, God purposed to destroy the Israelites because of their great sin of idolatry. (See Deuteronomy 9:12–21.) While Moses was receiving the law at God's hands, Aaron was swept away by the strong, popular tide of unbelief and sin. The very being of Israel was imperiled. All seemed lost except Moses and prayer, and prayer became more effective and wonder-working on behalf of Israel than Aaron's magic rod. God determined to destroy Israel and Aaron, for His anger grew hot. It was a fearful and critical hour. But prayer was the levee that held back heaven's desolating fury. God's hand was held fast by the prayers of Moses, the mighty intercessor.

Moses was set on delivering Israel. He prayed for forty days and forty nights; it was a long and exhaustive struggle. Not for one moment did he relax his hold on God. Not for one moment did he leave his place at the feet of God, even for food. Not for one moment did he moderate his demand or ease his cry. Israel's existence was in the balance. The wrath of almighty God had to be stayed. Israel had to be saved at all cost. And Israel *was* saved. Moses would not let God alone. And so, today, we can look back and give the credit for the present race of the Jews to the praying of Moses centuries ago.

Persevering prayer always wins; God yields to persistence and fidelity. He has no heart to say no to prayer, such as Moses did. God's purpose to destroy Israel was actually changed by the praying of this man of God. This illustrates how much just one praying person is worth in this world, and how much depends on him.

Daniel, in Babylon, refused to obey the decree of the king. (See Daniel 6:1–23.) The king had decreed that no one could ask any petition of any god or man for thirty days. But Daniel shut his eyes to the decree that would shut him off from his prayer room; he refused to allow fear of consequences to deter him from calling on God. So, he *"kneeled upon his knees three times a day"* (Daniel 6:10) and prayed as he had done before, putting in God's hands all the consequences of disobeying the king.

There was nothing impersonal about Daniel's praying. It always had an objective, and it was an appeal to a great God who could do all things.

Why Prayer Is Important to God 133

Daniel did not pamper himself or look for a feeling to urge him to pray. In the face of the dreadful decree that could hurl him from his high position into the lion's den, *"he kneeled upon his knees three times a day...and gave thanks before his God, as he did beforetime"* (Daniel 6:10). The gracious result was that prayer laid its hands upon an almighty arm, which intervened in that den of vicious lions. God closed their mouths and preserved His servant Daniel, who had been true to Him and who had called on Him for protection.

Daniel's praying was an essential factor in defeating the king's decree and in defeating the wicked, envious rulers who had tried to trap him. They wanted to destroy him and remove him from his powerful position in the kingdom, but Daniel's prayers prevailed!

TWO:

PUTTING GOD TO WORK

For since the beginning of the world men have not heard, nor perceived by the ear, neither has the eye seen, O God, beside You, what He has prepared for him that waits for Him. —Isaiah 64:4

When I use the expression, "putting God to work," I mean that God has placed Himself under the law of prayer and has obligated Himself to answer prayer. God has ordained prayer, and He will do things through people as they pray that He would not do otherwise. Prayer is a specific, divine appointment, an ordinance of heaven. By prayer, God purposes to carry out His gracious designs on earth and to execute and make effective the plan of salvation.

When I say that prayer puts God to work, I am simply saying that we have it in our power to move God to work by prayer. Prayer moves God to do works among people—in His own way, of course—that He would not do if the prayers were not made. Thus, while prayer moves God to work, at the same time God puts prayer to work. Since God has ordained prayer, and since prayer involves people and has no existence apart from people, then, logically, people's prayers are the one force that puts God to work in human affairs.

As we allude to prayer and read about prayer in the Scriptures, let us keep in mind these fundamental truths.

If prayer puts God to work on earth, then, by the same token, prayerlessness excludes God from the world's affairs and prevents Him from working. If prayer moves God to work in this world's affairs, then prayerlessness excludes God from everything concerning people. Prayerlessness leaves man as the mere creature of circumstances, at the mercy of blind fate, and without help of any kind from God. It leaves man with the tremendous responsibilities and difficult problems of the world, with all of its sorrows and burdens and afflictions, without any God at all. In reality, the denial of prayer is the denial of God Himself, for God and prayer are so inseparable that they can never be divorced.

Prayer affects three different spheres of existence: the divine, the angelic, and the human. It puts God to work, it puts angels to work, and it puts people to work. It lays its hands upon God, angels, and people. What a wonderful reach there is in prayer! It brings into play the forces of heaven and earth. God, angels, and people are subjects of this wonderful law of prayer, and all three deal with the possibilities and the results of prayer.

God has placed Himself under the law of prayer to such an extent that He is induced to work among people in a way in which He does not work if they do not pray. Prayer takes hold of God and influences Him to work. This is the meaning of prayer as it concerns God. This is the doctrine of prayer, or else there is no value whatsoever in prayer.

Prayer puts God to work in all things prayed for. While man in his weakness and poverty waits, trusts, and prays, God undertakes the work. *"For since the beginning of the world men have not heard, nor perceived by the ear, neither has the eye seen, O God, beside You, what He has prepared for him that waits for Him"* (Isaiah 64:4).

Jesus Christ commits Himself to the force of prayer. *"Whatsoever you shall ask in My name,"* He says, *"that will I do, that the Father may be glorified in the Son. If you shall ask any thing in My name, I will do it"* (John

14:13–14). And, again, *"If you abide in Me, and My words abide in you, you shall ask what you will, and it shall be done to you"* (John 15:7).

The promise of God is committed to nothing as strongly as it is to prayer. The purposes of God are not dependent on any other force as much as this force of prayer. The Word of God expounds on the necessity and results of prayer. The work of God halts or advances according to the strength of prayer. Prophets and apostles have urged the utility, force, and necessity of prayer. For example, Isaiah 62:6–7 says,

> *I have set watchmen upon your walls, O Jerusalem, which shall never hold their peace day nor night: you that make mention of the LORD, keep not silence, and give Him no rest, till He establish, and till He make Jerusalem a praise in the earth.*

Prayer, with its antecedents and attendants, is the one and only condition of the final triumph of the gospel. The fact that it is the one and only condition honors the Father and glorifies the Son. Little praying and poor praying have weakened Christ's power on earth, postponed the glorious results of His reign, and retired God from His sovereignty.

Prayer puts God's work in His hands and keeps it there. It looks to Him constantly and depends on Him implicitly to further His own cause. Prayer is simply faith resting in, acting with, leaning on, and obeying God. This is why God loves it so well, why He puts all power into its hands, and why He so highly esteems people of prayer.

Every movement for the advancement of the gospel must be created by and inspired by prayer. Prayer precedes and accompanies all the movements of God as an invariable and necessary condition.

In this sense, God makes prayer identical in force and power with Himself, and He says to those on earth who pray, in essence, "You are on the earth to carry on My cause. I am in heaven, the Lord of all, the Maker of all, the Holy One of all. Now whatever you need for My cause, ask Me, and I will do it. Shape the future by your prayers, and concerning all that you need for present supplies, command Me. (See Isaiah 45:11.) I made heaven and earth and all things in them. (See Acts 14:15.) Ask for great things. *'Open your mouth wide, and I will fill it'* (Psalm 81:10). It is My work that you are doing. It concerns My cause. Be prompt and full in praying. Do not abate your asking, and I will not wince or abate My giving."

Everywhere in His Word, God bases His actions on prayer. Everywhere in His Word, His actions and attitude are shaped by prayer. To quote all the Scripture passages that prove the direct relationship of prayer to God, would be to transfer whole pages of the Bible to this study. Man has personal relations with God, and prayer is the divinely appointed means by which man comes into direct connection with God. By His own ordinance, God binds Himself to hear our prayers. God bestows His great blessings on His children when they seek them along the avenue of prayer.

When Solomon closed the great prayer he offered at the dedication of the temple, God appeared to him, approved him, and laid down the universal principles of His actions. In 2 Chronicles 7:12–15, we read,

And the LORD appeared to Solomon by night, and said to him, I have heard your prayer, and have chosen this place to Myself for a house of sacrifice. If I shut up heaven that there be no rain, or if I command the locusts to devour the land, or if I send pestilence among My people; if My people, which are called by My name, shall humble themselves, and pray, and seek My face, and turn from their wicked ways; then will I hear from heaven, and will forgive their sin, and will heal their land. Now My eyes shall be open, and My ears attent to the prayer that is made in this place.

In His purposes concerning the Jews in the Babylonian captivity, God asserts His unfailing principles:

For thus says the Lord, That after seventy years be accomplished at Babylon I will visit you, and perform My good word toward you, in causing you to return to this place. For I know the thoughts that I think toward you, says the Lord, thoughts of peace, and not of evil, to give you an expected end. Then shall you call upon Me, and you shall go and pray to Me, and I will hearken to you. And you shall seek Me, and find Me, when you shall search for Me with all your heart.

(Jeremiah 29:10–13)

> *Man has personal relations with God, and prayer is the divinely appointed means by which man comes into direct connection with God. By His own ordinance, God binds Himself to hear our prayers. God bestows His great blessings on His children when they seek them along the avenue of prayer.*

In Bible terminology, prayer means calling on God for things we desire, asking God for things. Thus, we read, *"Call to Me, and I will answer you, and show you great and mighty things, which you know not"* (Jeremiah 33:3). *"Call upon Me in the day of trouble: I will deliver you"* (Psalm 50:15). *"Then shall you call, and the* LORD *shall answer; you shall cry, and He shall say, Here I am"* (Isaiah 58:9).

Prayer is revealed as a direct application to God for some temporal or spiritual good. It is an appeal to God to intervene in life's affairs for the good of those for whom we pray. God is recognized as the source and fountain of all good, and prayer implies that all His good is held in His keeping for those who call on Him in truth.

The fact that prayer is an appeal to God, communication with God, and communion with God, comes out strongly and simply in the praying of Old Testament saints. Abraham's intercession for Sodom is a striking illustration of the nature of prayer. (See Genesis 18:20–33; 19:24–25.) It is an example of communication with God and intercession for man. Abraham encountered God's plan to destroy Sodom, and his soul within him was greatly moved because of his great interest in that fated city. His nephew and family resided there. God's purpose to destroy the city had to be changed; God's decree to destroy its evil inhabitants had to be revoked.

It was no small undertaking that faced Abraham when he decided to beseech God to spare Sodom. Abraham set about to change God's purpose and to save Sodom along with the other cities of the plain. It was certainly a most difficult and delicate work for him—to undertake using his influence with God to save those doomed cities.

He used the plea that there may be righteous people in Sodom, and he appealed to the infinite uprightness of God not to destroy the righteous with the wicked: *"That be far from You to do after this manner, to slay the righteous with the wicked…shall not the Judge of all the earth do right?"* (Genesis 18:25). With what deep self-abasement and reverence did Abraham begin his high and divine work! He stood before God in solemn awe and meditation, and then he drew near to God and spoke. He asked God to spare Sodom if there were fifty righteous people in the city, and he kept reducing the number until it was down to ten. He advanced step by step in faith, in demand, and in urgency, and God granted every request that he made.

It has been well said that Abraham stopped asking before God stopped granting. It seems that Abraham had a kind of optimistic view of the piety of Sodom. He scarcely expected when he undertook this matter to have it end in failure. He was very much in earnest, and he had every encouragement to press his case. When he made his final request, he thought that surely with Lot, his wife, his daughters, his sons, and his sons-in-law, he had his ten righteous people for whose sake God would spare the city. But, alas! The count failed when the final test came. There were not ten righteous people in that large population.

In his goodness of heart, Abraham overestimated the number of pious people in that city. Otherwise, God might possibly have saved it if he had reduced his figures still further. But this much is true: even if he did not save Sodom by his persistent praying, the purposes of God were postponed for a season.

This is a representative case of Old Testament praying, and it discloses God's mode of working through prayer. It further shows how God is moved to work in this world in answer to prayer, even when it comes to changing His purposes concerning a sinful community. This praying of Abraham was no mere performance—no dull, lifeless ceremony—but an earnest plea, a strong entreaty, one person with another Person. Its purpose was to have an influence, to secure a desired end.

How full of meaning is this remarkable series of intercessions made by Abraham! Here we have arguments designed to convince God; here we have pleas to persuade God to change His purpose. We see deep humility, but we see holy boldness and perseverance as well. We see how Abraham kept advancing in his requests because God kept granting each petition. Here we have large requests encouraged by large answers. God stays and answers as long as Abraham stays and asks. To Abraham, God is existent, approachable, and all-powerful; furthermore, He defers to people, acts favorably on their desires, and grants them favors asked for. Not to pray is to deny God—to deny His existence, His nature, and His purposes toward mankind.

God has given us specific prayer promises and has outlined their breadth, certainty, and limitations. Jesus Christ urges us into the presence of God with these prayer promises by the assurance not only that God will answer, but that no other being but God can answer. He urges us toward God because only by prayer can we move God to take a hand in earth's affairs and induce Him to intervene on our behalf.

Jesus said, *"All things, whatsoever you shall ask in prayer, believing, you shall receive"* (Matthew 21:22). This all-inclusive condition not only urges us to pray for all things, everything great and small, but it points us to and limits us to God. Who but God can cover the whole range of universal things? Who but God gives us the whole thesaurus of earthly and heavenly good from which to ask? Who but God can assure us with certainty that we will receive the very thing for which we ask?

It is Jesus Christ, the Son of God, who commands us to pray, and it is He who puts Himself and all He has so fully in the answer. It is He who puts Himself at our service and answers our demands when we pray. Jesus puts Himself and the Father at our command in prayer; He promises to come directly into our lives and to work for our good. Also, He promises to answer the demands of two or more believers who agree in prayer about any one thing.

> *If two of you shall agree on earth as touching any thing that they shall ask, it shall be done for them of My Father which is in heaven.*
> (Matthew 18:19)

None but God could put Himself in a covenant so binding as that, for only God could fulfill such a promise and reach to its exacting and all-controlling demands. Only God can keep these promises.

God needs prayer, and people need prayer, too. It is indispensable to God's work in this world, and it is essential to getting God to work in earth's affairs. So, God binds people to pray by the most solemn obligations. God commands people to pray; therefore, not to pray is plain disobedience to an imperative command of almighty God. Prayer is such a prerequisite that the graces, the salvation, and the good of God are not bestowed on us unless we pray. Prayer is a high privilege, a royal prerogative. Manifold and eternal are the losses if we fail to exercise it. Prayer is the great, universal force that advances God's cause, the reverence that hallows God's name, and the establishment of God's kingdom in human hearts. These are created and affected by prayer.

One of the essential fortifiers of the gospel is prayer. Without prayer, the gospel can neither be preached effectively, proclaimed faithfully, experienced in the heart, nor practiced in the life. The reason is very simple: by leaving prayer out of the catalog of religious duties, we leave God out, too, and His work cannot progress without Him.

The things God purposed to do under King Cyrus of Persia, prophesied by Isaiah many years before Cyrus was born, were conditioned on prayer. God declares His purpose, power, independence, and defiance of obstacles, but His people still must pray. His omnipotent and absolutely infinite power encourages prayer. He has been ordering all events, directing all conditions, and creating all things so that He might answer prayer, and then He turns Himself over to His praying ones to be commanded. Then all the results and power He holds in His hands will be bestowed in lavish and unmeasured generosity to answer prayers and to make prayer the mightiest energy in the world.

The passage concerning Cyrus in Isaiah 45 is too lengthy to be quoted in its entirety, but it is well worth reading. It closes with strong words about prayer, words that are the climax of all that God says concerning His purposes in connection with Cyrus:

> *Thus says the Lord, the Holy One of Israel, and his Maker, Ask Me of things to come concerning My sons, and concerning the work of My hands command you Me. I have made the earth, and created man upon it: I, even My hands, have stretched out the heavens, and all their host have I commanded.* (Isaiah 45:11–12)

The book of Job also tells of the importance of prayer. In the conclusion of the story of Job, we see how God intervenes on behalf of Job and tells his friends to present themselves before Job so that he may pray for them. *"My wrath is kindled against you* [Eliphaz], *and against your two friends"* (Job 42:7) is God's statement, with the further words added: *"My servant Job shall pray for you: for him will I accept"* (Job 42:8). It is a striking illustration of God intervening to deliver Job's friends in answer to Job's prayer.

I have heretofore spoken of prayer affecting God, angels, and people. Christ wrote no books while living. Memoranda, notes, sermon-writing, and sermon-making were alien to Him. Autobiography was not to His taste. The revelation to John was His last utterance. In the book of Revelation, we have a depiction of the great importance, the priceless value, and the high position that prayer has in the progress of God's church in the world. This depiction reveals the angels' interest in the prayers of the saints and in accomplishing the answers to those prayers:

> *And another angel came and stood at the altar, having a golden censer; and there was given to him much incense, that he should offer it with the prayers of all saints upon the golden altar which was before the throne. And the smoke of the incense, which came with the prayers of the saints, ascended up before God out of the angel's hand. And the angel took the censer, and filled it with fire of the altar, and cast it into the earth: and there were voices, and thunderings, and lightnings, and an earthquake.* (Revelation 8:3–5)

Translated into the prose of everyday life, these words show how the business of salvation is carried on by and made up of the prayers of God's saints on earth. The passage discloses how these prayers come back to earth in flaming power and produce mighty commotions, influences, and revolutions.

Praying men and women are essential to almighty God in all His plans and purposes. God's plans, secrets, and cause have never been committed to prayerless people. Neglect of prayer has always brought loss of faith and loss of love. Failure to pray has been the destructive, inevitable cause of backsliding and estrangement from God. Prayerless people have stood in the way of God fulfilling His Word and doing His will on earth. They tie the divine hands and interfere with God in His gracious designs. As praying people are a help to God, so prayerless people are a hindrance to Him.

I stress the scriptural view of the necessity of prayer even at the cost of repeating myself. The subject is too important for repetition to weaken or tire, too vital to be trite or tame. We must feel it anew. The fires of prayer have burned low. Ashes, not flames, are on its altars.

No insistence in the Scriptures is more pressing than that we must pray. No exhortation is more often reiterated, none is more hearty, none is more solemn and stirring, than to pray. No principle is more strongly and broadly declared than that which urges us to pray. There is no duty to which we are more strongly obliged than that of praying. There is no command more imperative and insistent than that of praying. Are you praying in everything without ceasing? (See 1 Thessalonians 5:17.) Are you praying in your prayer closet, hidden from the eyes of others? Are you praying always and everywhere? These are personal, pertinent, and all-important questions for every soul.

God's Word shows us, through many examples, that God intervenes in this world in answer to prayer. How clear it is, when the Bible is consulted, that the almighty God is brought directly into the things of this world by the prayers of His people. Jonah fled from duty and took ship for a distant port, but God followed him. By a strange providence this disobedient prophet was cast out of the ship, and the God who sent him to Nineveh prepared a fish to swallow him. In the fish's belly he cried out to the God against whom he had sinned, and God intervened and caused the fish to vomit Jonah out onto dry land. Even the fishes of the great deep are subject to the law of prayer.

Likewise, the birds of the air are subject to this same law. Elijah had foretold to Ahab the coming of a prolonged drought, and food and water became scarce. God sent him to the brook Cherith and said to him,

> It shall be, that you shall drink of the brook; and I have commanded the ravens to feed you there…. And the ravens brought him bread and flesh in the morning, and bread and flesh in the evening; and he drank of the brook.
> (1 Kings 17:4, 6)

144 E. M. Bounds on Prayer & Spiritual Warfare

This is a man who later shut and opened the rain clouds by prayer. Can anyone doubt that this man of God was praying at this time, when so much was at stake? God intervened through the birds of the air this time, and He strangely moved them to take care of His servant so that he would not lack food and water.

David, in an evil hour, instead of listening to the advice of Joab, his prime minister, yielded to the suggestion of Satan. (See 1 Chronicles 21:1–14.) He took a census, thus displeasing God. So, God told him to choose one of three evils as a retribution for his folly and sin. He chose pestilence. Pestilence came among the people in violent form, and David went to prayer.

And David said to God, Is it not I that commanded the people to be numbered? even I it is that have sinned and done evil indeed; but as for these sheep, what have they done? let Your hand, I pray thee, O Lord my God, be on me, and on my father's house; but not on Your people, that they should be plagued. (1 Chronicles 21:17)

Although God had been greatly grieved by David's sin, He could not resist this appeal from a penitent and prayerful spirit. God was moved by prayer to put His hand on the springs of disease and stop the fearful plague. God was put to work by David's prayer.

Numbers of other cases could be named, but these are sufficient. God seems to have taken great pains in His Word to show how He interferes in human affairs in answer to the prayers of His saints.

At this point, a question might arise in some overcritical minds about the so-called "laws of nature." Those who raise this question are not strong believers in prayer; they think there is a conflict between what they call the laws of nature and the law of prayer. These people make nature a sort of imaginary god entirely separate from the almighty God. What is nature anyway? It is but the creation of God, the Maker of all things. And what are the laws of nature but the laws of God, through which He governs the material world? Since the law of prayer is also the law of God, there cannot possibly be any conflict between the two sets of laws, but prayer and nature must work in perfect harmony.

Prayer does not violate any natural law. God may set aside one law for the higher working of another law, and this He may do when He answers prayer. Or, God may answer prayer by working through the course of natural law. But, whether we understand it or not, God is over and above all nature. He can and will answer prayer in a wise, intelligent, and just manner, even though man may not comprehend it. So, in no sense is there any conflict between God's different laws when God intervenes in human affairs in answer to prayer.

Along this line of thought, another word might be said. I wrote something to which there can be no objection: prayer accomplishes things. However, it is not prayer itself that accomplishes things, but it is God working through it. Prayer is the instrument; God is the active agent. Prayer itself does not interfere in earth's affairs, but prayer moves God to intervene and do things. Prayer moves God to do things that He would not otherwise do.

It is like saying, "*faith has saved you*" (Luke 7:50). This simply means that God, through the faith of the sinner, saves him, faith being only the instrument that brings salvation to him.

THREE:

THE NECESSITY FOR PRAYING PEOPLE

Praying always with all prayer and supplication in the Spirit, and watching thereto with all perseverance and supplication for all saints.
—Ephesians 6:18

Meanwhile praying also for us, that God would open to us a door of utterance, to speak the mystery of Christ, for which I am also in bonds: that I may make it manifest, as I ought to speak.
—Colossians 4:3–4

One of the most pressing needs in our day is for people whose faith, prayers, and study of the Word of God have been vitalized. We need people whose hearts have written on them a transcript of the Word. We need people who will give forth the Word as the incorruptible seed that lives and abides forever. (See 1 Peter 1:23.)

A critical unbelief has eclipsed the Word of God. Nothing more is needed to clear up this haze than for the pulpit to pledge unwavering allegiance to the Bible and to fearlessly proclaim its truth. Without this the preacher fails, and his congregation becomes confused and unstable. The pulpit has done its mightiest work in the days of its unswerving loyalty to the Word of God.

In close connection with this, we must have preachers of prayer, preachers in high and low places who hold to and practice scriptural praying. While the pulpit must hold to its unswerving loyalty to the Word of God, it must, at the same time, be loyal to the doctrine of prayer, which that same Word illustrates and enforces upon mankind.

Christian schools, colleges, and education, considered simply as such, cannot be regarded as leaders in carrying forward the work of God's kingdom in the world. They have neither the right, the will, nor the power to do the work. This is to be accomplished by the preached Word, delivered in the power of the Holy Spirit sent down from heaven, sown with prayerful hands, and watered with the tears of praying hearts. This is the divine law, and we must follow it. We will follow the Lord.

Men and women are needed for the great work of soul saving, and they are commanded to go. (See Mark 16:15.) It is no angelic or impersonal force that is needed. Human hearts baptized with the spirit of prayer must bear the burden of this message. Human tongues on fire as the result of earnest, persistent prayer must declare the Word of God to dying people.

The church today needs praying people to meet the fearful crisis that is facing her. The crying need of the times is for people in increased numbers—Godfearing people, praying people, Holy Spirit people, people who can endure hardship. We need people who will not count their lives dear unto themselves (see Acts 20:24) but count all things as loss for the excellency of the knowledge of Jesus Christ, the Savior (see Philippians 3:8). The people who are so greatly needed in this age of the church are those who have learned the business of praying—learned it on their knees, learned it in the need and agony of their own hearts.

Praying people are the one commanding need of this day, as of all other days, if God is to intervene in the world. People who pray are, in reality, the only religious people. People of prayer are the only people who can, and do, represent God in this world. No cold, irreligious, prayerless person can claim the right. He misrepresents God in all His work and all His plans.

Praying people are the one commanding need of this day, as of all other days, if God is to intervene in the world. People who pray are, in reality, the only religious people. People of prayer are the only people who can, and do, represent God in this world. No cold, irreligious, prayerless person can claim the right. He misrepresents God in all His work and all His plans.

Praying people are the only people who have influence with God, the only people to whom God commits Himself and His gospel. Praying people are the only people in whom the Holy Spirit dwells, for the Holy Spirit and prayer go hand in hand. The Holy Spirit never descends upon prayerless people. He never fills them. He never empowers them. There is nothing whatsoever in common between the Spirit of God and people who do not pray. The Spirit dwells only in an atmosphere of prayer.

In doing God's work, there is no substitute for praying. People of prayer cannot be replaced with other kinds of people. People of financial skill, people of education, people of worldly influence—none of these can possibly substitute for people of prayer. The life, the vigor, and the motive power of God's work is formed by praying people. A diseased heart is not a more fearful symptom of approaching death than nonpraying people are of spiritual atrophy.

The people to whom Jesus Christ committed the fortunes and destiny of His church were people of prayer. To no other kind of people has God ever committed Himself. The apostles were preeminently men of prayer. They gave themselves to prayer. They made praying their chief business. It was first in importance and first in results. God never has, and He never will, commit the weighty interests of His kingdom to people who do not make prayer a conspicuous and controlling factor in their lives.

People who do not pray never rise to any eminence of piety. People of piety are always people of prayer. People are never noted for the simplicity and strength of their faith unless they are preeminently people of prayer. Piety flourishes nowhere so rapidly and so profusely as in the prayer closet. The prayer closet is "the garden of faith."

The apostles allowed no duty, however sacred, to so busy them that it infringed on their time and prevented them from making prayer the main thing. The Word of God was ministered with apostolic fidelity and zeal. It was spoken by people with apostolic commissions, people who had been baptized by the fiery tongues of Pentecost. The Word was pointless and powerless unless people were freshly clothed with power by continuous and mighty prayer. The seed of God's Word must be saturated in prayer to make it germinate. It grows more readily and anchors more deeply when it is soaked with prayer.

The apostles were praying people themselves. They were also teachers of prayer, and they trained their disciples in the school of prayer. They urged their disciples to pray, not only that they might attain to the loftiest eminence of faith, but that they might be the most powerful factors in advancing God's kingdom.

Jesus Christ is the divinely appointed Leader of God's people, and no single thing in His life proves His eminent fitness for that office as much as His habit of prayer. Nothing is more food for thought than Christ's continual praying, and nothing is more conspicuous about Him than prayer. His campaigns were arranged, His victories gained, in the struggles and communion of His all-night praying. His praying rent the heavens. Moses and Elijah and the Transfiguration glory waited on His praying. His miracles and His teaching had their force from the same source. Gethsemane's praying crimsoned Calvary with serenity and glory. His prayer made the history and hastens the triumphs of His church. What an inspiration and command to pray is Christ's life! What a comment on its worth! How He shames our lives by His praying!

Like all those who have drawn God nearer to the world and lifted the world nearer to God, Jesus was a man of prayer. God made Him a Leader and Commander of His people. His leadership was one of prayer. A great Leader He was, because He was great in prayer.

All great leaders for God have fashioned their leadership in the wrestlings of their prayer closets. Many great people have led and molded the church without being great in prayer, but they were great only in their plans, great for their opinions, great for their organization, great by natural gifts, great by genius or character. However, they were not great for God.

But Jesus Christ was a great Leader for God. His was the great leadership of great praying. God was greatly in His leadership because prayer was greatly in it. We would do well to be taught by Him to pray, and to pray more and more.

Herein has been the secret of the people of prayer in the past history of the church: their hearts were after God, their desires were on Him, and their prayers were addressed to Him. They communed with Him, sought nothing of the world, sought great things of God, wrestled with Him, conquered all opposing forces, and opened up the channel of faith deep and wide between themselves and heaven. And all this was done by the use of prayer. Holy meditations, spiritual desires, heavenly longings—these swayed their intellects, enriched their emotions, and filled and enlarged their hearts. And all this was so because they were, first of all, people of prayer.

The people who have thus communed with God and have sought after Him with their whole hearts have always risen to consecrated eminence. In fact, no person has ever risen to this eminence without his flames of holy desire all dying to the world and all glowing for God and heaven. Nor have they ever risen to the heights of higher spiritual experiences unless prayer and the spirit of prayer have been conspicuous and controlling factors in their lives.

The entire consecration of many of God's children stands out distinctly like towering mountain peaks. Why is this? How did they ascend to these heights? What brought them so near to God? What made them so Christlike? The answer is easy—prayer. They prayed much, prayed long, and drank deeper and deeper still. They asked, they sought, and they knocked, until heaven opened its richest inner treasures of grace to them. Prayer was the Jacob's Ladder by which they scaled those holy and blessed heights and by which the angels of God came down and ministered to them.

The men and women of spiritual character and strength always valued prayer. They took time to be alone with God. Their praying was no hurried performance. They had many serious needs to be relieved and many weighty pleas to offer. They had to secure many great answers to prayer. They had to do much silent waiting before God, and much patient asking and asking over again. Prayer was the only channel through which the supply of their needs came, and it was the only way to utter pleas.

The only acceptable waiting before God of which they knew anything was prayer. They valued praying. It was more precious to them than all jewels, more excellent than any good, and more valued than the greatest good of earth. They esteemed it, valued it, and prized it. They pressed it to its farthest limits, tested its greatest results, and secured its most glorious heritage. To them, prayer was the one great thing to be appreciated and used.

The apostles, above everything else, were praying people, and they left the stamp of their prayer example and teaching upon the early church. But the apostles are dead, and times and people have changed. They have no successors by official assignment or heirship. And we do not have a commission, in our times, to make other apostles. No, the apostles' successors are those who pray.

Unfortunately, the times are not prayerful times. God's cause just now is in dire need of praying leaders. Other things may be needed, but this is the crying demand of these times and the urgent, first need of the church.

This is the day of great wealth and wonderful material resources in the church. But, unfortunately, the abundance of material resources is a great enemy and a severe hindrance to strong spiritual forces. It is an invariable law that the presence of attractive and influential material resources creates a trust in them and, by the same inevitable law, creates distrust in the spiritual forces of the gospel. They are two masters that cannot be served at the same time. (See Matthew 6:24.) For the degree to which the mind is fixed on one, it will be drawn away from the other. The days of great financial prosperity in the church have not been days of great religious prosperity. Wealthy people and praying people are not synonymous terms.

Paul, in the second chapter of his first epistle to Timothy, emphasized the need for people who pray. In his estimation, church leaders are to be conspicuous for their praying. Of necessity, prayer must shape their characters, and prayer must be one of their distinguishing characteristics. Prayer ought to be one of their most powerful elements, so much so that it cannot be hidden. Prayer ought to make church leaders notable. Character, official duty, reputation, and life—all should be shaped by prayer. The mighty forces of prayer lie in its praying leaders in a marked way. The standing obligation to pray rests in a special sense on church leaders. The church would be wise to discover this important truth and give prominence to it.

It can be written as a rule that God needs, first of all, leaders in the church who will put prayer first, people with whom prayer is habitual and characteristic, people who know the primacy of prayer. But, even more than having a habit of prayer, church leaders are to be filled to overflowing with prayer. Their lives should be made and molded by prayer; their hearts should be made up of prayer. These are the people—the only people—God can use in the furtherance of His kingdom and in the implanting of His message in the hearts of men.

FOUR:

GOD'S NEED FOR PEOPLE WHO PRAY

We do what He commands. We go where He wants us to go. We speak what He wants us to speak. His will is our law. His pleasure our joy. He is, today, seeking the lost, and He would have us seek with Him. He is shepherding the lambs, and He wants our cooperation. He is opening doors in heathen lands, and He wants our money and our prayers. —*Anonymous*

As we proceed on the subject of prayer, we now declare that it demands prayer leadership to hold the church to God's aims and to prepare it for God's uses. Prayer leadership preserves the spirituality of the church, just as prayerless leaders make for unspiritual conditions. The church is not necessarily spiritual by the mere fact of its existence, nor by its vocation. It is not held to its sacred vocation by generation, nor by succession. Like the new birth, it is *"not of blood, nor of the will of the flesh, nor of the will of man, but of God"* (John 1:13).

The church is not necessarily spiritual because it is concerned with and deals in spiritual values. It may hold its confirmations by the thousand, it may multiply its baptisms, and it may administer its sacraments innumerable times, and yet be as far from fulfilling its true mission as human conditions can make it.

This present world's general attitude retires prayer to insignificance and obscurity. By this attitude, salvation and eternal life are put in the background. It cannot be too often affirmed, therefore, that the principal need of the church is neither people of money nor people of intelligence, but people of prayer. Leaders in the realm of religious activity are to be judged by their praying habits, not by their money or social position. Those who are placed in the forefront of the church's business must be, first of all, people who know how to pray.

God does not conduct His work solely with people of education, wealth, or business capacity. Neither can He carry on His work through people of large intellects or great culture, nor yet through people of great social eminence and influence. All these qualities can be useful in God's work, provided they are not regarded as being primary. People possessing only these qualities cannot lead in God's work nor control His cause. People of prayer, before anything else, are indispensable to the furtherance of the kingdom of God on earth. No other sort will fit in the scheme or do the deed. People, great and influential in other things but small in prayer, cannot do the work that God has set out for His church to do in this world.

People of prayer, before anything else, are indispensable to the furtherance of the kingdom of God on earth. No other sort will fit in the scheme or do the deed. People, great and influential in other things but small in prayer, cannot do the work that God has set out for His church to do in this world.

People who represent God and who stand here in His stead, people who are to build up His kingdom in this world, must be, in an eminent sense, people of prayer. Whatever else they may have, whatever else they may lack, they must be people of prayer. Having everything else and lacking prayer, they will fail. Having prayer and lacking all else, they can succeed. Prayer must be the most conspicuous and the most potent factor in the character and conduct of people who undertake divine commission. God's business requires people who are versed in the business of praying.

It must be kept in mind that the praying to which the disciples of Christ are called by scriptural authority, is a valiant calling. The people God wants, and on whom He depends, must work at prayer just as they work at their worldly callings. They must follow through in this business of praying, just as they do in their secular pursuits. Diligence, perseverance, heartiness, and courage must all be in it if it is to succeed.

Everything secured by gospel promise, defined by gospel measure, and represented by gospel treasure is in prayer. All heights are scaled by it, all doors are opened to it, all victories are gained through it, and all grace is obtained through it. Heaven has all its good and all its help for people who pray. How marked and strong is the command of Christ that sends people from the parade of public giving and public praying to the privacy of their prayer closets, where with shut doors and in encircling silence they are alone in prayer with God!

In all ages, those who have carried out the divine will on earth have been people of prayer. The days of prayer are God's prosperous days. His heart, His oath, and His glory are committed to one proclamation: that every knee should bow to Him. (See Philippians 2:10.) The day of the Lord, in a preeminent sense, will be a day of universal prayer.

God's cause does not suffer because of lack of divine ability, but because of lack of prayer ability in man. God's action is just as much bound up in prayer today as it was when He said to Abimelech, "[Abraham] *shall pray for you, and you shall live*" (Genesis 20:7). So it was when God said to Job's friends, "*My servant Job shall pray for you: for him will I accept*" (Job 42:8).

God's great plan for the redemption of mankind depends as much on prayer now as it did when the Father first decreed the plan. Prayer makes the plan of redemption prosper and succeed. For God gives an imperative, universal, and eternal condition: "*Ask of Me, and I shall give You the heathen for Your inheritance, and the uttermost parts of the earth for your possession*" (Psalm 2:8).

In many places, an alarming state of things has come to pass, in that many church members are not praying men and women. Many of those occupying prominent positions in church life are not praying people. It is greatly to be feared that much of the work of the church is being done by those who are perfect strangers to the prayer closet. No wonder the work does not succeed.

While it may be true that many in the church say prayers, it is equally true that their praying is of the stereotyped order. Their prayers may be charged with sentiment, but they are tame, timid, and without fire or force. This sort of praying is even done by some of the few people who attend prayer meetings. Those whose names are found looming large in our great churches are not people noted for their praying habits. Yet, the entire fabric of the work in which they are engaged has to, inevitably, depend on the adequacy of prayer. This lack of praying creates a crisis like that of a country admitting to an invading enemy that it cannot fight and knows nothing about weapons of war.

In all God's plans for human redemption, He purposes that people pray. We are to pray in every place—in the church, in the prayer closet, in the home. We are to pray on sacred days and on secular days. All things are dependent on the measure of people's praying.

Prayer is the mainspring of life. We pray as we live; we live as we pray. Life will never be finer than the quality of the prayer closet. The mercury of life will rise only by the warmth of the prayer closet. Persistent nonpraying will eventually depress the temperature of life below zero.

If you were to measure and weigh the conditions of prayer, you would readily discover why more people do not pray. The conditions are so perfect, so blessed, that it is a rare character who can meet them. A heart full of love, a heart that holds even its enemies in loving contemplation and prayerful concern, a heart from which all bitterness, revenge, and envy are purged—how rare! Yet, this is the only condition of mind and heart in which a man can expect to be powerful in prayer.

There are certain conditions laid down for authentic praying. People are to pray, *"lifting up holy hands"* (1 Timothy 2:8), hands here being the symbol of life. Hands unsoiled by stains of evildoing are the emblem of a life unsoiled by sin. With a clean life, people are to come into the presence of God; thus they are to approach the throne of the Highest, where they can *"obtain mercy, and find grace to help in time of need"* (Hebrews 4:16).

Here, then, is one reason why people do not pray. They are too worldly in heart and too secular in life to enter the prayer closet; and even when they enter there, they cannot offer the *"effectual fervent prayer of a righteous man* [which] *avails much"* (James 5:16).

Again, hands are the symbols of supplication. Outstretched hands stand for an appeal for help. It is the silent yet eloquent attitude of a helpless soul standing before God, appealing for mercy and grace. Hands, too, are symbols of activity, power, and conduct. Hands outstretched to God in prayer must be *"holy hands"* (1 Timothy 2:8), unstained hands. The word *"holy"* here means undefiled, unspotted, untainted, and religiously observing every obligation.

How remote is all this from the character of sin-loving, worldly-minded, fleshly-disposed people, soiled by fleshly lusts, spotted by worldly indulgence, unholy in heart and conduct! "He who seeks equity must do equity" is the maxim of earthly courts. Even so, he who seeks God's good gifts must practice God's good deeds. This is the maxim of heavenly courts.

Prayer is sensitive, and it is always affected by the character and conduct of the one who prays. Water cannot rise above its own level, and a spotless prayer cannot flow from a spotted heart. Straight praying is never born of crooked conduct. The character of a person gives character to his supplication. The cowardly heart cannot do brave praying. Soiled people cannot make clean, pure supplications.

It is neither words, nor thoughts, nor ideas, nor feelings that shape praying, but it is character and conduct. People must walk in an upright fashion in order to be able to pray well. Bad character and unrighteous living break down praying until it becomes meaningless. Praying takes its tone and vigor from the life of the man or woman exercising it. When character and conduct are at a low ebb, praying can barely live, much less thrive.

The man of prayer, whether layman or preacher, is God's right-hand man. In the realm of spiritual affairs, he creates conditions, begins movements, and brings things to pass.

By the fact and condition of their creation and redemption, all people are under obligation to pray. Every person *can* pray, and every person *should* pray. But when it comes to the affairs of the kingdom, let it be said at once that a prayerless person in the church of God is like a paralyzed organ in the physical body. He is out of place in the communion of saints, out of harmony with God, and out of accord with His purposes for mankind. A prayerless person handicaps the vigor and life of the whole system, just as a demoralized soldier is a menace to his army in the day of battle. The absence of prayer lessens the life-giving current of the soul, cripples faith, sets aside holy living, and shuts out heaven.

The Holy Scriptures draw a sharp line between praying saints and nonpraying people. The following was written about John Fletcher of Madeley—one of the praying saints:

> He was far more abundant in his public labors than the greater part of his companions in the holy ministry. Yet these bore but little proportion to those internal exercises of prayer and supplication to which he was wholly given up in private, which were almost uninterruptedly maintained from hour to hour. He lived in the spirit of prayer, and whatever employment in which he was engaged, this spirit of prayer was constantly manifested through them all.

> Without this he neither formed any design, nor entered upon any duty. Without this, he neither read nor conversed. Without this he neither visited nor received a visitor. There have been seasons of supplications in which he appeared to be carried out far beyond the ordinary limits of devotion, when, like his Lord upon the Mount of Transfiguration, while he continued to pour out his mighty prayer, the fashion of his countenance has been changed, and his face has appeared as the face of an angel.

O God, raise up more people of prayer like John Fletcher! How we need, in these times, people through whom God can work!

FIVE:

PRAYERLESS CHRISTIANS

If there was ever a time when Peter, James and John needed to remain awake, it was in Gethsemane. If James had persisted in keeping awake, it might have saved him from being decapitated a few years later. If Peter had stirred himself to really intercede for himself and others, he would not have denied his Christ that night in the palace of Caiaphas.
                                                                    —*Anonymous*

There is great need in this day for Christians in the business world to infuse their mundane affairs with the spirit of prayer. There is a great army of successful businesspeople in Christ's church, and it is high time they attended to this matter. We need to put God into business. In other words, we need to put the realization and restraint of His presence and His fear into all the secularities of life.

We need the atmosphere of the prayer closet to pervade our places of business. The sanctity of prayer is needed to fill our workplaces. We need the spirit of Sunday carried over to Monday and continued until Saturday.

160 *E. M. Bounds on Prayer & Spiritual Warfare*

But this cannot be done by prayerless people; we need people of prayer. We need businesspeople to go about their concerns with the same reverence and responsibility with which they enter the prayer closet. We need people who are devoid of greed and who carry God with them, with all their hearts, into the secular affairs of life.

Worldlings imagine prayer to be too impotent a thing to battle with business methods and worldly practices. Against such a misleading doctrine Paul sets the whole commands of God, the loyalty to Jesus Christ, the claims of pious character, and the demands of the salvation of the world. We must pray, and we must put strength and heart into our praying. Prayer is part of the primary business of life, and God has called His people to it first of all.

Praying people are God's agents on earth, the representatives of the government of heaven, called to a specific task on the earth. While it is true that the Holy Spirit and the angels are agents of God in carrying forward the redemption of the human race, yet among them there must be praying people. For such people God has great use. He can make much of them, and in the past He has done wonderful things through them. These are God's instruments in carrying out His great purposes on the earth. They are God's messengers, watchmen, shepherds, and workmen, who need not be ashamed. Fully equipped for the great work to which they are appointed, they honor God and bless the world.

Above all things, Christian men and women must, primarily, be leaders in prayer. No matter how conspicuous they may be in other activities, they fail if they are not conspicuous in prayer. They must give their brains and hearts to prayer. People who shape the program of Christ's church, who map out its line of activity, should, themselves, be shaped by prayer. People controlling the finances, thought, and action of the church should all be people of prayer.

In order for God's work to progress to completion, there are two basic principles: God's ability to give and people's ability to ask. Failure in either one would be fatal to the success of God's work on earth. God's inability to do or to give would put an end to redemption. People's failure to pray would, just as surely, set a limit on the plan. But, God's ability to do and to give has never failed and *cannot* fail, but people's ability to ask can fail and often does.

Therefore, the slow progress that is being made toward the realization of a world won for Christ lies entirely with people's limited asking. There is need for the entire church of God to get busy praying. The church upon its knees would bring heaven upon the earth.

The wonderful ability of God to do for us was expressed by Paul in one of his most comprehensive statements: *"And God is able to make all grace abound toward you; that you, always having all sufficiency in all things, may abound to every good work"* (2 Corinthians 9:8).

Study that remarkable statement—*"God is able to make all grace abound."* That is, He is able to give such sufficiency that we may abound—overflow—to every good work. Why are we not more fully overflowing? The answer is lack of prayer ability. "[We] *have not, because* [we] *ask not"* (James 4:2). We are feeble, weak, and impoverished because of our failure to pray. God is restrained in doing because we are restrained by our failure to pray. All failures in securing heaven are traceable to lack of prayer or misdirected prayer.

Prayer must be broad in its scope; it must plead for others. Intercession for others is the hallmark of all true prayer. When prayer is confined to self and to the sphere of one's personal needs, it dies by reason of its littleness, narrowness, and selfishness. Prayer must be broad and unselfish, or it will perish. Prayer is the soul of a person stirred to plead with God for others. In addition to being interested in the eternal interests of one's own soul, it must, in its very nature, be concerned for the spiritual and eternal welfare of others. A man is most able to pray for himself when he has compassion and concern for others.

> *Intercession for others is the hallmark of all true prayer. When prayer is confined to self and to the sphere of one's personal needs, it dies by reason of its littleness, narrowness, and selfishness. Prayer must be broad and unselfish, or it will perish. Prayer is the soul of a person stirred to plead with God for others.*

In the second chapter of 1 Timothy, the apostle Paul spoke to those who occupied positions of influence and places of authority. He urged them with singular and specific emphasis to give themselves to prayer. *"I will therefore that men pray every where"* (1 Timothy 2:8). This is the high calling of the men of the church, and no other calling is so engaging, so engrossing, and so valuable that we can afford to relieve Christian men from the all-important vocation of secret prayer. Nothing whatsoever can take the place of prayer. Nothing whatsoever can atone for the neglect of praying. This is of supreme importance, and it should be given first priority.

No person is so high in position or in grace to be exempt from the obligation to pray. No person is too big to pray, no matter who he is or what office he holds. The king on his throne is as much obligated to pray as the peasant in his cottage. No one is so high and exalted in this world, or so lowly and obscure, that he is excused from praying. Everyone's help is needed in doing the work of God, and the prayer of each praying person helps to swell the whole. Those who are leaders in place, in gifts, and in authority are to be chiefs in prayer.

Civil and church leaders shape the affairs of this world. Therefore, civil and church leaders themselves need to be shaped personally in spirit, in heart, in conduct, in truth, and in righteousness, by the prayers of God's people. This is in direct line with Paul's words:

> *I exhort therefore, that, first of all, supplications, prayers, intercessions, and giving of thanks, be made for all men; for kings, and for all that are in authority.* (1 Timothy 2:1–2)

It is a sad day for righteousness when church politics, instead of holy praying, shapes the administration of the church and elevates people to place and power.

Why must we pray for all people? Because God wills the salvation of all people. God's children on earth must link their prayers to God's will. Prayer is meant to carry out the will of God. God's will is that all people would be saved. His heart is set on this one thing. Our prayers must be the creation and exponent of God's will. We are to grasp humanity in our praying as God grasps humanity in His love, His interest, and His plans to redeem them. Our sympathies, prayers, wrestlings, and ardent desires must run parallel with the will of God and be broad, generous, worldwide, and godlike. A Christian must in all things, first of all, be conformed to the will of God, but nowhere should this royal devotion be more evident than in the salvation of the human race. This high partnership with God, as His agents on earth, is to have its fullest, richest, and most effective exercise in prayer for all people.

Believers are to pray for all people, especially for rulers in church and state, *"that we may lead a quiet and peaceable life in all godliness and honesty"* (1 Timothy 2:2). Peace on the outside and peace on the inside. Praying calms disturbing forces, allays tormenting fears, and brings conflict to an end. Prayer tends to do away with turmoil. Even if there are external conflicts, it is well to have deep peace within the citadel of the soul. *"That we may lead a quiet and peaceable life."* Prayer brings inner calm and furnishes outward tranquility. If there were praying rulers and praying subjects worldwide, they would allay turbulent forces, make wars to cease, and cause peace to reign.

Believers must pray for all people so that we may lead lives *"in all godliness and honesty,"* that is, with godliness and seriousness. Godliness means to be like God. It means to be godly, to have godlikeness, to have the image of God stamped on the inner nature, and to show the same likeness in our conduct and character. Almighty God is the very highest model, and to be like Him is to possess the highest character. Prayer molds us into the image of God. At the same time it tends to mold others into the same image in proportion to our praying for them.

Prayer means to be like God. To be godlike is to love Christ and love God, to be one with the Father and the Son in spirit, character, and conduct. Prayer means to stay with God until you are like Him. Prayer makes a person godly, and it puts within him *"the mind of Christ"* (1 Corinthians 2:16), the mind of humility, self-surrender, service, pity, and prayer. If we really pray, we will become more like God, or else we will quit praying.

"Men [are to] *pray every where"*—in the prayer closet, in the prayer meeting, around the family altar—and they are to do it, *"lifting up holy hands, without wrath and doubting"* (1 Timothy 2:8). Here is not only the obligation laid upon people to pray, but instructions on how they should pray. People must pray *"without wrath."* In other words, people must pray

without bitterness against their neighbors or fellow believers, without the stubbornness of a strong will, without hard feelings, without an evil desire or emotion kindled by fires in the carnal nature. Praying is not to be done by these questionable things or in company with such evil feelings, but "without" them, aloof and entirely separate from them.

This is the sort of praying we are called upon to do. It is the sort that God hears and the kind that prevails with God and accomplishes things. Such prayers in Christians' hands become divine agencies in God's hands for carrying on God's gracious purposes and executing His designs in redemption.

Prayer has a higher origin than man's nature. This is true whether we mean man's nature as separate from the angelic nature, or man's carnal nature, unrenewed and unchanged. Prayer does not originate in the realm of the carnal mind. Such a nature is entirely foreign to prayer simply because "the carnal mind is enmity against God" (Romans 8:7).

It is by the new spirit that we pray, the new spirit sweetened by the sugar of heaven, perfumed with the fragrance of the upper world, and invigorated by a breath from the crystal sea. The new spirit is native to the skies, panting after the heavenly things, and inspired by the breath of God. The new spirit produces praying from which all the old juices of the carnal, unregenerate nature have been expelled. It is praying in which the fire of God has created the flame that has consumed worldly lusts. At the same time, the juices of the Spirit have been injected into the soul. Praying that is by the new spirit is entirely divorced from wrath.

People are also to pray "without...doubting" (1 Timothy 2:8). The Revised Version puts it, "without...disputing." Praying people must have faith in God and belief in God's Word without question. There must be no doubting or disputing in the mind. There must be no opinions, no hesitancy, no questioning, no reasoning, no intellectual quibbling, no rebellion, but a strict, steadfast loyalty of spirit to God, a life of loyalty in heart and intellect to God's Word.

God is closely related to people who have a living, transforming faith in Jesus Christ. These are God's children. A father loves his children, supplies their needs, hears their cries, and answers their requests. A child believes his father, loves him, trusts in him, and asks him for what he needs, believing without doubting that his father will hear his requests. God answers the prayers of His children. Their troubles concern Him, and their prayers awaken Him. Their voices are sweet to Him. He loves to hear them pray, and He is never happier than to answer their prayers.

Prayer is intended for God's ear. It is not people but God who hears and answers prayer. Prayer covers the whole range of human need. Hence, *"in every thing by prayer and supplication with thanksgiving let your requests be made known to God"* (Philippians. 4:6). Prayer includes the entire range of God's ability. *"Is any thing too hard for the Lord?"* (Genesis 18:14). Prayer does not apply to one favored segment of man's need, but it reaches to and embraces the entire circle of his needs, simply because God is the God of the whole man. God has pledged Himself to supply the needs of the whole man: physical, intellectual, and spiritual. *"But my God shall supply all your need according to His riches in glory by Christ Jesus"* (Philippians 4:19). Prayer is the child of grace, and grace is for the whole man and for every one of the children of men.

SIX:

PRAYING FOR OTHERS

Our Redeemer was in the Garden of Gethsemane. His hour was come. He felt as if He would be strengthened somewhat, if He had two or three disciples near Him. His three chosen disciples were within a stone's throw of the scene of His agony; but they were all asleep that the Scripture might be fulfilled—*"I have trodden the winepress alone; and of the people there was none with me"* (Isaiah 63:3). The eight, in the distance, were good and true disciples; but they were only ordinary men, or men with a commonplace call.

—*Alexander Whyte*

No insistence in the Bible is more pressing than the command it lays upon people to pray. No exhortation contained therein is heartier, more solemn, or more stirring. No principle is more strongly stressed than *"men ought always to pray, and not to faint"* (Luke 18:1).

In view of this command, it is pertinent to ask if the majority of Christians are praying men and women. Is prayer a fixed course in the churches? In the Sunday school, the home, and the colleges, do we have any graduates in the school of prayer? Is the church producing those who have

Praying for Others 167

diplomas from the great university of prayer? This is what God requires, what He commands. It is those who possess such qualifications that He must have to accomplish His purposes and to carry out the work of His kingdom on earth.

And it is earnest praying that needs to be done. Languid praying, without heart or strength, with neither fire nor tenacity, defeats its own avowed purpose. The prophet of past times lamented that in a day that needed strenuous praying, there was no one who stirred up himself to take hold of God. (See Isaiah 64:7). Christ charges us *not to faint* (Luke 18:1) in our praying. Laxity and indifference are great hindrances to prayer, both to the practice of praying and the process of receiving. It requires a brave, strong, fearless, and insistent spirit to engage in successful prayer.

Trying to pray for too many things also interferes with effectiveness. Offering too many petitions breaks unity and breeds neglect. Prayers should be specific and urgent. Too many words, like too much width, causes shallowness and sandbars. A single objective that absorbs the whole being and inflames the entire person is the properly constraining force in prayer.

It is easy to see how prayer was a decreed factor in the dispensations before the coming of Jesus, how their leaders had to be men of prayer, and how God's mightiest revelations of Himself were revelations made through prayer. It is also easy to see how Jesus Christ, in His personal ministry and in His relationship to God, was great and constant in prayer. His labors and dispensation overflowed with fullness in proportion to His prayers. The possibilities of His praying were unlimited, as were the possibilities of His ministry. The necessity of His praying was equaled only by the constancy with which He practiced it during His earthly life.

The dispensation of the Holy Spirit is a dispensation of prayer in a preeminent sense. Here prayer has an essential and vital role. Without depreciating the possibilities and necessities of prayer in all the preceding dispensations of God in the world, it must be declared that it is in this latter dispensation that the exercises and demands of prayer are given their greatest authority. Furthermore, prayer's possibilities are rendered unlimited, and its necessity unavoidable.

In these days we have sore need of a generation of praying people, a band of men and women through whom God can bring His greatest movements more fully into the world. The Lord our God is not restricted within Himself, but He is restricted in us by reason of our little faith and weak praying. A breed of Christians is greatly needed who will seek tirelessly after God, who will give Him no rest, day and night, until He hearkens to their cries. The times demand people who are all athirst for God's glory, who are unselfish in their desires, who are quenchless for God, who seek Him late and early, and who will give themselves no rest until *"the whole earth be filled with His glory"* (Psalm 72:19).

> *In these days we have sore need of a generation of praying people, a band of men and women through whom God can bring His greatest movements more fully into the world. The Lord our God is not restricted within Himself, but He is restricted in us by reason of our little faith and weak praying. A breed of Christians is greatly needed who will seek tirelessly after God, who will give Him no rest, day and night, until He hearkens to their cries.*

Men and women are needed whose prayers will give to the world the utmost power of God, whose prayers will make His promises blossom with rich and full results. God is waiting to hear us, and He challenges us to pray that He might work. He is asking us today, as He asked His ancient Israel, to *"prove [Him] now herewith"* (Malachi 3:10). Behind God's Word is God Himself. We read in Isaiah 45:11,

> *Thus says the LORD, the Holy One of Israel, and his Maker, Ask Me of things to come concerning My sons, and concerning the work of My hands command you Me.*

It is as though God places Himself in the hands and at the disposal of His people who pray, and indeed He does.

The dominant element of all praying is faith that is conspicuous, cardinal, and emphatic. Without such faith it is impossible to please God (see Hebrews 11:6) and equally impossible to pray.

There is a current perception of spiritual duties that tends to separate the pulpit and the pew. The perception is that the pulpit should bear the entire burden of spiritual concerns, while the pew should be concerned only with secular and worldly duties. Such a view needs drastic correction. God's cause, obligations, efforts, and successes lie with equal pressure on pulpit and pew.

The person in the pew is not taxed with the burden of prayer as he ought to be, and as he must be, before any new visitation of power can come to the church. The church will never be wholly for God until the pews are filled with praying people. The church cannot be what God wants it to be until the members that are leaders in business, politics, law, and society are also leaders in prayer.

God began His early movements in the world with people of prayer. Abraham, a leader of God's cause, was preeminently a praying man. God chose Abraham to be the father of the race that became His chosen people in the world for hundreds of years. This was the race to whom God committed His oracles and from whom sprang the promised Messiah.

When we consider Abraham's conduct and character, we readily see how prayer ruled and swayed this great leader of God's people. *"Abraham planted a grove in Beersheba, and called there on the name of the LORD, the everlasting God"* (Genesis 21:33). It is an outstanding fact that wherever he pitched his tent and camped for a season with his household, there he erected an altar of sacrifice and of prayer. His was a personal and a family religion, in which prayer was a prominent and abiding factor.

Prayer is the medium of divine revelation. It is through prayer that God reveals Himself to the spiritual soul today, just as in the Old Testament days He made His revelations to the people who prayed. God shows Himself to the person who prays.

"God is with you in all that you do" (Genesis 21:22). This was the clear conviction of Abraham's peers, and they gladly would have made a covenant with him. It was the commonly held belief that Abraham was not only

a man of prayer, but a man whose prayers God would answer. This is the summary and secret of divine rule in the church. In all ages God has ruled the church by prayerful people. When prayer fails, the divine rulership fails.

As we have seen, Abraham, the father of the faithful, was a prince and a priest in prayer. He had remarkable influence with God. God held back His vengeance while Abraham prayed. His mercy was suspended and conditioned on Abraham's praying. His visitations of wrath were removed by the praying of this ruler in Israel. The movements of God were influenced by the prayers of Abraham, the friend of God. Abraham's righteous prayerfulness permitted him to share in the secrets of God's counsels, while the knowledge of these secrets lengthened and intensified his praying. With Abraham the altar of sacrifice was close to the altar of prayer. With him the altar of prayer sanctified the altar of sacrifice. To Abimelech God said, "[Abraham] *is a prophet, and he shall pray for you, and you shall live*" (Genesis 20:7).

Christian people must pray for others. On one occasion Samuel said to the people, "*Moreover as for me, God forbid that I should sin against the* LORD *in ceasing to pray for you*" (1 Samuel 12:23). Fortunately, these sinful Israelites, who had rejected God and desired a human king, had a man of prayer.

One way to increase personal grace is to pray for others. Intercessory prayer is a means of grace to those who exercise it. It is in the paths of intercessory prayer that we enter the richest fields of spiritual growth and gather priceless riches. To pray for others is of divine appointment, and it represents the highest form of Christian service.

People must pray, and people must be prayed for. The Christian must pray for all things, of course, but prayers for people are infinitely more important, just as people are infinitely more important than things. Also, prayers for people are far more important than prayers for things because people more deeply involve God's will and the work of Jesus Christ. People are to be cared for, sympathized with, and prayed for, because sympathy, pity, compassion, and care accompany and precede prayer for people.

All this makes praying a real business, not child's play, not a secondary affair, not a trivial matter, but a serious business. The people who have made a success of praying have made a business of praying. It is a process demanding the time, thought, energy, and hearts of mankind. Prayer is business for time, business for eternity. It is our business to pray, transcending all other business and taking precedence over all other vocations, professions, or occupations. Our praying concerns not only ourselves, but all people and their greatest interests, and even the salvation of their immortal souls. Praying is a business that takes hold of eternity and the things beyond the grave. It is a business that involves earth and heaven. All worlds are touched by prayer, and all worlds are influenced by prayer. It has to do with God and people, angels and devils.

Jesus was preeminently a leader in prayer, and His praying is an incentive to pray. How prominently prayer stands out in His life! The leading events of His earthly career are distinctly marked by prayer. The wonderful experience and glory of the Transfiguration was preceded by prayer, and it was the result of the praying of our Lord. (See Luke 9:28–35.) We do not know what words He used as He prayed, nor do we know what He prayed for. But I believe it was night, and long into its hours the Master prayed. It was while He prayed that the darkness fled and His form was lit with unearthly splendor. Moses and Elijah came to yield to Him not only the palm of law and prophecy, but the palm of praying.

None other prayed as Jesus did, nor did any have such a glorious manifestation of the divine presence. None other heard so clearly the revealing voice of the Father: *"This is My beloved Son: hear Him"* (Luke 9:35). Oh, to be with Christ in the school of prayer; then we would be happy disciples indeed!

How many of us have failed to come to this glorious Mount of Transfiguration because we were unacquainted with the transfiguring power of prayer! It is the going apart to pray and the long, intense seasons of prayer that make the face shine, transfigure the character, and make even dull, earthly garments glisten with heavenly splendor. But more than this: it is real praying that makes eternal things real, close, and tangible, and real praying brings the glorified visitors and the heavenly visions. Transfigured lives would not be so rare if there were more of this transfigured praying, and these heavenly visits would not be so few.

How difficult it seems to be for the church to understand that the whole scheme of redemption depends on people of prayer. The work of our Lord, while here on the earth, as well as the work of the apostle Paul, was to develop, by teaching and example, people of prayer, to whom the future of the church would be committed. How strange that instead of learning this simple and all-important lesson, the modern church has largely overlooked it. We need to turn afresh to that wondrous leader of spiritual Israel, our Lord Jesus Christ, who by example and precept instructs us to pray. And we need to turn to the apostle Paul, who, by virtue of his praying habits and prayer lessons, is a model to God's people in every age and place.

SEVEN:

PREACHERS AND PRAYER

Of course, the preacher is above all others distinguished as a man of prayer. He prays as an ordinary Christian, else he were a hypocrite. He prays more than ordinary Christians, else he were disqualified for the office he has undertaken. If you as ministers are not very prayerful, you are to be pitied. If you become lax in sacred devotion, not only will you need to be pitied but your people also, and the day cometh in which you will be ashamed and confounded. Our seasons of fastings and prayer at the Tabernacle have been high days indeed; never has heaven's gate stood wider; never have our hearts been nearer the central glory.   —*Charles Spurgeon*

Preachers are God's leaders. They are divinely called to their holy office and high purpose and, primarily, are responsible for the condition of the church. Just as Moses was called of God to lead Israel out of Egypt through the wilderness into the Promised Land, so also God calls His ministers to lead His spiritual Israel through this world to the heavenly land. They are divinely commissioned to leadership, and they are, by precept and example, to teach God's people what God would have them be. Paul's counsel to the young preacher Timothy is this:

> *Let no man despise your youth; but be you an example of the believers, in word, in conversation, in charity, in spirit, in faith, in purity.*
>
> (1 Timothy 4:12)

God's ministers shape the church's character and give tone and direction to its life. In Revelation chapters two and three, the prefacing sentence in the letters to each of the seven churches in Asia reads, *"To the angel of the church...."* This seems to indicate that the angel—the minister—was in the same state of mind and condition of life as the membership, and, moreover, the minister was largely responsible for the spiritual condition of the church. The angel in each case was the preacher, teacher, or leader.

The first Christians knew this full well and felt this responsibility. In their helplessness, which they consciously felt, they cried out, *"And who is sufficient for these things?"* (2 Corinthians 2:16), for the tremendous responsibility pressed upon their hearts and heads. The only reply to such a question was, *"God only"* (Mark 2:7). So, they were compelled by necessity to look beyond themselves for help and to throw themselves on prayer to secure God. More and more, as they prayed, they felt their responsibility; and more and more, by prayer they got God's help. They realized that their sufficiency was in God.

Prayer belongs in a very high and important sense to the ministry. It takes vigor and elevation of character to administer the prayer office. Praying prophets have frequently been at a premium in the history of God's people. In every age the demand has been for leaders in Israel who pray. God's watchmen must always and everywhere be people of prayer.

It ought to be no surprise for ministers to be often found on their knees seeking divine help for the responsibilities of their call. These are the true prophets of the Lord, and they stand as mouthpieces of God to a generation of wicked and worldly-minded men and women. Praying preachers are the boldest, the truest, and the swiftest ministers of God. They mount up highest and are nearest to Him who has called them. They advance more rapidly, and in Christian living they are most like God.

Praying preachers are the boldest, the truest, and the swiftest ministers of God. They mount up highest and are nearest to Him who has called them. They advance more rapidly, and in Christian living they are most like God.

In reading the Gospels, we cannot help being impressed by the supreme effort made by our Lord to rightly instruct the twelve apostles. He instructed them in all the things that would prepare them for the tremendous tasks ahead of them. His consideration was for the church, that it would have people, holy in life and in heart, who would know full well the origin of their strength and power in the work of the ministry. A large part of Christ's teaching was addressed to these chosen apostles, and the training of the Twelve occupied much of His thought and time. In all that training, prayer was laid down as a basic principle.

We find the same thing to be true in the life and work of the apostle Paul. Though he edified the churches to whom he ministered and wrote, it was his purpose to instruct and prepare ministers to whom the interests of God's people would be committed. Paul wrote two epistles to Timothy, who was a young preacher, and one to Titus, who was also a young minister. It appears that Paul's design was to give each of them needed instruction to rightly do the work of the ministry to which they had been called by the Spirit of God. Underlying these instructions was the foundation stone of prayer. Unless they were men of prayer, by no means would they be able to *"show* [themselves] *approved unto God,* [workmen] *that need*[ed] *not to be ashamed, rightly dividing the word of truth"* (2 Timothy 2:15).

The highest welfare of the church of God on earth depends largely on the ministry, and so God has always been jealous of His watchmen—His preachers. His concern has been for the character of the people who minister at His altars in holy things. They must be people who lean on Him, who look to Him, and who continually seek Him for wisdom, help, and power to effectively do the work of the ministry. So, He has designed people of prayer for the holy office, and He has relied on them successively to perform the tasks He has assigned them.

God's great works are to be done as Christ did them; they are to be done, indeed, with increased power received from the ascended and exalted Christ. These works are to be done by prayer. People must do God's work in God's way and to God's glory, and prayer is necessary for its successful accomplishment.

The thing far above all other things in the equipment of the preacher is prayer. Before everything else he must be a person who makes a specialty of prayer. A prayerless preacher is a misnomer. He has either missed his calling, or he has grievously failed God, who called him into the ministry.

God wants people who are not dullards, who *"study to show* [themselves] *approved"* (2 Timothy 2:15). Preaching the Word is essential, social qualities are not to be underestimated, and education is good. But under and above all else, prayer must be the main plank in the platform of the one who goes forth to preach the unsearchable riches of Christ to a lost and hungry world.

The one weak spot in our church institutions lies just here. Prayer is not regarded as being the primary factor in church life and activity; and other things, good in their places, are made primary. This should not be. First things need to be put first, and the first thing in the equipment of a minister is prayer.

Our Lord is the pattern for all preachers, and with Him prayer was the law of life. By it He lived. It was the inspiration of His toil, the source of His strength, and the spring of His joy. With our Lord prayer was no sentimental episode, nor a pleasing prelude, nor an interlude, nor an afterthought, nor a form. For Jesus, prayer was exacting, all-absorbing, and paramount. To Him it was the call of a sweet duty, the satisfying of a restless yearning, the preparation for heavy responsibilities, and the meeting of a vigorous need.

This being so, the disciple must be as his Lord, the servant as his Master. As the Lord Himself was, so also His disciples must be. Our Lord Jesus Christ chose His twelve apostles only after He had spent a night in praying, and we may rest assured that He sets the same high value on those He calls into His ministry today.

No feeble or secondary place was given to prayer in the ministry of Jesus. It comes first—emphatic, conspicuous, and controlling. Having prayerful habits, having a prayerful spirit, given to long, solitary communion with God, Jesus was above all else a man of prayer. The crux of His earthly history, in New Testament terminology, is condensed to a single statement, found in Hebrews 5:7:

Who in the days of His flesh, when He had offered up prayers and supplications with strong crying and tears to Him that was able to save Him from death, and was heard in that He feared.

Let Jesus's ministers be like their Lord and Master, whose they are and whom they serve. (See Acts 27:23.) Let Him be their pattern, their example, their leader, and their teacher. In some places much reference is made to "following Christ," but it is confined to the following of Him in modes and ordinances, as if salvation were wrapped up in the specific way of doing a thing. "The path of prayer Thyself hath trod"[1] is the path along which we are to follow Him; no other path will do.

Jesus was given as a leader to the people of God, and never has any leader more exemplified the worth and necessity of prayer. Even though he was equal in glory with the Father, and anointed and sent on His special mission by the Holy Spirit, Jesus still prayed. His incarnate birth, His high commission, His royal anointing—all these were His, but they did not relieve Him from the exacting claims of prayer. Rather, they tended to impose these claims upon Him with greater authority. He did not ask to be excused from the burden of prayer; He gladly accepted it, acknowledged its claims, and voluntarily subjected Himself to its demands.

Not only was His leadership preeminent, but His praying was preeminent. Had it not been, His leadership would have been neither preeminent nor divine. If, in true leadership, prayer had been dispensable, then certainly Jesus could have dispensed with it. But He did not, nor can any of His followers who desire effectiveness in Christian activity do other than follow their Lord.

While Jesus Christ was personally under the law of prayer and while His parables and miracles were exponents of prayer, He focused on teaching

---

1. "Prayer Is the Soul's Sincere Desire," hymn by James Montgomery (1818).

His disciples the specific art of praying. He said little or nothing about how to preach or what to preach. But, He spent both His strength and His time in teaching people how to speak to God, how to commune with Him, and how to be with Him. He knew very well that he who has learned the craft of talking to God will be well versed in talking to people.

Turning aside for a moment, we observe that prayer was the secret of the wonderful success of the early Methodist preachers, who were far from being learned people. But with all their limitations, they were people of prayer, and they did great things for God.

The ability to talk to people is measured by the ability with which a preacher can talk to God for people. He who does not plow in his prayer closet will never reap in his pulpit.

We must always emphasize that Jesus Christ trained His disciples to pray. This is the real meaning of the saying, "the training of the Twelve." We must remember that Christ taught the world's preachers more about praying than He did about preaching. Prayer was the great factor in the spreading of His gospel. Prayer preserved and made effective all other factors. He did not discount preaching when He stressed praying, but rather He taught that preaching is utterly dependent on prayer.

"The Christian's trade is praying," declared Martin Luther. Every Jewish boy had to learn a trade. Jesus Christ learned two: the trade of a carpenter and the trade of praying. The one trade served earthly uses; the other served His divine and higher purposes. Jewish custom committed Jesus as a boy to the trade of a carpenter; the law of God bound Him to praying from His earliest years and remained with Him to the end.

Christ is the Christian's example, and every Christian must imitate Him. Every preacher must be like his Lord and Master and must learn the trade of praying. He who learns well the trade of praying, masters the secret of the Christian art; and he becomes a skilled workman in God's workshop, one who does not need to be ashamed, a worker together with his Lord and Master.

"Pray without ceasing" (1 Thessalonians 5:17) is the trumpet call to the preachers of our time. If the preachers will clothe their thoughts with the

atmosphere of prayer, if they will prepare their sermons on their knees, a gracious outpouring of God's Spirit will come upon the earth.

The one indispensable qualification for preaching is the gift of the Holy Spirit, and it was for the bestowal of this indispensable gift that the disciples were charged to stay in Jerusalem. Receiving this gift is absolutely necessary if ministry is to be successful. This is why the first disciples were commanded to stay in Jerusalem until they received it. This is why they sought the gift with urgent and earnest prayerfulness. They obeyed their Lord's command to stay in that city until they were clothed with *"power from on high"* (Luke 24:49). Immediately after He had left them for heaven, they sought to secure it by continued and earnest prayer. *"These all with one accord continued stedfastly in prayer, with the women, and Mary the Mother of Jesus, and with his brethren"* (Acts 1:14 RV).

John refers to this same thing in his first epistle. He says, *"You have an unction from the Holy One"* (1 John 2:20). It is this divine unction that preachers of the present day should sincerely desire and pray for, remaining unsatisfied until the blessed gift is richly bestowed.

Another allusion to this same important procedure was made by our Lord shortly after His resurrection, when He said to His disciples, *"But you shall receive power, after that the Holy Ghost is come upon you"* (Acts 1:8). At the same time Jesus directed the attention of His disciples to the statement of John the Baptist concerning the Spirit. John had said, *"I indeed baptize you with water…He shall baptize you with the Holy Ghost, and with fire"* (Luke 3:16). This is identical to the *"power from on high"* (Luke 24:49) for which Jesus had commanded them to stay in the city of Jerusalem. Alluding to John the Baptist's words, Jesus said, *"For John truly baptized with water; but you shall be baptized with the Holy Ghost not many days from now"* (Acts 1:5). Peter at a later date said of our Lord, *"God anointed* [Him] *with the Holy Ghost and with power"* (Acts 10:38).

These are the divine statements to preachers of that day about the mission and ministry of the Holy Spirit, and the same divine statements apply with equal force to the preachers of today. God's ideal minister is a God-called, divinely anointed, Spirit-touched man. He is separated unto God's work; set apart from secularities and questionable affairs; baptized from above; marked, sealed, and owned by the Spirit; and devoted to his Master and His ministry. These are the divinely appointed requisites for a preacher of the Word; without them he is inadequate and inevitably unfruitful.

Today, there is no scarcity of preachers who deliver eloquent sermons on the need and nature of revival, who advance elaborate plans for the spread of the kingdom of God. But the praying preachers are rare. The greatest benefactor this age can have is a person who will bring the preachers, the church, and the people back to the practice of real praying. The reformer needed just now is the praying reformer. The leader Israel requires is one who, with clarion voice, will call the ministry back to their knees.

There is considerable talk in the air about revival. However, we need the vision to see that the revival we need, and the only one worth having, is the one that is born of the Holy Spirit. This kind of revival brings deep conviction for sin and regeneration for those who seek God's face. Such a revival comes at the end of a season of real praying. It is utter folly to discuss or expect a revival without the Holy Spirit operating in His distinctive office, and this is conditioned on much earnest praying. Such a revival will begin in pulpit and pew alike; it will be promoted by both preacher and layman working in harmony with God.

The heart is the vocabulary of prayer, the life is the best commentary on prayer, and the outward conduct is the fullest expression of prayer. Prayer builds the character; prayer perfects the life. And this the ministry needs to learn as thoroughly as the laymen. There is but one rule for both.

The general body of Christ's disciples was averse to prayer, having little taste for it and having little harmony with Him in the deep things of prayer and its mightier struggles. Therefore, the Master had to select a circle of three more apt scholars—Peter, James, and John—who had more relish for this divine work. He took them aside that they might learn the lesson of prayer. These men were nearer to Jesus, more like Him, and more helpful to Him because they were more prayerful.

Blessed, indeed, are those disciples whom Jesus Christ, in this day, calls into a more intimate fellowship with Himself, and who, readily responding to the call, are found much on their knees before Him. Distressing, indeed, is the condition of the Christians who, in their hearts, are averse to exercising the ministry of prayer.

All the great eras of our Lord, historical and spiritual, were made or fashioned by His praying. So, also, His plans and great achievements were born in prayer and filled with the spirit thereof. As was the Master, so also must His servant be; as his Lord did in the great eras of His life, so should the disciple do when faced by important crises. "To your knees, O Israel!" should be the clarion call to the ministry of this generation.

The highest form of religious life is attained by prayer. The richest revelations of God—Father, Son, and Spirit—are made, not to the learned, the great, or the noble of earth, but to people of prayer. *"For you see your calling, brethren, how that not many wise men after the flesh, not many mighty, not many noble, are called"* (1 Corinthians 1:26). God makes known His deep things and reveals the higher things of His character to the lowly, inquiring, praying ones. And, again, it must be said that this is as true of preachers as of laymen. It is the spiritual person who prays, and to praying ones God makes His revelations through the Holy Spirit.

Praying preachers have always brought the greater glory to God and have moved His gospel onward with its greatest, speediest rate and power. A nonpraying preacher and a nonpraying church might flourish outwardly and advance in many aspects. Both preacher and church might even become synonyms for success. But unless success rests on a foundation of prayer, it will eventually crumble into death and decay.

"You have not, because you ask not" (James 4:2) is the solution of all spiritual weakness both in the personal life and in the pulpit. Either that or it is, *"You ask, and receive not, because you ask amiss"* (v. 3). Real praying lies at the foundation of all the real success that the ministry has in the things of God. The stability, readiness, and energy with which God's kingdom is established in this world are dependent on prayer. God has made it so, and therefore God is eager for people to pray. He is especially concerned that His chosen ministers should be people of prayer, and so He gives this wonderful statement in order to encourage His ministers to pray:

And I say to you, Ask, and it shall be given you; seek, and you shall find; knock, and it shall be opened to you. For every one that asks receives; and he that seeks finds; and to him that knocks it shall be opened. (Luke 11:9–10)

Thus, both command and direct promise give accent to His concern that they should pray. Pause and think on these familiar words: *"Ask, and it shall be given you."* That verse itself would seem to be enough to set us all, laymen and preachers, to praying. These words are so direct, simple, and unlimited. They open all the treasures of heaven to us, simply by asking for them.

We should study the prayers of Paul, who was primarily a preacher to the Gentiles; otherwise, we can have only a feeble view of the great necessity for prayer and of how much it is worth in the life and work of a minister. Furthermore, we will have only a very limited view of the possibilities of the gospel to enrich, strengthen, and perfect Christian character, as well as equip preachers for their high and holy task. Oh, when will we learn the simple yet all-important lesson that the one great thing needed in the life of a preacher to help him in his personal life, to keep his soul alive to God, and to give efficacy to the Word he preaches, is real, constant prayer!

Paul, with prayer uppermost in his mind, assured the Colossians that *"Epaphras...[is] always laboring fervently for you in prayers, that you may stand perfect and complete in all the will of God"* (Colossians 4:12). He prayed that they may come to this high state of grace, *"complete in all the will of God."* So, prayer was the force that was to bring them to that elevated, vigorous, and stable state of heart.

This is in line with Paul's teaching to the Ephesians: *"And He gave some...pastors and teachers; for the perfecting of the saints, for the work of the ministry, for the edifying of the body of Christ"* (Ephesians 4:11–12). These verses evidently affirm that the whole work of the ministry is not merely to induce sinners to repent, but it is also the *"perfecting of the saints."* So, Epaphras labored fervently in prayers for this thing. Certainly, he was himself a praying man, for he earnestly prayed for these early Christians.

The apostles put forth their efforts in order that Christians should honor God by the purity and consistency of their outward lives. Christians were to reproduce the character of Jesus Christ. They were to perfect His image in themselves, incorporate His character, and reflect His behavior in all their attitudes and conduct. They were to be *"imitators of God, as beloved children"* (Ephesians 5:1 rv), to be holy as He was holy. (See 1 Peter 1:16.)

Thus, even laymen were to preach by their conduct and character, just as the ministry preached with their mouths.

To elevate the followers of Christ to these exalted heights of Christian experience, the apostles were in every way true in the ministry of God's Word—in the ministry of prayer, in holy zeal, in burning exhortation, in rebuke and reproof. Added to all these, sanctifying all these, invigorating all these, and making all these beneficial, they centered on and exercised constantly the force of mightiest praying. *"Night and day praying exceedingly"* (1 Thessalonians 3:10) means praying superabundantly, beyond measure, and with intense earnestness.

...night and day praying exceedingly that we might see your face, and might perfect that which is lacking in your faith? Now God Himself and our Father, and our Lord Jesus Christ, direct our way to you. And the Lord make you to increase and abound in love one toward another, and toward all men, even as we do toward you: to the end He may establish your hearts unblamable in holiness before God, even our Father, at the coming of our Lord Jesus Christ with all His saints.
(verses 10–13)

It was after this fashion that these apostles, the first preachers in the early church, labored in prayer. And only those who labor after the same fashion are the true successors of these apostles. This is the true, scriptural "apostolic succession": the succession of simple faith, earnest desire for holiness of heart and life, and zealous praying. These are the things today that make the ministry strong, faithful, and effective and make *"a workman that needs not to be ashamed, rightly dividing the word of truth"* (2 Timothy 2:15).

Jesus Christ, God's leader and commander of His people, lived and suffered under this law of prayer. All His personal conquests in His life on earth were won by obedience to this law. And the conquests won by His representatives since He ascended to heaven, were gained only when this condition of prayer was heartily and fully met. Christ was under this one prayer condition. His apostles were under the same prayer condition. His saints are under it, and even His angels are under it. By every token, therefore, preachers are under the same prayer law. Not for one moment are they relieved or excused from obedience to the law of prayer. It is their very life, the source of their power, the secret of their religious experience and communion with God.

Christ could do nothing without prayer. Christ could do all things by prayer. The apostles were helpless without prayer. They were absolutely dependent on it for success in defeating their spiritual foes. Like Christ, they could do all things by prayer.

EIGHT:

PRAYERLESSNESS IN THE PULPIT

Henry Martyn laments that "want of private devotional reading and shortness of prayer through incessant sermonmaking had produced much strangeness between God and his soul." He judges that he had dedicated too much time to public ministrations and too little to private communion with God. He was much impressed with the need of setting apart times for fasting and devoting times to solemn prayer. Resulting from this he records, "Was assisted this morning to pray for two hours."   *—E. M. Bounds*

All God's saints came to their sainthood by the way of prayer. The saints could do nothing without prayer. We can go further and say that the angels in heaven can do nothing without prayer, but can do all things by praying. These messengers of the Highest are largely dependent on the prayers of the saints for the sphere and power of their usefulness. Prayer opens avenues for angelic usefulness and creates missions for them on the earth. And, as it is with all the apostles, saints, and angels in heaven, so it is with preachers. The preachers, also called the angels of the churches, can do nothing without prayer, which opens doors of usefulness and gives power and point to their words.

How can a preacher preach effectively, make impressions on hearts and minds, and have fruits in his ministry, if he does not get his message first-hand from God? How can he deliver a fitting message without having his faith quickened, his vision cleared, and his heart warmed by his communion with God?

It would be well for all of us, in connection with this thought, to read again Isaiah's vision. As he waited and confessed and prayed before the throne, the angel touched his lips with a live coal from God's altar.

> *Then flew one of the seraphims to me, having a live coal in his hand, which he had taken with the tongs from off the altar: and he laid it upon my mouth, and said, Lo, this has touched your lips; and your iniquity is taken away, and your sin purged.* (Isaiah 6:6–7)

Oh, the need there is for present-day preachers to have their lips touched with a live coal from the altar of God! This fire is brought to the mouths of those prophets who are of a prayerful spirit and who wait in the secret place for the appointed angel to bring the living flame. Preachers of Isaiah's character received visits from an angel who brought live coals to touch their lips. Prayer always brings the living flame in order to unloose tongues, to open *"door[s] of utterance"* (Colossians 4:3), and to open great and effective doors of doing good. This, above all else, is the great need of the prophets of God.

As far as the abiding interests of religion are concerned, a pulpit without a prayer closet will always be a barren thing. Blessed is the preacher whose pulpit and prayer closet are close to each other, and who goes from the one into the other.

To consecrate no place to prayer is to make a beggarly showing, not only in praying, but in holy living; for secret prayer and holy living are so closely joined that they can never be separated. A preacher or a Christian may live a decent, religious life without secret prayer, but decency and holiness are two widely different things. And holiness is attained only by secret prayer.

A preacher may preach in an official, entertaining, and learned way without prayer, but there is a great distance between this kind of preaching and the sowing of God's precious seed.

A preacher may preach in an official, entertaining, and learned way without prayer, but there is a great distance between this kind of preaching and the sowing of God's precious seed.

We cannot declare too often or too strongly that prayer, involving all of its elements, is the one prime condition of the success of Christ's kingdom and that all else is secondary and incidental. Only prayerful preachers, prayerful men, and prayerful women can advance this gospel with aggressive power. Only they can put conquering forces into it. Preachers may be sent out by the thousand, and their equipment may be ever so complete; but unless they are skilled in the trade of prayer, trained to its martial and exhaustive exercise, their going will be lacking in power and effectiveness. Moreover, unless the men and women who are behind these preachers, who furnish their equipment, are men and women whose prayers are serious labor, their efforts will be vain and fruitless.

Prayer should be the inseparable accompaniment of all missionary effort, and prayer must be the one piece of equipment of the missionaries as they go out to their fields of labor and begin their delicate and responsible tasks. Prayer and missions go hand in hand. A prayerless missionary is a failure before he goes out, while he is out, and when he returns to his native land. A prayerless board of missions, too, needs to learn the necessity of prayer.

Added to all the missionary speeches, the money raised for missions, and the dozens being sent out to needy fields, is prayer. Missions has its root in prayer, and missions must have prayer in all of its plans. Prayer must precede, go with, and follow all of its missionaries and laborers.

Prayer enthrones God as sovereign and elevates Jesus Christ to sit with Him. If Christian preachers had used the power of prayer to its fullest, long before this *"the kingdoms of this world* [would have] *become the kingdoms of our Lord, and of His Christ"* (Revelation 11:15).

Huge difficulties face the church in its great work on earth, and almost superhuman and complex obstacles stand in the way of evangelizing the world. In the face of all this, God encourages us by His strongest promises: *"Call to Me, and I will answer you, and show you great and mighty things, which you know not"* (Jeremiah 33:3). God commits Himself to answer the specific prayer, but He does not stop there. The revelations of God to him who is of a prayerful spirit go far beyond the limits of the actual praying.

He says, *"Ask Me of things to come concerning My sons, and concerning the work of My hands command you Me"* (Isaiah 45:11). Think over that remarkable pledge of God to those who pray: *"Command you Me."* He actually places Himself at the command of praying preachers and a praying church. This is a sufficient answer to all doubts, fears, and unbelief. This is a wonderful inspiration to do God's work in God's way—by prayer.

Furthermore, as if to fortify even more the faith of His ministry and of His church, to protect against any temptation to doubt or be discouraged, He declares by the mouth of the great apostle to the Gentiles, *"[He] is able to do exceeding abundantly above all that we ask or think"* (Ephesians 3:20).

It is unquestionably taught that, in going forward with their God-appointed tasks, preachers can command God in their prayers. To pray is to command His ability, His presence, and His power. *"Certainly I will be with you"* (Exodus 3:12) is the reply to every sincere, inquiring minister of God. All of God's called workers in the ministry are privileged to stretch their prayers into regions where neither words nor thoughts can go. They are permitted to expect from Him beyond their praying. For their praying, they can expect God Himself and then, in addition, *"great and mighty things, which you know not"* (Jeremiah 33:3).

Real, live, heart praying by the power of the Spirit—praying that is direct, specific, ardent, and simple—is the kind of praying that legitimately belongs to the pulpit. This is the kind demanded just now of the preachers who stand in the pulpit. There is no school in which to learn to pray in public except the prayer closet. Preachers who have learned to pray in the prayer closet have mastered the secret of pulpit praying. It is but a short step from secret praying to effective, live, pulpit praying. Good pulpit praying follows good secret praying. An empty prayer closet makes for cold, spiritless, formal praying in the pulpit.

Oh, preacher, study how to pray, not by studying the forms of prayer, but by attending the school of prayer on your knees before God. Here is where we learn not only how to pray before God, but also how to pray in the presence of people. He who has learned the way to the prayer closet has discovered the way to pray in the pulpit.

How easily we become businesslike and mechanical in the most sacred undertakings! Henry Martyn learned the lesson so hard to learn, that the cultivation and perfection of personal righteousness is the prime factor in the preacher's success. Likewise, he that learns another lesson so hard to learn—that live, spiritual, effective pulpit praying is the outgrowth of regular secret praying—has learned his lesson well. Moreover, his work as a preacher will depend on his praying.

The great need of the hour is for good prayers in the pulpit as well as good preachers. Just as live, spiritual preaching is the kind that impresses and moves men, so live, spiritual praying in the pulpit moves and impresses God. The preacher is called not only to preach well, but also to pray well. Not that he is called to pray after the fashion of the Pharisees, who love to stand in public and pray so that they may be seen and heard of men. (See Matthew 6:5). The right sort of pulpit praying is far removed from pharisaical praying, as far as light is from darkness, as far as heat is from cold, as far as life is from death.

Preaching is the very loftiest work possible for a person to do. And praying goes hand in hand with preaching. It is a mighty, lofty work. Preaching is a lifegiving work, sowing the seeds of eternal life. Oh, may we do it well, do it after God's order, and do it successfully! May we do it divinely well, so that when the end comes, the solemn close of earthly probation, we may hear from the Great Judge of all the earth, *"Well done, good and faithful servant…enter you into the joy of your lord"* (Matthew 25:23).

When we consider this great question of preaching, we are led to exclaim, "With what reverence, simplicity, and sincerity it ought to be done!" What truth in the inward parts is demanded in order that it be done acceptably to God and with profit to men! How real, true, and loyal those who practice it must be! How great the need to pray as Christ prayed, with strong cryings, tears, and godly fear!

Oh, may preachers do the real thing of preaching, with no sham, with no mere form of words, with no dull, cold, professional discourses. May they give themselves to prayerful preaching and prayerful praying! Preaching that gives life is born of praying that gives life. Preaching and praying always go together, like Siamese twins, and can never be separated without death to one or the other, or death to both.

This is not the time for kid-glove methods or sugarcoated preaching. This is no time for playing the gentleman as a preacher, nor for putting on the garb of the scholar in the pulpit. We want to disciple all nations, destroy idolatry, crush the defiant forces of Islam, and destroy the tremendous forces of evil now opposing the kingdom of God. Brave people, true people, praying people—afraid of nothing but God—are the kind needed just now. There will be no smiting the forces of evil that now hold the world in bondage, no lifting of the degraded hordes of paganism to light and eternal life, by any but praying people. All others are merely playing at religion, make-believe soldiers with no armor or ammunition, who are absolutely helpless in the face of a wicked and opposing world. None but soldiers and bond servants of Jesus Christ can possibly do this tremendous work.

"Endure hardness, as a good soldier of Jesus Christ" (2 Timothy 2:3), cries the great apostle. This is no time to think of self, to consult with dignity, to confer with flesh and blood (see Galatians 1:16), to think of ease, or to shrink from hardship, grief, and loss. This is the time for toil, suffering, and self-denial. We must lose all for Christ in order to gain all for Christ. (See Philippians 3:8). People are needed in the pulpit, as well as in the pew, who are bold enough to take up and firm enough to sustain the consecrated cross. Here is the sort of preachers God wants, and this sort is born of much praying. For no prayerless preacher is sufficient for these things. Only praying preachers can meet the demand and be equal to the emergency.

The gospel of Jesus has neither relish nor life in it when spoken by prayerless lips or handled by prayerless hands. Without prayer, the doctrines of Christ degenerate into dead orthodoxy. Preaching them without the aid of the Spirit of God, who comes into the preacher's messages only by prayer, is nothing more than mere lecturing with no life, no grip, and no force. It amounts to nothing more than pure rationalism or sickly sentimentalism. *"But we will give ourselves continually to prayer, and to the ministry of the word"* (Acts 6:4) was the settled and declared purpose of the apostolic ministry. The kingdom of God waits on prayer, and prayer puts wings on and power into the gospel. By prayer, it moves forward with conquering force and rapid advance.

If prayer is left out, the preacher rises to no higher level than the lecturer, the politician, or the secular teacher. That which distinguishes him from all other public speakers is the fact of prayer. Because prayer deals with God, the preacher has God with him, while other speakers do not need God with them to make their public messages effective. The preacher above everything else is a spiritual person, a person of the Spirit, and he deals with spiritual things. And this implies that he has to do with God in his pulpit work in a high and holy sense. This can be said of no other public speaker. So, prayer must of necessity go with the preacher and his preaching. Pure intellectuality is the only qualification for other public speakers. Spirituality, which is born of prayer, belongs to the preacher.

In the Sermon on the Mount, Jesus Christ often speaks of prayer. It stands out prominently in His words on that occasion. The lesson of prayer that He taught was one of hallowing God's name, of advancing God's kingdom. We are to long for the coming of the kingdom of God. It is to be longed for, and it must be first in our communication with God. God's will must have its royal way in the hearts and wills of those who pray. The point of urgency is made by our Lord that people are to pray in earnest—by asking, seeking, knocking—in order to hallow God's name, bring His will to pass, and forward His kingdom.

And let it be kept in mind that while this prayer lesson has to do with all people, it has a special application to the ministry; for it was the twelve would-be preachers who made the request, *"Lord, teach us to pray, as John also taught his disciples"* (Luke 11:1). So, primarily, Jesus's reply was spoken first to twelve men just starting their work as ministers. Jesus was talking, as Luke records it, to preachers. He also speaks to the preachers of this day. How He pressed these twelve men into the ministry of prayer! Present-day ministers need the same lesson to be taught to them, and they need the same urgency pressing them to make prayer their habit of life.

Regardless of all a preacher may claim for himself, or how many good things may be put down to his credit, a prayerless preacher will never master God's truth, which he is called upon to declare with all fidelity and plainness of speech. Blind and blinding will he be if he lives a prayerless life. A prayerless ministry cannot know God's truth and, not knowing it, cannot teach it to ignorant people. He who teaches us the path of prayer must first of all walk in the same path. A preacher cannot teach what he does not know. The preacher who is a stranger to prayer will be a blind leader of the blind. Prayer opens the preacher's eyes, and prayer keeps them open to the evil of sin, the peril of sin, and the penalty of sin. A blind leader leading the blind will be the vocation of the one who is prayerless in his own life.

The best and the greatest offering that the church and the ministry can make to God is an offering of prayer. If the preachers of the twentieth century will learn well the lesson of prayer and use it fully in all its exhaustless effectiveness, the Millennium will come to its noon before the century closes.

The Bible preacher prays. He is filled with the Holy Spirit, filled with God's Word, and filled with faith. He has faith in God; he has faith in God's only begotten Son, his personal Savior; and he has implicit faith in God's Word. He cannot do otherwise than pray. He cannot be other than a person of prayer. The breath of his life and the throb of his heart are prayer. The Bible preacher lives by prayer, loves by prayer, and preaches by prayer. His bended knees in the place of secret prayer advertise what kind of a preacher he is.

Preachers may lose faith in God, lose faith in Jesus Christ as their personal and present Savior, become devoid of the peace of God, and let the joy of salvation go out of their hearts, yet be unconscious of it. How needful for the preacher to be continually examining himself and to be checking his religious state and his personal relationship with God!

The preachers, like the philosophers of old, may defer to a system and then earnestly contend for it even after they have lost all faith in its great facts. Preachers may preach in the pulpit with hearts of unbelief; they may minister at the altars of the church while being alien to the most sacred and vital principles of the gospel.

It is a comparatively easy task for preachers to become so absorbed in the material and external affairs of the church that they lose sight of their own souls, forget the necessity of life-giving prayer, and lose the inward sweetness of the Christian experience.

Prayer makes much of preaching, and we must make much of prayer. The character of our praying will determine the character of our preaching. Serious praying will give serious weight to preaching. Prayer makes preaching strong, gives it unction, and makes it stick. In every beneficial ministry, prayer has been a serious business.

It cannot be said with too much emphasis: the preacher must be pre-eminently a person of prayer. He must learn to pray. He must have such an estimate of prayer and its great worth that he feels he cannot afford to omit it from his list of private duties. His heart must be attuned to prayer, while he himself touches the highest note of prayer. Only in the school of prayer can the heart learn to preach. No gifts, no learning, no brainpower can atone for the failure to pray. No earnestness, no diligence, no study, no amount of social service will supply its lack. Talking to people for God may be a great thing, and it may be very commendable. But talking to God for people is far more valuable and commendable.

The power of Bible preaching does not lie solely in superlative devotion to God's Word and jealous passion for God's truth. Both of these are essential, valuable, and helpful. But, above these things, a preacher must have a sense of the divine presence. He must be conscious of the divine power of God's Spirit on him and in him. For the great work of preaching, he must have an anointing, an empowering, a sealing of the Holy Spirit, making him speak God's words and giving him the energy of God's right hand. Such a preacher can say,

> Your words were found, and I did eat them; and Your word was to me the joy and rejoicing of my heart: for I am called by Your name, O LORD God of hosts. (Jeremiah 15:16)

NINE:

EQUIPPED BY PRAYER

Go back! Back to that upper room; back to your knees; back to searching of heart and habit, thought and life; back to pleading, praying, waiting, till the Spirit of the Lord floods the soul with light, and you are *"endued with power from on high"* (Luke 24:49). Then go forth in the power of Pentecost, and the Christlife shall be lived, and the works of Christ shall be done. You shall open blind eyes, cleanse foul hearts, break men's fetters, and save men's souls. In the power of the indwelling Spirit, miracles become the commonplace of daily living. —*Samuel Chadwick*

Almost the last words uttered by our Lord before His ascension were those addressed to the eleven disciples. They were words which really were spoken to, and directly had to do with, preachers. These words indicated very clearly the power these people needed in order to preach the gospel, beginning at Jerusalem. These vital words of Jesus are recorded in Luke 24:49: *"And, behold, I send the promise of My Father upon you: but tarry you in the city of Jerusalem, until you be endued with power from on high."*

Two things are very clearly set forth in these urgent directions. The first thing is the power of the Holy Spirit, for which they must wait. This was to be received after their conversion. This power was an indispensable requisite, equipping them for the great task set before them.

The second thing is the truth that the *"promise of My Father,"* this *"power from on high,"* would come to them after they had waited in earnest, continuous prayer. A reference to Acts 1:14 will reveal that these same men, with the women, *"continued with one accord in prayer and supplication,"* and so continued until the Day of Pentecost when the power from on high descended upon them.

This power from on high is as important to those early preachers as it is to present-day preachers. This power was not the force of a mighty intellect, holding in its grasp great truths, flooding them with light, and forming them into verbal shapeliness and beauty. Nor was it the acquisition of great learning. Nor was it the result of a speech, faultless and complete by the rules of rhetoric. It was none of these things. This spiritual power was not held then, nor is it held now, in the keeping of any earthly sources of power. Human forces are essentially different in source and character; they are not a result of this power from on high. On the contrary, the transmission of such power is directly from God.

Power from on high is a bestowal, in rich measure, of the force and energy that pertains only to God. The Master transmits this power to His messenger only in answer to the longing, wrestling attitude of his soul. The messenger is conscious of his own impotency and seeks the omnipotence of the Lord he serves. He seeks God's power in order that he may more fully understand the given Word and preach it to his fellowmen.

The power from on high may be found in combination with all sources of human power, but it is not to be confused with them, is not dependent on them, and must never be superseded by them. Whatever human gift, talent, or force a preacher may possess, it is not to be made paramount, or even conspicuous. It must be hidden, lost, and overshadowed by this power from on high. The forces of intellect and culture may all be present, but without this inward, heaven-given power, all spiritual effort is vain and unsuccessful.

196 E. M. Bounds on Prayer & Spiritual Warfare

Even when lacking the other equipment but having this power from on high, a preacher cannot help but succeed. It is the one essential, all-important, vital force that a messenger of God must possess to give wings to his message, to put life into his preaching, and to enable him to speak the Word with power and acceptance.

I need to clarify something here. Distinctions need to be kept in mind. We must think clearly about the meaning of our terms. Power from on high means the *"unction from the Holy One"* (1 John 2:20) resting on and abiding in the preacher. This is not so much a power that bears witness to a person being the child of God as it is a preparation for delivering the Word to others. Also, unction must be distinguished from pathos. (Pathos causes an emotional response in the hearer; unction causes a spiritual response.) Pathos may exist in a sermon in which unction is entirely absent. So also unction may be present and pathos absent. Both may exist together, but they are not to be confused, nor should they be made to appear to be the same thing. Pathos promotes emotion, tender feeling, sometimes tears. Quite often it results when a sad story is told or when the tender side is appealed to. But pathos is neither the direct nor the indirect result of the Holy Spirit resting upon the preacher as he preaches.

However, unction is. Here we are given the evidence of the workings of an undefinable agency in the preacher; these workings result directly from the presence of this power from on high. Unction is deep, conscious, lifegiving, and carrying. It gives power and point to the preached Word. It is the element in a sermon that arouses, stirs, convicts, and moves the souls of sinners and saints. This is what the preacher requires, the great equipment for which he should wait and pray. This *"unction from the Holy One"* delivers from dryness, saves from superficiality, and gives authority to preaching. It is the one quality that distinguishes the preacher of the gospel from other people who speak in public; it is that which makes a sermon unique, unlike any other public address.

Prayer is the language of a person burdened with a sense of need. It is the voice of the beggar, conscious of his poverty, asking of another the things he needs. It is not only the language of lack, but of *felt* lack, of lack consciously realized. *"Blessed are the poor in spirit"* (Matthew 5:3) means not only that poverty of spirit brings the blessing, but also that poverty of spirit is realized, known, and acknowledged. Prayer is the language of those who need something—something which they, themselves, cannot supply but which God has promised them—and so they ask.

In the end, poor praying and prayerlessness amount to the same thing; for poor praying proceeds from a lack of the sense of need, while prayerlessness has its origin in the same soil. Not to pray is to declare there is nothing needed and to admit there is no realization of a need. This is what magnifies the sin of prayerlessness. It represents an attempt at instituting an independence of God, a self-sufficient ruling of God out of the life. It is a declaration made to God that we do not need Him and hence do not pray to Him.

This is the state in which the Holy Spirit, in His messages to the seven churches in Asia, found the Laodicean church. The "Laodicean state" has come to stand for one in which God is ruled out, expelled from the life, put out of the pulpit. The entire condemnation of this church is summed up in one expression: *"Because you say, I...have need of nothing"* (Revelation 3:17). This is the most alarming state into which a person, a church, or a preacher can come. Trusting in its riches, in its social position, in its outward and material things, the church at Laodicea omitted God, leaving Him out of their church plans and church work. They declared, by their acts and by their omission of prayer, *"I...have need of nothing."*

All of it was traceable to a prayerless state of heart, for no one can read this word of the Spirit to the Laodicean church and not see that the very core of their sin was prayerlessness. How could a church given to prayer openly and arrogantly declare, *"I...have need of nothing,"* in the face of the Spirit's assertion that it needed everything: *"You...know not that you are wretched, and miserable, and poor, and blind, and naked"* (Revelation 3:17)?

In addition to their sins of self-sufficiency and independence of God, the Laodiceans were spiritually blind. Oh, what dullness of sight, what blindness of soul! These people were prayerless, and they did not know the import of such prayerlessness. They lacked everything that makes up spiritual life and force and self-denying piety, and they vainly supposed themselves to need nothing but material wealth. Thus, they tried to make temporal possessions a substitute for spiritual wealth. They left God entirely out of their activities. They relied on human and material resources to do the work that is possible only to divine and supernatural intervention through prayer.

Nor let it be forgotten that this letter (in common with the other six letters) was primarily addressed to the preacher in charge of the church. All this strengthens the impression that the *"angel of the church"* (Revelation 3:14) himself was in this lukewarm state. He himself was living a prayerless life, relying on things other than God, practically saying, *"I...have need of nothing"* (v. 17). For these words are the natural expression of the spirit of him who does not pray, who does not care for God, and who does not feel the need of Him in his life and work and preaching. Furthermore, the words of the Spirit seem to indicate that the *"angel of the church"* at Laodicea was indirectly responsible for this sad condition into which the Laodicean church had fallen.

May not this sort of a church be found in modern times? Could we not discover some preachers who fall under a condemnation similar to that of the *"angel of the church"* at Laodicea?

Preachers of the present age excel those of the past in many, possibly in all, human elements of success. They are well abreast of the age in learning, research, and intellectual vigor. But these things neither ensure power from on high nor guarantee a righteous life or a thriving religious experience. These purely human gifts do not bring with them an insight into the deep things of God, a strong faith in the Scriptures, or an intense loyalty to God's divine revelation.

The presence of these earthly talents, even in the most commanding and impressive form and richest measure, do not in the least abate the necessity for the added endowment of the Holy Spirit. Herein lies the great danger menacing the pulpit of today. All around us we see a tendency to substitute human gifts and worldly attainments for that supernatural, inward power that comes from heaven in answer to earnest prayer.

In many instances modern preaching seems to fail in the very thing that should distinguish true preaching, that is essential to its being, and that alone can make it a powerfully aggressive agency. It lacks, in short, power from on high, which alone can make it a living thing. It fails to become the channel through which God's saving power can appeal to people's consciences and hearts.

Quite often, modern preaching fails to reach people because it does not have a potent influence that disturbs people in their sleep of security and awakens them to a sense of need and of peril. There is a growing need of an appeal that will quicken and arouse the conscience from its ignoble stupor, an appeal that will give the conscience a sense of wrongdoing and a corresponding sense of repentance. There is need of a message that searches into the secret places of a man's being, dividing, as it were, the joints and the marrow and laying bare the mysterious depths before himself and his God. (See Hebrews 4:12.)

Much of our present-day preaching lacks power to infuse new blood into the heart and veins of faith, to arm with courage and skill for the battle against the powers of darkness, and to get a victory over the forces of the world. Such high and noble ends can never be accomplished by human qualifications. Nor can these great results be secured by a pulpit clothed only with the human elements of power, however gracious, comfortable, and helpful they may be.

The Holy Spirit is needed. He alone can equip the ministry for its difficult and responsible work in and out of the pulpit. Oh, that the present-day ministry may come to see that its one great need is an outpouring of power from on high. May they see that this one need can be secured only by the use of God's appointed means of grace—the ministry of prayer.

Prayer is needed by the preacher in order that his personal relationship with God may be maintained, for there is no difference between him and any other person as far as his personal salvation is concerned. This he must work out *with fear and trembling* (Philippians 2:12) just as all other people must do. Thus, prayer is of vast importance to the preacher in order that he may possess a growing religious experience. Prayer enables him to live such a life that his character and conduct will back up his preaching and give force to his message.

A person must have prayer in preparing to preach, for no minister can preach effectively without prayer. He also has use for prayer in praying for others. Paul was a notable example of a preacher who constantly prayed for those to whom he ministered.

But we come, now, to another sphere of prayer: people praying for the preacher. *"Brethren, pray for us"* (1 Thessalonians 5:25). This is the cry that Paul set in motion, and this has been the cry of spiritually-minded preachers—those who know God and who know the value of prayer—in all succeeding ages. No amount of success or failure must abate the cry. No amount of refinement and no abundance of talents must cause that cry to cease. The learned preacher, as well as the unlearned, has equal need to call out to the people he serves, *"Meanwhile praying also for us"* (Colossians 4:3).

Such a cry voices the felt need of a preacher's heart, a preacher who feels the need for his people to be in harmony with him. Such a cry is the expression of the inner soul of a preacher who feels his insufficiency for the tremendous responsibilities of the pulpit. He realizes his weakness and his need of the divine unction, and therefore he throws himself upon the prayers of his congregation and calls out to them, *"Praying always with all prayer and supplication in the Spirit...and for me, that utterance may be given to me"* (Ephesians 6:18–19). It is the cry of the preacher who deeply feels in his heart that he must have this prayer made specifically for him so that he may do his work in God's own way.

When this request to a people to pray for the preacher is cold, formal, and official, it freezes instead of bearing fruit. To be ignorant of the necessity for the cry, is to be ignorant of the sources of spiritual success. To fail to stress the cry, and to fail to have responses to it, is to sap the sources of spiritual life. Preachers must sound out the cry to the church of God. Saints everywhere and of every kind and of every faith speedily respond and pray for the preacher. The imperative need of the work demands it. *"Pray for us"* (1 Thessalonians 5:25) is the natural cry of the hearts of God's called ministers, the faithful preachers of the Word.

Saintly praying in the early church helped apostolic preaching mightily, and it rescued apostolic believers from many severe troubles. It can do the same thing today. It can open doors for apostolic labors; it can open doors for apostolic lips to utter bravely and truly the gospel message. Apostolic movements wait their ordering from prayer, and avenues long closed are opened to apostolic entrance by and through the power of prayer. The messenger receives his message and is schooled as to how to carry and deliver the message by prayer. The forerunner of the gospel, and that which prepares the way, is prayer, not only by the praying of the messenger himself, but by the praying of the church of God.

Writing along this line in his second epistle to the Thessalonians, Paul was general at first in his request and said, *"Brethren, pray for us."* Then he became more minute and particular:

> *Finally, brethren, pray for us, that the word of the Lord may have free course, and be glorified, even as it is with you: and that we may be delivered from unreasonable and wicked men: for all men have not faith.* (2 Thessalonians 3:1–2)

In the Revised Version, *"have free course"* is replaced by the word *"run."* *"The word"* means doctrine, and the idea conveyed is that this doctrine of the gospel is running a race. In other words, it is being rapidly propagated. This verse is an exhortation to exert one's self, to strive hard, to expend strength. Thus, the prayer for the spread of the gospel gives the same energy to the Word of the Lord as the greatest output of strength gives success to the racer. Prayer in the pew gives the preached Word energy, attainment, and success. Preaching without the backing of mighty praying is as limp and worthless as can be imagined. Prayerlessness in the pew is a serious hindrance to the running of the Word of the Lord.

The preaching of God's Word fails to run and be glorified from many causes. The difficulty may lie with the preacher himself, if his outward conduct is out of harmony with the rule of the Scriptures and his own profession. He must live the Word and not just preach the Word; his life must be in harmony with his sermon. The preacher's spirit and behavior out of the pulpit must run parallel with the Word of the Lord spoken in the pulpit. Otherwise, a man is an obstacle to the success of his own message.

Again, the Word of the Lord may fail to run, may be seriously encumbered and crippled, by the inconsistent lives of those who are the hearers of it. Bad living in the pew will seriously cripple the Word of the Lord as it attempts to run on its appointed course. Unrighteous lives among the laity heavily weigh down the Word of the Lord and hamper the work of the ministry.

Yet, prayer will remove this unrighteous living that seriously handicaps the preached Word. It will tend to do this in a direct way or in an indirect way. For just as you set laymen to praying, for the preacher or even for themselves, it awakens conscience, stirs the heart, and tends to correct evil ways and promote good living. No one will pray for long and continue in sin. Prayer breaks up bad living, and bad living breaks down prayer. Praying goes into bankruptcy when a person goes into sin. Obeying the cry of the preacher, "*Brethren, pray for us,*" gets people to do that which will induce right living in them; it tends to break them away from sin.

For these reasons it is worth a great deal to get the laity to pray for the ministry. Prayer helps the preacher, is an aid to the sermon, assists the hearer, and promotes right living in the pew. Prayer also moves the one who prays for the preacher and for the Word of the Lord. It moves him to use all his influence to remove any hindrance to the Word which he may see and which lies in his power to remove.

But prayer reaches the preacher directly. God hears the praying of a church for its minister. Prayer for the preached Word is a direct aid to it. Prayer for the preacher gives wings, as well as feet, to the gospel. Prayer makes the Word of the Lord go forward strongly and rapidly. It takes the shackles off of the message and gives it a chance to run straight to the hearts of sinners and saints alike. It opens the way, clears the track, and furnishes a free course.

The failure of many a preacher may be found just here. He is hampered, hindered, and even crippled by a prayerless church. Non praying church workers stand in the way of the Word preached; they become veritable stumbling blocks in the way of the Word, definitely preventing its reaching the hearts of the unsaved.

Unbelief and prayerlessness go together. It is written of our Lord in Matthew's Gospel that when He entered into His own country, "*He did not many mighty works there because of their unbelief*" (Matthew 13:58). Mark puts it a little differently but gives the same idea:

> *And He could there do no mighty work, save that He laid His hands upon a few sick folk, and healed them. And he marveled because of their unbelief.* (Mark 6:5–6)

Unquestionably, the unbelief of that people hindered our Lord in His gracious work and tied His hands. And, if that is true, we would not be stretching the Scriptures to say that the unbelief and prayerlessness of a church can tie the hands of its preacher and prevent him from doing many great works in the salvation of souls and in edifying saints.

Prayerlessness, therefore, as it concerns the preacher, is a very serious matter. If it exists in the preacher himself, then he ties his own hands and makes his own preaching of the Word ineffective and void. If prayerless people are found in the pew, then they hurt the preacher, rob him of an invaluable help, and interfere seriously with the success of his work.

How great the need of a praying church to help move forward the preaching of the Word of the Lord! Both pew and pulpit are jointly concerned in this preaching business. It is a co-partnership. The two go hand in hand. One must help the other; one can hinder the other. Both must work in perfect accord. Otherwise, serious damage will result, and God's plan concerning the preacher and the preached Word will be defeated.

> *How great the need of a praying church to help move forward the preaching of the Word of the Lord! Both pew and pulpit are jointly concerned in this preaching business. It is a co-partnership. The two go hand in hand. One must help the other; one can hinder the other. Both must work in perfect accord. Otherwise, serious damage will result, and God's plan concerning the preacher and the preached Word will be defeated.*

TEN:

THE PREACHER'S CRY: "PRAY FOR US!"

That the true apostolic preacher must have the prayers of others—good people—to give to his ministry its full quota of success, Paul is a preeminent example. He asked, he coveted, he pleaded in an impassioned way for the help of all God's saints. He knew that in the spiritual realm as elsewhere, in union there is strength; that the consecration and aggregation of faith, desire, and prayer increased the volume of spiritual force until it became overwhelming and irresistible in its power. Units of prayer combined, like drops of water, make an ocean that defies resistance.   —*E. M. Bounds*

To what extent does praying for the preacher help preaching? It helps him personally and officially. It helps him to maintain a righteous life; it helps him in preparing his message; and it helps the Word he preaches to run to its appointed goal, unhindered and unhampered.

A praying church creates a spiritual atmosphere most favorable to preaching. What preacher who knows anything about the real work of preaching doubts the veracity of this statement? The spirit of prayer in a congregation produces an atmosphere supercharged with the Spirit of the Highest, removes obstacles, and gives the Word of the Lord the right-of-way. The very attitude of such a congregation constitutes an environment most encouraging and favorable to preaching. It renders preaching an easy task; it enables the Word to run quickly and without friction, propelled by the warmth of souls engaged in prayer.

People in the pew given to praying for the preacher, are like the poles that hold up the wires along which the electric current runs. They are not the power, nor are they the specific agents in making the Word of the Lord effective. But they hold up the wires along which the divine power runs to the hearts of men. They give liberty to the preacher and keep him from being hampered. They make conditions favorable for the preaching of the gospel.

Many preachers have had much experience and know the truth of these statements. Yet, how hard they have found it to preach in some places! This was because they had no *"door of utterance"* (Colossians 4:3) and were hampered in their delivery, there appearing no response whatsoever to their appeals. On the other hand, at other times thought flowed easily, words came freely, and there was no failure in speaking. The preacher "had liberty," as the old men say.

The preaching of the Word to a prayerless congregation falls at the very feet of the preacher. It has no traveling force; it stops because the atmosphere is cold, unsympathetic, and unfavorable to its running to the hearts of men and women. There is nothing to help it along. Just as some prayers never rise above the head of the one who prays, so the preaching of some preachers goes no farther than the front of the pulpit from which it is delivered. It takes prayer in the pulpit and prayer in the pew to make preaching arresting, lifegiving, and soul-saving.

The Word of God is inseparably linked with prayer. The two are joined together, twins from birth and twins through life. The apostles found themselves absorbed by the sacred and pressing duty of distributing the alms of the church, until time was not left for them to pray. They directed that other men be appointed to do this task so that they would be better able to give themselves continually to prayer and to the ministry of the Word.

Likewise, the church's prayer for the preacher is also inseparably joined to preaching. A praying church is an invaluable help to the faithful preacher. The Word of the Lord runs in such a church, and it is glorified by the saving of sinners, by the reclaiming of backsliders, and by the sanctifying of believers. Paul connected the Word of God closely to prayer in writing to Timothy:

> For every creature of God is good, and nothing to be refused, if it be received with thanksgiving: for it is sanctified by the word of God and prayer. (1 Timothy 4:4–5)

And so the Word of the Lord depends on prayer for its rapid spread and for its full, glorious success.

Paul indicated that prayer transforms the ills that come to the preacher: "*For I know that this shall turn to my salvation through your prayer, and the supply of the Spirit of Jesus Christ*" (Philippians 1:19). It was through their prayers that these benefits would come to him. So, it is through the prayers of a church that the pastor will be the beneficiary of large spiritual things.

In the epistle to the Hebrews, Paul asked the Hebrew Christians to pray for him. He based his request on the grave and eternal responsibilities of the office of a preacher:

> Obey them that have the rule over you, and submit yourselves: for they watch for your souls, as they that must give account, that they may do it with joy, and not with grief: for that is unprofitable for you. Pray for us: for we trust we have a good conscience, in all things willing to live honestly. (Hebrews 13:17–18)

How little the church understands the fearful responsibility attached to the office and work of the ministry! "*For they watch for your souls, as they that must give account.*" Preachers are God's watchmen, appointed to warn when danger is near. They are God's messengers, sent to rebuke, reprove, and exhort with all long-suffering. They are ordained as shepherds to protect the sheep against devouring wolves. How responsible is their position! And they are to give account to God for their work; they are to face a day of reckoning. How they need the prayers of those to whom they minister! And who should be more ready to do this praying than God's people, His own church, those who are presumably in harmony with the minister and his all-important work, divine in its origin?

Among the last messages of Jesus to His disciples are those found in the fourteenth, fifteenth, and sixteenth chapters of John's Gospel. In the fourteenth, as well as in the others, are some very specific teachings about prayer, designed for the disciples' help and encouragement in their future work. We must never forget that these last discourses of Jesus Christ were given to disciples alone, away from the busy crowds, and seem primarily intended for them in their public ministry. In reality, they were words spoken to preachers, for these eleven men were to be the first preachers of the new dispensation.

With this thought in mind, we are able to see the tremendous importance given to prayer by our Lord. We can see the high place He gave it in the lifework of preachers, not only preachers in His day, but also preachers in future generations.

First, our Lord proposes that He will pray for these disciples that the Father might send them another Comforter, *even the Spirit of truth, whom the world cannot receive* (John 14:17). He preceded this statement by a direct command to them to pray, to pray for anything, with the assurance that they would receive what they asked for. (See John 14:13–14.)

If, therefore, there was value in their own praying and in our Lord's interceding for them, then, of course, it would be worthwhile in the future for their people to pray for them. It is no wonder, then, that the apostle Paul took the key from our Lord; several times he broke out with the urgent exhortation, *Pray for us* (1 Thessalonians 5:25; 2 Thessalonians 3:1).

True praying done by the laymen helps in many ways, but in one particular way. It very much helps the preacher to be brave and true. Read Paul's request to the Ephesians:

> *Praying always with all prayer and supplication in the Spirit, and watching thereto with all perseverance and supplication for all saints; and for me, that utterance may be given to me, that I may open my mouth boldly, to make known the mystery of the gospel, for which I am*

an ambassador in bonds: that therein I may speak boldly, as I ought to speak. (Ephesians 6:18–20)

We do not know the extent to which the prayers of the church helped Paul be bold and true. But, it is unquestionable that through the prayers of the Christians at Ephesus, Colossae, and Thessalonica, he received much aid in preaching the Word. He would have been deprived of this aid had these churches not prayed for him. Likewise, in modern times the gift of ready and effective preaching has been bestowed upon a preacher through the prayers of the church.

The apostle Paul did not desire to fall short of that most important quality in a preacher of the gospel, namely, boldness. He was no coward or chameleon or man pleaser, but still he needed prayer. Prayer would give him courage to declare the whole truth of God. Prayer would keep him from fearing men and declaring the truth in an apologetic, hesitating way. He desired to remove himself as far as possible from an attitude of fear. His constant desire and effort was to declare the gospel with freedom and consecrated boldness. *"That I may open my mouth boldly, to make known the mystery of the gospel...that therein I may speak boldly, as I ought to speak"* (Ephesians 6:18–20). It would appear that, at times, he was really afraid that he might exhibit cowardice or be affected by the fear of man. But to speak boldly was his great desire.

This is a day that has urgent need for people from the mold of the great apostle—people of courage, brave and true. We need people who are not swayed by the fear of man. We need people who are not reduced to silence or apology by the dread of consequences. One way to secure these people is for the pew to engage in earnest prayer for the preachers.

> *This is a day that has urgent need for people from the mold of the great apostle—people of courage, brave and true. We need people who are not swayed by the fear of man. We need people who are not reduced to silence or apology by the dread of consequences. One way to secure these people is for the pew to engage in earnest prayer for the preachers.*

In Paul's word to the Ephesian elders, given when on his way to Jerusalem, Paul cleared himself from the charge of bloodguiltiness, in that he had not failed to declare the whole counsel of God to them. (See Acts 20:26–27.) To the Philippian believers, also, he said that through their prayers he would prove to be neither ashamed nor afraid. (See Philippians 1:19–20.)

Nothing, perhaps, can be more detrimental to the advancement of the kingdom of God than a timid or doubtful statement of revealed truth. The man who states only half of what he believes is the same as the man who states all but only half believes. No coward can preach the gospel and declare the whole counsel of God. To do that, a man must be ready to do battle, not from passion, but from deep conviction, strong conscience, and complete courage. Faith is in the custody of a gallant heart; timidity always surrenders to a brave spirit.

Paul prayed, and prevailed on others to pray, that he might be a man of resolute courage, brave enough to do everything but sin. The result of this mutual praying is that history has no finer example of courage in a minister of Jesus Christ than that displayed in the life of the apostle Paul. He stands in the premier position as a fearless, uncompromising, Godfearing preacher of the gospel.

God seems to have taken great pains with His prophets of old to save them from fear while they were delivering His messages to mankind. He sought in every way to safeguard His spokesmen from the fear of man. By means of command, reasoning, and encouragement, He sought to render them fearless and true to their high calling.

One of the besetting temptations of a preacher is the fear of man. Unfortunately, not a few surrender to this fear. Either they remain silent at times when they should be boldly eloquent, or they deliver a stern mandate softened with smooth words. *"The fear of man brings a snare"* (Proverbs 29:25). With this sore temptation, Satan often assails the preacher of the Word, and there are few who have not felt the force of this temptation. It is the duty of ministers of the gospel to face this temptation with resolute courage, to steel themselves against it, and, if need be, to trample it underfoot. To this important end, the preacher should be prayed for by his church. He needs deliverance from fear, and prayer can drive fear away and free his soul from its bondage.

In the seventeenth chapter of the book of Exodus, we have a striking picture of the preacher's need for prayer, and for what a people's prayers can do for him. Israel and Amalek were in battle, and the contest was severe and close. Moses stood on top of the hill and held up his rod, the symbol of power and victory. As long as Moses held up the rod, Israel prevailed, but when he let down the rod, Amalek prevailed. The outcome of the battle was at stake. Aaron and Hur came to the rescue, and when Moses' hands were heavy, these two men *"stayed up his hands...until the going down of the sun. And Joshua discomfited Amalek and his people"* (Exodus 17:12–13).

This incident is a striking illustration of how a people may sustain their preacher by prayer. It further illustrates how victory comes when the people pray for their preacher.

Some of the Lord's very best men in Old Testament times had to be encouraged by almighty God not to be afraid. Moses himself was not free from the fear that harasses and compromises a leader. God told him, in these words, to go to Pharaoh: *"Come now therefore, and I will send you to Pharaoh, that you may bring forth My people the children of Israel out of Egypt"* (Exodus 3:10). But Moses, largely through fear, began to offer objections and excuses for not going. Finally, God became angry with him and said that He would send Aaron along to do the talking, for Moses had insisted that he was *"slow of speech, and of a slow tongue"* (Exodus 4:10). But the fact was, Moses was afraid of the face of Pharaoh. It took God some time to circumvent his fears and nerve him to face the Egyptian monarch and deliver God's message to him.

Joshua, too, the successor of Moses and a man seemingly courageous, needed to be fortified by God against fear, lest he should shrink from duty and be reduced to discouragement and timidity. God said to him,

> Have not I commanded you? Be strong and of a good courage; be not afraid, neither be you dismayed: for the LORD your God is with thee wherever you go. (Joshua 1:9)

Jeremiah, a good and true man, was sorely tempted to fear. He had to be warned and strengthened, lest he should prove false to his charge.

When God ordained him to be a prophet to the nations, Jeremiah began to excuse himself on the ground that he could not speak, saying, *"I am a child"* (Jeremiah 1:6). Therefore, the Lord had to safeguard him from the temptation of fear so that he might not prove faithless. God said to His servant,

> *You therefore gird up your loins, and arise, and speak to them all that I command you: be not dismayed at their faces, lest I confound you before them.* (Jeremiah 1:17)

Since these great men of old were so beset with this temptation and disposed to shrink from duty, we need not be surprised that preachers of our own day are found in a similar case. The devil is the same in all ages, and human nature has not undergone any change. How needful, then, that we pray for the leaders of our Israel, especially that they may receive the gift of boldness and speak the Word of God with courage.

No wonder Paul insisted so vigorously that the believers pray for him. Prayer would give him an open door to preach, deliverance from the fear of man, and holy boldness in preaching the Word.

The challenge and demand of the world in our own day is that Christianity be made practical. The demand is for precepts to be expressed in practice, for principles to be brought down from the realm of the ideal to the levels of everyday life. This can be done only by praying men who, being much in harmony with their ministers, will not cease to bear them up in their prayers before God.

All alone, a preacher cannot meet the demands made upon him, any more than the vine can bear grapes without branches. The men who sit in the pews are to be the fruit bearing ones. They are to translate the "ideal" of the pulpit into the "real" of daily life and action. But they will not do it, they cannot do it, if they are not devoted to God and given to much prayer. Devotion to God and devotion to prayer are one and the same thing.

ELEVEN:

MODERN EXAMPLES OF PRAYER

When the dragonfly rends his husk and harnesses himself in a clean plate of sapphire mail, his is a pilgrimage of one or two sunny days over the fields and pastures wet with dew, yet nothing can exceed the marvelous beauty in which he is decked. No flowers on earth have a richer blue than the pure colour of his cuirass. So is it in the high spiritual sphere. The most complete spiritual loveliness may be obtained in the shortest time, and the stripling may die a hundred years old, in character and grace.

—*History of David Brainerd*

God has not confined Himself to Bible days in showing what can be done through prayer. In modern times, also, He is seen to be the same prayer-hearing God as before. Even in these latter days He has not left Himself without witness. Religious biographies and church history alike furnish us with many noble examples and striking illustrations of prayer. These examples show us prayer's necessity, its worth, and its fruits.

All these examples also encourage the faith of God's saints and urge them on to more and better praying. God has not confined Himself to Bible times in using praying people to further His cause on earth. He has placed Himself under obligation to answer our prayers just as much as He did the saints of old. A selection from these praying saints of modern times will show us how they valued prayer, what it meant to them, and what it meant to God.

Take, for example, Samuel Rutherford, a Scottish preacher, exiled to the north of Scotland, forbidden to preach, and banished from his home and pastoral charge. Rutherford lived between 1600 and 1661. He was a member of the Westminster Assembly, principal of New College, and rector of St. Andrews' University. He is said to have been one of the most moving and affectionate preachers of his time, or, perhaps, of any age of the church. Men said of him, "He is always praying." Concerning his and his wife's praying, one wrote,

> He who had heard them either pray or speak, might have learned to bemoan his ignorance. Oh, how many times have I been convinced by observing them of the evil of insincerity before God and unsavoriness in discourse! He so prayed for his people that he himself says, "There I wrestled with the Angel and prevailed." (See Genesis 32:24–28.)

Rutherford was ordered to appear before Parliament to answer the charge of high treason, even though he was a man of scholarly attainments and rare genius. At times, he was depressed and gloomy, especially when he was first silenced and banished from preaching, for there were many murmurings and charges against him. But his losses and crosses were so sanctified that Christ became more and more to him. Marvelous are his statements of his estimation of Christ. This devoted man of prayer wrote many letters during his exile to preachers, to state officers, to lords temporal and spiritual, to honorable and holy men, to honorable and holy women. These were precious letters, all breathing an intense devotion to Christ and all born of great devotion to prayer.

Ardor and panting after God have been characteristics of great souls in all ages of the church, and Samuel Rutherford was a striking example of this fact. He showed that he who always prays will be enveloped in devotion and will be joined to Christ in bonds of holy union.

Then there was Henry Martyn—scholar, saint, missionary, and apostle to India. Martyn was born on February 18, 1781 and sailed for India on August 31, 1805. He died at Tokai, Persia, October 16, 1812. Here is part of what he said about himself while a missionary:

> What a knowledge of man and acquaintance with the Scriptures, and what communion with God and study of my own heart ought to prepare me for the awful work of a messenger from God on business of the soul.

Someone said of this consecrated missionary:

> Oh, to be able to emulate his excellencies, his elevation of piety, his diligence, his superiority to the world, his love for souls, his anxiety to improve on all occasions to do souls good, his insight into the mystery of Christ, and his heavenly temper! These are the secrets of the wonderful impression he made in India.

It is interesting and profitable to note some of the things that Martyn records in his diary. Here is an example:

> The ways of wisdom appear more sweet and reasonable than ever, and the world more insipid and vexatious. The chief thing I mourn over is my want of power, and lack of fervour in secret prayer, especially when attempting to plead for the heathen. Warmth does not increase within me in proportion to my light.

If Henry Martyn, so devoted, ardent, and prayerful, lamented his lack of power and fervor in prayer, how our cold and feeble praying ought to lower us into the very dust! Alas, how rare are such praying men in the church of our own day!

Again, I quote an entry from his diary. He had been quite ill, but he had recovered, and he was filled with thankfulness because it had pleased God to restore him to life and health again.

Not that I have yet recovered my former strength, but I consider myself sufficiently restored to prosecute my journey. My daily prayer is that my late chastisement may have its intended effect and make me, all the rest of my days, more humble and less self-confident.

Selfconfidence has often led me down fearful lengths and would, without God's gracious interference, prove my endless perdition. I seem to be made to feel this evil of my heart more than any other at this time. In prayer, or when I write or converse on the subject, Christ appears to me my life and my strength; but at other times I am thoughtless and bold, as if I had all life and strength in myself. Such neglects on our part are a diminution of our joys.

Among the last entries in this consecrated missionary's journal we find the following:

In solitude, I sat in the orchard and thought, with sweet comfort and peace, of my God—my Company, my Friend, my Comforter. Oh, when shall time give place to eternity!

Note the words "in solitude." Away from the busy haunts of men, in a lonely place, like his Lord, he went out to meditate and pray.

Brief as this summary is, it suffices to show how fully and faithfully Henry Martyn exercised his ministry of prayer. The following may well serve to end our portrayal of him:

By daily weighing the Scriptures, with prayer, he waxed riper and riper in his ministry. Prayer and the Holy Scriptures were those wells of salvation out of which he drew daily the living water for his thirsty immortal soul. Truly may it be said of him, he prayed *"always with all prayer and supplication in the Spirit, and watch*[ed] *thereto with all perseverance"* (Ephesians 6:18).

David Brainerd, the missionary to the Indians, is a remarkable example of a praying man of God. Robert Hale said this about him:

Such invincible patience and selfdenial; such profound humility, exquisite prudence, indefatigable industry; such devotedness to

God, or rather such absorption of the whole soul in zeal for the divine glory and the salvation of men, is scarcely to be paralleled since the age of the Apostles. Such was the intense ardour of his mind that it seems to have diffused the spirit of a martyr over the common incidents of his life.

Dr. A. J. Gordon spoke thus of Brainerd:

In passing through Northampton, Massachusetts, I went into the old cemetery, swept off the snow that lay on the top of the slab, and I read these simple words:

"Sacred to the memory of David Brainerd, the faithful and devoted missionary to the Susquehanna, Delaware and Stockbridge Indians of America, who died in this town, October 8, 1747."

That was all there was on the slab. Now that great man did his greatest work by prayer. He was in the depths of those forests alone, unable to speak the language of the Indians, but he spent whole days literally in prayer.

What was he praying for? He knew he could not reach these savages, for he did not understand their language. If he wanted to speak at all, he must find somebody who could vaguely interpret his thought. Therefore he knew that anything he could do must be absolutely dependent upon God. So he spent whole days in praying, simply that the power of the Holy Ghost might come upon him so unmistakably that these people would not be able to stand before him.

What was his answer? Once he preached through a drunken interpreter, a man so intoxicated that he could hardly stand up. This was the best he could do. Yet scores were converted through that sermon. We can account for it only that it was the tremendous power of God behind him.

Now this man prayed in secret in the forest. A little while afterward, William Carey read about his life, and by its impulse he went to India. Payson read it as a young man, over twenty years old, and he said that he had never been so impressed by anything in his life as by the story of Brainerd. Murray McCheyne read it, and he likewise was impressed by it.

But all I want is simply to enforce this thought, that the hidden life, a life whose days are spent in communion with God, in trying to reach the source of power, is the life that moves the world. Those living such lives may be soon forgotten. There may be no one to speak a eulogy over them when they are dead. The great world may take no account of them. But by and by, the great moving current of their lives will begin to tell, as in the case of this young man, who died at about thirty years of age. The missionary spirit of this nineteenth century is more due to the prayers and consecration of this one man than to any other one.

So I say. And yet the most remarkable thing is that Jonathan Edwards, who watched over him all those months while he was slowly dying of consumption, should also say: "I praise God that it was in His Providence that he should die in my house, that I might hear his prayers, and that I might witness his consecration, and that I might be inspired by his example."

When Jonathan Edwards wrote that great appeal to Christendom to unite in prayer for the conversion of the world, which has been the trumpet call of modern missions, undoubtedly it was inspired by this dying missionary.

John Wesley bore this testimony about David Brainerd's spirit:

I preached and afterward made a collection for the Indian schools in America. A large sum of money is now collected. But will money convert heathens? Find preachers of David Brainerd's spirit, and nothing can stand before them. But without this, what will gold or silver do? No more than lead or iron.

Some selections from Brainerd's diary will be of value to show what manner of man he was:

My soul felt a pleasing yet painful concern, lest I should spend some moments without God. Oh, may I always live to God! In the evening I was visited by some friends, and we spent the time in prayer, and such conversation as tended to edification. It was a comfortable season to my soul. I felt an ardent desire to spend every moment with God.

God is unspeakably gracious to me continually. In time past, He has given me inexpressible sweetness in the performance of duty. Frequently, my soul has enjoyed much of God, but has been ready to say, "Lord, it is good to be here," and so indulge sloth while I have lived on the sweetness of my feelings. But of late God has been pleased to keep my soul hungry almost continually, so that I have been filled with a kind of pleasing pain. When I really enjoy God, I feel my desires of Him the more insatiable, and my thirstings after holiness the more unquenchable.

Oh, that I may feel this continual hunger, and not be retarded, but rather animated, by every cluster from Canaan, to reach forward in the narrow way, for the full enjoyment and possession of the heavenly inheritance! Oh, may I never loiter in my heavenly journey!

It seems as if such an unholy wretch as I never could arrive at that blessedness, to be holy as God is holy. At noon I longed for sanctification and conformity to God. Oh, that is the one thing, the all!

Toward night I enjoyed much sweetness in secret prayer, so that my soul longed for an arrival in the heavenly country, the blessed paradise of God.

If someone should ask about the secret of David Brainerd's heavenly spirit, his deep consecration, and his exalted spiritual state, the answer can be found in the last sentence of the preceding quote. He was given to "much…secret prayer," and he was so close to God in his life and spirit that prayer brought much sweetness to his inner soul.

We have cited the foregoing cases to illustrate the fundamental fact that God's great servants are devoted to the ministry of prayer. They are God's agents on earth who serve Him in this way, and they carry on His work by this holy means.

Louis Harms was born in Hanover in 1809. There came a time when he was powerfully convicted of sin. He said, "I have never known what fear was. But when I came to the knowledge of my sins, I quaked before the wrath of God, so that my limbs trembled." He was mightily converted to God by reading the Bible.

Rationalism, a dead orthodoxy, and worldliness blinded the multitudes in Hermansburgh, the town where he lived. His father, a Lutheran minister, died, and Harms became his successor. He began with all the energy of his soul to work for Christ and to develop a church of a pure, strong type. The fruit was soon evident. There was a quickening on every hand; attendance at public services increased; reverence for the Bible grew; conversation about sacred things revived. Meanwhile, infidelity, worldliness, and dead orthodoxy vanished like a passing cloud.

Harms proclaimed a conscious and present Christ, the Comforter, in the full energy of His mission, which is the revival of apostolic piety and power. The entire neighborhood began to attend church regularly; the Sabbath was restored to its sanctity and hallowed with strict devotion; homes began to have family devotions; and when the noon bell sounded, every head was bowed in prayer. In a very short time the whole aspect of the town was entirely changed.

The revival in Hermansburgh was essentially a prayer revival. It was brought about by prayer and yielded fruits of prayer in a rich and abundant harvest.

William Carvosso, an old-time Methodist leader, was one of the best examples in modern times of what the religious life of Christians was probably like in the apostolic age. He was a prayer leader, a class leader, a steward, and a trustee, but he never aspired to be a preacher. Yet, a preacher he was of the very first quality, and he was a master in the art and science of soul saving. He was a singular example of a man learning the simplest rudiments late in life. Up until the age of sixty-five, he had never written a single sentence. Yet, he later wrote letters that would make volumes, and he wrote a book that was regarded as a spiritual classic in the great worldwide Methodist church.

Not a page nor a letter, it is believed, was ever written by him on any other subject but religion. Here are some of his brief statements, which give us an insight into his religious character. "I want to be more like Jesus." "My soul thirsteth for Thee, O God." "I see nothing will do, O God, but being continually filled with Thy presence and glory."

This was the continual cry of his inner soul, and this was the strong inward impulse that moved the outward man. One time he exclaimed, "Glory to God! This is a morning without a cloud." Cloudless days were native to his sunny religion and his joyful spirit. Continual prayer and turning all conversation toward Christ in all company and in every home, was the law he always followed.

On the anniversary of his spiritual birth, he remembered his salvation experience with great joyousness of spirit, and he broke forth:

Blessed be Thy name, O God! The last has been the best of the whole. I may say with Bunyan, "I have got into that land where the sun shines night and day." I thank Thee, O my God, for this heaven, this element of love and joy, in which my soul now lives.

Here is a sample of Carvosso's spiritual experiences, of which he had many:

I have sometimes had seasons of remarkable visitation from the presence of the Lord. I well remember one night when in bed being so filled, so overpowered with the glory of God, that had there been a thousand suns shining at noonday, the brightness of that divine glory would have eclipsed the whole. I was constrained to shout aloud for joy. It was the overwhelming power of saving grace. Now it was that I again received the impress of the seal and the earnest of the Spirit in my heart. Beholding as in a glass the glory of the Lord, I was changed into the same image from glory to glory by the Spirit of the Lord. (See 2 Corinthians 3:18.) Language fails in giving but a faint description of what I there experienced. I can never forget it in time nor to all eternity.

Many years before I was sealed by the Spirit in a somewhat similar manner. While walking out one day, I was drawn to turn aside on the public road, and under the canopy of the skies, I was moved to kneel down to pray. I had not long been praying with

God before I was so visited from Him that I was overpowered by the divine glory, and I shouted till I could be heard at a distance. It was a weight of glory that I seemed incapable of bearing in the body, and therefore I cried out, perhaps unwisely, "Lord, stay Thy hand." In this glorious baptism these words came to my heart with indescribable power: "I have sealed thee unto the day of redemption." (See Ephesians 4:30.)

Oh, I long to be filled more with God! Lord, stir me up more in earnest. I want to be more like Jesus. I see that nothing will do but being continually filled with the divine presence and glory. I know all that Thou hast is mine, but I want to feel a close union. Lord, increase my faith.

Such was William Carvosso—a man whose life was saturated with the spirit of prayer, who lived on his knees, so to speak, and who belonged to that company of praying saints that has blessed the earth.

Jonathan Edwards must be placed among the praying saints—one whom God mightily used through the instrumentality of prayer. As in the instance of this great New Englander, purity of heart should be ingrained in the very foundation of every person who is a minister of the gospel. A sample of the statements of this mighty man of God is here given in the form of a resolution he wrote down:

Resolved to exercise myself in this all my life long, viz., with the greatest openness to declare my ways to God, and to lay my soul open to God—all my sins, temptations, difficulties, sorrows, fears, hopes, desires, and everything and every circumstance.

We are not surprised, therefore, that the result of such fervid and honest praying was to lead him to record in his diary:

It was my continual strife day and night, and my constant inquiry, how I should be more holy, and live more holily. The heaven I desired was a heaven of holiness. I went on with my eager pursuit after more holiness and conformity to Christ.

The character and work of Jonathan Edwards exemplified a great truth: prayer is the activating agency in every truly God-ordered work and life. He himself gives some particulars about his life as a boy. He might well be called the "Isaiah of the Christian Dispensation." There were united in him great mental powers, ardent piety, and devotion to study; these were unequaled except by his devotion to God. Here is what he said about himself:

> When a boy I used to pray five times a day in secret, and to spend much time in religious conversation with other boys. I used to meet with them to pray together. So it is God's will through His wonderful grace, that the prayers of His saints should be one great and principal means of carrying on the designs of Christ's kingdom in the world. Pray much for the ministers and the church of God.

Edwards used the great powers of his mind and heart to get God's people everywhere to unite in extraordinary prayer. His life, efforts, and character are an exemplification of his statement. He said,

> The heaven I desire is a heaven spent with God: an eternity spent in the presence of divine love, and in holy communion with Christ.

At another time he said,

> The soul of a true Christian appears like a little white flower in the spring of the year, low and humble on the ground, opening its bosom to receive the pleasant beams of the sun's glory, rejoicing as it were in a calm rapture, diffusing around a sweet fragrance, standing peacefully and lovingly in the midst of other flowers.

Again, he wrote,

"The heaven I desire is a heaven spent with God:
an eternity spent in the presence of divine love,
and in holy communion with Christ."
—*Jonathan Edwards*

Once, having ridden out into the woods for my health, I alighted from my horse in a retired place, for my manner has been to walk for divine contemplation and prayer. I had a view, that for me was extraordinary, of the glory of the Son of God as Mediator between God and man, and of His wonderful, great, full, pure, and sweet grace and love, and His meek and gentle condescension. This grace that seemed so calm and sweet, appeared also great above the heavens. The person of Christ appeared ineffably excellent with an excellency great enough to swallow up all thought and conception, which continued, as near as I can judge, about an hour. It kept me the greater part of the time in a flood of tears and weeping aloud. I felt an ardency of soul to be, what I know not otherwise how to express, emptied and annihilated, to lie in the dust; to be full of Christ alone, to love Him with my whole heart.

As it was with Jonathan Edwards, so it is with all great intercessors. They come into that holy, elect condition of mind and heart by a thorough self-dedication to God, and by periods of God's revelation to them, which make distinct, marked eras in their spiritual history. These eras are never to be forgotten. During these eras faith *"mount[s] up with wings as eagles"* (Isaiah 40:31). The intercessor has a new and fuller vision of God; a stronger grasp of faith; a sweeter, clearer vision of all things heavenly and eternal; and a blessed intimacy with, and access to, God.

TWELVE:

MORE MODERN EXAMPLES OF PRAYER

Edward Bounds did not merely pray well that he might write well about prayer. He prayed for long years upon subjects to which easygoing Christians rarely give a thought. He prayed for objects which men of less faith are ready to call impossible. Yet from these continued, solitary prayer vigils, year by year there arose a gift of prayer-teaching equaled by few men. He wrote transcendently about prayer because he was transcendent in its practice.

—*C. L. Chilton Jr.*

Lady Maxwell was a contemporary of John Wesley, and she was a fruit of Methodism in its earlier phases. She was a woman of refinement, of culture, and of deep piety. Separating herself entirely from the world, she sought and found the deepest religious experience, and she was a woman fully set apart to God.

Her life was one of prayer, of complete consecration to God, of living to bless others. She was noted for her systematic habits of life, which entered into and controlled her religion. Her time was economized and ordered for God. She arose at four o'clock in the morning and attended preaching at five o'clock. After breakfast she held a family service. Then, from eleven to twelve o'clock she observed a season of intercessory prayer. The rest of the day was given to reading, visiting, and acts of benevolence. Her evenings were spent in reading. At night, before retiring, religious services were held for the family, which sometimes were spent in praising God for His mercies.

Rarely has God been served with more intelligence or out of a richer experience, a nobler zeal, or a greater nobility of soul. Strongly, spiritually, and ardently attached to Wesley's doctrine of entire dedication, she sought it with persistency and a never-flagging zeal. She obtained it by faith and prayer, and she illustrated it in a life as holy and as perfect as is given to mortals to reach. If Wesley's teaching of entire dedication had, today, models and teachers like Lady Maxwell of Edinburgh and John Fletcher of Madeley, it would not be so misunderstood. No, it would commend itself to the good and pure everywhere by holy lives, if not by its phraseology.

Lady Maxwell's diary yields some rich counsel for secret prayer, holy experience, and consecrated living. One of the entries reads as follows:

Of late I feel painfully convinced that I do not pray enough. Lord, give me the spirit of prayer and of supplication. Oh, what a cause of thankfulness it is that we have a gracious God to whom to go on all occasions! Use and enjoy this privilege, and you can never be miserable. Who gives thanks for this royal privilege? It puts God in everything, His wisdom, power, control, and safety. Oh, what an unspeakable privilege is prayer! Let us give thanks for it. I do not prove all the power of prayer that I wish.

Thus, we see that the remedy for nonpraying is *praying*. The cure for little praying is more praying. Praying can procure all things necessary for our good.

For this excellent woman, praying embraced everything and included everything. To one of her most intimate friends she wrote,

I wish I could provide you with a proper maid, but it is a difficult matter. You have my prayers for it, and if I hear of one I will let you know.

So small a matter as a friend's need for a maid was not too small for her to take to God in prayer.

In the same letter, she tells her friend that she wants "more faith. Cry mightily for it, and stir up the gift of God that is in you." (See 2 Timothy 1:6.)

Whether the need was a small, secular thing like a servant, or a great spiritual grace, prayer was the means to attain that end and supply that need. She wrote to a dear correspondent,

There is nothing so hurtful to the nervous system as anxiety. It preys upon the vitals and weakens the whole frame, and what is more than all, it grieves the Holy Spirit.

Her remedy, again, for a common evil, was prayer.

How prayer lifts the burden of care by bringing in God to relieve, possess, and hold!

The apostle said,

Be careful for nothing; but in every thing by prayer and supplication with thanksgiving let your requests be made known to God. And the peace of God, which passes all understanding, shall keep your hearts and minds through Christ Jesus. (Philippians 4:6–7)

These verses tell us that God keeps and protects us. Picture a besieged and distressed garrison, unable to protect the fort from attacking enemies, when suddenly strong reinforcements come pouring in. Into the heart oppressed, distracted, and discouraged, true prayer brings God, who holds it in perfect peace and perfect safety. Lady Maxwell fully understood this truth, not only theoretically, but, even better, experientially.

Christ Jesus is the only cure for needless care and over anxiety of soul, and we secure God, His presence, and His peace by prayer. Care is so natural and so strong that no one but God can drive it out. It takes the presence and personality of God Himself to expel the care and to enthrone quietness and peace. When Christ comes in with His peace, all tormenting fears leave. Trepidation and vexing anxieties surrender to Christ's reign of peace, and all disturbing elements depart.

> *Christ Jesus is the only cure for needless care and over anxiety of soul, and we secure God, His presence, and His peace by prayer. Care is so natural and so strong that no one but God can drive it out. It takes the presence and personality of God Himself to expel the care and to enthrone quietness and peace. When Christ comes in with His peace, all tormenting fears leave. Trepidation and vexing anxieties surrender to Christ's reign of peace, and all disturbing elements depart.*

Anxious thought and care assault the soul, and feebleness, faintness, and cowardice are within. Prayer reinforces with God's peace, and the heart is kept by Him. *"You will keep him in perfect peace, whose mind is stayed on You"* (Isaiah 26:3). All now is safety, quietness, and assurance. *"The work of righteousness shall be peace; and the effect of righteousness quietness and assurance for ever"* (Isaiah 32:17).

But to ensure this great peace, prayer must pass into strenuous, insistent, personal supplication, and thanksgiving must bloom into full flower. Our exposed condition of heart must be brought to the knowledge of God *"by prayer and supplication with thanksgiving"* (Philippians 4:6). The peace of God will keep the heart and thoughts fixed and fearless. Peace—deep, exhaustless, wide, flowing like a river—will come in.

Referring again to Lady Maxwell, we remember her words:

God is daily teaching me more simplicity of spirit, and He makes me willing to receive all as His unmerited gift. He is teaching me to call on Him for everything I need, as I need it, and He supplies my wants according to existing needs. But I have certainly felt more of it this last eighteen months than in former periods. I wish to *"pray without ceasing"* (1 Thess. 5:17). I see the necessity of praying always, and not fainting (Luke 18:1).

Again, we recall her words: "I wish to be much in prayer. I greatly need it. The prayer of faith shuts or opens heaven. Come, Lord, and turn my captivity." If we felt the need of prayer as this saintly woman did, we could be like her in her saintly ascension. Prayer truly shuts or opens heaven. Oh, for a quality of faith that would test to the uttermost the power of prayer!

Lady Maxwell uttered a great truth when she said,

When God is at work, either among a people or in the heart of an individual, the adversary of souls is peculiarly at work also. A belief of the former should prevent discouragement, and a fear of the latter should stir us up to much prayer. Oh, the power of faithful prayer! I live by prayer! May you prove its sovereign efficacy in every difficult case.

A record among Lady Maxwell's writings shows us that in prayer and meditation she obtained enlarged views of the full salvation of God. What is thus discovered in prayer, faith goes out after, and according to faith's strength are its returns.

I daily feel the need of the precious blood of sprinkling [she said] and dwell continually under its influence, and most sensibly feel its sovereign efficacy. It is by momentary faith in this blood alone that I am saved from sin. Prayer is my chief employ.

If this last statement, "Prayer is my chief employ," had ever been true of all of God's people, this world would have been by this time quite another world; and God's glory, instead of being dim, shadowy, and only in spots, would now shine with universal and unrivaled brilliance and power.

Here is another record of her fervent and faithful praying: "Lately, I have been favoured with a more ardent spirit of praying than almost ever formerly."

We need to study the words "favoured with a more ardent spirit of praying," for they are pregnant words. The spirit of prayer, the ardent spirit of prayer, and the more ardent spirit of prayer—all these are of God. They

More Modern Examples of Prayer 229

are given in answer to prayer. The spirit of prayer and the more ardent spirit are the result of fervent, persistent, secret prayer.

At another time Lady Maxwell declared that secret prayer was the means whereby she derived the greatest spiritual benefit.

> I do indeed prove it to be an especial privilege. I could not live without it, though I do not always find comfort in it. I still ardently desire an enlarged sphere of usefulness, and find it comfortable to embrace the opportunities afforded me.

An "enlarged sphere of usefulness" is certainly a proper theme of intense prayer, but that prayer must always be accompanied by an embracing of the opportunities one already has.

Many pages could be filled with extracts from Lady Maxwell's diary about the vital importance and the nature of prayer, but we must conclude. For many years she was in fervent supplication for a larger sphere of usefulness, but all these years of ardent praying may be condensed into one paragraph:

> My whole soul has been thirsting after a larger sphere of action [she said] agreeably to the promises of a faithful God. For these few last weeks I have been led to plead earnestly for more holiness. Lord, give me both, that I may praise Thee.

These two things—more work and more holiness—must go together. They are one, and they are not to be separated. The desire for a larger field of work without the accompanying desire for more consecration is perilous, and it may be supremely selfish, the offspring of spiritual pride.

John Fletcher, also a contemporary of John Wesley, was intimately associated with this founder of Methodism. Fletcher was a scholar of courtesy and refinement; a strong, original thinker; a speaker of simple eloquence and truth. What qualified him as a spiritual leader was his exceedingly great faith in God, his nearness to God, and his perfect assurance of a dear, unquestioned relationship with his Lord. Fletcher had profound convictions about the truth of God, possessed a perpetual communion with his Savior, and was humble in his knowledge of God. He was a man of deep spiritual insight into the things of God, and his thorough earnestness, his truth, and his consecration marked him as a man of God. He was well equipped to be a leader in the church.

Unceasing prayer was the sign and secret of Fletcher's sainthood, as well as its power and influence. His whole life was one of prayer. So intently was his mind fixed on God that he sometimes said, "I would not rise from my seat without lifting up my heart to God." A friend related the fact that whenever they met, Fletcher's first greeting was, "Do I meet you praying?" If they were talking about theology, in the midst of it he would stop abruptly and say, "Where are our hearts now?" If the misconduct of any person who was absent was mentioned, he would say, "Let us pray for him."

The very walls of his room, so it was said, were stained by the breath of his prayers. Spiritually, Madeley was a dreary, desolate desert when he went to live there, but it was so revolutionized by his prayers that it bloomed and blossomed like the garden of the Lord. A friend of his thus wrote of Fletcher:

> Many of us have at times gone with him aside, and there we would continue for two or three hours, wrestling like Jacob for the blessing, praying one after another. And I have seen him on these occasions so filled with the love of God that he could contain no more, but would cry out, "O my God, withhold Thy hand or the vessel will burst!" His whole life was a life of prayer.

John Foster, a man of exalted piety and deep devotion to God, said this about prayer while on his deathbed:

> "*Pray without ceasing*" (1 Thessalonians 5:17) has been the sentence repeating itself in my silent thoughts, and I am sure that it will be, it must be, my practice till the last conscious hour of my life. Oh, why was it not my practice throughout that long, indolent, inanimate half century past! I often think mournfully of the difference it would have made in me. Now there remains so little time for a genuine, effective spiritual life.

The Reformation of the fifteenth century owes its origin to prayer. In all of Martin Luther's lifework—its beginning, continuance, and ending— he was devoted to prayer. The secret of his extraordinary activity is found in this statement: "I have so much work to do that I cannot get along without giving three hours daily of my best time to prayer." Another one of his sayings was, "It takes meditation and prayer to make a clergyman." His everyday motto was, "He that has prayed well, has studied well."

Another time he confessed his lack by saying, "I was short and superficial in prayer this morning." How often is this the case with us! Remember that the source of decline in religion and the proof of decline in a Christian life is found right here, in "short and superficial" praying. Such praying foretells and causes coldness between us and God.

William Wilberforce once said of himself,

I have been keeping too late hours, and hence have had but a hurried half hour to myself. I am lean and cold and hard. I had better allow more time, say two hours, or an hour and a half, daily to religious exercises.

A person must be very skillful and regular in long praying for his short prayers not to be superficial. Short prayers make shallow lives. Longer praying would work like magic in many a decayed spiritual life. A holy life would not be so difficult and rare if our praying were not so brief, cold, and superficial.

George Müller, that remarkable man of such simple yet strong faith in God, was a man of prayer and Bible reading. He was the founder and promoter of the noted orphanage in England, which cared for hundreds of orphan children. He conducted the institution solely by faith and prayer. He never asked a man for anything, but he simply trusted in the providence of God, and it is a well-known fact that the orphans at the home never lacked any good thing. From his newsletter he always excluded money matters, and financial difficulties found no place in it. Nor would he mention the sums that had been given him, nor the names of those who had made contributions. He never spoke of his needs to others or asked for a donation.

The story of his life and the history of this orphanage read like a chapter from the Scriptures. The secret of his success is found in this simple statement made by him: "I went to my God and prayed diligently, and I received what I needed." That was the simple course that he pursued. There was nothing he insisted on with more earnestness than that, no matter what the expenses were or how suddenly they increased, he must not beg for anything. There was nothing that he told more excitedly than that he had prayed for every need he had ever had in his great work. His was a work of continuous and persevering praying, and he always confidently claimed that God had guided him throughout it all. His work was a proof of the power of simple faith, divine providence, answered prayer. A stronger proof cannot be found in church history or religious biography.

John Wesley, in writing to a friend one time, helped, urged, and prayed. Here are John Wesley's own words:

> Have you received a gleam of light from above, a spark of faith? If you have, let it not go! Hold fast by His grace that earnest of your inheritance. Come just as you are, and come boldly to the throne of grace. You need not delay. Even now the bowels of Jesus yearn over you. What have you to do with tomorrow? I love you today. And how much more does He love you? "He pities still His wandering sheep, and longs to bring you to His fold." Today hear His voice, the voice of Him that speaks as never man spake.

The seekings of Madame Guyon after God were sincere, and her yearnings were strong and earnest. She went to a devout Franciscan friar for advice and comfort. She stated her convictions and told him of her long and fruitless seeking. After she had finished speaking to him, the friar remained silent for some time, in inward meditation and prayer. Then he said to her,

> Your efforts have been unsuccessful, because you have sought without what you can only find within. Accustom yourself to seek God in your heart, and you will not fail to find Him.

Charley G. Finney said this about prayer:

> When God has specially promised the thing, we are bound to believe we shall receive it when we pray for it. You have no right to put in an "if," and say, "Lord, if it be Thy will, give me Thy Holy Spirit." This is to insult God. To put an "if" in God's promise when God has put none there, is tantamount to charging God

with being insincere. It is like saying, "O God, if Thou art in earnest in making these promises, grant us the blessing we pray for."

We may fittingly conclude this book by quoting a word of Adoniram Judson's, the noted missionary to Burma. Speaking of the prevailing power of prayer, he said,

"Nothing is impossible," said one of the seven sages of Greece, "to industry." Let us change the word, "industry," to "persevering prayer," and the motto will be more Christian and more worthy of universal adoption. God loves importunate prayer so much that He will not give us much blessing without it. God says, "*Behold, I will do a new thing; now it shall spring forth; shall ye not know it? I will even make a way in the wilderness, and rivers in the desert....This people have I formed for myself; they shall show forth my praise*" (Isaiah 43:19, 21).

BOOK THREE:

POWER THROUGH PRAYER

ONE:

THE DIVINE CHANNEL OF POWER

Study universal holiness of life. Your whole usefulness depends on this, for your sermons last only an hour or two; your life preaches all week. If Satan can make you a covetous minister, a lover of praise, of pleasure, of good eating, he has ruined your ministry. Give yourself to prayer, and get your texts, your thoughts, your words from God. Luther spent his best three hours in prayer.

—Robert Murray McCheyne

We are continually striving to create new methods, plans, and organizations to advance the church. We are ever working to provide and stimulate growth and efficiency for the gospel.

This trend of the day has a tendency to lose sight of the man. Or else he is lost in the workings of the plan or organization. God's plan is to make much of the man, far more of him than of anything else. Men are God's method.

The church is looking for better methods; God is looking for better men. "*There was a man sent from God, whose name was John*" (John 1:6). The dispensation that heralded and prepared the way for Christ was bound up in that man John. "*Unto us a child is born, unto us a son is given*" (Isaiah 9:6). The world's salvation comes out of that cradled Son.

> *The church is looking for better methods;*
> *God is looking for better men.*

When Paul appealed to the personal character of the men who rooted the gospel in the world, he solved the mystery of their success. The glory and efficiency of the gospel depend on the men who proclaim it. When God declares that "*the eyes of the LORD run to and fro throughout the whole earth, to show himself strong in the behalf of them whose heart is perfect toward him*" (2 Chronicles 16:9), He declares the necessity of men. He acknowledges His dependence on them as a channel through which He can exert His power on the world.

This vital, urgent truth is one that this age of machinery is apt to forget. The forgetting of it is as detrimental to the Word of God as removing the sun from its sphere would be. Darkness, confusion, and death would ensue.

What the church needs today is not more or better machinery, not new organizations or more novel methods. She needs men whom the Holy Spirit can use—men of prayer, men mighty in prayer. The Holy Spirit does not flow through methods, but through men. He does not come on machinery, but on men. He does not anoint plans, but men—men of prayer!

An eminent historian has said that the accidents of personal character have more to do with the revolutions of nations than either philosophic historians or democratic politicians will allow. This truth fully applies to the gospel of Christ and the character and conduct of the followers of Christ—Christianize the world, and you transfigure nations and individuals. It is eminently true of the preachers of the gospel.

The character as well as the fortunes of the gospel are committed to the preacher. He either makes or mars the message from God to man. The preacher is the golden pipe through which the divine oil flows. The pipe must not only be golden, but open and flawless. This way the oil may have a full, unhindered, and unwasted flow.

The man makes the preacher. God must make the man. The messenger is, if possible, more than the message. The preacher is more than the sermon. The preacher *makes* the sermon. As life-giving milk from the mother's bosom is no more than the mother's life, so all the preacher *says* is tinctured, impregnated, by what the preacher *is*. The treasure is in earthen vessels, and the taste of the vessel may permeate and discolor the treasure.

The man—the whole man—lies behind the sermon. Preaching is not the performance of an hour; it is the outflow of a life. It takes twenty years to make a sermon because it takes twenty years to make the man. The true sermon is a thing of life. The sermon grows because the man grows. The sermon is forceful because the man is forceful. The sermon is holy because the man is holy. The sermon is full of the divine anointing because the man is full of the divine anointing.

Paul termed it *"my gospel"* (Romans 2:16). It was not that he had slanted it with his personal eccentricities or selfish understanding, but the gospel was laid up in the heart and lifeblood of Paul as a personal trust to be executed by his Pauline traits—to be set aflame and empowered by the fiery energy of his fiery soul. Paul's sermons—what were they? Where were they? Skeletons, scattered fragments, afloat on the sea of inspiration! But the man Paul—greater than his sermons—lives forever, in full form, feature, and stature, with his molding hand on the church. The preacher is only a voice. The voice in silence dies; the text is forgotten; the sermon fades from memory, but the preacher lives.

In its life-giving forces, the sermon cannot rise above the man. Dead men preach dead sermons, and dead sermons kill. Everything depends on the spiritual character of the preacher. Under the Jewish dispensation, the high priest had "Holiness to the Lord" inscribed in jeweled letters on a golden frontlet. So, too, every preacher in Christ's ministry must be molded into and mastered by this same holy motto. It is a shame that the Christian ministry has less holiness of character and aim than the Jewish priesthood.

240 E. M. Bounds on Prayer & Spiritual Warfare

Jonathan Edwards, the famous missionary, said, "I went on with my eager pursuit after more holiness and conformity to Christ. The heaven I desired was a heaven of holiness."[1]

The gospel of Christ does not move by popular waves. It has no self-propagating power. It moves as the men who have charge of it move. The preacher must live the gospel. Its divine, most distinctive features must be embodied in him. The constraining power of love must be in the preacher as a projecting, extraordinary, all-commanding, and self-oblivious force. The energy of self-denial must be his being—his heart, blood, and bones. He must go forth as a man among men, clothed with humility, abiding in meekness, wise as a serpent, and harmless as a dove. He must wear the bonds of a servant with the spirit of a king and the simplicity and sweetness of a child.

The preacher must throw himself—with all the abandon of a perfect, self-emptying faith and a self-consuming zeal—into his work for the salvation of men. The men who take hold of and shape a generation for God must be hearty, heroic, compassionate, and fearless martyrs. If they are timid timeservers, place seekers, men pleasers, men fearers; if their faith in God or His Word is weak; and if their denial may be broken by any phrase of self or the world, they cannot take hold of the church or the world for God.

The preacher's sharpest and strongest preaching should be to himself. His most difficult, delicate, laborious, and thorough work must be with himself. The training of the Twelve was the great, difficult, and enduring work of Christ. Preachers are not sermon makers, but men makers and saint makers. Only he who has made himself a man and a saint is well trained for this business. God does not need great talents, great learning, or great preachers, but men great in holiness, great in faith, great in love, great in fidelity, great for God. He needs men who are always preaching holy sermons in the pulpit and living holy lives out of it. These can mold a great generation for God.

After this order, the early Christians were formed. They were men of solid mold, preachers after the heavenly type—heroic, stalwart, soldierly,

---

1. Jonathan Edwards, "Personal Narrative," c. 1740, in *The Life and Character of the Late Rev. Mr. Jonathan Edwards*, comp. Samuel Hopkins, 1765

saintly. To them, preaching meant self-denying, self-crucifying, serious, toilsome, martyr business. They applied themselves to it in a way that influenced their generation and formed in its womb a generation yet unborn for God. The preaching man is to be the praying man. Prayer is the preacher's mightiest weapon. An almighty force in itself, it gives life and force to all.

The real sermon is made in the prayer closet. The man—God's man— is made in the closet. His life and his most profound convictions are born in his secret communion with God. The burdened and tearful agony of his spirit, his weightiest and sweetest messages, are received when alone with God. Prayer makes the man; prayer makes the preacher; prayer makes the pastor.

The pulpit of this day is weak in praying. The pride of learning is in opposition to the dependent humility of prayer. In the pulpit, prayer is all too often only official—a performance for the routine of service. In the modern pulpit, prayer is not the mighty force it was in Paul's life or ministry. Every preacher who does not make prayer a mighty factor in his own life and ministry is weak as a factor in God's work and is powerless to advance God's cause in this world.

TWO:

OUR SUFFICIENCY IS OF GOD

But, above all, George Fox excelled in prayer. The inwardness and weight of his spirit, the reverence and solemnity of his address and behavior, and the fewness and fullness of his words have often struck even strangers with admiration as they used to reach others with consolation. The most awful living, reverend frame I ever felt or beheld, I must say, was his prayer. And truly it was a testimony. He knew and lived nearer to the Lord than other men, for they that know Him most will see most reason to approach Him with reverence and fear. —William Penn

By a slight perversion, the sweetest graces may bear the bitterest fruit. The sun gives life, but sunstrokes are death. Preaching is to give life, but it may kill. The preacher holds the keys; he may lock as well as unlock. Preaching is God's great institution for the planting and maturing of spiritual life. When properly executed, its benefits are untold. When wrongly executed, no evil can exceed its damaging results.

It is an easy matter to destroy the flock if the shepherd is unwary or the pasture is destroyed. It is easy to capture the citadel if the watchmen are asleep or the food and water are poisoned. As preachers are invested with such gracious prerogatives, exposed to great evils, involving so many grave responsibilities, it would be a parody on the shrewdness of the Devil—a libel on his character and reputation—if he did not use his master influences to adulterate the preacher and the preaching. In the face of all this, Paul's exclamatory question, *"Who is sufficient for these things?"* (2 Corinthians 2:16), is never out of place.

Paul said,

Our sufficiency is of God; who also hath made us able ministers of the new testament; not of the letter, but of the spirit: for the letter killeth, but the spirit giveth life. (2 Corinthians 3:5–6)

The true ministry is God-touched, God-enabled, and God-made. The Spirit of God is on the preacher in anointing power. The fruit of the Spirit is in his heart. The Spirit of God has vitalized the man and the Word; his preaching gives life, gives life as the spring gives life. His words give life as the resurrection gives life. His sermons give ardent life as the summer gives ardent life. His preaching gives fruitful life as the autumn gives fruitful life. The life-giving preacher is a man of God whose soul is continually following after God. His eye looks only to God; and in him, by the power of God's Spirit, the flesh and the world have been crucified. His ministry is like the generous flood of a life-giving river.

The preaching that kills is unspiritual preaching. The ability of the preaching is not from God. Lower sources than God have given it energy and stimulant. The Spirit is not evident in the preacher, nor his preaching. Many kinds of forces may be projected and stimulated by preaching that kills, but they are not spiritual forces. They may resemble spiritual forces but are only the shadow, the counterfeit. They may seem to have life, but the life is false. The preaching that kills is the letter. It may be shapely and orderly, but it is the letter still—the dry, husky letter; the empty, bald shell. The letter may have the germ of life in it, but it has no breath of spring to evoke it. They are winter seeds, as hard as the winter's soil, as icy as the winter's air. They will neither thaw nor germinate.

This letter preaching has the truth. But even divine truth has no life-giving energy alone. It must be energized by the Spirit, with all God's forces behind it. Truth unquickened by God's Spirit deadens as much as, or more than, error. It may be the truth, but without the Spirit, its shade and touch are deadly. Its truth is error, its light darkness. The letter preaching is unanointed, neither mellowed nor oiled by the Spirit.

> *Preaching must be energized by the Spirit,*
> *with all God's forces behind it.*

There may be tears, but tears cannot run God's machinery. Tears may be nothing but superficial expression. There may be feelings and earnestness, but it is the emotion of the actor and the earnestness of the attorney. The preacher may be moved by the kindling of his own sparks, be eloquent over his own exegesis, and be earnest in delivering the product of his own brain, but the message of his words may be dead and fruitless. The professor may imitate the fire of the apostles; brains and nerves may feign the work of God's Spirit; and by these forces the letter may glow and sparkle like an illuminated text, but the glow and sparkle will be as barren as the field sown with pearls. The death-dealing element lies behind the words, behind the sermon, behind the occasion, behind the manner, behind the action.

The great hindrance is in the preacher himself. He does not find within himself the mighty, life-creating forces. There may be no deficiency in his orthodoxy, honesty, cleanness, or earnestness, but somehow the man—the inner man—in his secret places has never broken down and surrendered to God. His inner life is not a great highway for the transmission of God's message, God's power.

Somehow, self—not God—rules in the holy of holiest. Somewhere, all unconscious to himself, some spiritual nonconductor has touched his inner being. The divine current has been arrested. His inner being has never felt its thorough spiritual bankruptcy, its utter powerlessness. He has never learned to cry out with an ineffable cry of self-despair and helplessness until God's power and fire come in, fill, purify, and empower. Self-esteem—self-ability in some wicked form—has defamed and violated the temple that should be held sacred for God.

Life-giving preaching costs the preacher much—death to self, crucifixion to the world, the travail of his own soul. Only crucified preaching can give life. Crucified preaching can come only from a crucified man.

THREE:

MAN'S MOST NOBLE EXERCISE

During this affliction I examined my life in relation to eternity closer than I had done when in the enjoyment of health. In the examination relative to the discharge of my duties toward my fellowmen as a man, a Christian minister, and an officer of the church, I stood approved by my own conscience. But, in relation to my Redeemer and Savior, the result was different. My returns of gratitude and loving obedience bear no proportion to my obligations for redeeming, persevering, and supporting me through the vicissitudes of life from infancy to old age. The coldness of my love to Him who first loved me and has done so much for me overwhelmed and confused me. And, to complete my unworthy character, I had not only neglected to improve the grace given to the extent of my duty and privilege but, for want of that improvement, had, while abounding in perplexing care and labor, declined from first zeal and love. I was confounded, humbled myself, implored mercy, and renewed my covenant to strive and devote myself unreservedly to the Lord.

—Bishop McKendree

The preaching that kills may be, and often is, orthodox—dogmatically, inviolably orthodox. We love orthodoxy. It is good. It is the best. It is the clean, clear-cut teaching of God's Word. It is the trophies won by truth in its conflict with error, the levees that faith has raised against the desolating floods of honest or reckless misbelief or unbelief. But, orthodoxy, clear and hard as a crystal, suspicious and militant, may be nothing but the letter, well shaped, well named, and well learned—the letter that kills. Nothing is so dead as a dead orthodoxy—too dead to speculate; too dead to think, study, or pray.

The preaching that kills may have insight and grasp of principle. It may be scholarly and critical in taste. It may be fluent in all the minor details of the derivation and grammar of the letter. It may be able to trim the letter into its perfect pattern and illuminate it as Plato and Cicero may have done. It may study the letter as a lawyer studies his textbooks to form his brief or to defend his case. And yet it may still be like a frost, a killing frost. Letter preaching may be eloquent, embellished with poetry and rhetoric, sprinkled with prayer, spiced with sensation, illuminated by genius, and yet these may merely be the chaste, costly mountings—the rare and beautiful flowers—that coffin the corpse.

The preaching that kills may be without scholarship. It may be unmarked by any freshness of thought or feeling, clothed in tasteless generalities or dull specialities. It may be slovenly, savoring neither closet nor study, graced neither by thought, nor expression, nor prayer. Under such preaching, how wide and utter the desolation! How profound the spiritual death!

This letter preaching deals with the surface and shadow of things, not the things themselves. It does not penetrate the inner part. It has no deep insight into, no strong grasp of, the hidden life of God's Word. It is true to the outside. But the outside is the hull that must be broken and penetrated to obtain the kernel. The letter may be dressed so as to attract and be fashionable, but the attraction is not toward God, nor is the fashion for heaven.

The failure is in the preacher. God has not made him. He has never been in the hands of God like clay in the hands of the potter. He has been busy working on the sermon, its thought and finish, its drawing and impressive forces. But the deep things of God have never been sought, studied, fathomed, experienced by him. He has never stood before the *"throne, high and lifted up"* (Isaiah 6:1). He has never heard the seraphim song or seen the vision, nor has he felt the rush of that awesome holiness. He has never cried out in utter abandon and despair under the sense of weakness and guilt. He has never had his life renewed or his heart touched, purged, and inflamed by the live coal from God's altar.

> *Without prayer,*
> *the preacher creates death and not life.*

His ministry may draw people to him, to the church, and to the form and ceremony. But no true drawings to God—no sweet, holy, divine communion—is induced. The church has been adorned, but not edified. It has pleased, but not sanctified. Life is suppressed. The city of our God becomes the city of the dead—the church a graveyard, not an embattled army. Praise and prayer are stifled; worship is dead. The preacher and the preaching have helped sin, not holiness. They have populated hell, not heaven.

Preaching that kills is prayerless preaching. Without prayer, the preacher creates death and not life. The preacher who is feeble in prayer is feeble in life-giving forces. The preacher who has retired from prayer as a conspicuous and largely prevailing element in his own character has stripped his preaching of its distinctive, life-giving power. There is and will be professional praying, but professional praying helps the preaching to do its deadly work. Professional praying chills and kills both preaching and praying.

Much of the lax devotion and lazy, irreverent attitudes in congregational praying is attributable to professional praying in the pulpit. The prayers in many pulpits are long, discursive, dry, and inane. Without anointing or heart, they fall like a killing frost on all the graces of worship.

Death-dealing prayers they are. Every trace of devotion has perished under their breath. The more dead they are, the longer they grow.

A plea for short praying, live praying, real heart praying, praying by the Holy Spirit—direct, specific, ardent, simple, anointed in the pulpit—is in order. A school to teach preachers how to pray, as God counts praying, would be more beneficial to true piety, true worship, and true preaching than all theological schools.

Stop! Pause! Consider! Where are we? What are we doing? Preaching to kill? Praying to kill?

Praying to God! The great God, the Maker of all worlds, the Judge of all men! What reverence, what simplicity, what sincerity, what truth in the inward parts is demanded! How real we must be! How hearty! Prayer to God: the most noble exercise, the loftiest effort of man, the most real thing! We will forever discard accursed preaching and prayer that kills, and we will do the real thing. Life-giving preaching brings the mightiest force to bear on heaven and earth. It draws on God's exhaustless and open treasure for the need and beggary of man.

FOUR:

TALKING TO GOD
FOR MEN

Let us often look at Brainerd, an American missionary to the native Indians, in the woods of America, pouring out his very soul before God for the perishing heathen without whose salvation nothing could make him happy. Prayer—secret, fervent, believing prayer—lies at the root of all personal godliness. A competent knowledge of the language where a missionary lives, a mild and winning temper, a heart given up to God in close religion—these, these are the attainments that, more than all knowledge or all other gifts, will fit us to become the instruments of God in the great work of human redemption. —Carey's Brotherhood

There are two extreme tendencies in the ministry. The one is to shut itself out from fellowship with the people. The monk and the hermit are illustrations of this. They shut themselves out from men to be more with God. They failed, of course. Our being with God is of use only as we expend its priceless benefits on men.

Too often Christian leaders shut themselves in their studies and become students—bookworms, Bible experts, and sermon makers. They are noted for literature, thought, and sermons; but the people and God, where are they? Out of heart, out of mind. Preachers who are great thinkers, great students, must be the greatest of pray-ers. If they are not, they will be the greatest of backsliders, heartless professionals, rationalistic, less than the least of preachers in God's estimate.

The other tendency is to popularize the ministry thoroughly. It is no longer God's, but a ministry of affairs, of the people. The minister does not pray because his mission is to the people. If he can move the people, create a sensation in favor of religion, and an interest in church work, he is satisfied. His personal relationship to God is no factor in his work. Prayer has little or no place in his plans. The disaster and ruin of such a ministry cannot be computed by earthly mathematics. What the preacher is in prayer to God—for himself, for his people—so is his power for real good to men, his true fruitfulness, and his true fidelity to God—for time and for eternity.

It is impossible for the preacher to keep his spirit in harmony with the divine nature of his high calling without much and constant prayer. It is a serious mistake to think that the preacher, by duty and laborious fidelity to the work and routine of the ministry, can keep himself trim and fit for his high calling. Even sermon making—incessant and taxing as an art, as a duty, as a work, or as a pleasure—will engross, harden, and estrange the heart from God by neglect of prayer. The scientist loses God in nature. The preacher may lose God in his sermon.

Prayer freshens the heart of the preacher, keeps it in tune with God and in sympathy with the people. It lifts his ministry out of the chilly air of a profession, revitalizes routine, and moves every wheel with the ease and power of a divine anointing.

Charles Spurgeon has said,

Of course the preacher is above all others distinguished as a man of prayer. He prays as an ordinary Christian, else he were a hypocrite. He prays more than ordinary Christians, else he were disqualified for the office he has undertaken. If you as ministers are not very prayerful, you are to be pitied. If you become lax in sacred devotion, not only will you need to be pitied, but your people also, and the day approaches in which you will be ashamed and confounded. All our libraries and studies are mere emptiness compared with our prayer closets. Our seasons of fasting and prayer at the tabernacle have been high days indeed; never has heaven's gate stood wider; never have our hearts been nearer the central glory.

The praying that makes a prayerful ministry is not the meager praying added only as flavoring to give it a pleasant taste. But the praying must be in the body, form, blood, and bones. Prayer is no petty duty put into a corner. It is no piece-meal performance made out of the fragments of time that have been snatched from business and other engagements of life. The best of our time, and the heart of our time and strength, must be given to prayer. This does not mean that the closet is absorbed in the study or swallowed up in the activities of ministerial duties. But it means the closet first, the study and activities second. In this way, both the study and the activities are freshened and made efficient by the closet.

Prayer that affects one's ministry must touch one's life. The praying that gives color and bent to character is no pleasant, hurried pastime. It must enter as strongly into the heart and life as Christ's *"strong crying and tears"* (Hebrews 5:7) did. It must draw the soul into an agony of desire as Paul's did. It must be an in-wrought fire and force like the *"effectual fervent prayer"* (James 5:16) of James. The praying must be of that quality that, when put into the golden censer and incensed before God, works mighty, spiritual struggles and revolutions.

Prayer is not a little habit pinned onto us while we were tied to our mother's apron strings. Neither is it a little, decent quarter-of-a-minute's grace said over an hour's dinner. But it is a most serious work of our most serious years. It engages more of time and appetite than our longest dinings or richest feasts. The prayer that makes much of our preaching must itself be made much of. The character of our praying will determine the character of our preaching. Light praying will make light preaching. Prayer makes preaching strong, gives it an anointing, and makes it stick. In every ministry that is righteously working for good, prayer has always been a serious business.

The preacher must primarily be a man of prayer. In the school of prayer, only the heart can learn to preach. No learning can make up for the failure to pray. No earnestness, no diligence, no study, no gifts will supply its lack.

Give the best of your time and strength to prayer.

Talking to men for God is a great thing, but talking to God for men is still greater. He who has not learned well how to talk to God for men will never talk well—with real success—to men for God. More than this, prayerless words, both in and out of the pulpit, are deadening.

FIVE:

HOW TO GET RESULTS FOR GOD

You know the value of prayer: It is precious beyond all price. Never, never neglect it. —Sir Thomas Buxton

Prayer is the first thing, the second thing, the third thing necessary to a minister. Pray; then, my dear brother, pray, pray, pray. —Edward Payson

Prayer, in the preacher's life, study, and pulpit, must be a conspicuous and all-impregnating force, an all-coloring ingredient. It must play no secondary role, be no mere coating. The preacher is called to be with his Lord *"all night in prayer"* (Luke 6:12). To train himself in self-denying prayer, he is charged to look to his Master, who, *"rising up a great while before day... went out, and departed into a solitary place, and there prayed"* (Mark 1:35).

The preacher's study ought to be a closet, a Bethel, an altar, a vision, and a ladder, so that every thought might ascend heavenward before it goes manward. Likewise, every part of the sermon should be scented by the air of heaven and made serious because God was in the study.

Just as the steam engine never moves until the fire is kindled, so preaching—with all its machinery, perfection, and polish—is at a dead standstill, spiritually, until prayer has kindled and created the steam. The texture, fineness, and strength of the sermon are rubbish unless the mighty impulse of prayer is in it, through it, and behind it. The preacher must, by prayer, put God in the sermon. The preacher must, by prayer, move God toward the people before he can move the people to God by his words. The preacher must have had audience and ready access to God before he can have access to the people. An open way to God for the preacher is the surest pledge of an open way to the people.

It is necessary to iterate and reiterate that prayer, as a mere habit, as a performance gone through by routine or in a professional way, is a dead and rotten thing. Such praying has no connection with the praying for which we plead. We stress true praying that engages and sets on fire every high element of the preacher's being. We emphasize prayer that is born of vital oneness with Christ in the fullness of the Holy Spirit and that springs from the deep, overflowing fountains of His tender compassion.

We seek prayer composed of undying solicitude for man's eternal good, and a consuming zeal for the glory of God. The preacher needs a thorough conviction of his difficult and delicate work and of his imperative need of God's mightiest help. Praying grounded on these solemn and profound convictions is the only true praying. Preaching backed by such praying is the only preaching that sows the seeds of eternal life in human hearts and builds men up for heaven.

It is true that, with little or no praying, there may be popular, pleasant, captivating, and intellectual preaching that avails a small amount of good. But the preaching that secures God's end must be born of prayer from the initial conception to the actual presentation. It must be delivered with the energy and spirit of prayer. It must be followed, made to germinate, and kept in vital force in the hearts of the hearers by the preacher's prayers, long after the occasion has passed.

We may excuse the spiritual poverty of our preaching in many ways, but the true reason for it is the lack of urgent prayer for God's presence in the power of the Holy Spirit. There are innumerable preachers who can deliver masterful sermons, but the effects are short-lived. They do not affect the regions of the spirit where the fearful war between God and Satan, heaven and hell, is being waged because they are not made powerfully militant and spiritually victorious by prayer.

The preachers who gain mighty results for God are the men who have prevailed in their pleadings with God *before* venturing to plead with men. The preachers who are the mightiest in their closets with God are the mightiest in their pulpits with men.

Preachers are human and are often exposed to or involved in the strong currents of human emotions and problems. Praying is spiritual work, and human nature does not like taxing, spiritual work. Human nature wants to sail to heaven under a pleasant breeze and a full, smooth sea. Prayer is humbling work. It abases intellect and pride, crucifies vainglory, and signals our spiritual bankruptcy. All these are hard for flesh and blood to bear. It is easier not to pray than to bear them, and so we come to one of the crying evils of these times, maybe of all times: little or no praying. Of these two evils, perhaps little praying is worse than no praying. Little praying is a kind of make-believe, a salve for the conscience, a farce, and a delusion.

> *God commits the keys of His kingdom to those who devote time to prayer.*

The little regard we give prayer is evident from the little time we spend in it. The time given to prayer by the average preacher scarcely counts in light of how the remaining time is delegated to daily chores. Not infrequently, the preacher's only praying is by his bedside—in his nightclothes, ready for bed. Perchance, he gets in a few additional prayers before he is dressed in the morning. How feeble, vain, and little is such praying compared with the time and energy devoted to praying by holy men in and out of the Bible! How poor and meager our petty, childish praying is beside the habits of the true men of God in all ages! God commits the keys of His kingdom to men who think that praying is their main business and who devote time to it according to this high estimate of its importance. By these men He works His spiritual wonders in this world. Great praying is the sign and seal of God's great leaders. It is the most earnest of the conquering forces with which God will crown their labors.

The preacher is commissioned to pray as well as to preach. His mission is incomplete if he does not do both well. The preacher may speak with all the eloquence of men and of angels, but unless he can pray with a faith that draws all heaven to his aid, his preaching will be *as sounding brass, or a tinkling cymbal*" (1 Corinthians 13:1). It will be useless for permanent, God-honoring, soul-saving purposes.

SIX:

GREAT MEN OF PRAYER

The principal cause of my leanness and unfruitfulness is due to an unaccountable backwardness to pray. I can write or read or converse or hear with a ready heart. But, prayer is more spiritual and inward than any of these, and the more spiritual any duty is, the more my carnal heart is apt to stray from it. Prayer and patience and faith are never disappointed. I have long since learned that if ever I was to be a minister, faith and prayer must make me one. When I can find my heart dissolved in prayer, everything else is comparatively easy.
—Richard Newton

It may be considered a spiritual axiom that, in every truly successful ministry, prayer is an evident and controlling force. It is evident and controlling in the life of the preacher, evident and controlling in the deep spirituality of his work. A ministry may be a very thought-provoking ministry without prayer. The preacher may secure fame and popularity without prayer. The whole machinery of the preacher's life and work may be run without the oil of prayer or with scarcely enough to grease one cog. But no ministry can be a spiritual one—securing holiness in the preacher and in his people—without prayer being made an evident and controlling force.

Indeed, the preacher who prays puts God into the work. God does not come into the preacher's work as a matter of course or on general principle, but He comes in by prayer and special urgency. It is as true of the preacher as of the penitent that God will be found the day that we seek Him with the whole heart. (See Jeremiah 29:13.) A prayerful ministry is the only ministry that brings the preacher into sympathy with the people. As essentially as prayer unites the human, it does the divine. A prayerful ministry is the only ministry qualified for the high offices and responsibilities of the preacher. Colleges, knowledge, books, theology, and preaching do not make a preacher, but praying does. The apostles' commission to preach was nothing until it was filled up by the praying that Pentecost resulted from. A prayerful minister has passed beyond the regions of the popular, beyond the man of mere affairs, secularities, and pulpit attractiveness. He has passed beyond the ecclesiastical organizer or leader and has entered into a more sublime and mightier region—the region of the spiritual.

Bible study should be bathed in prayer.

Holiness is the product of the prayerful preacher's work. Transfigured hearts and lives emblazon the reality of his work, its trueness and substantial nature. God is with him. His ministry is not based or built on worldly, surface principles. He is highly experienced and deeply learned in the things of God. His long, deep communings with God about His people, and the agony of his wrestling spirit, have crowned him as a prince in the things of God. The iciness of mere professionalism has long since melted under the intensity of his praying.

The superficial results of many a ministry and the deadness of others are to be found in the lack of praying. No ministry can succeed without much praying, and this praying must be fundamental, ever abiding, ever increasing. The text, the sermon, should be the result of prayer. The study

260 E. M. Bounds on Prayer & Spiritual Warfare

should be bathed in prayer, all its duties impregnated with prayer, its whole spirit the spirit of prayer.

"I am sorry that I have prayed so little" was the deathbed regret of one of God's chosen ones. That is a sad and remorseful regret for a preacher. "I want a life of greater, deeper, truer prayer," said the late Archbishop Tait.* So may we all say, and this may we all secure.

God's true preachers can be distinguished by one great feature: They are men of prayer. Often differing in many things, they have always had a common center. They may have started from different points and traveled by different roads, but they converge to one point: They are one in prayer. To them, God is the center of attraction, and prayer is the path that led to God. These men do not pray occasionally—not a little or at odd times— but they pray in such a way that their prayers enter into and shape their very characters. They pray so as to affect their own lives and the lives of others, and to cause the history of the church to influence the current of the times. They spend much time in prayer, not because they watch the shadow on the dial or the hands on the clock, but because it is to them so momentous and engaging a business that they can scarcely quit.

Prayer is to them what it was to Paul—a striving with earnest effort of soul. It is to them what it was to Jacob—a wrestling and prevailing. It is to them what it was to Christ—strong crying and tears. They pray *always with all prayer and supplication in the Spirit, and watching thereunto with all perseverance* (Ephesians 6:18). *"The effectual fervent prayer"* (James 5:16) has been, and still is, the mightiest weapon of God's mightiest soldiers.

The statement that James made in regard to Elijah—that he

> was a man subject to like passions as we are, and he prayed earnestly that it might not rain: and it rained not on the earth by the space of three years and six months. And he prayed again, and the heaven gave rain, and the earth brought forth her fruit. (vv. 17–18)

—applies to all prophets and preachers who have moved their generation for God, and shows the instrument by which they worked their wonders.

Many private prayers must be short. Public prayers, as a rule, ought to be short and condensed. Also, there is often need for spontaneous, exclamatory prayer. However, in our private communions with God, time is essential to the value of the prayer. Much time spent with God is the secret of all successful praying.

Prayer that produces a powerful influence is the mediate or immediate product of much time spent with God. Our short prayers are effective and efficient because long ones have preceded them. The short, prevailing prayer cannot be prayed by one who has not prevailed with God in a mightier struggle of long continuance. Jacob's victory of faith could not have been gained without that all-night wrestling.

God's acquaintance is not made hurriedly. He does not bestow His gifts on the casual or hasty comer and goer. To be much alone with God is the secret of knowing Him and of having influence with Him. God yields to the persistency of a faith that knows Him. He bestows His richest gifts on those who declare their desire for and appreciation of those gifts by the constancy as well as the earnestness of their importunity.

Christ, who in this as well as in other things is our example, spent many whole nights in prayer. His custom was to pray much. He had His habitual place to pray. Many long seasons of praying make up His history and character. Paul prayed day and night. Daniel's three daily prayers took time away from other important interests. David's morning, noon, and night praying was doubtless on many occasions very long and involved. While we have no specific account of the time these Bible saints spent in prayer, the indications are that they devoted much time to prayer, and on some occasions long seasons of praying were their custom.

We would not want anyone to think that the value of their prayers is measured by the clock. Our purpose is to impress on our minds the necessity of being much alone with God. And, if this feature has not been produced by our faith, then our faith is feeble and superficial.

The men who have most fully imitated Christ in their character and have most powerfully affected the world for Him have been men who spent so much time with God as to make it a notable feature of their lives. Charles Simeon, the English revivalist, devoted the hours from four to eight in the morning to God. John Wesley spent two hours a day in prayer. He began at four in the morning. One who knew him well wrote, "He thought prayer to be more his business than anything else, and I have seen him come out of his closet with a serenity of face next to shining."

John Fletcher, an English clergyman and author, stained the walls of his room by the breath of his prayers. Sometimes he would pray all night, always frequently and with great earnestness. His whole life was a life of prayer. "I would not rise from my seat," he said, "without lifting my heart to God." His greeting to a friend was always, "Do I meet you praying?" Martin Luther said, "If I fail to spend two hours in prayer each morning, the Devil gets the victory through the day. I have so much business, I cannot get on without spending three hours daily in prayer." He had a motto: "He that has prayed well has studied well."

Archbishop Leighton was so much alone with God that he seemed to be in a perpetual meditation. "Prayer and praise were his business and his pleasure," said his biographer. Bishop Thomas Ken was so much with God that his soul was said to be God-enamored. He was with God before the clock struck three every morning. Bishop Francis Asbury said, "I propose to rise at four o'clock as often as I can and spend two hours in prayer and meditation." Samuel Rutherford, the fragrance of whose piety is still rich, rose at three in the morning to meet God in prayer. Joseph Alleine, an English clergyman, arose at four o'clock for his business of praying until eight. If he heard other tradesmen going about their business before he was up, he would exclaim, "Oh, how this shames me! Does my Master not deserve more than theirs?" He who has well learned this practice of prayer draws to it at will, on sight, and with the acceptance of heaven's unfailing bank.

One of the holiest and most gifted of Scottish preachers said,

I ought to spend the best hours in communion with God. It is my noblest and most fruitful employment, and is not to be thrust into a corner. The morning hours, from six to eight, are the most uninterrupted and should be thus employed. After tea is my best hour, and that should be solemnly dedicated to God. I ought not to give up the good and old habit of prayer before going to bed; but guard must be kept against sleep. When I awake in the night, I ought to rise and pray. A little time after breakfast might be given to intercession.

This was the praying plan of Robert Murray McCheyne.

In their praying, the memorable Methodists shame us: "From four to five in the morning, private prayer; from five to six in the evening, private prayer."

John Welch, the holy and wonderful Scottish preacher, thought the day was ill spent if he did not spend eight or ten hours in prayer. He kept a blanket near his bed so that he might wrap himself when he arose to pray at night. His wife would complain when she found him lying on the ground weeping. He would reply, "O woman, I have the souls of three thousand to answer for, and I know not how it is with many of them!"

Bishop Wilson said, "In Henry Martyn's journal, the spirit of prayer— the time he devoted to the duty—and his fervor in it are the first things that strike me."

Edward Payson wore grooves into the hardwood floor where his knees pressed so often and so long. His biographer said,

> His continuing time in prayer, regardless of his circumstances, is the most noticeable fact in his history. It points out the duty of all who would rival his eminency. His distinguished and almost unin- terrupted success must no doubt be ascribed in a great measure to his ardent and persevering prayers.

The Marquis DeRenty, to whom Christ was most precious, ordered his servant to call him from his devotions at the end of half an hour. The servant at the time saw his face through an opening. It was marked with such holiness that he hated to arouse him. His lips were moving, but he was perfectly silent. The servant waited until an hour and a half had passed, then he called to him. The Marquis arose from his knees, saying that half an hour was so short when he was communing with Christ.

David Brainerd said, "I love to be alone in my cottage, where I can spend much time in prayer."

William Bramwell, famous in Methodist records for personal holiness, for his wonderful success in preaching, and for the marvelous answers to his prayers, would pray for hours at a time. He almost lived on his knees. He went over his circuits like a flame of fire. The fire was kindled by the time he spent in prayer. He often spent as much as four hours in a single season of prayer in retirement.

Bishop Andrewes spent the greatest part of five hours every day in prayer and devotion.

Sir Henry Havelock, a distinguished British soldier, always spent the first two hours of each day alone with God. If they were to break camp at six o'clock, he would rise at four.

Earl Cairns, an Irish lawyer, rose daily at six o'clock to spend an hour and a half in Bible study and prayer before conducting family worship at a quarter to eight.

Dr. Adoniram Judson's success in God's work, as an American missionary in India, is attributable to the fact that he gave much time to prayer. He said on this point,

> Arrange your affairs, if possible, so that you can leisurely devote two or three hours every day, not merely to devotional exercises, but to the very act of secret prayer and communion with God. Endeavor seven times a day to withdraw from business and company, and lift up your soul to God in private retirement. Begin the day by rising after midnight and devoting some time amid the silence and darkness of the night to this sacred work. Let the hour of opening dawn find you at the same work. Let the hours of nine, twelve, three, six, and nine at night witness the same. Be resolute in His cause. Make all practical sacrifices to maintain it. Consider that your time is short and that business and company must not be allowed to rob you of your God.

Impossible! we say. Fanatical directions! Yet Adoniram Judson impressed an empire for Christ. He laid the foundations of God's kingdom with imperishable granite in the heart of Burma. He was successful—one of the few men who mightily impressed the world for Christ. Many men of greater gifts and genius and learning than he have made no such impression. Their religious work resembles footsteps in the sand, but his work endures as if it were engraved in stone. The secret of its profoundness and endurance is found in the fact that he gave time to prayer. He kept the iron red-hot with prayer, and God's skill molded it with enduring power. No man who is not a man of prayer can do a great and enduring work for God, and no man can be a man of prayer without giving much time to prayer.

Is it true that prayer is simply a compliance with habit—dull and mechanical? Is it petty performance into which we are trained until tameness, shortness, and superficiality are its chief elements?

Canon Liddon, the English orator, has asked,

Is it true that prayer is, as is assumed, little else than the half-passive play of sentiment that flows languidly on through the minutes or hours of easy reverie? Let those who have really prayed give the answer. They sometimes describe prayer as a wrestling together with an unseen power that may last late into the night hours, or even to the break of day, as it was with Jacob. And, like St. Paul, they sometimes refer to common intercession as a concerted struggle. They have, when praying, their eyes fixed on the Great Intercessor in Gethsemane, on the drops of blood that fall to the ground in that agony of resignation and sacrifice. Importunity is the essence of successful prayer. Importunity means not dreaminess but sustained work. It is through prayer especially that the kingdom of heaven suffers violence and the violent take it by force.

It was a saying of the late Bishop Hamilton that:

a man is not likely to do much good in prayer if he does not begin by looking on it in the light of a work to be prepared for and persevered with all the earnestness that we bring to bear on subjects that in our opinion are at once more interesting and most necessary.

SEVEN:

"EARLY WILL I SEEK THEE"

I ought to pray before seeing anyone. Often when I sleep long, or meet with others early, it is eleven or twelve o'clock before I begin secret prayer. This is a wretched system. It is unscriptural. Christ arose before day and went into a solitary place. David said, "Early will I seek Thee," and "My voice shalt Thou hear in the morning." Family prayer loses much of its power and sweetness, and I can do no good to those who come to seek from me. My conscience feels guilty, my soul unfed, my lamp not trimmed. Then, when in secret prayer, the soul is often out of tune. I feel it is far better to begin with God—to see His face first—to get my soul near Him before it is near another.
—Robert Murray McCheyne

The men who have done the most for God in this world have been early on their knees. He who fritters away the early morning—its opportunity and freshness—in other pursuits than seeking God will make poor headway seeking Him the rest of the day. If God is not first in our thoughts and efforts in the morning, He will be last during the remainder of the day.

Behind this early rising and early praying is the intense desire that urges us into this pursuit after God. Morning listlessness indicates a listless heart. The heart that is lax in seeking God in the morning has lost its relish for God. David's heart was ardent after God. He hungered and thirsted after God. He sought God early, before daylight. The bed and sleep could not chain his soul in its eagerness after God. Christ longed for communion with God, and so, rising a great while before day, He would go out to the mountain to pray. The disciples, when fully awake and ashamed of their indulgence, knew where to find Him. We find that men who have mightily impressed the world for God were early in seeking after Him.

If God is not first in our thoughts and efforts in the morning, He will be last during the remainder of the day.

A desire for God that cannot break the chains of sleep is a weak thing and will do little good for God. The desire for God that stays far behind the Devil and the world at the beginning of the day will never catch up.

It is not simply getting up that has brought men to the front and has made them leaders in God's hosts. It is the overwhelming desire that stirs and breaks all self-indulgent chains that does so. But getting up gives vent, increase, and strength to the desire. If they had lain in bed and indulged themselves, the desire would have been quenched. The desire aroused them and inspired them to reach out for God.

This heeding and acting on the call gave their faith its grasp on God, and their hearts the sweetest and fullest revelation of Him. This strength of faith and fullness of revelation made them saints by eminence. The halo of their sainthood has come down to us, and we have entered into the enjoyment of their conquests. But we take our fill in enjoyment of them, and not in imitating them. We build their tombs and write their epitaphs but are careful not to follow their examples.

We need a generation of preachers who seek God and seek Him early. We need men who give the freshness and dew of effort to God and in return secure the freshness and fullness of His power, that He may be as the dew to them—full of gladness and strength through all the heat and labor of the day. Our laziness after God is our crying sin. The children of this world are far wiser than we. They are at it early and late. We do not seek God with ardor and diligence. No man receives God who does not follow hard after Him, and no soul follows hard after God who is not after Him in the early morning.

EIGHT:

THE SECRET OF POWER

There is a manifest want of spiritual influence on the ministry of the present day. I feel it in my own case, and I see it in that of others. I am afraid there is too much of a low, managing, contriving, maneuvering temper of mind among us. We are laying ourselves out more than is expedient to meet one man's taste and another man's prejudices. The ministry is a grand and holy affair, and it should find in us a simple habit of spirit and a holy but humble indifference to all consequences. The leading defect in Christian ministers is want of a devotional habit.   —Richard Cecil

Never was there a greater need for saintly men and women. More imperative still is the call for saintly, God-devoted preachers. The world moves with gigantic strides. Satan has his hold and rule on the world, and he labors to make all its movements subserve his ends. Christianity must do its best work, present its most attractive and perfect models. By every means, modern sainthood must be inspired by the loftiest ideals and by the largest possibilities through the Spirit.

Paul lived on his knees so that the Ephesian church might measure the heights, breadths, and depths of an immeasurable saintliness and *"be filled with all the fulness of God"* (Ephesians 3:19). Epaphras laid himself out with the exhaustive toil and strenuous conflict of fervent prayer so that the Colossian church might *"stand perfect and complete in all the will of God"* (Colossians 4:12). Everywhere and everything in apostolic times was growing so that the people of God might each and *"all come in the unity of the faith, and of the knowledge of the Son of God, unto a perfect man, unto the measure of the stature of the fulness of Christ"* (Ephesians 4:13).

No premium was given to those who fell short of God's calling. No encouragement was offered to an old babyhood. The babies were to grow. The old, instead of feebleness and infirmities, were to bear fruit in old age and be fat and flourishing. The most divine thing in Christianity is holy men and women.

No amount of money, genius, or culture can move things for God. Holiness energizing the soul—the whole man aflame with love, with desire for more faith, more prayer, more zeal, more consecration—this is the secret of power. These we need and must have, and men must be the incarnation of this God-inflamed devotedness. God's advance has been stayed, His cause crippled, His name dishonored for their lack. Genius (though the loftiest and most gifted), education (though the most learned and refined), position, dignity, place, and honored names cannot move this chariot of our God. It is a fiery one, and only fiery forces can move it.

The genius of a Milton fails. The imperial strength of a Leo fails. But Brainerd's spirit could move it. Brainerd's spirit was on fire for God, on fire for souls. Nothing earthly, worldly, or selfish was able to quench the intensity of this all-impelling and all-consuming force and name.

Prayer is the creator as well as the channel of devotion. The spirit of devotion is the spirit of prayer. Prayer and devotion are united as soul and body are united, as life and heart are united. There is no real prayer without devotion, no devotion without prayer. The preacher must be surrendered to God in the holiest devotion. He is not a professional man; his ministry is not a profession. It is a divine institution, a divine devotion. He is devoted to God. His aim, aspirations, and ambitions are for God and to God; as such, prayer is as essential as food is to life.

The preacher, above everything else, must be devoted to God. The preacher's relationship to God is the insignia and credentials of his ministry. These must be clear, conclusive, and unmistakable. His must not possess a common, superficial piety. If he does not excel in grace, he does not excel at all. If he does not preach by life, character, and conduct, he does not preach at all. His piety may be light, his preaching as soft and as sweet as music, yet its weight will be a feather's weight—visionary, fleeting as the morning cloud or the early dew.

Devotion to God—there is no substitute for this in the preacher's character and conduct. Devotion to a church, to opinions, to an organization, to orthodoxy—these are paltry, misleading, and vain when they become the source of inspiration. God must be the mainspring of the preacher's effort, the fountain and crown of all his toil. The name and honor of Jesus Christ, the advance of His cause, must be all in all. The preacher must have no inspiration but the name of Jesus Christ, no ambition but to have Him glorified, no toil but for Him. Then prayer will be the source of his illuminations, the means of perpetual advancement, the gauge of his success. The continual aim, the only ambition the preacher can cherish, is to have God with him.

Never has God's cause been in greater need of the perfect example of the possibilities of prayer than in this age. No age, no person, will demonstrate the gospel power except the ages or persons of deep and earnest prayer. A prayerless age will have only scant models of divine power. Prayerless hearts will never rise to these glorious heights. The age may be a better age than the past, but there is an infinite distance between the betterment of an age by the force of an advancing civilization and its betterment by the increase of holiness and Christlikeness by the energy of prayer.

The Jews were much better off when Christ came than in the ages before. It was the golden age of their pharisaical religion. Their golden, religious age crucified Christ. During the time before Christ, there was never more piety, never less praying; never more indulgence, never less sacrifice; never more idolatry, never less devotion to God; never more temple worship, never less God worship; never more lip service, never less heart service; never more churchgoers, never fewer saints.

It is the prayer force that makes saints. Holy characters are formed by the power of real praying. The more true saints, the more praying; the more praying, the more true saints.

God has now, and has had in the past, many of these devoted, prayerful preachers—men in whose lives prayer has been a mighty, controlling, conspicuous force. The world has felt their power. God has felt and honored their power. God's cause has moved mightily and swiftly by their prayers; holiness has shone out in their characters with a divine effulgence. God found one of the men he was looking for in David Brainerd, whose work and name have gone into history. He was no ordinary man but was capable of shining in any company. He was the peer of the wise and gifted ones, eminently suited to fill the most attractive pulpits and to labor among the most refined and cultured who were so anxious to secure him for their pastor.

> *The more true saints, the more praying; the more praying, the more true saints.*

Jonathan Edwards, the famous missionary and clergyman, bears testimony that Brainerd was:

> a young man of distinguished talents, had extraordinary knowledge of men and things, had rare conversational powers, excelled in his knowledge of theory, and was truly, for one so young, an extraordinary divine, and especially in all matters relating to practical Christianity. I never knew his equal of his age and standing for clear and accurate notions of the nature and essence of true Christianity. His manner in prayer was almost inimitable, such as I have very rarely known equaled. His learning was very considerable, and he had extraordinary gifts for the pulpit.

No more noble or inspiring a story has ever been recorded in earthly annals than that of David Brainerd. No miracle attests the truth of

Christianity with more divine force than the life and work of such a man. Alone in the savage wilds of America, struggling day and night with a mortal disease, unschooled in the care of souls, he fully established the worship of God. Hindered by having only a pagan interpreter through whom he preached to the Indians, strengthened by the Word of God in his heart and in his hands, he seized many for God's service. With his soul fired by the divine flame, and his mouth, heart, and mind always in prayer, he secured all the gracious results of his divine calling and devotion.

The Indians experienced a great change, from the very lowest form of an ignorant and debased heathenism to pure, devout, intelligent Christianity. All vice was reformed; the external duties of Christianity were at once embraced and acted on. Family prayer was set up; the Sabbath was instituted and joyously observed. The internal graces of Christianity were exhibited with growing sweetness and strength.

The cause of these results is found in David Brainerd himself—not in the conditions or accidents, but in the man Brainerd. He was God's man, acting for God, first and last and all the time. God could flow unhindered through him. The omnipotence of grace was neither arrested nor hindered by the conditions of his heart. The whole channel was broadened and cleaned out for God's fullest and most powerful passage. Thus God, with all His mighty forces, could come down on the hopeless, savage wilderness and transform it into His blooming and fruitful garden. Nothing is too hard for God to do if He can get the right kind of man to do it.

Brainerd lived a life of holiness and prayer. His diary is full of the record of his seasons of fasting, meditation, and retirement. The time he spent in private prayer amounted to many hours daily. "When I return home," he said,

> and give myself to meditation, prayer, and fasting, my soul longs for mortification, self-denial, humility, and divorcement from all things of the world. I have nothing to do with earth, but only labor in it honestly for God. I do not desire to live one minute for anything that earth can afford.

It was prayer that gave marvelous power to his life and ministry.

He prayed after this high order:

Feeling somewhat of the sweetness of communion with God and the constraining force of His love and how admirably it captivates the soul and makes all the desires and affections to center in God, I set apart this day for secret fasting and prayer to God, to direct and bless me with regard to the great work that I have in view of preaching the gospel and to ask that the Lord would return to me and show me the light of His countenance. I had little life and power in the forenoon. Near the middle of the afternoon, God enabled me to wrestle ardently in intercession for my absent friends, but just at night the Lord visited me marvelously in prayer. I think my soul was never in such agony before. I felt no restraint, for the treasures of divine grace were opened to me. I wrestled for absent friends, for the ingathering of souls, for multitudes of poor souls, and for many that I thought were the children of God, personally in many distant places. I was in such agony from sun half an hour high until near dark that I was wet all over with sweat, but yet it seemed to me I had done nothing. Oh, my dear Savior did sweat blood for poor souls! I longed for more compassion toward them. I felt still in a sweet frame, under a sense of divine love and grace, and went to bed in such a frame, with my heart set on God.

The men of mighty prayer are men of spiritual strength. Prayers never die. Brainerd's whole life was a life of prayer. By day and by night he prayed. Before preaching and after preaching, he prayed. Riding through the interminable solitudes of the forest he prayed. On his bed of straw he prayed. Retiring to the dense and lonely forest he prayed. Hour by hour, day after day, early morn and late at night, he was praying and fasting, pouring out his soul, interceding, communing with God. He was with God mightily in prayer and God was with him mightily. Because of this, he who is dead yet speaks and works and will continue to do so until the end comes. Among the glorious ones of that glorious day, he will be with the first.

Jonathan Edwards said of David Brainerd,

His life shows the right way to success in the works of the ministry. He sought it as the soldier seeks victory in a siege or battle; or as a man that runs a race for a great prize. Animated with love to Christ and souls, how did he labor? Always fervently, not only in word and doctrine, in public and in private, but in prayers by day and night, wrestling with God in secret and travailing in birth with unutterable groans and agonies, until Christ was formed in the hearts of the people to whom he was sent. Like a true son of Jacob, he persevered in wrestling through all the darkness of the night, until the breaking of the day!

NINE:

POWER THROUGH PRAYERS

For nothing reaches the heart but what is from the heart, or pierces the conscience but what comes from a living conscience.

—William Penn

In the morning I was more engaged in preparing the head than the heart. This has been frequently my error, and I have always felt the evil of it, especially in prayer. Reform it, then, O Lord! Enlarge my heart, and I shall preach.　　　　—Robert Murray McCheyne

A sermon that has more head infused into it than heart will not come home with efficacy to the hearers.　　　　—Richard Cecil

Prayer, with its manifold and many-sided forces, helps the mouth to utter the truth in its fullness and freedom. The preacher is to be prayed for because the preacher is made by prayer. The preacher's mouth is to be prayed for—his mouth is to be opened and filled by prayer. A holy mouth is made by praying, by much praying. A brave mouth is made by praying, by much praying. The church and the world, God and heaven, owe much to Paul's mouth. Paul's mouth owed its power to prayer.

How manifold, illimitable, valuable, and helpful prayer is to the preacher in so many ways, at so many points, in every way! One great value is that it helps his heart.

Praying makes the preacher a heart-preacher. Prayer puts the preacher's whole heart into the preacher's sermon. Prayer puts the preacher's sermon into the preacher's heart.

The heart makes the preacher. Men of great hearts are great preachers. Men of bad hearts may do a measure of good, but this is rare. The hireling and the stranger may help the sheep at some points, but it is the good shepherd with the good shepherd's heart who will bless the sheep and fill the full measure of the shepherd's place.

We have emphasized sermon preparation until we have lost sight of the important thing to be prepared—the heart. A prepared heart is much better than a prepared sermon. A prepared heart will *make* a prepared sermon.

Volumes have been written stating the detailed mechanics of sermon making. We have become possessed with the idea that this scaffolding is the building. The young preacher has been taught to exhaust all of his strength on the form, taste, and beauty of his sermon as a mechanical and intellectual product. We have thereby cultivated a vicious taste among the people and raised the clamor for talent instead of grace. We have emphasized eloquence instead of piety, rhetoric instead of revelation, reputation and brilliance instead of holiness. By it, we have lost the true idea of preaching. We have lost preaching power and the pungent conviction for sin. We have also lost the rich experience, the elevated Christian character, and the divine authority over consciences and lives that always results from genuine preaching.

> *We have emphasized eloquence instead of piety, reputation instead of holiness.*

It would not do to say that preachers study too much. Some of them do not study at all; others do not study enough. Many do not study the right way to show themselves workmen approved of God. (See 2 Timothy 2:15.) But our great lack is not in the head culture, but in heart culture. Not lack of knowledge, but lack of holiness is our sad and telling defect—not that we know too much, but that we do not meditate enough on God and His Word, and we do not watch and fast and pray enough. The heart is the great hindrance to our preaching. Words pregnant with divine truth do not find our hearts to be conducive. Arrested, they fall flat and powerless.

Can ambition that lusts after praise and position preach the gospel of Him who made Himself of no reputation and took on the form of a servant? (See Philippians 2:7.) Can the proud, the vain, the egotistical preach the gospel of Him who was meek and lowly? (See Matthew 11:29.) Can the bad-tempered, passionate, selfish, hard, worldly man preach the doctrine that is based on long-suffering, self-denial, and tenderness, and that imperatively demands separation from enmity and crucifixion to the world? Can the hireling—official, heartless, and perfunctory—preach the gospel that demands that the Shepherd give His life for the sheep? Can the covetous man, who counts salary and money, preach the gospel until he has cleansed his heart and can say in the spirit of Christ and Paul in the words of Wesley, "I count it dung and dross; I trample it under my feet; I (yet not I, but the grace of God in me) esteem it just as the mire of the streets; I desire it not; I seek it not"? (See Philippians 3:7–9.)

God's revelation does not need the light of human genius, the polish and strength of human culture, the brilliancy of human thought, the force of human brains to adorn or enforce it. But it does demand the simplicity, docility, humility, and faith of a child's heart.

It was this surrender and subordination of intellect and genius to the divine and spiritual forces that made Paul peerless among the apostles. It was this that gave Wesley his power.

Our great need is heart preparation. Again, Luther held it as an axiom: "He who has prayed well has studied well."

I am not saying that men are not to think and use their intellects, but he who cultivates his heart the most will use his intellect the best. I am not saying that preachers should not be students, but I am saying that their great study should be the Bible; and, he who has kept his heart with diligence studies the Bible best. I am not saying that the preacher should not know men, but he who has fathomed the depths and intricacies of his own heart will be more adept in the knowledge of human nature.

I am saying that while the channel of preaching is the mind, its fountain is the heart. You may broaden and deepen the channel, but if you do not look well to the purity and depth of the fountain, you will have a dry or polluted channel. Almost any man of average intelligence has sense enough to preach the gospel, but very few have grace enough to do so. He who has struggled with his own heart and conquered it; who has taught it humility, faith, love, truth, mercy, sympathy, courage; who can pour the rich treasures of the human heart thus trained all surcharged with the power of the gospel, on the consciences of his hearers—such a person will be the truest, most successful preacher in the esteem of his Lord.

The heart is the savior of the world. Heads do not save. Genius, brains, brilliancy, strength, natural gifts do not save. The gospel flows through hearts. All the mightiest forces are heart forces. All the sweetest and loveliest graces are heart graces. Great hearts make great characters; great hearts make divine characters. God is love. There is nothing greater than love, nothing greater than God. Hearts make heaven; heaven is love. There is nothing higher, nothing sweeter, than heaven. It is the heart and not the head that makes God's great preachers. The heart counts for much in every way in Christianity. The heart must speak from the pulpit. The heart must hear in the pew. In fact, we serve God with our hearts. Head homage does not conduct current in heaven.

We believe that one of the serious and most popular errors of the modern pulpit is the inclusion of more thought than prayer—more head than heart—in its sermons. Big hearts make big preachers; good hearts make good preachers. A theological school to enlarge and cultivate the heart is the golden desire of the gospel. The pastor binds his people to him and rules his people by his heart. They may admire his gifts; they may be proud of his ability; they may be affected for the time by his sermons. But the stronghold of his power is his heart. The throne of his power is his heart. His scepter is love.

The Good Shepherd gives His life for the sheep. Heads never make martyrs. It is the heart that surrenders the life to love and fidelity. It takes great courage to be a faithful pastor, but the heart alone can supply this courage. Gifts and genius may be brave, but they are the gifts and genius of the heart and not of the head.

It is easier to fill the head than it is to prepare the heart. It is easier to make a brain sermon than a heart sermon. It was heart that drew the Son of God from heaven. It is heart that will draw men to heaven. The world needs men of heart to sympathize with its woe, to kiss away its sorrows, to feel compassion for its misery, and to alleviate its pain. Christ was eminently the Man of Sorrows (see Isaiah 53:3) because He was preeminently the Man of Heart.

"Give Me your heart" is God's requisition of men. "Give me your heart!" is man's demand of man.

A professional ministry is a heartless ministry. When salary plays a great part in the ministry, the heart plays little part. We may make preaching our business and not put our hearts in the business. He who puts self to the front in his preaching puts heart to the rear. He who does not sow with his heart in his study will never reap a harvest for God. The closet is the heart's study. We will learn more about how to preach and what to preach there than we can learn in our libraries. *"Jesus wept"* (John 11:35) is the shortest and biggest verse in the Bible. It is he who goes forth weeping (not preaching great sermons), *"bearing precious seed, [who will] doubtless come again with rejoicing, bringing his sheaves with him"* (Psalm 126:6).

Praying gives sense, brings wisdom, and broadens and strengthens the mind. The prayer closet is a perfect school teacher and schoolhouse for the preacher. Thought is not only brightened and clarified in prayer, but thought is also born in prayer. We can learn more in an hour of praying, when truly praying, than from many hours of rigorous study. There are books in the closet that can be found and read nowhere else. Revelations are made in the closet that are made nowhere else.

TEN:

UNDER THE DEW
OF HEAVEN

One bright blessing that private prayer brings down upon the ministry is an indescribable and inimitable something—an anointing from the Holy One. If the anointing that we bear comes not from the Lord of Hosts, we are deceivers, since only in prayer can we obtain it. Let us continue instant, constant, fervent in supplication. Let your fleece lie on the threshing-floor of supplication until it is wet with the dew of heaven. —Charles Spurgeon

Alexander Knox, a Christian philosopher in the days of Wesley, during the time of the great Methodist revival, wrote,

It is strange and lamentable, but I truly believe that except among Methodists and Methodistic clergymen, there is not much interesting preaching in England. The clergy, too generally, have absolutely lost the art. When I was in this country two years ago, I did not hear a single preacher who taught me as my own great masters did, but such as are deemed Methodistic. And I now despair of getting an atom of heart instruction from any other quarter. The Methodist preachers (although I may not always approve of all their expressions) do most assuredly diffuse this religion, true and undefiled.

I felt real pleasure last Sunday. I can bear witness that the preacher did at once speak the words of truth and soberness. There was no eloquence—the honest man never dreamed of such a thing—but there was far better: a cordial communication of vitalized truth. I say *vitalized* because what he declared to others it was impossible not to feel he lived himself. He was truly anointed.

This anointing is the art of preaching. The preacher who never had this anointing never had the art of preaching. The preacher who has lost this anointing has lost the art of preaching. Whatever other arts he may have and retain—the art of sermon making, the art of eloquence, the art of great, clear thinking, the art of pleasing an audience—he has lost the divine art of preaching. This anointing makes God's truth powerful and interesting, draws, attracts, edifies, convicts, and saves.

This same anointing, or unction, vitalizes God's revealed truth, makes it living and life-giving. God's truth, spoken without this anointing, is too light; it is dead and deadening. Though abounding in truth, though weighty with thought, though sparkling with rhetoric, though pointed by logic, though powerful by earnestness, without this divine anointing it issues death, not life. Spurgeon has said,

I wonder how long we might beat our brains before we could plainly put into words what is meant by preaching with unction. Yet he who preaches knows its presence, and he who hears soon detects its absence. Samaria, in famine, typifies a discourse without it. Jerusalem, with her feast of fat things, full of marrow (see Isaiah 25:6), may represent a sermon enriched with it. Everyone knows what the freshness of the morning is when orient pearls abound on every blade of grass, but who can describe it, much less produce it of itself? Such is the mystery of spiritual anointing. We know, but we cannot tell others, what it is. It is as easy as it is foolish to counterfeit it. Unction is a thing that you cannot manufacture, and its counterfeits are worse than worthless. Yet it is, in itself, priceless and beyond measure needful if you wish to edify believers and bring sinners to Christ.

Anointing is that indefinable, indescribable something that an old, renowned Scottish preacher explained in this manner:

There is sometimes something in preaching that cannot be described either in matter or expression, and cannot be described what it is, or from where it comes, but with a sweet violence it pierces into the heart and affections and comes immediately from the Lord; but if there is any way to obtain such a thing it is by the heavenly disposition of the speaker.

We call it *unction*, or *anointing*. It is this anointing that makes the Word of God

quick, and powerful, and sharper than any twoedged sword, piercing even to the dividing asunder of soul and spirit, and of the joints and marrow, and...a discerner of the thoughts and intents of the heart.
(Hebrews 4:12)

It is this anointing that gives the words of the preacher such point, sharpness, and power, and that creates such friction and stir in many a dead congregation.

The same truths have been told in the strictness of the letter, smooth as human oil could make them. But no signs of life—not a pulse—are evident. All is as peaceful as the grave and equally as dead. The same preacher, in the meanwhile, receives a baptism of this anointing; divine inspiration is on him. The letter of the Word has been embellished and fired by this mysterious power, and the throbbings of life begin—life that receives or life that resists. The anointing pervades and convicts the conscience and breaks the heart.

This divine anointing is the feature that separates and distinguishes true gospel preaching from all other methods of presenting the truth. It creates a wide spiritual chasm between the preacher who has it and the one who does not. It supports and impregnates revealed truth with all the energy of God. Anointing is simply allowing God to be in His own Word and on His own preacher. By mighty, great, and continual prayerfulness, it is the preacher's entire potential. It inspires and clarifies his intellect, gives insight, grasp, and projecting power. It gives the preacher heart power, which is greater than head power, and tenderness, purity, and force flow from the heart by it. Growth, freedom, fullness of thought, directness, and simplicity of utterance are the fruits of this anointing.

Often, earnestness is mistaken for this anointing. He who has the divine anointing will be earnest in the very spiritual nature of things, but there may be a great deal of earnestness without the least bit of anointing.

Earnestness and anointing look alike from some points of view. Earnestness may be readily and without detection substituted or mistaken for unction. It requires a spiritual eye and a spiritual taste to discriminate.

Earnestness may be sincere, serious, ardent, and persevering. It goes at a thing with a good will, pursues it with perseverance, and urges it with vehemence—puts force in it. But all these forces do not rise higher than the mere human. The *man* is in it, the whole man, with all that he has of will and heart, of brains and genius, of planning, working, and talking. He has set himself to some purpose that has mastered him, and he pursues to master it. There may be none of God in it. There may be little of God in it because there is so much of the man in it. He may present pleas in support of his earnest purpose that please, touch, move, or overwhelm with the conviction of their importance. In all this earnestness, he may move along earthly ways, being propelled by human forces only. Its altar is made by earthly hands, and its fire kindled by earthly flames.

It was once said of a rather famous preacher of gifts, who interpreted Scripture to fit his fancy or purpose, that he "grows very eloquent over his own exegesis." Oftentimes men grow exceedingly earnest over their own plans or movements. Earnestness may be selfishness in disguise.

What, then, is the anointing? It is the indefinable aspect of preaching that makes it preaching. It is that which distinguishes and separates preaching from all mere human speeches and presentations. It is the divine quality in preaching. It makes the preaching sharp to those who need sharpness. It cleanses as the dew those who need to be refreshed. It is well described as

> ...a two-edged sword
> Of heavenly temper keen.
> And double were the wounds it made
> Where'er it glanced between.
> 'Twas death to sin; 'twas life
> To all who mourned for sin.
> It kindled and it silenced strife,
> Made war and peace within.

This anointing comes to the preacher not in the study but in the closet. It is heaven's distillation in answer to prayer. It is the sweetest exhalation of the Holy Spirit. It impregnates, suffuses, softens, percolates, cuts, and soothes. It carries the Word like dynamite. It makes the Word a soother, an arraigner, a revealer, a searcher. It makes the hearer a culprit or a saint, makes him weep like a child and live like a giant. It opens his heart and his purse as gently, yet as strongly, as the spring opens the leaves. This anointing is not the gift of genius. It is not found in the halls of learning. No eloquence can woo it. No industry can win it. No orthodox hands can bestow it. It is the gift of God, the signet sent to His own messengers. It is heaven's knighthood given to the chosen, true, and brave ones who have sought this anointed honor through many hours of tearful, wrestling prayer.

Earnestness is good and impressive; genius is gifted and great; thought kindles and inspires, but it takes a divine endowment—a more powerful energy than earnestness, genius, or thought—to break the chains of sin. It takes more to win estranged and depraved hearts to God, to repair the breaches, and to restore the church to her old ways of purity and power. Nothing but holy anointing can do this.

Nothing but holy anointing can win depraved hearts to God.

In the Christian system, unction is the anointing of the Holy Spirit, separating the believer for God's work and qualifying him for it. This anointing is the one divine enablement by which the preacher accomplishes the unique and saving ends of preaching. Without it, no true spiritual results are accomplished. The results and forces in preaching do not rise above the results of unsanctified speech. Without anointing, the preacher is as potent as the pulpit itself.

This divine anointing on the preacher generates, through the Word of God, the spiritual results that flow from the gospel. Without this anointing, these results are not secured. Many pleasant impressions may be made, but these all fall far below the ends of gospel preaching. This anointing may be simulated; there are many things that look like it. There are many results that resemble its effects, but they are foreign to its results and to its nature. The fervor or softness excited by a moving or emotional sermon may look like the movements of the divine anointing, but it has no pungent, penetrating, heartbreaking force. No heart-healing balm exists in these superficial, sympathetic, emotional movements. They are not radical—neither sin-searching nor sin-curing.

This divine anointing is the one distinguishing feature that separates true gospel preaching from all other methods of presenting truth. It supports and interpenetrates the revealed truth with all the force of God. It illumines the Word; it broadens and enriches the intellect, and empowers it to grasp and understand the Word. It qualifies the preacher's heart and brings it to that condition of tenderness, purity, force, and light necessary to secure the highest results. This anointing gives the preacher liberty and enlargement of thought and soul—a freedom, fullness, and directness of utterance that can be secured by no other process.

Without this anointing on the preacher, the gospel has no more power to propagate itself than any other system of truth. This is the seal of its divinity. Anointing on the preacher puts God in the gospel. Without the anointing, God is absent, and the gospel is left to the low and unsatisfactory forces that the ingenuity, interest, or talents of men can devise to enforce and project its doctrines.

It is in this element that the pulpit more often fails than in any other element. It lapses just at this all-important point. It may be full of knowledge, brilliance, eloquence, and charm. Sensationalism, or even less offensive methods, may attract large crowds. Mental power may impress and enforce truth with all its resources. But without this anointing each and all of these will merely be like the fretful assault of the waters on a Gibraltar. Spray and foam may cover and spangle, but the rocks are still there, unimpressed and immovable. The human heart can no more be rid of its hardness and sin by these human forces than these rocks can be swept away by the ocean's ceaseless flow.

This anointing is the consecration force, and its presence the continuous test of that consecration. It is this divine anointing of the preacher that secures his consecration to God and His work. Other forces and motives may call him to the work, but only this is consecration. A separation to God's work by the power of the Holy Spirit is the only consecration recognized by God as legitimate.

The anointing—the divine unction, this heavenly anointing—is what the pulpit needs and must have. This divine and heavenly oil put on it by the imposition of God's hand must soften and lubricate the whole man— heart, head, and spirit. It must mightily separate him from all earthly, secular, worldly, selfish motives and aims, separating him to everything that is pure and Godlike.

It is the presence of this anointing in the preacher that creates the stir and friction in many a congregation. The same truths have been told in the strictness of the letter, but no effect has been seen, no pain or pulsation felt. All is as quiet as a graveyard. Another preacher comes, and this mysterious influence is on him. The letter of the Word has been tried by the Spirit; the throes of a mighty movement are felt. It is the unction that pervades and stirs the conscience and breaks the heart. Unctionless preaching makes everything hard, dry, acrid, and dead.

This anointing is more than a memory or an era of the past. It is a present, realized, conscious fact. It belongs to the experience of the man as well as to his preaching. It is that which transforms him into the image of his divine Master, as well as that by which he declares the truths of Christ with power. It is so much the power in the ministry that it makes all else seem feeble and vain without it. By its presence, it atones for the absence of all other forces.

This anointing is not an inalienable gift; it is a conditional gift. Its presence is perpetuated and increased by the same process by which it was at first secured—by unceasing prayer to God, by impassioned desires after

God, by seeking it with tireless zeal, by deeming all else loss and failure without it.

This anointing comes directly from God in answer to prayer. Only praying hearts are filled with this holy oil. Only praying lips are anointed with this divine unction.

Prayer, much prayer, is the price of the anointing on preaching. Prayer, much prayer, is the sole condition of keeping this anointing. Without unceasing prayer, the anointing never comes to the preacher. Without perseverance in prayer, the anointing, like overkept manna, breeds worms.

ELEVEN:

THE EXAMPLE OF THE APOSTLES

Give me one hundred preachers who fear nothing but sin and desire nothing but God, and I care not a straw whether they be clergymen or laymen; such alone will shake the gates of hell and set up the kingdom of heaven on earth. God does nothing but in answer to prayer.

—John Wesley

The apostles knew the necessity and worth of prayer to their ministry. They knew that their high commission as apostles—instead of relieving them from the necessity of prayer—committed them to it by a more urgent need. They were exceedingly jealous when some other important work exhausted their time and prevented their praying as they ought. As a result, they appointed laymen to look after the delicate and engrossing duties of ministering to the poor so that they (the apostles) might, unhindered, give themselves *continually to prayer, and to the ministry of the word*" (Acts 6:4). Prayer was put first, and their relation to prayer was strongly stated—they gave themselves to it. They made a business of it, surrendering themselves to praying, putting fervor, urgency, perseverance, and time into it.

How holy, apostolic men devoted themselves to this divine work of prayer! *"Night and day praying exceedingly"* (1 Thessalonians 3:10), said Paul. The consensus of apostolic devotedness is, "We will give ourselves continually to prayer."

How these New Testament preachers laid themselves out in prayer for God's people! How they put God in full force into their churches by their praying! These holy apostles did not vainly think that they had met their high and solemn duties by faithfully delivering God's Word. But, their preaching was made effective and lasting by the fervor and insistence of their praying.

Apostolic praying was as taxing, toilsome, and imperative as apostolic preaching. They prayed mightily day and night to bring their people to the highest regions of faith and holiness. They prayed even mightier still to hold them to this high spiritual altitude. The preacher who has never learned in the school of Christ the high and divine art of intercession for his people will never learn the art of preaching. Though homiletics be poured into him by the ton, and though he may be the most gifted genius in sermon making and sermon delivery, he will never preach as the apostles did if he does not pray as they did.

The prayers of apostolic, saintly leaders do much in making saints of those who are not apostles. If the church leaders in later years had been as particular and fervent in praying for their people as the apostles were, the sad, dark times of worldliness and apostasy would not have marred the history of the world and arrested the advance of the church. Apostolic praying makes apostolic saints and keeps apostolic times of purity and power in the church.

TWELVE:

WHAT GOD
WOULD HAVE

If some Christians who have been complaining of their ministers had said and acted less before men and had applied themselves with all their might to cry to God for their ministers—had, as it were, risen and stormed heaven with their humble, fervent, and incessant prayers for them—they would have been much more in the way of success.   —Jonathan Edwards

Somehow the practice of praying for the preacher has fallen into disuse or become discounted. Occasionally we have heard the practice referred to as a discredit of the ministry. Some think of it as being a public declaration of the inefficiency of the ministry. Perhaps praying for the preacher offends the pride of learning and self-sufficiency. But these *ought* to be offended and rebuked if a ministry is so derelict as to allow them to exist.

Prayer, to the preacher, is not simply the duty or a privilege of his profession. It is a necessity. Air is not more necessary to the lungs than prayer is to the preacher. It is absolutely necessary for the preacher to pray. It is an absolute necessity that the preacher be prayed for. These two propositions are wedded into a union that ought never to know any divorce. *The preacher must pray; the preacher must be prayed for.* It will take all the praying he can do, and all the praying he can get done, to meet the fearful responsibilities and gain the largest, truest success in his great work. Next to cultivation of the spirit and the presence of prayer in his own life—both in their most intense forms—the true preacher greatly covets the prayers of God's people.

The more holy a man is, the more he values prayer. He sees clearly that God gives Himself to the praying ones and that the measure of God's revelation to the soul is proportionate to the soul's longing, importunate prayer for God. Salvation never finds its way to a prayerless heart. The Holy Spirit never abides in a prayerless spirit. Preaching never edifies a prayerless soul. Christ knows nothing of prayerless Christians. The gospel cannot be extended by a prayerless preacher. Gifts, talents, education, eloquence, and God's call cannot lessen the demand of prayer but only intensify the necessity for the preacher to pray and to be prayed for. The more the preacher's eyes are opened to the nature, responsibility, and difficulties in his work, the more he will see, and if he is a true preacher, he will feel the necessity of prayer even more strongly. He will not only feel the increasing demand to pray himself, but he will also feel compelled to call on others to help him by their prayers.

What loftiness of soul, what purity and elevation of motive, what unselfishness, what self-sacrifice, what exhaustive toil, what enthusiasm of spirit, what divine sensitivity are necessary to be an intercessor for men!

The preacher is to lay himself out in prayer for his people—not that they might simply be saved but that they might be mightily saved. The apostles laid themselves out in prayer so that the believers' sights might be perfect. They did this not because the people lacked a meager relish for the things of God but so that they *might be filled with all the fulness of God* (Ephesians 3:19). Paul did not rely on his apostolic preaching to secure this end. For this cause, he bowed his knees to the Father of our Lord Jesus Christ. (See verse 14.) Paul's praying carried Paul's converts farther along the highway of sainthood than Paul's preaching did.

Epaphras did as much or more by prayer for the Colossian saints than by his preaching. He labored fervently, always in prayer for them, that they might *"stand perfect and complete in all the will of God"* (Colossians 4:12).

Preachers are preeminently God's leaders. They are primarily responsible for the condition of the church. They shape its character, give tone and direction to its life.

Much depends on these leaders. They shape the times and the institutions. The church is divine; the treasure it encases is heavenly. But it bears the imprint of the human. The treasure is in earthen vessels, and it tastes of the vessel. The church of God makes, or is made by, its leaders. In any case, the church will be what its leaders are: spiritual if they are spiritual, secular if they are secular, conglomerate if its leaders are a mixture of the two.

Israel's kings gave character to Israel's piety. A church rarely revolts against or rises above the religion of its leaders. Strong spiritual leaders—men of holy might—at the lead are tokens of God's favor. Disaster and weakness follow the wake of feeble or worldly leaders. The Israelites fell low when God gave them children for princes and babes to rule over them. The prophets predict unhappiness when children oppress God's Israel and enemies rule over them.

Times of spiritual leadership are times of great spiritual prosperity to the church. Prayer is one of the eminent characteristics of strong spiritual leadership. Men of mighty prayer are men of might, and they shape the outcome of things. Their power with God has the conquering tread.

How can a man who does not get his message fresh from God in the closet expect to preach? How can he preach without having his faith quickened, his vision cleared, and his heart warmed by his closeting with God? Alas for the pulpit lips that are untouched by this closet flame! (See Isaiah 6:1–7.) They will forever be dry and without the anointing. Divine truths will never come with power from such lips. As far as the real interests of Christianity are concerned, a pulpit without a prayer closet will always be a barren thing.

A preacher may preach in an official, entertaining, or learned way, without prayer, but there is an immeasurable distance between this kind of preaching and the sowing of God's precious seed with holy hands and prayerful, weeping hearts.

Paul was an illustration of these things. If any man could extend or advance the gospel by personal force, by brainpower, by culture, by personal grace, by God's apostolic commission, God's extraordinary call, that man was Paul. Paul exemplified the fact that the preacher must be a man given to prayer. Paul preeminently demonstrated that the true apostolic preacher must have the prayers of other good people to give to his ministry its full quota of success. Paul asked, he coveted, he pleaded in an impassioned way for the help of all God's saints.

Paul knew that in the spiritual realm—as elsewhere—in union there is strength. He knew that the concentration and aggregation of faith, desire, and prayer increased the volume of spiritual force until it became overwhelming and irresistible in its power. Units of prayer combined, like drops of water, make an ocean that defies resistance. So Paul, with his clear and full understanding of spiritual dynamics, decided to make his ministry as impressive, eternal, and irresistible as the ocean by gathering all the scattered units of prayer and precipitating them on his ministry.

The reason for Paul's prominence in labors and results, and his impact on the church and the world, may be that he was able to center more prayer on himself and his ministry than others were. To his brethren at Rome he wrote,

Now I beseech you, brethren, for the Lord Jesus Christ's sake, and for the love of the Spirit, that ye strive together with me in your prayers to God for me. (Romans 15:30)

To the Ephesians he said,

Praying always with all prayer and supplication in the Spirit, and watching thereunto with all perseverance and supplication for all saints; and for me, that utterance may be given unto me, that I may open my mouth boldly, to make known the mystery of the gospel. (Ephesians 6:18–19)

To the Colossians he emphasized,

Withal praying also for us, that God would open unto us a door of utterance, to speak the mystery of Christ, for which I am also in bonds: that I may make it manifest, as I ought to speak. (Colossians 4:3–4)

To the Thessalonians he said sharply and strongly, *"Brethren, pray for us"* (1 Thessalonians 5:25).

Paul called on the Corinthian church to help him: *"Ye also helping together by prayer for us"* (2 Corinthians 1:11). This was to be part of their work. They were to apply themselves vigorously to the helping hand of prayer.

Paul, in an additional and closing charge to the Thessalonian church about the importance and necessity of their prayers, said,

Finally, brethren, pray for us, that the word of the Lord may have free course, and be glorified, even as it is with you: and that we may be delivered from unreasonable and wicked men.

(2 Thessalonians 3:1–2)

He impressed upon the Philippians that all his trials and opposition could be made subservient to the spread of the gospel by the efficiency of their prayers for him. (See Philippians 1:12–20.) Philemon was to prepare a lodging for him, for through Philemon's prayer, Paul was to be his guest. (See Philemon 22.)

Paul's attitude about this question illustrates his humility and his deep insight into the spiritual forces that project the gospel. More than this, it teaches a lesson for all times—that if Paul was so dependent on the prayers of God's saints to give his ministry success, how much greater the necessity that the prayers of God's saints be centered on the ministry of today!

Paul did not feel that this urgent plea for prayer lowered his dignity, lessened his influence, or depreciated his piety. What if it did? Let dignity go; let influence be destroyed; let his reputation be marred—he must have their prayers. Called, commissioned, chief of the apostles as he was, all his equipment was imperfect without the prayers of his people. He wrote letters everywhere, urging them to pray for him. Do you pray for your preacher? Do you pray for him in secret? Public prayers are of little worth unless they are founded on or followed up by private praying. The praying ones are to the preacher as Aaron and Hur were to Moses. They hold up his hands and decide the issue that is so fiercely raging around them.

The plea and purpose of the apostles were to stir the church to praying. They did not ignore the grace of cheerful giving. They were not ignorant of the place that religious activity and work occupied in the spiritual life. But not one or all of these, in apostolic estimate or urgency, could at all compare in necessity and importance to prayer. The most sacred and urgent pleas were used—the most fervid exhortation—the most comprehensive and arousing words were uttered, to enforce the all-important obligation and necessity of prayer.

"Put the saints everywhere to praying" is the burden of the apostolic effort and the keynote of apostolic success. Jesus Christ strove to do this in the days of His personal ministry. As He was moved by infinite compassion at the ripened fields of the earth perishing for lack of laborers—and pausing in His own praying—He tried to awaken the sensibilities of His disciples to the duty of prayer as He charged them, *Pray ye therefore the Lord of the harvest, that he will send forth labourers into his harvest*" (Matthew 9:38). The Bible also says, *"And he spake a parable unto them to this end, that men ought always to pray, and not to faint"* (Luke 18:1).

Our devotions are not measured by the clock, but time is of their essence. The ability to wait and stay and press essentially belongs to our fellowship with God. Haste, everywhere unseeming and damaging, is often, to an alarming extent, a part of the great business of communion with God. Short devotions are the bane of deep piety. Calmness, grasp, and strength are never the companions of haste. Short devotions deplete spiritual vigor, arrest spiritual progress, sap spiritual foundations, and blight the root and bloom of the spiritual life. They are the prolific source of backsliding, the sure indication of a superficial piety; they deceive, blight, rot the seed, and impoverish the soil.

It is true that Bible prayers in word and print are short, but the praying men of the Bible were with God through many sweet and holy wrestling hours. They won by few words but long waiting. The prayers Moses recorded may be short, but Moses prayed to God with fastings and mighty cryings for forty days and nights.

The statement of Elijah's praying may be condensed to a few brief paragraphs. But doubtless, Elijah, who prayed earnestly, spent many hours of fiery struggle and lofty communion with God before he could, with assured boldness, say to Ahab, *"There shall not be dew nor rain these years, but according to my word"* (1 Kings 17:1). The Bible record of Paul's prayers is short, but Paul prayed exceedingly night and day. (See 1 Thessalonians 3:10.)

To be little with God is to be little for God.

The Lord's Prayer is a divine epitome for infant lips, but Christ Jesus often prayed all night before His work was done. His all-night and long-sustained devotions gave His work its finish and perfection, and His character the fullness and glory of its divinity.

Spiritual work is taxing work, and men are loath to do it. Praying, true praying, costs an outlay of serious attention and time, a payment that flesh and blood do not relish. Few people are made of such strong fiber that they will make a costly outlay when inferior work will pass just as well in the market. We can habituate ourselves to our beggarly praying until it looks good to us. At least it presents a decent front and quiets the conscience—the deadliest of opiates! We can become lax in our praying and not realize the peril until the damage has been done. Hasty devotions make weak faith, feeble convictions, and questionable piety. To be little *with* God is to be little *for* God. To cut the praying short makes the whole Christian character short, miserly, and slovenly.

It takes much time for the fullness of God to flow into the spirit. Short devotions cut the pipe of God's full flow. It takes time spent in the secret places to receive the full revelation of God. Little time and much hurrying will mar the picture.

Henry Martyn, the English missionary, lamented that "lack of private devotional reading and shortness of prayer through incessant sermon making has produced much strangeness between God and my soul." He judged that he had dedicated too much time to public ministrations and too little to private communion with God. He was very convicted concerning the need to set apart and devote time for fasting and solemn prayer.

Resulting from this, he recorded, "I was assisted this morning to pray for two hours."

Said William Wilberforce, the peer of kings,

I must secure more time for private devotions. I have been living far too public for me. The shortening of private devotions starves the soul; it grows lean and faint. I have been keeping too late hours.

Of a failure in Parliament, he said,

Let me record my grief and shame, and all, probably, from private devotions having been contracted, and so God let me stumble.

More solitude and earlier hours were his remedy.

More time and early hours devoted to prayer would revive and invigorate many a decayed spiritual life. More time and early hours for prayer would be manifest in holy living. A holy life would not be so rare or so difficult a thing if our devotions were not so short and hurried. A Christlike temper, or attitude, in its sweet and passionless fragrance, would not be so alien and hopeless a heritage if our stay in the prayer closet were lengthened and intensified.

We live shabbily because we pray meagerly. Plenty of time to feast in our prayer closets will bring marrow and fatness to our lives. (See Psalm 63:3–6.) Our ability to stay with God in our prayer chambers directly relates to our ability to stay with God out of the prayer chamber. Hasty closet visits are deceptive and defaulting. We are not only deluded by them, but we are losers by them in many ways and in many rich legacies. Tarrying in the closet instructs and wins. We are taught by it, and the greatest victories are often the results of great waiting—waiting until words and plans are exhausted. Silent and patient waiting gains the crown. Jesus Christ asks with an affronted emphasis, "*Shall not God avenge his own elect, which cry day and night unto him?*" (Luke 18:7).

To pray is the greatest thing we can do; and to do it well, there must be calmness, time, and deliberation. Otherwise, it is degraded into the smallest and dullest of things. True praying has the largest results for good, and poor praying, the least. We cannot do too much real praying; we cannot do too little of the imitation. We must learn anew the worth of prayer—enter anew the school of prayer. There is nothing that takes more time to learn. And if we want to learn the wondrous art, we must not offer a fragment here and there—"A little talk with Jesus," as the tiny saintlets sing—but we must demand and hold with an iron grasp the best hours of the day for God and prayer, or there will be no praying worth the name.

This, however, is not a day of prayer. Few men pray. Prayer is defamed by preacher and priest. In these days of hustle and bustle, of electricity and steam, men will not take time to pray. There are preachers who "say prayers" as a part of their program, on regular or state occasions, but who "stirreth up himself to take hold" (Isaiah 64:7) of God? Who prays as Jacob prayed—until he is crowned as a prevailing, princely intercessor? Who prays as Elijah prayed—until all the locked-up forces of nature were unsealed and a famine-stricken land bloomed as the garden of God? Who prays as Jesus Christ prayed—as out upon the mountain He "continued all night in prayer to God" (Luke 6:12)? The apostles gave themselves "continually to prayer" (Acts 6:4)—the most difficult thing to get men or even the preachers to do.

There are laymen who will give their money—some of them in rich abundance—but they will not give themselves to prayer, without which their money is only a curse. There are plenty of preachers who will preach and deliver great and eloquent addresses on the need of revival and the spread of the kingdom of God. But there are many who will do that without prayer, which makes all preaching and organizing worse than vain. Prayer is out-of-date, almost a lost art. The greatest benefactor this age could have is the man who will bring the preachers and the church back to prayer.

The apostles could only glimpse the great importance of prayer before Pentecost. But the Spirit coming and filling at Pentecost elevated prayer to its vital and all-commanding position in the gospel of Christ. Now the call of prayer to every saint is the Spirit's loudest and most urgent call. Sainthood's piety is made, refined, and perfected by prayer. The gospel moves with slow and timid pace when the saints are not at their prayers early and late and long.

Where are the Christlike leaders who can teach the modern saints how to pray and can put them at it? Do we know that we are raising up a prayerless set of saints? Where are the apostolic leaders who can put God's people to praying? Let them come to the front and do the work, and it will be the greatest work that can be done. An increase in educational facilities and a great increase in money will be a curse to Christianity if they are not sanctified by more and better praying than we are doing.

More praying will not come as a matter of course. The campaign for the twentieth- or thirtieth-century fund will hinder our praying if we are not careful. Nothing but a specific effort from a praying leadership will avail. The chief ones must lead in the apostolic effort to root, or plant deeply, the vital importance and fact of prayer in the heart and life of the church. Only praying leaders can have praying followers. Praying apostles will beget praying saints. A praying pulpit will beget praying pews. We greatly need somebody who can set the saints to this business of praying. We are not a generation of praying saints. Nonpraying saints are a beggarly gang of saints who have neither the zeal nor the beauty nor the power of real saints. Who will restore this breach? He who can set the church to praying will be the greatest of reformers and apostles.

We put it as our most sober judgment that the great need of the church in this and all ages is men of commanding faith, unsullied holiness, marked spiritual vigor, and consuming zeal. Their prayers, faith, lives, and ministries will be of such a radical and aggressive form as to work spiritual revolutions that will form eras in individual and church life.

We do not need men who arouse sensational stirs by novel devices, nor do we need those who attract by a pleasing entertainment. Rather, we need men who can stir things, work revolutions by the preaching of God's Word, and, by the power of the Holy Spirit, cause revolutions that change the whole current of events. Natural ability and educational advantages do not figure as factors in this matter; however, capacity for faith, the ability to pray, the power of thorough consecration, and the ability of self-denial are all important factors. Also required are an absolute losing of oneself in God's glory and an ever present and insatiable yearning and seeking after all the fullness of God. We need men who can set the church ablaze for

God, not in a noisy, showy way, but with an intense and quiet heat that melts and moves everything for God.

God can work wonders if He has a suitable man. Men can work wonders if they let God lead them. The full endowment of the Spirit that turned the world upside down would be eminently useful in these latter days. Men who can stir things mightily for God, whose spiritual revolutions change the whole aspect of things, are the universal need of the church.

The church has never been without these men. They adorn its history. They are the standing miracles of God's presence in the church. Their example and history are an unfailing inspiration and blessing. An increase in their number and power should be our desire.

That which has been done in spiritual matters can be done again, and be done better. This was Christ's view. He said,

> Verily, verily, I say unto you, He that believeth on me, the works that I do shall he do also; and greater works than these shall he do; because I go unto my Father. (John 14:12)

The past has not exhausted the possibilities nor the demands for doing great things for God. The church that is dependent on its past history for its miracles of power and grace is a fallen church.

God wants elect men, men of whom self and the world have been severely crucified. Their bankruptcy has so totally ruined self and the world that there is neither hope nor desire of recovery. God wants men who, by this insolvency and crucifixion, have turned toward Him with perfect hearts.

Let us pray without ceasing that God's promise concerning the results of prayer will come to fruition beyond what we have even hoped for.

BOOK FOUR:

PRAYER AND SPIRITUAL WARFARE

ONE:

PRAYER AND FAITH

A dear friend of mine who was quite a lover of the hunt, told me the following story. "Rising early one morning," he said, "I heard the barking of a number of dogs chasing deer. Looking at a large open field in front of me, I saw a young fawn making its way across the field and giving signs that its race was almost run. It leaped over the rails of the enclosed place and crouched within ten feet of where I stood. A moment later two of the hounds came over, and the fawn ran in my direction and pushed its head between my legs. I lifted the little thing to my breast, and, swinging round and round, fought off the dogs. Just then I felt that all the dogs in the West could not and would not capture that fawn after its weakness had appealed to my strength." So is it, when human helplessness appeals to Almighty God. I remember well, when the hounds of sin were after my soul, that at last I ran into the arms of Almighty God.
—A. C. Dixon

Whenever a study of the principles of prayer is made, lessons concerning faith must accompany it. Faith is the essential quality in the heart of any man who desires to communicate with God. He must believe and stretch out his hands in faith for that which he cannot see or prove. Prayer is actually faith claiming and taking hold of its natural, immeasurable inheritance. True godliness is just as important in the realm of faith as it is in the area of prayer. Moreover, when faith ceases to pray, it ceases to live.

Faith does the impossible because it lets God undertake for us, and nothing is impossible with God. How great—without qualification or limitation, the power of faith is! If doubt can be banished from the heart and unbelief is made a stranger there, what we ask from God will surely come to pass. A believer has granted to him *"whatsoever he saith"* (Mark 11:23).

Prayer throws faith on God and God on the world. Only God can move mountains, but faith and prayer move God. In the cursing of the fig tree, our Lord demonstrated His power. (See Matthew 21:19–22.) Following that, He went on to say that large powers were committed to faith and prayer, not to kill but to make alive, not to blast but to bless.

At this point in our study, we need to emphasize some words of Jesus that are the very keystone of the arch of faith and prayer. The first is found in Mark 11:24: *"Therefore I say unto you, What things soever ye desire, when ye pray, believe that ye receive them, and ye shall have them."* We should think about that statement: *"Believe that ye receive them, and ye shall have them."* A faith that realizes, appropriates, and *takes* is described here. This faith is an awareness of God, an experienced communion, a real fact.

Is faith growing or declining as the years go by? Does faith stand strong and firm as sin abounds and the love of many grows cold? Does faith keep its hold as religion becomes a mere formality and worldliness becomes victorious? The question our Lord asked may appropriately be ours. *"When the Son of man cometh,"* He asked, *"shall he find faith on the earth?"* (Luke 18:8). We believe that He will, and it is our job today to see to it that the lamp of faith is trimmed and burning, until He returns.

Faith is the foundation of Christian character and the security of the soul. When Jesus was looking toward Peter's denial and cautioning him against it, He said to His disciple, *"Simon, Simon, behold, Satan hath desired to have you, that he may sift you as wheat: but I have prayed for thee, that thy faith fail not"* (Luke 22:31–32).

Our Lord was stating a central truth. It was Peter's faith He was seeking to guard. He knew that when faith breaks down, the foundations of spiritual life give way, and the entire structure of religious experience falls. It was Peter's faith that needed guarding. That is why Christ was concerned for the welfare of His disciple's soul and was determined to strengthen Peter's faith by His own victorious prayer.

Faith is the foundation of Christian character and the security of the soul.

Peter, in his second epistle, had this same idea in mind when he wrote of growing in grace as a measure of safety in the Christian life and as fruitfulness. *"And beside this,"* he declared, *"giving all diligence, add to your faith virtue; and to virtue knowledge; and to knowledge temperance; and to temperance patience; and to patience godliness"* (2 Peter 1:5–6).

In this addition process, faith was the starting point, the basis of the other graces of the Spirit. Faith was the foundation on which other things were built. Peter did not urge his readers to add to works or gifts or virtues but to *faith*. In this business of growing in grace, much depends on starting right. There is a divine order. Peter was aware of it. He went on to say that we are to give constant care to making our calling and election secure. (See 2 Peter 1:10.) This election is made sure by adding to faith that which is done by constant, earnest praying. Faith is kept alive by prayer. Every step in this adding of grace to grace is accompanied by prayer.

Faith that creates powerful praying is the faith that centers itself on a powerful Person. Faith in Christ's ability to *do* and to do *greatly* is the faith that prays greatly. In this way the leper laid hold of the power of Christ. *"Lord, if thou wilt,"* he cried, *"thou canst make me clean"* (Matthew 8:2). In this instance, we are shown how a faith centered in Christ's ability to *do* obtained the healing power.

It was concerning this very point that Jesus questioned the blind men who came to Him for healing: *"Believe ye that I am able to do this?"* He

308 *E. M. Bounds on Prayer & Spiritual Warfare*

asked. *"They said unto Him, Yea, Lord. Then touched he their eyes, saying, According to your faith be it unto you"* (Matthew 9:28–29).

It was because He wanted to inspire faith in His ability to *do* that Jesus left behind Him that last, great statement, which, in the final analysis, is a ringing challenge to faith. *"All power,"* He declared, *"is given unto me in heaven and in earth"* (Matthew 28:18).

Again, faith is obedient. It goes when commanded, as did the nobleman who came to Jesus when his son was grievously sick. (See John 4:46–53.)

Likewise, such faith acts. Like the man who was born blind, it goes to wash in the pool of Siloam when *told* to wash. Like Peter on the Sea of Galilee, it instantly casts the net where Jesus commands, without question or doubt. Such faith promptly takes away the stone from the grave of Lazarus. A praying faith keeps the commandments of God and does those things that are pleasing in His sight. It asks, "Lord, what will you have me to do?" and answers quickly, "Speak, Lord, your servant hears." Obedience helps faith, and faith helps obedience. To do God's will is essential to true faith, and faith is necessary to absolute obedience.

Yet, faith is often called upon to wait patiently before God and is prepared for God's seeming delays in answering prayer. Faith does not grow disheartened because prayer is not immediately honored. It takes God at His Word and lets Him take what time He chooses in fulfilling His purposes and in carrying on His work. There are bound to be delays and long days of waiting for true faith, but faith accepts the conditions. It knows there will be delays in answering prayer and regards such delays as times of testing where it is privileged to show that it is made of courage and stern stuff.

The case of Lazarus was an instance where there was delay and where the faith of two good women was sorely tried. Lazarus was critically ill, and his sisters sent for Jesus. But, without any known rea son, our Lord delayed going to the relief of His sick friend. The plea was urgent and touching: *"Lord, behold, he whom thou lovest is sick"* (John 11:3). But the Master was not moved by it, and the women's earnest request seemed to fall on deaf ears. What a trial of faith! Furthermore, our Lord's delay appeared to bring about hopeless disaster. While Jesus tarried, Lazarus died.

But the delay of Jesus was used in the interest of a greater good. Finally, He made His way to the home in Bethany.

Then said Jesus unto them plainly, Lazarus is dead. And I am glad for your sakes, that I was not there, to the intent ye may believe; nevertheless let us go unto him. (John 11:14–15)

Fear not, O tempted and tried believer. Jesus will come, if patience is exercised and faith holds fast. His delay will serve to make His coming more richly blessed. Pray on. Wait on. You cannot fail. If Christ delays, wait for Him. In His own good time, He will come and will not be late.

Delay is often the test and the strength of faith. How much patience is required when these times of testing come! Yet, faith gathers strength by waiting and praying. Patience has its perfect work in the school of delay. In some instances, delay is of the very nature of the prayer. God has to do many things before He gives the final answer. They are things that are essential to the lasting good of the person who is requesting the favor from Him.

Jacob prayed with purpose and eagerness to be delivered from Esau. But, before that prayer could be answered, there was much to be done with and for Jacob. He had to be changed as well as Esau. Jacob had to be made into a new man before Esau could be. Jacob had to be converted to God before Esau could be converted to Jacob.

Among the brilliant sayings of Jesus concerning prayer, none is more interesting than this:

Verily, verily, I say unto you, He that believeth on me, the works that I do shall he do also; and greater works than these shall he do; because I go unto my Father. And whatsoever ye shall ask in my name, that will I do, that the Father may be glorified in the Son. If ye shall ask any thing in my name, I will do it. (John 14:12–14)

How wonderful these statements are of what God will do in answer to prayer! What great importance these ringing words have when prefaced with solemn truth! Faith in Christ is the basis of all working and all praying. All wonderful works depend on wonderful praying, and all praying is done in the name of Jesus Christ. The amazing, simple lesson is this praying in the name of the Lord Jesus! All other conditions are of little value. Everything else is given up except Jesus. The name of Christ—the person of our Lord and Savior Jesus Christ—must be supremely sovereign in the hour of prayer.

If Jesus dwells at the source of my life—if the flow of His life has replaced all of my life—then He can safely commit the praying to my will. If absolute obedience to Him is the inspiration and force of every movement of my life, then He will pledge Himself, by a duty as deep as His own nature, that whatever is asked will be granted. Nothing can be clearer, more distinct, more unlimited both in application and extent, than the plea and urgency of Christ: *"Have faith in God"* (Mark 11:22).

Faith covers worldly as well as spiritual needs. Faith scatters excessive anxiety and needless care about what will be eaten, what will be drunk, and what will be worn. Faith lives in the present and regards the day as being *"sufficient unto...the evil thereof"* (Matthew 6:34). It lives day by day and scatters all fears for tomorrow. Faith brings great peace of mind and perfect peace of heart.

> *Thou wilt keep him in perfect peace, whose mind is stayed on thee: because he trusteth in thee.*   (Isaiah 26:3)

When we pray, *"Give us this day our daily bread"* (Matthew 6:11), we are, in a measure, shutting tomorrow out of our prayer. We do not live for tomorrow, but for today. We do not look for tomorrow's grace or tomorrow's bread. Those who live in the present thrive best and get the most out of life. Those who pray best pray for today's, not tomorrow's, needs. Our prayer for tomorrow's needs may be unnecessary because they may not exist at all!

True prayers are born out of present trials and present needs. Bread for today is enough. Bread given for today is the strongest pledge that there will be bread tomorrow. Victory today is the assurance of victory tomorrow. Our prayers need to be focused on the present. We must trust God today and leave tomorrow entirely with Him. The present is ours; the future belongs to God. Prayer is the task and duty of each new day—daily prayer for daily needs.

As every day demands its bread, so every day demands its prayer. No amount of praying done today will be sufficient for tomorrow's praying. On the other hand, no praying for tomorrow is of any great value to us today. Today's manna is what we need; tomorrow God will see that our needs are supplied. This is the faith that God seeks to inspire.

So leave tomorrow, with its cares, needs, and troubles, in God's hands. There is no storing up of tomorrow's grace or tomorrow's praying. We cannot lay hold of today's grace to meet tomorrow's needs. We cannot have tomorrow's grace; we cannot eat tomorrow's bread; we cannot do tomorrow's praying. *"Sufficient unto the day is the evil thereof"* (Matthew 6:34). And, certainly, if we possess faith, sufficient also will be the good.

TWO:

PRAYER THAT GETS RESULTS

The guests at a certain hotel were being made uncomfortable by the repeated banging on a piano by a little girl who possessed no musical knowledge. They complained to the owner with the hope of having the annoyance stopped. "I am sorry you are annoyed," he said, "but the girl is the child of one of my very best guests. I can hardly ask her not to touch the piano. But her father, who is away for a day or so, will return tomorrow. You can approach him and have the matter settled." When the father returned, he found his daughter in the reception room thumping on the piano. He walked up behind the child, put his arms over her shoulders, took her hands in his, and produced some beautiful music. So may it be with us, and so will it be someday. Just now, we can produce only clamor and disharmony; but, one day, the Lord Jesus will take hold of our hands of faith and prayer and use them to bring forth the music of the skies.

—Anonymous

Genuine, authentic faith must be definite and free of doubt. It is not general in character or a mere belief in the being, goodness, and power of God. It is a faith that believes that the things that *"he saith shall come to pass"* (Mark 11:23). As faith is specific, so the answer will also be definite. *"He shall have whatsoever he saith"* (Mark 11:23). Faith and prayer select the things, and God pledges Himself to do the very things that faith and persistent prayer name and ask Him to accomplish.

The Revised Version translates Mark 11:24 this way: *"All things whatsoever ye pray and ask for, believe that ye have received them, and ye shall have them."* Perfect faith always has in its keeping what perfect prayer asks for. How large and unqualified this area of operation is—all things whatsoever! How definite and specific the promise is—*"ye shall have them"*!

Our major concern is our faith—the problems of its growth and the actions of its strong development. A faith that holds on to the very things it asks for, without wavering, doubt, or fear—that is the faith we need. We need faith, like a pearl of great price, in the process and practice of prayer.

The above statement about faith and prayer is of supreme importance. *Faith must be definite and specific.* It must be an unqualified, unmistakable request for the things asked for. It should not be a vague, indefinite, shadowy thing. It must be something more than an ideal belief in God's willingness and ability to do something for us. It should be a definite, specific asking for and expectation of the things for which we ask. Note Mark 11:23: *"Whosoever...shall not doubt in his heart, but shall believe that those things which he saith shall come to pass; he shall have whatsoever he saith."*

Just as the faith and the request is definite, so the answer will be definite. The giving is not something other than the things prayed for, but the actual things sought and named. *"He shall have whatsoever he saith."* It is a certainty: *"he shall have."* The granting is unlimited both in quality and quantity.

Faith and prayer select the subjects to be prayed for, thus determining what God is to do. *"He shall have whatsoever he saith."* Christ is ready to supply exactly and fully all the demands of faith and prayer. If the order to

God is clear, specific, and definite, God will fill it exactly in agreement with the terms put before Him.

Faith is not an abstract belief in the Word of God or a mere mental belief. It is not a simple agreement of the understanding and will or a passive belief in facts, no matter how sacred or thorough. Faith is an operation of God, a divine illumination, a holy energy planted by the Word of God and the Spirit in the human soul. It is a spiritual, divine principle that takes from the supernatural and makes it an understandable thing by the faculties of time and sense.

Faith deals with God and is conscious of God. It deals with the Lord Jesus Christ and sees Him as a Savior. It deals with God's Word and lays hold of the truth. It deals with the Spirit of God and is energized and inspired by its holy fire. God is the great objective of faith, for faith rests its whole weight on His Word. Faith is not an aimless act of the soul, but a looking to God and a resting on His promises. Just as love and hope always have an objective, so also has faith. Faith is not believing just *anything*. It is believing God, resting in Him, and trusting His Word.

Faith gives birth to prayer. It grows stronger, strikes deeper, and rises higher in the struggles and wrestling of mighty petitioning. Faith is *"the substance of things hoped for"* (Hebrews 11:1), the confidence and reality of the inheritance of the saints. Faith, too, is humble and persistent. It can wait and pray. It can stay on its knees or lie in the dust. It is the one great condition of prayer. The lack of faith lies at the root of all poor, feeble, little, unanswered praying.

The nature and meaning of faith is proven more in what it does than by any definition it is given. So, if we turn to the record of faith given to us in that great honor roll in Hebrews 11, we see something of the wonderful results of faith.

Faith gives birth to prayer. It grows stronger, strikes deeper, and rises higher in the struggles and wrestling of mighty petitioning.

What a glorious list it is of these men and women of faith! What marvelous achievements are recorded there and set to faith's credit! The inspired writer, exhausting his resources in cataloging the Old Testament saints who were such notable examples of wonderful faith, finally said,

And what shall I more say? for the time would fail me to tell of Gedeon, and of Barak, and of Samson, and of Jephthae; of David also, and Samuel, and of the prophets. (Hebrews 11:32)

Then the writer of Hebrews went on to tell of the unrecorded exploits brought about through the faith of the men of old, *"of whom the world was not worthy"* (v. 38). All these, he said, *"obtained a good report through faith"* (v. 39).

If we could only reproduce a race of saints with mighty faith and wonderful praying, what a glorious period of achievements would begin for the church and the world! The church does not need the intellectually great. The times do not demand wealthy men. People of great social influence are not what is required. Above everybody and everything else, the church and the whole wide world of humanity need men of faith and mighty prayer. We need men and women like the saints and heroes counted in Hebrews 11 who *"obtained a good report through faith."*

Today, many men obtain a good report because of their monetary donations and their great mental gifts and talents. But there are few who obtain a good report because of their great faith in God or because of the wonderful things that come about through their great praying. Today, as much as at any time, we need men of great faith and men who are great in prayer. These are the two chief virtues that make men great in the eyes of God. These two things create conditions of real spiritual success in the life and work of the church. It is our main concern to see that we keep this kind of quality faith before God. This kind of faith grasps and holds in its keeping the things for which it asks without doubt and fear.

Doubt and fear are the twin enemies of faith. Sometimes they actually take the place of faith, and, although we pray, it is a restless, disquieted, uneasy, complaining prayer that we offer. Peter failed to walk on the waters of Galilee because he allowed the waves to break over him and swamp the power of his faith. Taking his eyes off the Lord and looking at the water around him, he began to sink and cry for help—"Lord, save me, or I perish!"

Doubts and fears should never be cherished or hidden. No one should cherish the false idea that he is a martyr to fear and doubt. It is of no credit to man's mental ability to cherish doubt of God. No comfort can possibly be gotten from such a thought. Our eyes should be taken off ourselves. They should be removed from our own weakness and allowed to rest totally on God's strength. *"Cast not away therefore your confidence, which hath great recompense of reward"* (Heb. 10:35). A simple, confiding faith, lived out day by day, will drive fear away. A faith that casts its burden on the Lord each hour of the day will drive away misgiving and deliver from doubt.

"Be careful for nothing; but in every thing by prayer and supplication with thanksgiving let your requests be made known unto God" (Philippians 4:6). That is the divine cure for all fear, anxiety, and excessive concern for the soul. All these are closely related to doubt and unbelief. This is the divine prescription for securing the peace that passes all understanding and keeps the heart and mind in quietness and peace.

All of us need to pay attention and heed the caution given in Hebrews 3:12: *"Take heed, brethren, lest there be in any of you an evil heart of unbelief, in departing from the living God."* We need to guard against unbelief as we would against an enemy. Faith needs to be cultivated. We need to keep on praying, *"Lord, increase our faith"* (Luke 17:5), for faith is capable of increasing. Paul's tribute to the Thessalonians was that their faith grew exceedingly. (See 2 Thessalonians 1:3.) Faith is increased by exercise, by being put to use. It is nourished by painful trials.

> *That the trial of your faith, being much more precious than of gold that perisheth, though it be tried with fire, might be found unto praise and honour and glory at the appearing of Jesus Christ.* (1 Peter 1:7)

Faith grows by reading and meditating upon the Word of God. Most of all, faith thrives in an atmosphere of prayer.

It would be good if we stop and ask ourselves, Do I have faith in God; do I have *real* faith—faith that keeps me in perfect peace about the things of the earth and heaven? This is the most important question a man can propose and expect to be answered. And there is another question closely related to it in significance and importance: Do I really pray to God so that He hears me and answers my prayers; and do I truly pray to God so that I get directly from God the things I ask of Him?

It was said that Augustus Caesar found Rome a city of wood and left it a city of marble. The pastor who succeeds in changing his people from a prayerless to a prayerful people has done a greater work than Augustus did in changing a city from wood to marble. After all, this is the major work of the preacher. Primarily, he is dealing with prayerless people, of whom it is said, "*God is not in all* [their] *thoughts*" (Psalm 10:4).

The pastor meets such people everywhere all the time. His main business is to turn them from being forgetful about God, from lacking faith, from being prayerless, into people who habitually pray, believe in God, remember Him, and do His will. The preacher is not sent simply to persuade men to join the church or to get them to do better. He is sent to get them to pray, to trust God, and to keep God ever before their eyes so that they may not sin against Him.

The work of the ministry is to change unbelieving sinners into praying, believing saints. The call goes out by divine authority, "*Believe on the Lord Jesus Christ, and thou shalt be saved*" (Acts 16:31). We catch a glimpse of the tremendous importance of faith and the great value God has put on it when we remember that He has made it the one essential condition of being saved. "*For by grace are ye saved through faith*" (Ephesians 2:8). So, when we think about the great importance of prayer, we find faith standing immediately by its side. By faith we are saved, and by faith we *stay* saved. Prayer introduces us to a life of faith. Paul declared that the life he lived, he lived by faith in the Son of God, who loved him and gave Himself for him (see Galatians 2:20)—that he walked by faith and not by sight (see 2 Corinthians 5:7).

Prayer is absolutely dependent on faith. It has virtually no existence apart from it and accomplishes nothing unless it is faith's inseparable companion. Faith makes prayer effective and, in a certain important sense, must precede it. "*For he that cometh to God must believe that he is, and that he is a rewarder of them that diligently seek him*" (Hebrews 11:6).

Before prayer ever starts toward God, before its petition is chosen and its requests made known, faith must have gone on ahead. It must have had

318 *E. M. Bounds on Prayer & Spiritual Warfare*

its belief in the existence of God stated. It must have given its consent to the gracious truth that God is a rewarder of those who diligently seek His face.

This is the primary step in praying. In this regard, while faith does not bring the blessing, it puts prayer in a position to ask for it. It leads to another step of understanding by helping the petitioner believe that God is able and willing to bless.

Faith starts prayer working. It clears the way to the mercy seat. It gives assurance, first of all, that there is a mercy seat and that the High Priest waits there for us to come with our prayers. Faith opens the way for prayer to approach God. But it does more. Faith accompanies prayer with every step it takes. Faith is prayer's inseparable companion. When requests are made to God, faith turns the asking into obtaining. And faith follows prayer, since the spiritual life into which a believer is led by prayer is a life of faith. Faith, not a life of works, is the one prominent characteristic of the experience that believers are brought into through prayer.

Faith makes prayer strong and gives it patience to wait on God. Faith believes that God is a rewarder. No truth is more clearly revealed and none is more encouraging in Scripture than this. Even the prayer closet has its promised reward: "*Thy Father which seeth in secret himself shall reward thee openly*" (Matthew 6:4). The most insignificant service given to a disciple in the name of the Lord surely receives its reward. Faith gives its hearty consent to this precious truth.

Yet, faith is narrowed down to one particular thing. It does not believe that God will reward everybody. It does not believe that He is a rewarder of all who pray, but that He is a rewarder of those who "*diligently seek him*" (Hebrews 11:6). Faith rests its case on diligent prayer. It gives assurance and encouragement to diligent seekers after God, for it is they alone who are richly rewarded when they pray.

We constantly need to be reminded that faith is the one inseparable condition of successful praying. There are other conditions, but faith is the final, essential condition of true praying, as it is written: "*But without faith it is impossible to please him*" (v. 6).

James put this truth very plainly:

If any of you lack wisdom, let him ask of God, that giveth to all men liberally, and upbraideth not; and it shall be given him. But let him ask in faith, nothing wavering. For he that wavereth is like a wave of the sea driven with the wind and tossed. For let not that man think that he shall receive any thing of the Lord. (James 1:5–7)

Doubting is always forbidden because it stands as an enemy to faith and hinders effective praying. Paul gave us a priceless truth relative to the conditions of successful praying. He said, *"I will therefore that men pray every where, lifting up holy hands, without wrath and doubting"* (1 Timothy 2:8).

All questioning must be guarded against and avoided. Fear and doubt have no place in true praying. Faith must assert itself and tell these enemies of prayer to depart.

Faith cannot be assigned too much authority, but prayer is the scepter that signals power. There is much spiritual wisdom in the following advice written by a famous saint:

Do you want to be free from the bondage of corruption? Do you want to grow in grace in general and grow in grace in particular? If you do, your way is plain. Ask God for more faith. Beg Him morning, noon, and night, while you walk by the road, while you sit in the house, when you lie down, and when you rise up. Beg Him simply to impress divine things more deeply on your heart, to give you more and more of *"the substance of things hoped for"* and of *"the evidence of things not seen"* (Hebrews 11:1).

Great incentives to pray are furnished in Scripture. Our Lord closed His teaching about prayer with the assurance and promise of heaven. The presence of Jesus Christ in heaven and the preparation He is making there for His saints help the weariness of praying. The assurance that He will come again to receive the saints strengthens and sweetens its difficult work! These things are the star of hope to prayer. They wipe away its tears and put the sweet odor of heaven into the bitterness of its cry. The spirit of a pilgrim makes praying easier. An earthbound, earth-satisfied spirit cannot pray. The flame of spiritual desire in such a heart has either gone out or is smoldering in a faint glow. The wings of its faith are clipped, its eyes are filmed, its tongue is silenced. But they who, in immovable faith and unceasing prayer, wait continually upon the Lord *do* renew their strength, *do* mount up with wings as eagles, *do* run and are not weary, *do* walk and not faint. (See Isaiah 40:31.)

THREE:

PRAYER AND TRUSTING GOD

One evening I left my office in New York with a bitterly cold wind in my face. I had with me (as I thought) my thick, warm muffler, but when I proceeded to button up against the storm, I found that it was gone. I turned back, looked along the streets, searched my office, but in vain. I realized that I must have dropped it, and I prayed to God that I would find it; for such was the state of the weather that it would be running a great risk to proceed without it. I looked again up and down the surrounding streets, but without success. Suddenly, I saw a man on the opposite side of the road holding out something in his hand. I crossed over and asked him if that was my muffler. He handed it to me saying, "It was blown to me by the wind." He who rides upon the storm had used the wind as a means of answering prayer.

—William Horst

Prayer does not stand alone. It is not an isolated duty or an independent principle. It lives in fellowship with other Christian duties. It is married to other principles and is a partner with other graces. But prayer is firmly joined to faith. Faith gives it color and tone, shapes its character, and secures its results.

Trust is faith that has become absolute, approved, and accomplished. When all is said and done, there is a sort of risk in faith and its exercise. But trust is firm belief; it is faith in full bloom. Trust is a conscious act, a fact of which we are aware. According to the scriptural concept, it is the eye of the newborn soul and the ear of the renewed soul. It is the feeling of the soul—the spiritual sight, hearing, taste, and touch. All these have to do with trust. How bright, distinct, conscious, powerful, and scriptural such a trust is! How different, feeble, dry, and cold are many forms of modern beliefs in comparison! These modern beliefs do not bring awareness of their presence. They do not bring "*joy unspeakable and full of glory*" (1 Peter 1:8) from their exercise. They are, for the most part, adventures in the doubts of the soul. There is no safe, sure trust in anything. The whole transaction takes place in the area of *maybe* and *perhaps*.

Trust, like life, is feeling, though much more. An unfelt life is a contradiction. An unfelt trust is a misnaming and a false belief. Trust is the most felt of all qualities. It is *all* feeling, and it only works by love. An unfelt love is as impossible as an unfelt trust. The trust we are speaking about is a conviction. An unfelt conviction? How absurd!

Trust sees God doing things here and now. Yes, and more. It rises to a high place and looks into the invisible and the eternal. It realizes that God has done things and regards them as being already done. Trust brings eternity into the history and happenings of time. It transforms hope into the reality of fulfillment and changes promise into present possession. We know when we trust, just as we know when we see. We are conscious of our sense of touch. Trust sees, receives, holds. Trust is its own witness.

Yet, quite often, faith is too weak to obtain God's greatest good immediately. It has to wait in loving, strong, prayerful, pressing obedience until it grows in strength and is able to bring down the eternal into the areas of experience and time.

Up to this point, trust shapes all its forces. Here it holds. In the struggle, trust's grasp becomes mightier, and it grasps for itself all that God has done for it in His eternal wisdom and fullness of grace.

In the matter of waiting in mighty prayer, faith rises to its highest level and becomes the gift of God. It becomes the blessed character and expression of the soul that is secured by a constant fellowship with and tireless request to God.

Jesus Christ clearly taught that faith was the condition on which prayer was answered. When our Lord cursed the fig tree, the disciples were very surprised that its withering had actually taken place. Their remarks indicated their unbelief. It was then that Jesus said to them:

> *Have faith in God. For verily I say unto you, That whosoever shall say unto this mountain, Be thou removed, and be thou cast into the sea; and shall not doubt in his heart, but shall believe that those things which he saith shall come to pass; he shall have whatsoever he saith. Therefore I say unto you, What things soever ye desire, when ye pray, believe that ye receive them, and ye shall have them.* (Mark 11:22–24)

There is no place where trust grows so readily and richly as in the prayer closet. Its unfolding and development are rapid and wholesome when they are kept regularly and well. When these appointments are sincere, full, and free, trust grows increasingly. The eye and presence of God give active life to trust, just like the eye and presence of the sun make fruit and flower grow and all things glad and bright with fuller life.

Faith and trust in the Lord form the keynote and foundation of prayer. Primarily, it is not trust in the Word of God but rather trust in the person of God, for trust in the person of God must precede trust in the Word of God. *"Ye believe in God, believe also in me"* (John 14:1) is the demand our Lord makes on the personal trust of His disciples. The person of Jesus Christ must be central to the eye of trust. Jesus sought to impress this great truth on Martha when her brother lay dead in their home at Bethany. Martha stated her belief in the resurrection of her brother: *"Martha saith unto him, I know that he shall rise again in the resurrection at the last day"* (John 11:24).

Jesus lifted her trust above the mere fact of the resurrection, to His own person, by saying,

I am the resurrection, and the life: he that believeth in me, though he were dead, yet shall he live: and whosoever liveth and believeth in me shall never die. Believest thou this? She saith unto him, Yea, Lord: I believe that thou art the Christ, the Son of God, which should come into the world. (John 11:25–27)

Trust in a historical fact or a mere record may be a very passive thing, but trust in a person strengthens the quality. It bears fruit and supplies it with love. The trust that supplies prayer centers in a Person.

Trust goes even further than this. The trust that inspires our prayer must not only be one in the person of God, and of Christ, but also in their ability and willingness to grant the thing prayed for. It is not only, *"Trust in the* LORD*"* (Psalm 37:3), but also, *"for in the* LORD JEHOVAH *is everlasting strength"* (Isaiah 26:4).

The trust that our Lord taught as a condition of effective prayer is not from the head but from the heart. It is trust that does not doubt. Such trust has the divine assurance that it will be honored with large and satisfying answers. The strong promise of our Lord brings faith down to the present and counts on a present answer.

> *The trust that inspires our prayer must not only be one in the person of God, and of Christ, but also in their ability and willingness to grant the thing prayed for.*

Do we believe without a doubt? When we pray, do we believe that we will receive the things we ask for, not on a future day, but then and there? This is the teaching of this inspiring Scripture. How we need to pray, *"Lord, increase our faith"* (Luke 17:5) until doubt is gone and absolute trust claims the promised blessings as its very own.

This is no easy condition. It is only reached after many failures, much praying, many wailings, and much trial of faith. May our faith increase until we realize and receive all the fullness that there is in the name of Jesus, which guarantees to do so much.

Our Lord puts forth trust as the very foundation of praying. The background of prayer is trust. The whole purpose of Christ's ministry and work was dependent on absolute trust in His Father. The center of trust is God. Mountains of difficulties and all other hindrances to prayer are moved out of the way by trust and its strong follower, faith.

When trust is perfect and there is no doubt, prayer is simply the outstretched hand ready to receive. Trust perfected is prayer perfected. Trust looks to receive the thing asked for and gets it. Trust is not a belief that God *can* bless or that He *will* bless, but that He *does* bless, here and now. Trust always operates in the present tense. Hope looks toward the future. Trust looks to the present. Hope expects. Trust possesses. Trust receives what prayer acquires. So, what prayer needs, at all times, is abiding and abundant trust.

The disciples' unfortunate lack of trust and resulting failure to do what they were sent out to do is seen in the case of the lunatic son. His father brought him to nine of them while their Master was on the Mount of Transfiguration. The boy, sadly tormented, was brought to these men to be cured of his sickness. They had been commissioned to do this very kind of work. This was part of their mission. They tried to cast the demon from the boy but noticeably failed. The demon was too much for them. They were humiliated at their failure while their enemies were victorious.

During the incident, Jesus drew near. He was informed of the circumstances and conditions connected with it. Here is the account of what followed:

> *Then Jesus answered and said, O faithless and perverse generation, how long shall I be with you? how long shall I suffer you? bring him hither to me. And Jesus rebuked the devil; and he departed out of him: and the child was cured from that very hour. Then came the disciples to Jesus apart, and said, Why could not we cast him out?…Howbeit this kind goeth not out but by prayer and fasting.*
>
> (Matthew 17:17–19, 21)

326 E. M. Bounds on Prayer & Spiritual Warfare

Where was the difficulty of these men? They had been careless in cultivating their faith by prayer, and, as a result, their trust utterly failed. They did not trust God, Christ, or the authenticity of His mission or their own. It has been the same since, in many a crisis in the church of God. Failure has resulted from a lack of trust, a weakness of faith, and a lack of prayerfulness. Many failures in revival efforts have been traceable to the same cause. Faith has not been nurtured and made powerful by prayer. Neglect of the inner chamber is the solution of most spiritual failure. This is also true of our personal struggles with Satan when we attempt to cast out demons. Being on our knees in private fellowship with God is our only assurance that we will have Him with us in our personal struggles or in our efforts to convert sinners.

When people came to Him, our Lord put their trust in Him and the divinity of His mission in the forefront. He did not give a definition of trust. He did not furnish a theological discussion or analysis of it. He knew that men would see what faith was by what faith *did*. They would see from its free exercise that trust grew up, automatically, in His presence. It was the product of His work, His power, and His person. These furnished and created a favorable atmosphere for its exercise and development. Trust is altogether too simple for verbal definition. It is too sincere and spontaneous for theological terms. The very simplicity of trust is what staggers many people. They look for some great thing to come to pass, while all the time *"the word is nigh thee, even in thy mouth, and in thy heart"* (Romans 10:8).

When the sad news of his daughter's death was brought to Jairus, our Lord interrupted saying, *"Fear not: believe only, and she shall be made whole"* (Luke 8:50). To the woman with the issue of blood, who stood trembling before Him, He said, *"Daughter, be of good comfort: thy faith hath made thee whole; go in peace"* (v. 48).

As the two blind men followed Him, pressing their way into the house, He said, *"According to your faith be it unto you. And their eyes were opened"* (Matthew 9:29–30). When the paralytic was let down by four of his friends through the roof of the house where Jesus was teaching and placed before Him, it is recorded: *"And Jesus seeing their faith said unto the sick of the palsy; Son, be of good cheer; thy sins be forgiven thee"* (Matthew 9:2).

Prayer and Trusting God 327

When Jesus dismissed the centurion whose servant was seriously ill, He did it in a particular manner. The centurion had come to Jesus with the prayer that He speak the healing word without even going to his house. Jesus did the following: *"And Jesus said unto the centurion, Go thy way; and as thou hast believed, so be it done unto thee. And his servant was healed in the selfsame hour"* (Matthew 8:13). When the poor leper fell at Jesus' feet and cried out for relief saying, *"Lord, if thou wilt, thou canst make me clean"* (v. 2), Jesus immediately granted his request, and the man glorified Him with a loud voice.

The Syrophenician woman came to Jesus about her troubled daughter. Making the case her own, she prayed, *"Lord, help me"* (Matthew 15:25). Jesus honored her faith and prayer, saying, *"O woman, great is thy faith: be it unto thee even as thou wilt. And her daughter was made whole from that very hour"* (v. 28).

After the disciples had utterly failed to cast the demon out of the epileptic boy, the father of the boy came to Jesus with a sad, despairing cry, *"If thou canst do any thing, have compassion on us, and help us"* (Mark 9:22). But Jesus replied, *"If thou canst believe, all things are possible to him that believeth"* (v. 23).

Blind Bartimaeus, sitting by the wayside, heard our Lord as He passed by and cried out pitifully, *"Jesus, thou son of David, have mercy on me"* (Mark 10:47). The keen ears of our Lord immediately caught the sound of prayer. He said to the beggar, *"Go thy way; thy faith hath made thee whole. And immediately he received his sight, and followed Jesus in the way"* (v. 52).

Jesus spoke cheerful, soul-comforting words to the weeping, penitent woman who washed His feet with her tears and wiped them with her hair: *"Thy faith hath saved thee; go in peace"* (Luke 7:50).

One day Jesus healed ten lepers at one time, in answer to their united prayer, *"Jesus, Master, have mercy on us"* (Luke 17:13). He told them to go and show themselves to the priests. *"And it came to pass, that, as they went, they were cleansed"* (v. 14).

FOUR:

PRAYER AND DESIRE

There are those who will mock me and tell me to stick to my trade as a cobbler. They will tell me to not trouble my mind with philosophy and theology. But the truth of God did so burn in my bones that I took my pen in hand and began to set down what I had seen.
—Jacob Behmen

Desire is not merely a simple wish. It is a deep-seated desire and an intense longing for accomplishment. In the realm of spiritual affairs, it is an important addition to prayer. It is so important that one could almost say desire is an absolute essential of prayer. Desire precedes and accompanies prayer. Desire goes before prayer and is created and intensified by it. Prayer is the oral expression of desire. If prayer is asking God for something, then prayer must be expressed. Prayer comes out into the open. Desire is silent. Prayer is heard. The deeper the desire, the stronger the prayer. Without desire, prayer is a meaningless mumble of words. Such uninterested, formal praying, with no heart, feeling, or real desire accompanying it, is to be avoided like a plague. Its exercise is a waste of precious time, and no real blessing results from it.

Yet, even if it is discovered that desire is honestly absent, we should pray anyway. We ought to pray. The *ought* comes in, in order for desire and expression to be produced. God's Word commands it. Our judgment tells us we ought to pray—whether we feel like it or not—and not allow our feelings to determine our prayer habits. In such circumstances, we ought to pray for the *desire* to pray. This desire is God-given and heaven-born. We should pray for desire. Then, when desire has been given, we should pray according to its principles. The lack of spiritual desire should grieve us and lead us to mourn its absence. We should earnestly seek for its prize so that our praying would be an expression of "the soul's sincere desire."

A sense of need creates, or should create, earnest desire. The stronger the need before God, the greater the desire and the more earnest the prayer should be. The *"poor in spirit"* (Matthew 5:3) are highly competent to pray.

Hunger is an active sense of physical need. It prompts the request for food. In like manner, the inward awareness of spiritual need creates desire, and desire creates prayer. Desire is an inward longing for something that we do not possess and need. It is something that God has promised and that can be secured by earnest prayer at His throne of grace.

Spiritual desire, carried to a higher degree, is the evidence of the new birth. It is born in the renewed soul: *"As newborn babes, desire the sincere milk of the word, that ye may grow thereby"* (1 Peter 2:2).

The absence of this holy desire in the heart is proof that there has been a decline in spiritual joy or that the new birth has never taken place. *"Blessed are they which do hunger and thirst after righteousness: for they shall be filled"* (Matthew 5:6).

These heaven-given appetites are proof of a renewed heart and the evidence of a stirring spiritual life. Physical appetites are the characteristics of a living body, not a corpse. Spiritual desires belong to a soul made alive to God. As the renewed soul hungers and thirsts after righteousness, these holy, inward desires break out into earnest, petitioning prayer.

In prayer we are dependent on the name and power of Jesus Christ, our great High Priest. Searching the accompanying conditions and forces in prayer, we find its vital basis, which is seated in the human heart. It is not simply our need; it is the heart's desire for what we need and for what we feel urged to pray about. *Desire is the will in action.* It is a strong, conscious longing that is excited in the inner man for some great good. Desire exalts the object of its longing and sets the mind on it. It has choice, attitude, and fire in it. Prayer, based on these, is genuine and specific. It knows its need, feels and sees the thing that will meet it, and hurries to acquire it.

Holy desire is helped by devout study. Meditation on our spiritual need and on God's readiness and ability to correct it helps desire to grow. Serious thought practiced before praying increases desire. It makes prayer more insistent and tends to save us from the danger of private prayer— wandering thought. We fail much more in desire than in its outward expression. We keep the form while the inner life fades and almost dies.

One might ask whether the feebleness of our desire for God the Father, the Holy Spirit, and all the fullness of Christ is the cause of our lack of prayer. Do we really feel this inward hunger and desire for heavenly treasures? Do the inborn groanings of desire stir our souls to mighty wrestlings? Oh, the fire burns entirely too low. The flaming heat of the soul has been toned down to a lukewarmness. This, we should remember, was the major cause of the sad, desperate condition of the Laodicean Christians. Because of this condition, the awful condemnation is written about them: "[You are] *rich, and increased with goods, and* **have need of nothing;** *and knowest not that thou art wretched, and miserable, and poor, and blind, and naked*" (Revelation 3:17, emphasis added).

Again, we might ask, do we have that desire that presses us into close communion with God? Do we have the desire that is filled with silent pain that keeps us there through the agony of an intense, soul-stirred prayer? Our hearts need to be worked over, not only to get the evil out of them, but to get the good into them. They need to be worked over so that the foundation and inspiration to the incoming good is strong, moving desire. This holy, fervent flame in the soul awakens the interest of heaven, attracts God's attention, and places the inexhaustible riches of divine grace at the disposal of those who exercise it.

The dampening of the flame of holy desire is destructive to the vital, aggressive forces in church life. God expects to be represented by a fiery church or He is not, in any proper sense, represented at all. God Himself is all fire, and His church, if it is to be like Him, must also be like white heat.

The only things that His church can afford to be on fire about are the great, eternal interests of heaven-born, God-given faith.

Yet, holy desire does not have to be fussy in order to be consuming. Our Lord was the incarnate opposite of nervous excitability, the absolute opposite of intolerant or noisy speech. Still, the zeal of God's house consumed Him. And the world is still feeling the glow of His fierce, consuming flame. They are responding to it with an ever-increasing readiness and an even larger response.

A lack of passion in prayer is a sure sign of the lack of depth and the intensity of desire. The absence of intense desire is a sure sign of God's absence from the heart! To reduce fervor is to retire from God. He can and does tolerate in His children many things in the areas of weakness and mistakes. He can and will pardon sin when the repentant one prays.

But two things are intolerable to Him—insincerity and lukewarmness. Lack of heart and heat are two things He hates. He said to the Laodiceans, in unmistakable severity and condemnation: *"I would thou wert cold or hot. So then because thou art lukewarm, and neither cold nor hot, I will spue thee out of my mouth"* (Revelation 3:15–16).

This was God's precise judgment on the lack of fire in one of the seven churches. It is His accusation against individual Christians for the fatal lack of sacred zeal. Fire is the motivating power in prayer. Religious principles that do not come out of fire have neither force nor effect. Fire is the wing on which faith ascends. Passion is the soul of prayer. It is the *"effectual fervent prayer of a righteous man* [that] *availeth much"* (James 5:16). Love is kindled in a flame, and zeal is its life. Flame is the air that true Christian experience breathes. It feeds on fire. It can withstand anything except a weak flame. It dies, chilled and starved.

True prayer *must* be aflame. The Christian life and character need to be on fire. Lack of spiritual heat creates more unbelief than lack of faith does. If man is not wholly interested in the things of heaven, he is not interested in them at all. The fiery souls are those who conquer in the day of battle. They are those from whom the kingdom of heaven suffers violence and who take it by force (Matthew 11:12). The stronghold of God is taken only by those who storm it in worshipful earnestness and besiege it with fiery, unshakeable zeal.

Nothing short of being red-hot for God can keep the glow of heaven in our hearts during these chilly days. The early Methodists had no heating in their churches. They said that the flame in the pew and the fire in the pulpit must be sufficient to keep them warm. And we, today, need to have the live coal from God's altar and the consuming flame from heaven glowing in our hearts. This flame is not mental power or fleshly energy. It is divine, intense, dross-consuming fire in the soul. It is the very being of the Spirit of God.

No scholarship, pure speech, breadth of mental outlook, fluent language, or elegance can make up for the lack of fire. Prayer ascends by fire. Flame gives prayer access as well as wings. It gives prayer acceptance as well as energy. There is no incense without fire, no prayer without flame.

> *We, today, need to have the live coal from God's altar and the consuming flame from heaven glowing in our hearts. This flame is not mental power or fleshly energy. It is divine, intense, dross-consuming fire in the soul.*

Ardent desire is the basis of unceasing prayer. It is not a shallow, fickle tendency, but a strong yearning— an unquenchable desire that permeates, glows, burns, and fixes the heart. It is the flame of a present and active principle ascending up to God. It is ardor propelled by desire that burns its way to the throne of mercy and gets its request. It is the determination of desire that gives victory in a great struggle of prayer. It is the burden of a weighty desire that sobers, makes rest less, and reduces to quietness the soul just emerged from its mighty wrestlings. It is the inclusive character of desire that arms prayer with a thousand requests. It clothes it with an indestructible courage and an all-conquering power.

The Syrophenician woman is an object lesson of desire. The demanding widow represents desire gaining its end, overcoming obstacles that would be insurmountable to weaker instincts.

Prayer is not the rehearsal of a mere performance. It is not an indefinite, widespread demand. Desire, while it ignites the soul, holds it to the object sought. Prayer is a necessary phase of spiritual habit, but it ceases to be prayer when it is carried on by habit alone. Depth and strength of spiritual desire give intensity and depth to prayer. The soul cannot be unconcerned when some great desire heats and inflames it. The urgency of our desire holds us to the thing desired with a courage that refuses to be lessened or loosened. It stays, pleads, persists, and refuses to let go until the blessing has been given.

> Lord, I cannot let Thee go,
> Till a blessing Thou bestow;
> Do not turn away Thy face;
> Mine's an urgent, pressing case.

The secret of cowardice, the lack of demanding, and the scarcity of courage and strength in prayer lie in the weakness of spiritual desire. The failure of prayer is the fearful evidence of that desire having ceased to live. That soul whose desire for Him no longer pushes into the inner room, has turned from God. There is no successful prayer without consuming desire. Of course, there can be much *seeming* to pray, without desire of any kind.

Many things may be listed and much ground covered. But does desire make up the list? Does desire map out the region to be covered? The answer hangs on the issue of whether our petitioning is babbling or prayer. Desire is intense but narrow. It cannot spread itself over a wide area. It wants a few things and wants them badly. It wants them so badly that nothing but God's willingness to answer can bring it ease or contentment.

Desire shoots at its objective. There may be many things that are desired, but they are specifically and individually felt and expressed. David did not yearn for everything. He did not allow his desires to spread out everywhere and hit nothing. Here is the way his desires ran and found expression:

> *One thing have I desired of the LORD, that will I seek after; that I may dwell in the house of the LORD all the days of my life, to behold the beauty of the LORD, and to inquire in His temple.* (Psalm 27:4)

It is this singleness of desire, this definite yearning, that counts in praying and drives prayer directly to the core and center of supply.

In the Beatitudes, Jesus voiced the words that bear directly upon the inborn desires of a renewed soul with the promise that they will be granted. *"Blessed are they which do hunger and thirst after righteousness: for they shall be filled"* (Matthew 5:6).

This, then, is the basis of prayer that expects an answer. It is that strong, inward desire that has entered the spiritual appetite and demands to be satisfied. For us, it is entirely true and frequent that our prayers operate in the dry area of a mere wish or in the lifeless area of a memorized prayer. Sometimes our prayers are merely stereotyped expressions of set phrases and standardized dimensions. The freshness and life has gone out long ago.

Without desire, there is no burden of the soul, no sense of need, no enthusiasm, no vision, no strength, and no glow of faith. There is no strong pressure, no holding on to God with a deathless, despairing grasp—*"I will not let thee go, except thou bless me"* (Genesis 32:26). There is no total surrender as there was with Moses. Lost in the agony of a desperate, stubborn, and all - consuming request, he cried, *"Yet now, if thou wilt forgive their sin—; and if not, blot me, I pray thee, out of thy book which thou hast written"* (Exodus 32:32). Or, there was also John Knox when he pleaded, "Give me Scotland, or may I die!"

God draws very close to the praying soul. To see God, know God, and live for God—these form the objective of all true praying. So, praying is, after all, inspired to seek after God. Prayer desire is ignited to see God and have a clearer, fuller, sweeter, and richer revelation of God. To those who pray this way, the Bible becomes a new Bible and Christ a new Savior by the light and revelation of the prayer closet.

We affirm and reaffirm that burning desire because the best and most powerful gifts and graces of the Spirit of God are the real heritage of true praying. Self and service cannot be divorced. They cannot possibly be separated. More than that, desire must be made intensely personal. It must be centered on God with an insatiable hungering and thirsting after Him and His righteousness. *"My soul thirsteth for God, for the living God"* (Psalm 42:2). The essential prerequisite for all true praying is a deep-seated desire that seeks after God Himself. It remains unsatisfied until the choice gifts in heaven have been richly and abundantly given.

FIVE:

PRAYER AND ENTHUSIASM

St. Teresa rose off her deathbed to finish her work. She inspected, with all her quickness of eye and love of order, the whole house where she had been carried to die. She saw everything put in its proper place and everyone answering to their proper order. After that she attended to the divine offices of the day. Then she went back to her bed, summoned her daughter around her... and, with David's penitential prayers on her tongue, Teresa of Avila went forth to meet her Bridegroom. —Alexander Whyte

Prayer without burning enthusiasm stakes nothing on the issue, because it has nothing to stake. It comes with empty hands. These hands are listless, empty, and have never learned the lesson of clinging to the cross.

Prayer without enthusiasm has no heart in it. It is an empty thing, an unfit vessel. Heart, soul, and life must find a place in all real praying. Heaven must be made to feel the force of this crying unto God.

Paul was a notable example of the man who possesses a fervent spirit of prayer. His petitioning was all-consuming. It centered immovably upon the object of his desire and the God who was able to meet it.

Prayers must be red-hot. It is the fervent prayer that is effective and profitable. Coldness of spirit hinders praying. It takes fire to make prayers go. A warm soul creates a favorable atmosphere to prayer because it is favorable to fervency. Prayer ascends to heaven by fire. Yet, fire is not fuss, heat, or noise. Heat is intensity— something that glows and burns.

God wants warmhearted servants. The Holy Spirit comes *as a fire* to dwell in us. We are to be baptized with the Holy Spirit and with fire. (See Luke 3:16.) Fervency is warmth of soul. A phlegmatic temperament is detestable to vital experience. If our faith does not set us on fire, it is because we have frozen hearts. God dwells in a flame; the Holy Spirit descends in fire. To be absorbed in God's will and to be so in earnest about doing it that our whole being takes fire are the qualifying conditions of the man who would engage in effective prayer.

Our Lord warns us against feeble praying. *"Men ought always to pray, and not to faint"* (Luke 18:1), said Christ to His disciples. This means that we are to possess enough enthusiasm to carry us through the severe and long periods of pleading prayer. Fire makes one alert, vigilant, and brings him out more than a conqueror. The atmosphere about us is too heavily charged with resisting forces for limp and languid prayers to make headway. It takes heat, fervency, and meteoric fire to push through to the upper heavens where God dwells with His saints in light.

Many of the great Bible characters were notable examples of fervency of spirit when they were seeking God. The psalmist declared with great earnestness, *"My soul breaketh for the longing that it hath unto thy judgments at all times"* (Ps. 119:20). What strong heart desires are here! What earnest soul longings there are for the Word of the living God! An even greater fervency is expressed by him in another place:

> *As the hart panteth after the water brooks, so panteth my soul after thee, O God. My soul thirsteth for God, for the living God: when shall I come and appear before God?* (Psalm 42:1–2)

This is the word of a man who lived in a state of grace and had been deeply and supernaturally fulfilled in his soul.

Fervency before God counts in the hour of prayer and finds a speedy and rich reward at His hands. The psalmist gave us this statement of what God had done for the king, as his heart turned toward his Lord: *"Thou hast given him his heart's desire, and hast not withholden the request of his lips"* (Psalm 21:2).

At another time, he expressed himself directly to God in making his request: *"Lord, all my desire is before thee; and my groaning is not hid from thee"* (Psalm 38:9). What a cheerful thought! Our inward groanings, our secret desires, our heart longings are not hidden from the eyes of Him with whom we deal in prayer.

The incentive to fervency of spirit before God is precisely the same as it is for continued and earnest prayer. While fervency is not prayer, yet it comes out of an earnest soul and is precious in the sight of God. Fervency in prayer is the forerunner of what God will do by way of an answer. When we seek His face in prayer, God stands pledged to give us the desire of our hearts in proportion to the fervency of spirit we exhibit.

Fervency has its seat in the heart, not in the brain or intellectual faculties of the mind. Fervency, therefore, is not an expression of the intellect. Fervency of spirit is something far above poetical fancy or sentimental imagery. It is something besides preference, which contrasts likes with dislikes. Fervency is the pulse and movement of the emotional nature.

> *Fervency in prayer is the forerunner of what God will do by way of an answer. When we seek His face in prayer, God stands pledged to give us the desire of our hearts in proportion to the fervency of spirit we exhibit.*

It is not our job to create fervency of spirit at will, but we can ask God to implant it. Then, it is ours to nourish and cherish, guard against extinction, and prevent its lessening or decline. The process of personal salvation

Prayer and Enthusiasm 339

is not just to pray and express our desires to God. But it is to acquire a fervent spirit and seek to cultivate it. It is never wrong to ask God to create in us and keep alive the spirit of fervent prayer.

Fervency has to do with God, just as prayer has to do with Him. Desire always has an objective. If we desire at all, we desire *something*. The degree of enthusiasm with which we form our spiritual desires will always serve to determine the earnestness of our praying. In this relation, Adoniram Judson has said,

> A travailing spirit, the throes of a great burdened desire, belongs to prayer. A fervency strong enough to drive away sleep, which devotes and inflames the spirit and which retires all earthly ties, all this belongs to wrestling, prevailing prayer. The Spirit, the power, the air, and food of prayer is in such a spirit.

Prayer must be clothed with fervency, strength, and power. It is the force that, centered on God, determines the amount of Himself given out for earthly good. Men who are fervent in spirit are bent on attaining righteousness, truth, grace, and all other sublime, powerful graces that adorn the character of the authentic, unquestioned child of God.

God once declared the following message by the mouth of the prophet Hanani to Asa. Asa, at one time, had been true to God. But, through success and material prosperity, he lost his faith.

> *The eyes of the LORD run to and fro throughout the whole earth, to show himself strong in the behalf of them whose heart is perfect toward him. Herein thou hast done foolishly: therefore from henceforth thou shalt have wars.* (2 Chronicles 16:9)

God had heard Asa's prayer in early life; but because he had given up the life of prayer and simple faith, disaster and trouble came to him.

In Romans 15:30 we have the word *strive* in the request that Paul made for prayerful cooperation. In Colossians 4:12 we have the same word, but translated differently: "*Epaphras...always labouring fervently for you in prayers.*" Paul charged the Romans to strive together with him in prayer, that is, to help him with his struggle in prayer. The word *strive* means "to enter into a contest, to fight against adversaries." It also means "to engage with fervent zeal to endeavor to obtain."

These recorded instances of the exercise and reward of faith allow us to see that, in almost every instance, faith was blended with trust until the former was swallowed up in the latter. It is hard to properly distinguish the specific activities of these two qualities, faith and trust. But there is a point at which faith is relieved of its burden, so to speak, and trust comes along and says, "You have done your part. The rest is mine!"

In the incident of the barren fig tree, our Lord transfers the marvelous power of faith to His disciples.

To their exclamation, *"How soon is the fig tree withered away!"* (Matthew 21:20), He said,

> *If ye have faith, and doubt not, ye shall not only do this which is done to the fig tree, but also if ye shall say unto this mountain, Be thou removed, and be thou cast into the sea; it shall be done. And all things, whatsoever ye shall ask in prayer, believing, ye shall receive.*
>
> (Matthew 21:21–22)

When a believer achieves these magnificent proportions of faith, he steps into the realm of absolute trust. He stands without a tremor at the height of his spiritual outreaching. He has attained faith's top step, which is unswerving, unalterable, unquestionable trust in the power of the living God.

SIX:

PRAYER THAT IS PERSISTENT

How glibly we talk of praying without ceasing! Yet, we are quite ready to quit if our prayer remains unanswered for one week or a month! We assume that by a stroke of His arm or an action of His will, God will give us what we ask. It never seems to dawn on us that He is the Master of nature, as of grace, and that sometimes He chooses one way, and sometimes another, to do His work. It takes years, sometimes, to answer a prayer. When it is answered, we can look back to see that it did take years. But God knows all the time. It is His will that we pray and pray and still pray, and so come to know indeed what it is to pray without ceasing.

—Anonymous

Our Lord Jesus declared that *"men ought always to pray, and not to faint"* (Luke 18:1). The parable that comes after these words was taught with the intention of saving men from faintheartedness and weakness in prayer. Our Lord wanted to teach us to guard against negligence and to encourage and bring about persistence. We cannot have two opinions regarding the importance of the exercise of this indispensable quality in our praying.

Persistent prayer is a mighty move of the soul toward God. It is a stirring of the deepest forces of the soul toward the throne of heavenly grace. It is the ability to hold on, press on, and wait. Restless desire, restful patience, and strength to hold on are all embraced in it. It is not an incident or a performance, but a passion of soul. It is not something half-needed, but a sheer necessity.

The wrestling quality in persistent prayer does not spring from physical violence or fleshly energy. It is not an impulse of energy or a mere earnestness of the soul. It is an inward force or ability planted and roused by the Holy Spirit. Virtually, it is the intercession of the Spirit of God in us. It is *the effectual fervent prayer...[that] availeth much*" (James 5:16). The divine Spirit supplies every part of us with the energy of His own striving. This is the essence of the persistence that urges our praying at the mercy seat to continue until the fire falls and the blessing descends. This wrestling in prayer is not loud or vehement, but quiet, firm, and urgent. When there are no visible outlets for its mighty forces, it may be silent.

Nothing distinguishes the children of God so clearly and strongly as prayer. It is the one infallible mark and test of being a Christian. Christian people are prayerful. The worldly-minded are prayerless. Christians call on God. The world ignores God and does not call on His name. But even the Christian has to cultivate *continual* prayer. It must be habitual, but it must be much more than a habit. It is duty, yet it is one that rises far above and goes beyond the ordinary implications of the term. It is the expression of a relationship with God, a yearning for divine communion. It is the outward and upward flow of the inner life toward its original fountain. It is a statement of the soul's origin, a claiming of sonship that links man to the eternal.

Prayer has everything to do with molding the soul into the image of God. It also has everything to do with elevating and enlarging the measure of divine grace. It has everything to do with bringing the soul into complete communion with God. It has everything to do with enriching, broadening, and maturing the soul's experience of God. A man who does not pray cannot possibly be called a Christian. There is no possible way that he can claim any right to the term or its implied significance. If he does not pray, he is a sinner, pure and simple. Prayer is the only way the soul of man can enter into fellowship and communion with the source of all Christlike spirit and energy. Therefore, if he does not pray, he is not of the household of faith.

Even the Christian has to cultivate continual prayer. It must be habitual, but it must be much more than a habit. It is duty, yet it is one that rises far above and goes beyond the ordinary implications of the term. It is the expression of a relationship with God, a yearning for divine communion.

In this study, however, we will turn our attention to one phase of prayer—persistence. It is the pressing of our desires on God with urgency and perseverance. It is praying with the kind of courage and tension that neither relaxes nor stops until its cry is heard and its cause is won.

The man who has clear views of God, has scriptural conceptions of the divine character, appreciates his privilege of approach to God, and understands his inward need of all that God has for him will be eager, outspoken, and persistent. In Scripture, the duty of prayer is advocated in terms that are barely stronger than those in which the necessity for its persistence is mentioned. Praying that influences God is said to be the outpouring of the fervent, effectual righteous man. (See James 5:16.) It is prayer on fire. It does not have a feeble, flickering flame or a momentary flash, but it shines with a vigorous, steady glow.

The repeated intercessions of Abraham for the salvation of Sodom and Gomorrah present an early example of the necessity for and benefit derived from persistent prayer. The case of Jacob, wrestling all night with the angel, gives significant emphasis to the power of a dogged perseverance in prayer. It shows how, in spiritual things, persistence succeeds just as effectively as it does in matters relating to time and sense.

Moses prayed forty days and forty nights to stop the wrath of God against Israel. His example and success are a stimulus to present-day faith in its darkest hour. Elijah repeated his prayer seven times before the rain clouds appeared above the horizon and heralded the success of his prayer and the victory of his faith. On one occasion, Daniel, though faint and weak, pressed his case for three weeks before the answer and the blessing came. (See Daniel 10.)

During His earthly life, the blessed Savior spent many nights in prayer. In Gethsemane He presented the same petition three times with unshaken, urgent, yet submissive persistence. This called on every part of His soul and brought about tears and bloody sweat. His life crises were distinctly marked with, and His life victories were all won in, hours of persistent prayer. So, the servant is not greater than his Lord.

The parable of the persistent widow is a classic example of insistent prayer. We would do well to refresh our memories, at this point in our study, by reading the account from Scripture.

> *And he spake a parable unto them to this end, that men ought always to pray, and not to faint; saying, There was in a city a judge, which feared not God, neither regarded man: and there was a widow in that city; and she came unto him, saying, Avenge me of my adversary. And he would not for a while: but afterward he said within himself, Though I fear not God, nor regard man; yet because this widow troubleth me, I will avenge her, lest by her continual coming she weary me. And the Lord said, Hear what the unjust judge saith. And shall not God avenge his own elect, which cry day and night unto him, though he bear long with them? I tell you he will avenge them speedily.* (Luke 18:1–8)

This parable stresses the central truth of persistent prayer. The widow presses her case until the unjust judge yields. If this parable does not teach the necessity for persistence, it does not have any purpose or teaching. Take this one thought away, and you have nothing left worth recording. Beyond objection, Christ intended it to stand as evidence of the need that exists for insistent prayer.

We have the same teaching emphasized in the incident of the Syrophenician woman, who came to Jesus on behalf of her daughter. Here,

Prayer That Is Persistent 345

persistence is shown, not as rudeness, but as the persuasive equipment of humility, sincerity, and fervency. We are given a glimpse of a woman's clinging faith, her bitter grief, and her spiritual insight. The Master went to that Sidonian country so that this truth could be shown for all time: There is no cry as effective as persistent prayer, and there is no prayer to which God surrenders Himself so fully and so freely.

The persistence of this distressed mother won her the victory and brought about her request. Instead of being an offense to the Savior, it drew from Him a word of wonder and glad surprise: *"O woman, great is thy faith: be it unto thee even as thou wilt"* (Matthew 15:28).

He who does not push his plea does not pray at all. Cold prayers have no claim on heaven and no hearing in the courts above. Fire is the life of prayer, and heaven is reached by fiery persistence rising in an ascending scale. Going back to the case of the persistent widow, we see that her widowhood, friendlessness, and weakness did not count for anything with the unjust judge. Persistence was everything. *"Because this widow troubleth me,"* he said, *"I will avenge her* [speedily], *lest…she weary me."* Because the widow imposed upon the time and attention of the unjust judge, her case was won.

God waits patiently as, day and night, His elect cry to Him. He is moved by their requests a thousand times more than this unjust judge was. A limit is set to His waiting by the persistent praying of His people, and the answer is richly given. God finds faith in His praying child. He honors this faith that stays and cries by permitting its further exercise, so that it is strengthened and enriched. Then He rewards it in abundance.

The case of the Syrophenician woman is a notable instance of successful persistence. It is one that is highly encouraging to all who pray successfully. It is a remarkable example of insistence and perseverance to ultimate victory in the face of insurmountable obstacles and hindrances. But the woman overcame them all by heroic faith and persistent spirit. Jesus had gone over into her country, *"and would have no man know it"* (Mark 7:24). But she breaks through His purpose, violates His privacy, attracts His attention, and pours out to Him a distressing appeal of need and faith. Her heart was in her prayer.

At first, Jesus appears to pay no attention to her agony and ignores her cry for relief. He gives her neither eye nor ear nor word. Silence, deep and chilling, greets her impassioned cry. But she is not turned aside or disheartened. She holds on. The disciples, offended at her unseemly noise, inter cede for her, but they are silenced by the Lord's declaring that the woman is entirely outside the scope of His mission and His ministry.

But neither the failure of the disciples to gain her a hearing nor the despairing knowledge that she is barred from the benefits of His mission stop her. They serve only to lend intensity and increased boldness in her approach to Christ. She came closer, cutting her prayer in half, and fell at His feet. Worshipping Him, she made her daughter's case her own and cries with pointed brevity, *"Lord, help me!"* (Matthew 15:25). This last cry won her case. Her daughter was healed the same hour. Hopeful, urgent, and unwearied, she stays near the Master, insisting and praying until the answer is given. What a study in persistence, in earnestness. They were promoted and propelled under conditions that would have disheartened any but a heroic, constant soul.

In these parables of persistent praying, our Lord stated, for our information and encouragement, the serious difficulties that stand in the way of prayer. At the same time, He taught that persistence conquers all unfavorable circumstances and gets itself a victory over a whole host of obstacles.

He taught that an answer to prayer is conditional upon the amount of faith that goes into the petition. To test this, He will delay the answer. The super superficial pray-er sinks into silence when the answer is delayed, but the man of prayer hangs on and on. The Lord recognizes and honors his faith and gives him a rich, abundant answer to his faith-evidencing, persistent prayer.

SEVEN:

PRAYER THAT MOTIVATES GOD

Two-thirds of the praying we do is for that which would give us the greatest possible pleasure to receive. It is a sort of spiritual self-indulgence in which we engage and, as a consequence, is the exact opposite of self-discipline. God knows all this and keeps His children asking. In the process of time—His time—our petitions take on another aspect, and we, another spiritual approach. God keeps us praying until, in His wisdom, He is ready to answer. And no matter how long it may be before He speaks, it is, even then, far earlier than we have a right to expect or hope to deserve.

—Anonymous

The purpose of Christ's teachings is to declare that men are to pray earnestly. They are to pray with an earnestness that cannot be denied. Heaven has listening ears only for the wholehearted and the deeply earnest. Energy, courage, and perseverance must back the prayers that heaven respects and that God hears.

348 E. M. Bounds on Prayer & Spiritual Warfare

All these qualities of soul, so essential to effectual praying, are brought out in the parable of the man who went to his friend for bread at midnight. (See Luke 11:5–10.) This man went on his errand with confidence. Friendship promised him success. His cry was pressing. Truly, he could not go back empty-handed. The flat refusal shamed and surprised him. Here even friendship failed! But there was still something to be tried—stern resolution and fixed determination. He would stay and pursue his demand until the door was opened and the request granted. He proceeded to do this and, by persistence, secured what ordinary requesting had failed to obtain.

The success of this man, achieved in the face of a flat denial, was used by the Savior to illustrate the need for insistence in humble prayer before the throne of heavenly grace. When the answer is not immediately given, the praying Christian must gather courage at each delay. He must urgently go forward until the answer comes. The answer is assured, if he has the faith to press his petition with vigorous faith.

Negligence, faintheartedness, impatience, and fear will be fatal to our prayers. The Father's heart, hand, infinite power, and infinite willingness to hear and give to His children are waiting for the start of our insistence.

Persistent praying is the earnest, inward movement of the heart toward God. It is throwing the entire force of the spiritual man into the exercise of prayer. Isaiah lamented that no one stirred himself to take hold of God. There was much praying done in Isaiah's time, but it was too easy, indifferent, and complacent. There were no mighty moves by souls toward God. There was no array of sanctified energies bent on reaching and grappling with God. There was no energy to draw the treasures of His grace from Him. Forceless prayers have no power to overcome difficulties, win marked results, or gain complete victories. We must win God before we can win our plea.

Persistent praying is the earnest, inward movement of the heart toward God. It is throwing the entire force of the spiritual man into the exercise of prayer.

Isaiah looked with hopeful eyes to the day when faith would flourish and there would be times of real praying. When those times would come, the watchmen would not weaken their vigilance, but would cry day and night. And those who were the Lord's remembrancers would give Him no rest. (See Isaiah 62:6–7.) Their urgent, persistent efforts would keep all spiritual interests busy and make increasing demands on God's exhaustless treasures.

Persistent praying never faints or grows weary. It is never discouraged. It never yields to coward ice but is lifted up and sustained by a hope that knows no despair and a faith that will not let go. Persistent praying has patience to wait and strength to continue. It never prepares itself to quit praying, and it refuses to get up from its knees until an answer is received.

The familiar words of the great missionary Adoniram Judson are the testimony of a man who was persistent at prayer. He said,

I was never deeply interested in any object, never prayed sincerely and earnestly for it, but that it came at some time, no matter how distant the day. Somehow, in some shape, probably the last I would have devised, it came.

"*Ask, and it shall be given you; seek, and ye shall find; knock, and it shall be opened unto you*" (Matthew 7:7). These are the ringing challenges of our Lord in regard to prayer. These challenges are His explanation that true praying must stay and advance in effort and urgency until the prayer is answered and the blessing sought is received.

In the three words *ask, seek,* and *knock*, Jesus, by the order in which He places them, urges the necessity of persistence in prayer. Asking, seeking, and knocking are ascending rungs in the ladder of successful prayer. No principle is more definitely enforced by Christ than that successful prayer must have in it the quality that waits and perseveres. It must have in it the courage that never surrenders, the patience that never grows tired, and the resolution that never wavers.

In the parable of the friend at midnight, a most significant and instructive lesson in this respect is outlined. Chief among the qualities included in Christ's estimate of the highest and most successful form of praying are the following: unbeatable courage, ceaseless persistence, and stability of purpose.

Persistence is made up of intensity, perseverance, and patience. The apparent delay in answering prayer is the ground and demand of persistence. In Matthew we have the first recorded instance of the miracle of healing the blind. We have an illustration of the way in which our Lord did not seem to hear immediately those who sought Him. But the two blind men continued their crying and followed Him with their continual petition saying, "*Thou son of David, have mercy on us*" (Matthew 9:27). But He did not answer them and went into the house. The needy ones followed Him and, finally, gained their eyesight and their plea.

The case of blind Bartimaeus is a notable one in many ways. (See Mark 10:46–52.) It is especially remarkable for the show of persistence that this blind man exhibited in appealing to our Lord. His first crying, as it seems, was done as Jesus entered Jericho, and he continued it until Jesus came out of the place. It is a strong illustration of the necessity of persistent prayer. It is also an illustration of the success that comes to those who stake their all on Christ and do not give Him any peace until He grants them their hearts' desire.

Mark put the entire incident clearly before us. At first, Jesus seems not to hear. The crowd rebukes the noisy babbling of Bartimaeus. Despite the apparent unconcern of our Lord and the rebuke of an impatient, quick-tempered crowd, the blind beggar still cries. He increases the loudness of his cry until Jesus is impressed and moved. Finally, the crowd, as well as Jesus, listens to the beggar's cry and speaks in favor of his cause. He wins his case. His persistence wins even in the face of apparent neglect on the part of Jesus and despite opposition and rebuke from the surrounding crowd. His persistence won where halfhearted indifference would surely have failed.

Faith functions in connection with prayer and, of course, has its inseparable association with persistence. But the latter quality *drives* the prayer to the believing point. A persistent spirit brings a man to the place where faith takes hold, claims, and appropriates the blessing.

The absolute necessity of persistent prayer is plainly stated in the Word of God and needs to be stated and restated today. We are inclined to overlook this vital truth. Love of ease, spiritual laziness, and religious indifference all operate against this type of petitioning. Our praying, however, needs to be coaxed and pursued with an energy that never tires. It needs to have a persistency that will not be denied and a courage that never fails.

We also need to give thought to that mysterious fact of prayer—the certainty that there will be delays, denials, and seeming failures in connection with its exercise. We are to prepare for these and to permit them. However, we must not cease in our urgent praying. The praying Christian is like a brave soldier who, as the conflict grows more severe, exhibits a more superior courage than in the earlier stages of the battle. When delay and denial face him, he increases his earnest asking and does not stop until prayer prevails.

Moses furnished us with an excellent example of persistence in prayer. Instead of allowing his intimacy with God to release him from the necessity for persistence, he regarded it as something better to fit him for its exercise.

When Israel set up the golden calf, the wrath of God increased fiercely against them. Jehovah, bent on executing justice, said to Moses when He told him what He purposed to do, *"Let me alone"* (Exodus 32:10). But Moses would not let Him alone. He threw himself down before the Lord in an agony of intercession on behalf of the sinning Israelites. For forty days and nights he fasted and prayed. What a season of persistent prayer that was!

Jehovah was also angry with Aaron, who had acted as leader in this idolatrous business of the golden calf. But Moses prayed for Aaron as well as for the Israelites. If he had not prayed, both Israel and Aaron would have perished under the consuming fire of God's wrath.

That long period of pleading before God left a mighty impression on Moses. He had been in close relationship with God before, but his character never attained the greatness that marked it in the days and years following this long season of persistent intercession.

There can be no question about persistent prayer moving God and heightening human character. If we were more in agreement with God in this great command of intercession, our faces would shine more brightly.

Our lives and service would possess richer qualities that earn the goodwill of humanity and bring glory to the name of God.

EIGHT:

PRAYER AND CHRISTIAN CONDUCT

General Charles James Gordon, the hero of Khartoum, was a truly Christian soldier. Shut up in the Sudanese town, he gallantly held out for one year, but finally was overcome and slain. On his memorial in Westminster Abbey are these words: "He gave his money to the poor, his sympathy to the sorrowing, his life to his country, and his soul to God."
—Homer W. Hodge

Prayer governs conduct, and conduct makes character. Conduct is what we do; character is what we are. Conduct is the outward life; character is the unseen life, hidden within, yet evidenced by that which is seen. Conduct is external, seen from without; character is internal, operating within. In the economy of grace, conduct is the offspring of character. Character is the state of the heart; conduct is its outward expression. Character is the root of the tree; conduct is the fruit it bears.

Prayer is related to all the gifts of grace. Its relationship to character and conduct is that of a helper. Prayer helps to establish character and to fashion conduct. Both, for their successful continuance, depend on prayer. There may be a certain degree of moral character and conduct independent of prayer, but there cannot be any distinctive religious character and Christian conduct without it. Prayer helps where all other aids fail. The more we pray, the better we are, and the purer and better our lives become.

The very end and purpose of the atoning work of Christ is to create religious character and make Christian conduct.

Who gave himself for us, that he might redeem us from all iniquity, and purify unto himself a peculiar people, zealous of good works.

(Titus 2:14)

In Christ's teaching, it is not simply works of charity and deeds of mercy that He insists upon, but inward spiritual character. This much is demanded, and nothing short of it will suffice.

In the study of Paul's epistles, there is one thing that stands out clearly and unmistakably—the insistence on holiness of heart and righteousness of life. Paul did not seek to promote what is termed "personal work." The leading theme of his letters is not deeds of charity. Rather, it is the condition of the human heart and the blamelessness of the personal life that form the burden of Paul's writings.

It is character and conduct that are most important elsewhere in the Scriptures, too. The Christian religion deals with men who are lacking spiritual character and are unholy in life. It aims to change them so that they become holy in heart and righteous in life. It aims to change bad men into good men.

Here is where prayer enters and demonstrates its wonderful ability and fruit. Prayer drives toward this specific end. In fact, without prayer, no such supernatural change in moral character can ever be effected. The change from badness to goodness is not brought about *"by works of righteousness which we have done,"* but according to God's mercy, which saves us *"by the washing of regeneration"* (Titus 3:5). This marvelous change is brought to pass through earnest, persistent, faithful prayer. Any assumed form of Christianity that does not effect this change in the hearts of men is a delusion and a snare.

The office of prayer is to change the character and conduct of men. In countless instances, change has been brought about by prayer. At this point, prayer, by its credentials, has proven its divinity. Just as it is the office of prayer to effect this, it is the major work of the church to take hold of evil men and make them good. Its mission is to change human nature and character, influence behavior, and revolutionize conduct. The church is presumed to be righteous and should be engaged in turning men to righteousness.

The church is God's factory on earth. Its primary duty is to create and foster righteous character. This is its very first business. Its primary work is not to acquire members or amass numbers. Its aim is not to get money or engage in deeds of charity and works of mercy. Its work is to produce righteousness of character and purity of the outward life.

A product reflects and partakes of the character of the manufacturer that makes it. A righteous church with a righteous purpose makes righteous men. Prayer produces cleanliness of heart and purity of life. It can produce nothing else. Unrighteous conduct is born in prayerlessness. The two go hand in hand. Prayer and sinning cannot keep company with each other. One or the other must, of necessity, stop. Get men to pray, and they will quit sinning, because prayer creates a distaste for sinning. It works so much upon the heart that evildoing becomes repugnant. It lifts the entire nature to a reverent contemplation of high and holy things.

Prayer is based on character. What we are with God determines our influence with Him. It was the inner character, not the outward appearance, of such men as Abraham, Job, David, Moses, and others that had such great influence with God in the days of old. Today, it is not so much our words, but what we really are that counts with God. Conduct affects character, of course, and counts for much in our praying.

At the same time, character affects conduct to a far greater extent and has a superior influence over prayer. Our inner life gives color to our praying.

Bad living means bad praying and, in the end, no praying at all. We pray feebly because we live feebly. The stream of prayer cannot rise higher than the fountain of living. The force of the prayer closet is made up of the energy that emerges from the flowing streams of life. The weakness of living grows out of the shallowness and shoddiness of character.

Feebleness of living reflects its weakness in the praying hours. We simply cannot talk to God strongly, intimately, and confidently unless we are living for Him, faithfully and truly. The prayer closet cannot become sanctified to God when the life is alien to His laws and purpose. We must learn this lesson well. Righteous character and Christlike conduct give us a particular and preferential standing in prayer before God. The Word gives special emphasis to the part that conduct has in imparting value to our praying.

> *We simply cannot talk to God strongly, intimately, and confidently unless we are living for Him, faithfully and truly.*

> *Then shalt thou call, and the LORD shall answer; thou shalt cry, and he shall say, Here I am. If thou take away from the midst of thee the yoke, the putting forth of the finger, and speaking vanity.* (Isaiah 58:9)

The wickedness of Israel and their heinous practices were definitely cited by Isaiah as the reason why God would turn His ears away from their prayers. "*And when ye spread forth your hands, I will hide mine eyes from you: yea, when ye make many prayers, I will not hear: your hands are full of blood*" (Isaiah 1:15).

The same sad truth was declared by the Lord through the mouth of Jeremiah: "*Therefore pray not thou for this people, neither lift up a cry or prayer for them: for I will not hear them in the time that they cry unto me for their trouble*" (Jeremiah 11:14). Here, it is plainly stated that unholy conduct is a hindrance to successful praying. It is clearly suggested that, in order to have full access to God in prayer, there must be a total abandonment of conscious and premeditated sin.

We are commanded to pray, "*lifting up holy hands, without wrath and doubting*" (1 Timothy 2:8). We must pass the time we live here in a rigorous abstaining from evil if we are to keep our privilege of calling upon the Father. We cannot, by any process, divorce praying from conduct. *"And whatsoever we ask, we receive of him, because we keep his commandments, and do those things which are pleasing in his sight"* (1 John 3:22).

James declared that men ask and yet do not receive because they ask amiss and seek only the gratification of selfish desires. (See James 4:3.)

Our Lord's command to watch and pray always is to cover and guard all our conduct. Then we may come to our prayer closet with all its force secured by a vigilant guard kept over our lives.

> *And take heed to yourselves, lest at any time your hearts be overcharged with surfeiting, and drunkenness, and cares of this life, and so that day come upon you unawares.* (Luke 21:34)

Quite often, Christian experience collapses on the rock of conduct. Beautiful theories are marred by ugly lives. The most difficult thing about piety, because it is the most impressive, is to be able to live it. It is the life that counts. Our praying suffers, as do other phases of our religious experience, from bad living.

In early times, preachers were ordered to preach by their lives or not preach at all. Christians everywhere ought to be reminded to pray by their lives or not pray at all. The most effective preaching is not what is heard from the pulpit, but what is proclaimed quietly, humbly, and consistently. It is preaching that exhibits its excellencies in the home and in the community. Example preaches a far more effective sermon than instruction. The best preaching, even in the pulpit, is strengthened by the preacher living a godly life.

The most effective work done by people sitting in the pews is preceded by, and accompanied with, holiness of life, separation from the world, and severance from sin. Some of the strongest appeals are made with mute lips by godly fathers and saintly mothers. These parents, around the fireside, fear God, love His cause, and daily show their children and others around them the beauties and excellencies of Christian life and conduct.

The best prepared, most eloquent sermon can be marred and rendered ineffective by questionable practices in the preacher. The most active church worker can have the labor of his hands weakened by worldliness of spirit and inconsistency of life. Men preach by their lives, not by their words. Sermons are delivered, not so much in and from a pulpit, as they are in tempers, actions, and the thousand and one incidents that crowd the pathway of daily life.

Of course, the prayer of repentance is acceptable to God. He delights in hearing the cries of penitent sinners. But repentance involves not only sorrow for sin, but also turning away from wrongdoing and learning to do well. A repentance that does not produce a change in character and conduct is a mere sham that should deceive no one. Old things *must* pass away. All things *must* become new. (See 2 Corinthians 5:17.)

Praying that does not result in right thinking and right living is a farce. We have missed the whole office of prayer if it fails to purge character and correct conduct. We have failed entirely to understand the virtue of prayer if it does not bring about the revolutionizing of the life. In the very nature of things, we must either quit praying or quit our bad conduct. Cold, formal praying may exist side by side with bad conduct, but such praying, in God's estimation, is no praying at all. Our praying advances in power just as much as it rectifies the life. A prayerful life will grow in purity and devotion to God.

The character of the inner life is a condition of effective praying. As the life is, so the praying will be. An inconsistent life hinders praying and neutralizes what little praying we may do. Always, it is the prayer of the righteous man that avails much. (See James 5:16.) Indeed, one may go further and say that it is only the prayer of the righteous that avails anything at all, at any time. To have an eye to God's glory and to be possessed by an earnest desire to please Him in all our ways gives weight, influence, and power to prayer. To possess hands busy in His service and to have feet swift to run in the way of His commandments insure an audience with God. The oppression of our lives often breaks the force of our praying and, not infrequently, is as a door of brass in the face of prayer.

Praying must come out of a clean heart and be presented and urged with the *"lifting up [of] holy hands"* (1 Timothy 2:8). It must be strengthened by a life aiming, unceasingly, to obey God, to attain conformity to the divine law, and to come into submission to the divine will.

Let it not be forgotten that, while life is a condition of prayer, prayer is also the condition of righteous living. Prayer promotes righteous living and is the one great aid to uprightness of heart and life. The fruit of real praying is right living. Praying sets him who prays to the great business of working out his salvation with fear and trembling. (See Philippians 2:12.) It causes him to watch his temper, conversation, and conduct. It leads him to walk circumspectly and redeem the time. (See Ephesians 5:15–16.) It enables him to walk worthy of the vocation to which he is called, with all lowliness and meekness. (See Ephesians 4:1–2.) It gives him a high incentive to pursue his pilgrimage consistently by shunning every evil way to walk in the good. (See Psalm 199:101.)

NINE:

PRAYER AND OBEDIENCE

An obedience discovered itself in John Fletcher, which I wish I could describe or imitate. It produced in him a mind ready to embrace every cross with alacrity and pleasure. He had a singular love for the lambs of the flock and applied himself with the greatest diligence to their instruction for which he had a peculiar gift.... All his fellowship with me was so mingled with prayer and praise that every employment and every meal was, as it were, perfumed therewith.

—John Wesley

Under the Mosaic law, to obey was looked upon as being *"better than sacrifice, and to hearken than the fat of rams"* (1 Samuel 15:22). In Deuteronomy 5:29, Moses represented Almighty God declaring the importance He laid upon the exercise of this quality. Referring to the waywardness of His people, He cried,

> *O that there were such an heart in them, that they would fear me, and keep all my commandments always, that it might be well with them, and with their children for ever!*

Unquestionably, obedience is a high virtue, the quality of a soldier. To obey belongs, preeminently, to the soldier. It is his first and last lesson. He must learn how to practice it at all times without questioning or complaining. Obedience is faith in action. It is the outflow, the very test of love. *"He that hath my commandments, and keepeth them, he it is that loveth me"* (John 14:21).

Furthermore, obedience is love. *"If ye keep my commandments, ye shall abide in my love; even as I have kept my Father's commandments, and abide in his love"* (John 15:10). What a marvelous statement of the relationship created and maintained by obedience! The Son of God is held in the bosom of the Father's love by virtue of His obedience! The fact that allows the Son of God to ever abide in His Father's love is revealed in His own statement: *"For I do always those things that please him"* (John 8:29).

The gift of the Holy Spirit in full measure and in richer experience depends on loving obedience. *"If ye love me, keep my commandments"* is the Master's word. *"And I will pray the Father, and he shall give you another Comforter, that he may abide with you for ever"* (John 14:15–16).

Obedience to God is a condition of spiritual thrift, inward satisfaction, and stability of heart. Obedience opens the gates of the Holy City and gives access to the Tree of Life. *"Blessed are they that do his commandments, that they may have right to the tree of life, and may enter in through the gates into the city"* (Revelation 22:14).

What is obedience? It is doing God's will. It is keeping His commandments. How many of the commandments require obedience? To keep half of them and break the other half—is that real obedience? To keep all the commandments but one—is that obedience? The apostle James was very explicit on this point. *"Whosoever shall keep the whole law, and yet offend in one point, he is guilty of all"* (James 2:10).

The spirit that prompts a man to break one commandment is the spirit that may move him to break them all. God's commandments are a unit. To break one strikes at the principle that underlies and runs through the whole. He who does not hesitate to break a single commandment probably would, under the same stress and surrounded by the same circumstances, break them all.

Universal obedience of the race is demanded. Nothing short of absolute obedience will satisfy God. The keeping of all His commandments is the demonstration of obedience that God requires. But can we keep all of God's commandments? Can a man receive moral ability that helps him to obey every one of them? Certainly he can. By the same token, man can, through prayer, obtain ability to do this very thing.

Does God give commandments that men cannot obey? Is He so arbitrary, so severe, so unloving, that He issues commandments that cannot be obeyed? The answer is that, in all of Scripture, not a single instance is recorded of God having commanded any man to do a thing that was beyond his power. Is God so unjust and so inconsiderate to require of man something that he is unable to do? Certainly not. To infer it is to slander the character of God.

Let us think about this thought for a moment. Do earthly parents require their children to perform duties that they cannot do? Where is the father who would even think of being so unjust and so tyrannical? Is God less kind and just than faulty earthly parents? Are they better and more just than a perfect God? What a foolish and inconsistent thought!

In principle, obedience to God is the same quality as obedience to earthly parents. It implies, in general, the giving up of one's own way to follow that of another. It requires the surrender of the will to the will of another. It implies the submission of oneself to the authority and requirements of a parent. Commands, either from our heavenly Father or our earthly father, are directed by love. All such commands are in the best interests of those who are commanded. God's commands are not issued in severity or tyranny. They are always issued in love and in our interests. So, it is important for us to pay attention and obey them. In other words, God has issued His commands to us in order to promote our good.

It pays, therefore, to be obedient. Obedience brings its own reward. God has ordained it so. Since He has, even human reason can realize that He would never demand what is out of our power to perform.

Obedience is love fulfilling every command. It is love expressing itself. Obedience, therefore, is not a hard demand made on us. It is not any more than the service a husband renders to his wife or a wife renders to her husband. Love delights to obey and please whom it loves. There are no hardships in love. There may be demands, but there are no irritations. There are no impossible tasks for love.

> *God's commands are not issued in severity or tyranny. They are always issued in love and in our interests. So, it is important for us to pay attention and obey them. In other words, God has issued His commands to us in order to promote our good.*

How simply and matter-of-factly John said, "*And whatsoever we ask, we receive of him, because we keep his commandments, and do those things that are pleasing in his sight*" (1 John 3:22). This is obedience, running ahead of every command. It is love, obeying by anticipation. Those who say that men are bound to commit sin because of environment, heredity, or tendency greatly err, and even sin. God's commands are not grievous (1 John 5:3). Their ways are pleasant, and their paths are peaceful. The task that falls to obedience is not a hard one. "*For my yoke is easy, and my burden is light*" (Matthew 11:30).

Far be it from our heavenly Father to demand impossibilities of His children. It is possible to please Him in all things, for He is not hard to please. He is neither a hard master nor an austere lord, "*taking up that* [he] *laid not down, and reaping that* [he] *did not sow*" (Luke 19:22). Thank God it is possible for every child of God to please his heavenly Father! It is really much easier to please Him than to please men. Moreover, we may *know* when we please Him. This is the witness of the Spirit—the inward, divine assurance given to all the children of God that they are doing their Father's will and that their ways are well pleasing in His sight.

God's commandments are righteous and founded in justice and wisdom. "*Wherefore the law is holy, and the commandment holy, and just, and good*" (Romans 7:12). "*Just and true are thy ways, thou King of saints*" (Revelation 15:3). God's commandments, then, can be obeyed by all who seek supplies of grace that enable them to obey. These commandments

364 *E. M. Bounds on Prayer & Spiritual Warfare*

must be obeyed. God's government is at stake. God's children are under obligation to obey Him. Disobedience can not be permitted. The spirit of rebellion is the very essence of sin. It is denial of God's authority that God cannot tolerate. He has never done so. A declaration of His attitude was part of the reason why the Son of the Highest was made manifest among men.

> *For what the law could not do, in that it was weak through the flesh, God sending his own Son in the likeness of sinful flesh, and for sin, condemned sin in the flesh: that the righteousness of the law might be fulfilled in us, who walk not after the flesh, but after the Spirit.*
>
> (Romans 8:3–4)

If anyone complains that man under the Fall is too weak and helpless to obey these high commands of God, the answer is that, through the atonement of Christ, man is able to obey. The Atonement is God's enabling act. God places in us, through regeneration and the agency of the Holy Spirit, the enabling grace sufficient for all that is required of us under the Atonement. This grace is furnished without measure in answer to prayer.

So, while God commands, He, at the same time, stands pledged to give us all the necessary strength of will and grace of soul to meet His demands. Because this is true, man has no excuse for disobedience. He is immediately criticized for refusing or failing to secure necessary grace, whereby he may serve the Lord with reverence and godly fear.

Those who say it is impossible to keep God's commandments overlook one important consideration. It is the vital truth that, through prayer and faith, man's nature is changed and made partaker of the divine nature. All reluctance to obey God is taken out of him. His natural inability to keep God's commandments, growing out of his fallen and helpless state, is gloriously removed. By this radical change in his moral nature, a man receives power to obey God in every way and to yield full and glad allegiance. Then he can say, "*I delight to do thy will, O my God*" (Psalm 40:8). Not only is rebellion of the natural man removed, but he also receives a heart that gladly obeys God's Word.

There is no denying that the unrenewed man cannot obey God. But to declare that—after one is renewed by the Holy Spirit, has received a new

Prayer and Obedience 365

nature, and become a child of the King—he *cannot* obey God is to assume a ridiculous attitude. It is to show a lamentable ignorance of the work and implications of the Atonement.

Absolute and perfect obedience is the state to which the man of prayer is called. "*Lifting up holy hands, without wrath and doubting*" (1 Timothy 2:8) is the condition of obedient praying. Here, inward loyalty and love, together with outward cleanliness, are set forth as accompaniments of acceptable praying.

John gave the reason for answered prayer in the passage previously quoted: "*And whatsoever we ask, we receive of him, because we keep his commandments, and do those things that are pleasing in his sight*" (1 John 3:22). Because we have said that keeping God's commandments is the reason why He answers prayer, it is reasonable to assume that we *can* keep God's commandments. We *can* do those things that are pleasing to Him. Do you think God would make the keeping of His commandments a condition of effective prayer if He knew we could not keep His statutes? *Certainly not!*

Obedience can ask with boldness at the throne of grace. Those who exercise it are the only ones who can ask after that fashion. The disobedient folk are timid in their approach and hesitant in their supplication. They are stopped by their wrongdoing. The requesting, obedient child comes into the presence of his Father with confidence and boldness. His very consciousness of obedience gives him courage and frees him from the dread born of disobedience.

To do God's will without hesitation is the joy and the privilege of the successful praying man. He who has clean hands and a pure heart can pray with confidence. In the Sermon on the Mount, Jesus said, "*Not every one that saith unto me, Lord, Lord, shall enter into the kingdom of heaven, but he that doeth the will of my Father which is in heaven*" (Matthew 7:21). To this great deliverance may be added another: "*If ye keep my commandments, ye shall abide in my love: even as I have kept my Father's commandments, and abide in his love*" (John 15:10).

"The Christian's trade," said Martin Luther, "is prayer." But the Christian has another trade to learn before he proceeds to learn the secrets of the trade of prayer. He must learn well the trade of perfect obedience to the Father's will. Obedience follows love, and prayer follows obedience. The business of *real* obedience to God's commandments inseparably accompanies the business of *real* praying.

One who has been disobedient may pray. He may pray for pardoning mercy and the peace of his soul. He may come to God's feet with tears, confession, and a penitent heart. God will hear him and answer his prayer. This kind of praying does not belong to the child of God, but to the penitent sinner, who has no other way to approach God. It is the possession of the unjustified soul, not of him who has been saved and reconciled to God.

An obedient life helps prayer. It speeds prayer to the throne. God cannot help hearing the prayer of an obedient child. He has always heard His obedient children when they have prayed. Unquestioning obedience counts much in the sight of God, at the throne of heavenly grace. It acts like the flowing tides of many rivers. It gives volume and fullness of flow, as well as power, to the prayer closet. An obedient life is not simply a reformed life. It is not the old life primed and repainted. It is not a superficial churchgoing life or a flurry of activities. Neither is it an external conformation to the dictates of public morality. Far more than all this is combined in a truly obedient Christian God-fearing life.

A life of full obedience, a life that is settled on the most intimate terms with God, offers no hindrance to the prayer closet. Where the will is in full conformity to God's will and the outward life shows the fruit of righteousness like Aaron and Hur, such a life lifts up and sustains the hands of prayer.

If you have an earnest desire to pray well, you must learn how to obey well. If you have a desire to learn to pray, then you must have an earnest desire to learn how to do God's will. If you desire to pray to God, you must first have a consuming desire to obey Him. If you want to have free access to God in prayer, then every obstacle in the nature of sin or disobedience must be removed.

God delights in the prayers of obedient children. Requests coming from the lips of those who delight to do His will reach His ears with great speed. They incline Him to answer them promptly and abundantly. In themselves, tears are not rewarding. Yet, they have their uses in prayer. Tears should baptize our place of supplication.

The person who has never wept concerning his sins has never really prayed over his sins. Sometimes tears are a prodigal's only plea. But tears are for the past, for the sin and wrongdoing. There is another step and stage waiting to be taken. That step is unquestioning obedience. Until it is taken, prayer for blessing and continued sustenance will be of no avail.

Everywhere in Scripture, God is represented as disapproving disobedience and condemning sin. This is as true in the lives of His elect as it is in the lives of sinners. Nowhere does He approve of sin or excuse disobedience. God puts the emphasis always upon obedience to His commands. Obedience to them brings blessing. Disobedience meets with disaster. This is true in the Word of God from the beginning to the end. It is because of this that the men of prayer in the Bible had such influence with God. Obedient men have always been the closest to God. They are the ones who have prayed well and have received great things from God. They have brought great things to pass.

Obedience to God counts tremendously in the realm of prayer. This fact cannot be emphasized too much or too often. To plead for a faith that tolerates sinning is to cut the ground out from under the feet of effective praying. To excuse sinning by the plea that obedience to God is not possible to unregenerate men is to discount the character of the new birth and to place men where effective praying is not possible. At one time Jesus spoke out with a very pertinent and personal question that strikes right to the core of disobedience. He asked, *"Why call ye me, Lord, Lord, and do not the things which I say?"* (Luke 6:46).

He who prays must obey. The person who wants to get anything out of his prayers must be in perfect harmony with God. Prayer puts a spirit of obedience in those who sincerely pray. The spirit of disobedience is not of God and does not belong to God's praying people.

An obedient life is a great help to prayer. In fact, an obedient life is a necessity to prayer. The absence of an obedient life makes prayer an empty performance. A penitent sinner seeks pardon and salvation and has an answer to his prayers, even with a life stained with sin. However, God's royal intercessors come before Him with royal lives. Holy living promotes holy praying. God's intercessors, *"lifting up holy hands"* (1 Timothy 2:8), are the symbols of righteous, obedient lives.

TEN:

PRAYER AND FULL SURRENDER

Many exemplary men have I known, holy in heart and life, within my four score years. But one equal to John Fletcher—one so inwardly and outwardly obedient and devoted to God—I have not known.   —John Wesley

It is important to note that the praying that is given such a transcendent position, and from which great results are attributed, is not simply the saying of prayers, but holy praying. This is the *prayers of the saints* (Revelation 8:4). This is the prayers of the holy men and women of God. Behind such praying, giving to it energy and flame, are men and women who are wholly devoted to God. They are entirely separated from sin and fully separated to God. They always give energy, force, and strength to praying.

Our Lord Jesus Christ excelled in praying because He was supreme in saintliness. Entire dedication to God and full surrender, which carry the whole being in a flame of holy consecration, give wings to faith and energy to prayer. Full surrender opens the door to the throne of grace. It brings strong influence to bear on Almighty God.

The *"lifting up* [of] *holy hands"* (1 Timothy 2:8) is essential to Christlike praying. It is not, however, a holiness that only dedicates a closet to God. It does not merely set apart an hour to Him. It is a consecration that takes hold of the entire man. It dedicates the whole life to God.

Our Lord Jesus Christ, who was *"holy, harmless, undefiled, separate from sinners"* (Hebrews 7:26), had ready access to God in prayer. He had this free, full access because of His unquestioning obedience to His Father. Throughout His earthly life, His supreme care and desire was to do the will of His Father. This fact, coupled with another—the consciousness of having so ordered His life—gave Him confidence and assurance. It enabled Him to draw near to the throne of grace with unlimited confidence born of obedience, promised acceptance, audience, and answer.

Loving obedience puts us where we can ask anything in His name. It gives us the assurance that He will do it. (See John 14:14.) Loving obedience brings us into the prayer realm. It makes us beneficiaries of the wealth of Christ. We receive the riches of His grace through the Holy Spirit, who will abide with us and be in us. Cheerful obedience to God qualifies us to pray effectively.

This obedience that qualifies and is the forerunner of prayer must be loving and constant. It is always doing the Father's will and cheerfully following the path of God's commands.

In King Hezekiah's situation, it was a potent plea that changed God's decree that he should die and not live. The stricken ruler called upon God to remember how he had walked before Him in truth and with a perfect heart. With God, this counted. He listened carefully to the petition. As a result, death found its approach to Hezekiah barred for fifteen years.

Jesus learned obedience in the school of suffering. At the same time, He learned prayer in the school of obedience. Just as it is the prayer of a righteous man that avails much, so it is righteousness that is obedience to God. A righteous man is an obedient man. He can pray effectively. He can accomplish great things when he goes to his knees.

Remember that true praying is not mere sentiment, poetry, or eloquent speech. It does not consist of saying in sweet tones, "Lord, Lord." Prayer is not a mere form of words. It is not just calling upon a name. *Prayer is obedience.* It is founded on the unbending rock of obedience to God. Only those who obey have the right to pray. Behind the praying must be the doing. It is the constant doing of God's will in daily life that gives prayer its potency.

Our Lord plainly taught,

Not every one that saith unto me, Lord, Lord, shall enter the kingdom of heaven; but he that doeth the will of my Father which is in heaven. Many will say to me in that day, Lord, Lord, have we not prophesied in thy name? and in thy name have cast out devils? and in thy name done many wonderful works? And then will I profess unto them, I never knew you: depart from me, ye that worketh iniquity.

(Matthew 7:21–23)

No name, however precious and powerful, can protect and give effectiveness to prayer that is unaccompanied by doing God's will. Neither can the doing, without the praying, protect from divine disapproval. If the will of God does not master the life, the praying will be nothing but sickly sentiment. If prayer does not inspire, sanctify, and direct our work, then self-will enters and ruins both the work and worker.

How many great misconceptions there are of the true elements and functions of prayer! There are many who earnestly desire to obtain answers to their prayers but who go unrewarded and unblessed. They fix their minds on some promise of God. Then they endeavor by stubborn perseverance to summon enough faith to lay hold of it and claim it. This fixing the mind on some great promise may help in strengthening faith, but persistent and urgent prayer—prayer that expects and waits until faith grows exceedingly—must be added to this promise. Who is able and competent to do such praying except the man who readily, cheerfully, and continually obeys God?

Faith, in its highest form, is the attitude as well as the act of a soul surrendered to God. His Word and His Spirit dwell in that soul. It is true that faith must exist in some form or another in order to prompt praying. However, in its strongest form and in its greatest results, faith is the fruit of prayer. It is true that faith increases the ability and efficiency of prayer. It is likewise true that prayer increases the ability and effectiveness of faith. Prayer and faith work, act, and react one upon the other.

Obedience to God helps faith as no other attribute possibly can. When there is absolute recognition of the validity and supremacy of the divine commands, faith ceases to be an almost superhuman task. It requires no straining to exercise it. Obedience to God makes it easy to believe and trust God. Where the spirit of obedience totally saturates the soul and the will is perfectly surrendered to God, faith becomes a reality. It also does this where there is a fixed, unalterable purpose to obey God. Faith then becomes almost involuntary. After obedience it is the next natural step. It is easily and readily taken. The difficulty in prayer then is not with faith but with obedience, which is faith's foundation.

If we want to pray well and get the most out of our praying, we must look at our obedience. We must look at the secret springs of action and the loyalty of our hearts to God. Obedience is the groundwork of effective praying. This brings us near to God. The lack of obedience in our lives breaks down our praying. Quite often our lives are in rebellion. This places us where praying is almost impossible, except for pardoning mercy. Disobedient living produces extremely poor praying. Disobedience shuts the door of the prayer closet. It bars the way to the Holy of Holies. No man can pray—really pray—who does not obey.

> *Our will must be surrendered to God as a primary condition to all successful praying.*

Our will must be surrendered to God as a primary condition to all successful praying. Everything about us receives its coloring from our innermost character. Our secret will determines our character and controls our conduct. Our will, therefore, plays an important part in all successful praying. There can be no rich, true praying when the will is not wholly and fully surrendered to God. This unswerving loyalty to God is an utterly indispensable condition of the best, truest, and most effective praying. We have simply to Trust and obey.

> Trust and obey.
> For *there's no other way*
> To be happy in Jesus,
> But to trust and *obey!*

ELEVEN:

PRAYER AND SPIRITUAL WARFARE

David Brainerd was pursued by unearthly adversaries who were resolved to rob him of his reward. He knew he must never take off his armor, but lie down to rest with his [sandals] laced. The stains that marred the perfection of his lustrous dress and the spots of rust on his gleaming shield are imperceptible to us, but they were to him the source of much sorrow and ardency of yearning.

—*The Life of David Brainerd*

The description of the Christian soldier given by Paul in Ephesians 6 is compact and comprehensive. He is seen as always being in the conflict, which has many fluctuating seasons. There are seasons of prosperity and adversity, lightness and darkness, victory and defeat. He is to pray in all seasons and with all prayer. This is to be added to the armor when he goes into battle. At all times, he is to have the full armor of prayer. The Christian soldier, if he fights to win, must pray much. Only by this means is he able to defeat his long-standing enemy, Satan, and his many agents. *"Praying always with all prayer*" (Ephesians 6:18) is the divine direction given to him. This covers all seasons and includes all manner of praying.

Christian soldiers, fighting the good fight of faith (1 Timothy 6:12), have access to a place of retreat where they continually go for prayer. "*Praying always with all prayer*" is a clear statement of the essential need of much praying. It is also a statement of many kinds of praying, by him who, fighting the good fight of faith, wins out over all his foes in the end.

The Revised Version puts it this way:

> *With all prayer and supplication praying at all seasons in the Spirit... for all the saints, and on my behalf, that utterance may be given unto me in opening my mouth, to make known with boldness the mystery of the gospel, for which I am an ambassador in chains; that in it I may speak boldly, as I ought to speak.* (Ephesians 6:18–20)

It cannot be said too often that the life of a Christian is warfare, an intense conflict, a lifelong contest. It is a battle fought against invisible foes who are ever alert and seeking to entrap, deceive, and ruin the souls of men. The Bible calls men to life, not a picnic or holiday. It is no pastime or pleasure excursion. It entails effort, wrestling, and struggling. It demands putting out the full energy of the spirit in order to frustrate the foe and to come out, at last, more than a conqueror. It is no primrose path, no rose-scented flirting. From start to finish, it is war. The Christian warrior is compelled from the hour he first draws his sword to "*endure hardness, as a good soldier*" (2 Timothy 2:3).

What a misconception many people have of the Christian life! How little the average church member appears to know of the character of the conflict and of its demands on him! How ignorant he seems to be of the enemies he must encounter if he is to serve God faithfully, succeed in getting to heaven, and receive the crown of life! He scarcely seems to realize that the world, the flesh, and the devil will oppose his onward march. He hardly realizes that they will defeat him utterly, unless he gives himself to constant vigilance and unceasing prayer.

The Christian soldier does not wrestle against flesh and blood, but against spiritual wickedness in high places (Ephesians 6:12). Or, as the scriptural margin note in reads, "wicked spirits in high places" (RV, mg).

What a fearful array of forces are set against him! They desire to impede his way through the wilderness of this world to the doors of the Celestial City! It is no surprise, therefore, to find Paul, who understood the character of the Christian life so well, carefully and plainly urging Christians to *"put on the whole armour of God"* (v. 11). It is not surprising that Paul, who was so thoroughly informed as to the malignity and number of the foes that the disciple of the Lord must encounter, urged us to pray *"with all prayer and supplication in the Spirit"* (v. 18). The present generation would be wise if all who profess our faith could be persuaded to realize this all-important, vital truth, which is absolutely indispensable to a successful Christian life.

It is just at this point in today's Christianity that one may find its greatest defect. There is little or nothing of the soldier element in it. The discipline, self-denial, spirit of hardship, and determination so prominent in and belonging to the military life are lacking. Yet, the Christian life is warfare, all the way.

How comprehensive, pointed, and striking are all Paul's directions to the Christian soldier who is bent on defeating the devil and saving his soul alive. First of all, he must possess a clear idea of the character of the life into which he has entered. Then, he must know something of his foes— the adversaries of his immortal soul—their strength, their skill, their viciousness.

Knowing something of the character of the enemy and realizing the need of preparation to overcome them, he is prepared to hear the apostle's decisive conclusion:

> *Finally, my brethren, be strong in the Lord, and in the power of his might. Put on the whole armour of God, that ye may be able to stand against the wiles of the devil....Wherefore take unto you the whole armour of God, that ye may be able to withstand in the evil day, and having done all, to stand.* (Ephesians 6:10–11, 13)

All these directions end in a climax, and that climax is prayer. How can the brave warrior for Christ be made braver still? How can the strong soldier be made stronger still? How can the victorious fighter be made still more victorious?

Here are Paul's explicit directions to that end: *"Praying always with all prayer and supplication in the Spirit, and watching thereunto with all perseverance and supplication for all saints"* (Ephesians 6:18).

Prayer, and more prayer, adds to the fighting qualities and the more certain victories of God's good, fighting men. The power of prayer is most forceful on the battlefield in the midst of the noise and strife of the conflict. Paul was preeminently a soldier of the cross. For him, life was no flowery bed of ease. He was no parading, holiday soldier, whose only business was to put on a uniform for special occasions. His was a life of intense conflict, the facing of many adversaries, the exercise of unsleeping vigilance and constant effort. And in sight of the end, we hear him as he chanted his final song of victory, *"I have fought a good fight"* (2 Timothy 4:7). Reading between the lines, we see that he was more than a conqueror!

Paul indicated the nature of his soldier life, giving us some views of the kind of praying needed for such a career. He wrote,

Now I beseech you, brethren, for the Lord Jesus Christ's sake, and for the love of the Spirit, that ye strive together with me in your prayers to God for me; that I may be delivered from them that do not believe in Judaea. (Romans 15:30–31)

Paul *had* foes in Judea—foes who surrounded and opposed him in the form of unbelieving men, and this, added to other weighty reasons, led him to urge the Roman Christians to strive with him in prayer. That word *strive* indicates wrestling, the putting forth of great effort. This is the kind of effort and spirit that must possess the Christian soldier.

Here is a great soldier, in the great struggle, faced by malignant forces who seek his ruin. His strength is almost gone. What reinforcements can he count on? What can give help and bring success to a warrior in such a pressing emergency? It is a critical moment in the conflict. What strength can be added to the energy of his own prayers? The answer is—the prayers of others, even the prayers of his fellow believers who were at Rome. These, he believes, will bring him additional aid. He can then win his fight, overcome his adversaries, and, ultimately, prevail.

The Christian soldier is to pray in all seasons and under all circumstances. His praying must be arranged in order to cover his times of peace as well as his hours of active conflict. It must be available in his marching and his fighting. Prayer must diffuse all effort, permeate all ventures, decide all issues. The Christian soldier must be as intense in his praying as in his fighting, for his victories will depend much more on his praying than on his fighting.

Fervent supplication must be added to steady resolve. Prayer and supplication must supplement the armor of God. The Holy Spirit must aid the supplication with His own strenuous plea. And the soldier must pray in the Spirit. In this, as in other forms of warfare, eternal vigilance is the price of victory. Thus, watchfulness and perseverance must mark every activity of the Christian warrior.

The soldier's prayer must reflect his profound concern for the success and well-being of the whole army. The battle is not altogether a personal matter. Victory cannot be achieved for self alone. There is a sense in which the entire army of Christ is involved. The cause of God, His saints, their woes and trials, their duties and crosses—all should find a pleading voice in the Christian soldier when he prays. He does not dare to limit his praying to himself. Nothing dries up spiritual blessings so certainly and completely, nothing poisons the fountain of spiritual life so effectively, and nothing acts in such deadly fashion as selfish praying.

Note carefully that the Christian's armor will avail him nothing unless prayer is added. This is the pivot, the connecting link of the armor of God. This holds it together and renders it effective. God's true soldier plans his campaigns, arranges his battle forces, and conducts his conflicts with prayer. Prayer is all-important and absolutely essential to victory. Prayer should so saturate the life that every breath becomes a petition, every sigh a supplication. The Christian soldier must always be fighting. He should, of sheer necessity, be always praying.

God's true soldier plans their campaigns, arranges their battle forces, and conducts their conflicts with prayer. Prayer is all-important and absolutely essential to victory. Prayer should so saturate the life that every breath becomes a petition, every sigh a supplication.

The Christian soldier is compelled to constant guard duty. He is faced by a foe who never sleeps, who is always alert, and who is ever prepared to take advantage of the fortunes of war. Watchfulness is a fundamental principle with Christ's warrior; *"watch and pray"* (Matthew 26:41) is forever sounding in his ears. He cannot dare to be asleep at his post. Such a lapse brings him not only under the displeasure of the Captain of his salvation, but also exposes him to added danger. Watchfulness, therefore, imperatively constitutes the duty of the soldier of the Lord.

In the New Testament, there are three different words that are translated "watch." The first means "absence of sleep" and implies a wakeful frame of mind as opposed to listlessness. It is a command to keep awake, attentive, and vigilant. The second word means "fully awake"—a state induced by some rousing, active, cautious effort lest, through carelessness or laziness, some destructive calamity should suddenly evolve. The third word means "to be calm and collected in spirit," unemotional, untouched by confusing circumstances, cautious against all pitfalls and diversions.

All three words were used by Paul. Two of them are used in connection with prayer. Watchfulness intensified is a necessity for prayer. Watchfulness must guard and cover the whole spiritual man and prepare him for prayer. Everything resembling unpreparedness or non-vigilance is death to prayer.

In Ephesians 6:18, Paul gave prominence to the duty of constant watchfulness, *"watching thereunto with all perseverance and supplication."* "Watch," he said, *"watch,* WATCH!"

Sleepless alertness is the price one must pay for victory over his spiritual foes. Rest assured that the devil never falls asleep. He ever *"walketh about, seeking whom he may devour"* (1 Peter 5:8). Just as a shepherd must never be careless or unwatchful lest the wolf devour his sheep, so the Christian soldier must have his eyes wide open, implying his possession of a spirit that neither slumbers nor grows careless. The inseparable companions and safeguards of prayer are vigilance and watchfulness. In writing to the Colossians, Paul bracketed these inseparable qualities together: *"Continue in prayer, and watch in the same with thanksgiving"* (Colossians 4:2).

When will Christians more thoroughly learn the twofold lesson that they are called to a great warfare and that, in order to get the victory, they must give themselves to unsleeping watchfulness and unceasing prayer? *"Be sober, be vigilant; because your adversary the devil, as a roaring lion, walketh about, seeking whom he may devour"* (1 Peter 5:8).

God's church is a militant host. Its warfare is with unseen forces of evil. God's people compose an army fighting to establish His kingdom in the earth. Their aim is to destroy the sovereignty of Satan and, over its ruins, erect the kingdom of God, which is *"righteousness, and peace, and joy in the Holy Ghost"* (Romans 14:17). This militant army is composed of individual soldiers of the cross. The armor of God is needed for defense, and added prayer crowns the entire army.

Prayer is too simple, too obvious a duty, to need definition. Necessity gives being and shape to prayer. Its importance is so absolute that the Christian soldier's life, in all the breadth and intensity of it, should be one of prayer. The entire life of a Christian soldier—its being, intention, implication, and action—are all dependent on its being a life of prayer. Without prayer—no matter what else he has—the Christian soldier's life will be feeble and ineffective. Without prayer, he is an easy prey for his spiritual enemies.

Unless prayer has an important place in a Christian's life, his experience and influence will be powerless. Without prayer the Christian graces will wither and die. Without prayer, we may add, preaching is futile and fruitless. Christ is the Lawgiver of prayer, and Paul is His apostle of prayer. Both declare its primary importance and demonstrate the fact of its necessity. Their prayer directions cover all places, include all times, and comprehend all things. How, then, can the Christian soldier hope or dream of victory, unless he is fortified by its power? How can he fail if in addition to putting on the armor of God he is, at all times and seasons, *"watching thereunto with all perseverance and supplication for all saints"* (Ephesians 6:18)?

TWELVE:

PRAYER AND GOD'S PROMISES

In the Scriptures, we constantly encounter such words as "field," "seed," "sower," "reaper," "seedtime," "harvest." Employing such metaphors interprets a fact of nature by a parable of grace. The field is the world and the good seed is the Word of God. Whether the Word be spoken or written, it is the power of God unto salvation. In our work of evangelism, the whole world is our field, every creature the object of effort, and every book and tract, a seed of God. —David Fant, Jr.

God's Word is a record of prayer—of praying men and their achievements, of the divine warrant of prayer, and of the encouragement given to those who pray. No one can read the instances, commands, and examples of statements that concern themselves with prayer without realizing that the cause of God and the success of His work in this world are committed to prayer. Praying men have been God's appointed officers on earth. Prayerless men have never been used by Him.

A reverence for God's holy name is closely related to a high regard for His Word. This hallowing of God's name, the ability to do His will on earth as it is done in heaven, and the establishment and glory of God's kingdom are as much involved in prayer as when Jesus taught men the universal prayer. That *"men ought always to pray, and not to faint"* (Luke 18:1) is as fundamental to God's cause today as when Jesus Christ enshrined that great truth in the immortal setting of the parable of the persistent widow.

As God's house is called *"the house of prayer"* (Matthew 21:13), because prayer is the most important of its holy offices, so, by the same token, the Bible may be called the book of prayer. Prayer is the great theme and content of its message to mankind. God's Word is the basis of, the directory of, and the prayer of faith. Paul said,

> Let the word of Christ dwell in you richly in all wisdom; teaching and admonishing one another in psalms and hymns and spiritual songs, singing with grace in your hearts to the Lord.   (Colossians 3:16)

As the Word of Christ dwells richly in us, we become transformed. The result is that we become praying Christians. Faith is constructed of the Word and the Spirit, and faith is the body and substance of prayer.

In many of its aspects, prayer is dependent on the Word of God. Jesus says, *"If ye abide in me, and my words abide in you, ye shall ask what ye will, and it shall be done unto you"* (John 15:7).

The Word of God is the support upon which the lever of prayer is placed and by which things are mightily moved. God has committed Himself, His purpose, and His promise to prayer. His Word becomes the basis and the inspiration of our praying. Under certain circumstances, persistent prayer may bring additional assurance of His promises. It is said of the old saints that they *"through faith...obtained promises"* (Hebrews 11:33).

There would seem to be the capacity in prayer for going beyond the Word, beyond His promise, and into the very presence of God Himself.

Jacob wrestled, not so much with a promise, as with the Promiser. We must take hold of the Promiser, or else the promise is useless. Prayer may well be defined as the force that vitalizes and energizes the Word of God, by taking hold of God Himself. By taking hold of the Promiser, prayer releases the personal promise. *"There is none…that stirreth up himself to take hold of [me]"* (Isaiah 64:7) is God's sad lament. *"Let him take hold of my strength, that he may make peace with me"* (Isaiah 27:5) is God's recipe for prayer.

By scriptural authority, prayer may be divided into the petition of faith and that of submission. The prayer of faith is based on the written Word, for *"faith cometh by hearing, and hearing by the word of God"* (Romans 10:17). It inevitably receives its answer—the very thing for which it prays.

The prayer of submission is without a definite word of promise, so to speak. However, it takes hold of God with a lowly and contrite spirit and asks and pleads with Him for that which the soul desires. Abraham had no definite promise that God would spare Sodom. Moses had no definite promise that God would spare Israel. On the contrary, there was the declaration of His wrath and of His purpose to destroy. Still, the devoted leader gained his plea with God when he interceded for the Israelites with incessant prayers and many tears. Daniel had no definite promise that God would reveal to him the meaning of the king's dream, but he prayed specifically, and God answered definitely.

The Word of God is made effective and operative by the process and practice of prayer. The Word of the Lord came to Elijah, *"Go, show thyself unto Ahab; and I will send rain upon the earth"* (1 Kings 18:1). Elijah showed himself to Ahab, but the answer to his prayer did not come until he had pressed his fiery prayer upon the Lord seven times.

Paul had the definite promise from Christ that He would deliver him *"from the people, and from the Gentiles"* (Acts 26:17). Yet, we find that he exhorted the Romans in an urgent and solemn manner concerning this very matter:

> *Now I beseech you, brethren, for the Lord Jesus Christ's sake, and for the love of the Spirit, that ye strive together with me in your prayers to God for me; that I may be delivered from them that do not believe in Judaea; and that my service which I have for Jerusalem may be accepted of the saints.* (Romans 15:30–31)

The Word of God is a great help in prayer. If it is lodged and written in our hearts, it will form an outflowing current of prayer, full and irresistible.

Promises, stored in the heart, are to be the fuel from which prayer receives life and warmth. Just as coal, which has been stored in the earth, gives us comfort on stormy days and wintry nights, the Word of God stored in our hearts is the food by which prayer is nourished and made strong. Prayer, like man, cannot live by bread alone, *"but by every word that proceedeth out of the mouth of God"* (Matthew 4:4).

Unless the vital forces of prayer are supplied by God's Word, prayer, though earnest, even vociferous in its urgency, is flabby and void in reality. The absence of vital force in praying can be traced to the absence of a constant supply of God's Word to repair the waste and renew the life. He who wants to learn to pray well must first study God's Word and store it in his memory and thought.

When we consult God's Word, we find that no duty is more binding, more exacting, than that of prayer. On the other hand, we discover that no privilege is more exalted, no habit more richly owned of God. No promises are more radiant, more abounding, more explicit, more often reiterated, than those that are attached to prayer. *"All things whatsoever"* are received by prayer because *"all things whatsoever"* (Matthew 21:22) are promised. There is no limit to the provisions included in the promises to prayer and no exclusion from its promises. *"For every one that asketh receiveth"* (Luke 11:10). The word of our Lord is to this all-embracing effect: *"If ye shall ask any thing in my name, I will do it"* (John 14:14).

Here are some of the comprehensive and exhaustive statements of the Word of God about prayer, the things to be taken in by prayer, and the strong promise made in answer to prayer: *"Pray without ceasing"* (1 Thessalonians 5:17); *"continue in prayer"* (Colossians 4:2); *"continuing instant in prayer"* (Romans 12:12); *"in every thing by prayer...let your requests be made known unto God"* (Phil. 4:6); *"always to pray, and not to faint"* (Luke 18:1); *"men [should] pray every where"* (1 Timothy 2:8); *"praying always with all prayer and supplication"* (Ephesians 6:18).

What clear and strong statements those are that are put in the divine record to furnish us with a sure basis of faith and to urge, constrain, and encourage us to pray! How wide the range of prayer in the divine revelation! How these Scriptures incite us to seek the God of prayer, with all our needs, with all our burdens!

384 E. M. Bounds on Prayer & Spiritual Warfare

In addition to these statements left on record for our encouragement, the sacred pages teem with facts, examples, incidents, and observations, stressing the importance and the absolute necessity of prayer and putting emphasis on its all-prevailing power.

The greatest benefit of the rich promises of the Word of God should humbly be received by us and put to the test. The world will never receive the full benefits of the Gospel until this is done. Neither Christian experience nor Christian living will be what they ought to be until these divine promises have been fully tested by those who pray. By prayer, we bring these promises of God's holy will into the realm of the actual and the real.

If asked what is to be done in order to render God's promises real, the answer is that we must pray, until the words of the promise are fulfilled.

God's promises are too large to be mastered by aimless praying. When we examine ourselves, we discover that our praying does not rise to the demands of the situation. It is so limited that it is little more than a mere oasis amid the waste and desert of the world's sin. Who of us, in our praying, measures up to the promises of our Lord? *"Verily, verily, I say unto you, He that believeth on me, the works that I do shall he do also; and greater works than these shall he do; because I go unto my Father"* (John 14:12).

How comprehensive, how far reaching, how all-embracing! How much is here, for the glory of God, how much for the good of man! How much for the manifestation of Christ's enthroned power, how much for the reward of abundant faith! How great and gracious are the results that grow from the exercise of believing prayer!

Look at another of God's great promises and discover how we may be strengthened by the Word as we pray and on what firm ground we may stand to make our petitions to our God: *"If ye abide in me, and my words abide in you, ye shall ask what ye will, and it shall be done unto you"* (John 15:7). In these comprehensive words, God turns Himself over to the will of His people. When Christ becomes our all in all, prayer lays God's treasures at our feet.

Early Christianity had an easy and practical solution to the situation. The first Christians received all that God had to give. That simple, short solution is recorded in 1 John 3:22: *"Whatsoever we ask, we receive of him, because we keep his commandments, and do those things that are pleasing in his sight."*

Prayer coupled with loving obedience is the answer to all ends and all things. Prayer joined to the Word of God hallows and makes sacred all God's gifts. Prayer is not simply to receive things from God, but to make holy those things that already have been received of Him. It is not merely to *receive* a blessing, but also to be able to *give* a blessing. Prayer makes common things holy and secular things sacred. It receives things from God with thanksgiving and hallows them with thankful hearts and devoted service.

> *Prayer is not simply to receive things from God, but to make holy those things that already have been received of Him. It is not merely to receive a blessing, but also to be able to give a blessing. Prayer makes common things holy and secular things sacred. It receives things from God with thanksgiving and hallows them with thankful hearts and devoted service.*

In 1 Timothy 4:4–5, Paul gave us these words: *"For every creature of God is good, and nothing to be refused, if it be received with thanksgiving: for it is sanctified by the word of God and prayer."* God's good gifts are to be holy, not only by God's creative power, but also because they are made holy to us by prayer. We receive them, appropriate them, and sanctify them by prayer.

Doing God's will—having His Word abiding in us—is an imperative of effective praying. But, it may be asked, how are we to know what God's will is? The answer is by studying His Word (see 2 Timothy 2:15), by hiding it in our hearts (see Psalm 119:11), and by letting the Word dwell in us richly. (See Colossians 3:16.) *"The entrance of thy words giveth light"* (Psalm 119:130).

To know God's will in prayer, we must be filled with God's Spirit, who makes intercession for the saints according to the will of God. (See Romans 8:27.) To be filled with God's Spirit, to be filled with God's Word, is to know God's will. It is to be put in such a frame of mind and state of heart that it will enable us to read and correctly interpret the purposes of the infinite. Such filling of the heart with the Word and the Spirit gives us an insight into the will of the Father. It enables us to rightly discern His will and puts a disposition of mind and heart within us to make it the guide and compass of our lives.

Epaphras prayed that the Colossians might stand *"perfect and complete in all the will of God"* (Colossians 4:12). This is proof positive that not only can we know the will of God, but that we can know *all* the will of God. And not only can we know all the will of God, but we can *do* all the will of God. In addition, we can do all the will of God as an established habit instead of an occasional impulse. Still further, it shows us that we not only can do the will of God externally, but from the heart, cheerfully, without holding back from the intimate presence of the Lord.

THIRTEEN:

PRAYER AND GOD'S PROMISES

Some years ago a man was traveling in the wilds of Kentucky. He had with him a large sum of money and was well armed. He stayed at a log house one night but was much concerned with the rough appearance of the men who came and went from this abode. He retired early, but not to sleep. At midnight he heard the dogs barking furiously and the sound of someone entering the cabin. Peering through a chink in the boards of his room, he saw a stranger with a gun in his hand. Another man sat before the fire. The traveler concluded they were planning to rob him and prepared to defend himself and his property. Presently the newcomer took down a copy of the Bible, read a chapter aloud, and then knelt down and prayed. The traveler dismissed his fears, put his revolver away, and lay down to sleep peacefully until morning light. And all because a Bible was in the cabin and its owner a man of prayer.

—Rev. F. F. Shoup

Prayer means the success of the preaching of the Word. Paul clearly taught this in that familiar and pressing request he made to the Thessalonians: *"Finally, brethren, pray for us, that the word of the Lord may have free course, and be glorified"* (2 Thessalonians 3:1).

Prayer opens the way for the Word of God to run without hindrance. It creates the atmosphere that is favorable for the Word to accomplish its purpose. Prayer puts wheels under God's Word and gives wings to the angel of the Lord *"having the everlasting gospel to preach unto them that dwell on the earth, and to every nation, and kindred, and tongue, and people"* (Revelation 14:6). Prayer greatly helps the Word of the Lord.

The parable of the sower is a notable study of preaching, showing its differing effects and describing the diversity of hearers. The wayside hearers are many. The soil lies unprepared either by previous thought or prayer. As a consequence, the enemy easily takes away the seed (which is the Word of God). Dissipating all good impressions, Satan renders the work of the sower futile. If only the hearers would prepare the ground of their hearts beforehand by prayer and meditation, much of the current sowing would be fruitful.

The same applies to the stony-ground and thorny-ground hearers. Although the Word lodges in their hearts and begins to sprout, yet all is lost, chiefly because there is no prayer or watchfulness or cultivation following. The good-ground hearers are profited by the sowing, simply because their minds have been prepared for the reception of the seed. After hearing, they have cultivated the seed sown in their hearts by the exercise of prayer. All this gives particular emphasis to the conclusion of this striking parable: *"Take heed therefore how ye hear"* (Luke 8:18). In order that we can heed how we hear, we must give ourselves continually to prayer.

We have to believe that the success and effect of God's Word depend on prayer. *"So shall my word be that goeth forth out of my mouth: it shall not return unto me void, but it shall…prosper in the thing whereto I sent it"* (Isaiah 55:11).

In Psalm 19, David magnified the Word of God in six statements concerning it. The Word converts the soul, makes the simple wise, rejoices the heart, enlightens the eyes, endures eternally, and is altogether true and righteous. The Word of God is perfect, sure, right, and pure. It is heart-searching and, at the same time, purifying in its effect.

It is no surprise that after considering the deep spirituality of the Word of God, its power to search the inner nature of man, and its deep purity, the psalmist should close his dissertation with this passage:

> *Who can understand his errors? cleanse thou me from secret faults. Keep back thy servant also from presumptuous sins; let them not have dominion over me….Let the words of my mouth, and the meditation of my heart, be acceptable in thy sight, O LORD, my strength, and my redeemer.* (Psalm 19:12–14)

James recognized the deep spirituality of the Word and its inherent saving power in the following exhortation: "*Wherefore lay apart all filthiness and superfluity of naughtiness, and receive with meekness the engrafted word, which is able to save your souls*" (James 1:21).

And Peter talked along the same line when describing the saving power of the Word of God: "*Being born again, not of corruptible seed, but of incorruptible, by the word of God, which liveth and abideth for ever*" (1 Peter 1:23). Not only did Peter speak of being born again by the incorruptible Word of God, but he informed us that to grow in grace we must be like newborn babes, desiring or feeding on the "*sincere milk of the word*" (1 Peter 2:2).

Prayer invariably generates a love for the Word of God. Prayer leads people to obey the Word of God and puts an unspeakable joy into the obedient heart. Praying people and Bible-reading people are the same sort of folk. The God of the Bible and the God of prayer are one. God speaks to man in the Bible; man speaks to God in prayer. One reads the Bible to discover God's will. He prays in order to receive power to do that will. Bible reading and praying are the distinguishing traits of those who strive to know and please God.

> *Prayer invariably generates a love for the Word of God. Prayer leads people to obey the Word of God and puts an unspeakable joy into the obedient heart.*

Just as prayer generates a love for the Scriptures and causes people to begin to read the Bible, so prayer causes men and women to visit the house of God to hear the Scriptures expounded. Churchgoing is closely connected with the Bible, primarily because the Bible cautions us against *"forsaking the assembling of ourselves together, as the manner of some is"* (Heb. 10:25). Churchgoing also results because God's chosen minister explains and enforces the Scriptures upon his hearers. Prayer germinates a resolve in those who practice it to not forsake the church.

Prayer generates a churchgoing conscience, a church-loving heart, and a church-supporting spirit. Praying people take delight in the preaching of the Word and the support of the church. Prayer exalts the Word of God and gives it preeminence in those who faithfully and wholeheartedly call upon the name of the Lord.

Prayer draws its very life from the Bible. It places its security on the firm ground of Scripture. Its very existence and character depend on revelation made by God to man in His holy Word. Prayer, in turn, exalts this same revelation and turns men toward that Word. The nature, necessity, and all-comprehending character of prayer are based on the Word of God.

Psalm 119 is a directory of God's Word. With three or four exceptions, each verse contains a word that identifies or locates the Word of God. Quite often, the author broke out into supplication, several times praying, *"Teach me thy statutes"* (Psalm 119:12). He was so deeply impressed with the wonders of God's Word and with the need for divine illumination to see and understand the wonderful things recorded within that he fervently prayed, *"Open thou mine eyes, that I may behold wondrous things out of thy law"* (Psalm 119:18).

From the opening of this wonderful psalm to its close, prayer and God's Word are intertwined. Almost every phase of God's Word is touched on by this inspired writer. The psalmist was so thoroughly convinced of the deep spiritual power of the Word of God that he made this declaration: *"Thy word have I hid in mine heart, that I might not sin against thee"* (v. 11).

Here the psalmist found his protection against sinning. By having God's Word hidden in his heart and his whole being thoroughly impregnated with that Word, he was able to walk to and fro on the earth. He was safe from the attack of the enemy and strengthened from wandering away.

We find, furthermore, that the power of prayer creates a real love for the Scriptures and puts within men a nature that will take pleasure in the Word. In holy ecstasy the psalmist cried, *"O how I love thy law! it is my meditation all the day"* (v. 97). And again: *"How sweet are thy words unto my taste! yea, sweeter than honey to my mouth!"* (v. 103).

Do we relish God's Word? If so, then let us give ourselves continually to prayer. He who would have a heart for the reading of the Bible must not—dare not—forget to pray. A man who loves the Bible will also love to pray. A man who loves to pray will delight in the law of the Lord.

Our Lord was a man of prayer. He magnified the Word of God and often quoted the Scriptures. Right through His earthly life, Jesus observed Sabbath-keeping, churchgoing, and the reading of the Word of God. His prayer intermingled with them all: *"And he came to Nazareth, where he had been brought up: and, as his custom was, he went into the synagogue on the sabbath day, and stood up for to read"* (Luke 4:16).

Let it be said that no two things are more essential to a Spirit-filled life than Bible reading and secret prayer. They will help you to grow in grace, to obtain joy from living a Christian life, and to be established in the way of eternal peace. To neglect these all-important duties means leanness of soul, loss of joy, absence of peace, dryness of spirit, and decay in all that pertains to spiritual life. Neglecting these things paves the way for apostasy and gives the enemy an advantage such as he is not likely to ignore.

Reading God's Word regularly and praying habitually in the secret place of the Most High puts one where he is absolutely safe from the attacks of the enemy of souls. It guarantees him salvation and final victory through the overcoming power of the Lamb.

FOURTEEN:

PRAYER AND THE HOUSE OF GOD

And dear to me the loud "Amen," Which echoes through the blest abode— Which swells, and sinks, then swells again, Dies on the walls—but lives with God!

Prayer affects places, times, occasions, and circumstances. It has to do with God and with everything that is related to God. It has an intimate and special relationship to His house. A church should be a sacred place, set apart from all unhallowed and secular uses, for the worship of God. As worship is prayer, the house of God is a place set apart for worship. It is no common place. It is where God dwells, where He meets with His people, and where He delights in the worship of His saints.

Prayer is always proper in the house of God. When prayer is a stranger there, it ceases to be God's house at all. Our Lord put particular emphasis on what the church is to be when He cast out the buyers and sellers in the temple. He repeated the words from Isaiah: *"It is written, My house shall be called the house of prayer"* (Matthew 21:13). He makes prayer preeminent above all else in the house of God. Those who sidetrack prayer or seek to minimize it pervert the church of God and make it something less than it is ordained to be.

Prayer is perfectly at home in the house of God. It is no stranger, no mere guest; it belongs there. It has a peculiar affinity for the place. It has a divine appointment to be there.

The inner chamber is a sacred place for personal worship. The house of God is a holy place for united worship. The prayer closet is for individual prayer. The house of God is for mutual, united prayer. Yet, even in the house of God, there is the element of private worship. God's people are to worship Him and pray to Him, personally, even in public worship. The church is for the united prayer of kindred, yet individual, believers.

The life, power, and glory of the church is prayer. The life of its members is dependent on prayer. The presence of God is secured and retained by prayer. The very place is made sacred by its ministry. Without it, the church is lifeless and powerless. Without it, even the building itself is nothing more than any other structure. Prayer converts even the bricks, mortar, and lumber into a sanctuary, a Holy of Holies, where the Shekinah dwells. Prayer separates it, in spirit and in purpose, from all other buildings. Prayer gives a peculiar sacredness to the building, sanctifies it, sets it apart for God, and conserves it from all common and mundane affairs.

With prayer, the house of God becomes a divine sanctuary. So the tabernacle, moving about from place to place, became the Holy of Holies, because God and prayer were there. Without prayer, the building may be costly, perfect in its structure, attractive to the eye, but it comes down to the human, with nothing divine in it, and is on a level with all other buildings.

Without prayer, a church is like a body without spirit; it is a dead, inanimate thing. A church with prayer in it has God in it. When prayer is set aside, God is outlawed. When prayer becomes an unfamiliar exercise, then God Himself is a stranger there.

As God's house is a house of prayer, the divine intention is that people should leave their homes and go to meet Him in His own house. The building is set apart for prayer. God has made a special promise to meet His people there. It is their duty to go there for that specific end. Prayer should be the chief attraction for all spiritually-minded churchgoers. While it is conceded that the preaching of the Word has an important place in the house of God, prayer is its predominant, distinguishing feature. Not that all other places are sinful or evil in themselves or in their uses— they are secular and human, having no special conception of God in them.

The church is, essentially, spiritual and divine. The work belonging to other places is done without special reference to God. He is not specifically recognized or called upon. In the church, however, God is acknowledged, and nothing is done without Him. Prayer is the one distinguishing mark of the house of God. As prayer distinguishes the Christian from unsaved people, so prayer distinguishes God's house from all other houses. It is a place where faithful believers meet with their Lord.

As God's house is a house of prayer, prayer should enter into and underlie everything that is done there. Prayer belongs to every sort of work relating to the church. As God's house is a house where the business of praying is carried on, so is it a place where the business of making praying people out of prayerless people is done. The house of God is a divine workshop, and there the work of prayer goes on; or the house of God is a divine schoolhouse, in which the lesson of prayer is taught, where men and women learn to pray, and where they graduate from the school of prayer.

Any church that calls itself the house of God but fails to magnify and teach the great lesson of prayer should change its teaching to conform to the divine prayer pattern, or it should change the name of its building to something other than a church.

On an earlier page, I referred to the finding of the Book of the Law that was given to Moses from the Lord. How long that book had been there, we do not know. But when tidings of its discovery were carried to Josiah, he tore his clothes and was greatly disturbed. He lamented the neglect of God's Word and saw, as a natural result, the iniquity that abounded throughout the land.

And then, Josiah thought of God and commanded Hilkiah, the priest, to go and make inquiry of the Lord. Such neglect of the word of the law was too serious a matter to be treated lightly. God must be sought. Josiah and his nation needed to repent.

Go ye, inquire of the LORD *for me, and for the people, and for all Judah, concerning the words of this book that is found: for great is the wrath of the* LORD *that is kindled against us, because our fathers have not hearkened unto the words of this book, to do according unto all that which is written concerning us.* (2 Kings 22:13)

However, that was not all. Josiah was bent on promoting a revival of religion in his kingdom. He gathered all the elders of Jerusalem and Judah together for that purpose. When they had come together, the king went into the house of the Lord and read all the words of the Book of the Covenant that was found in the house of the Lord.

With this righteous king, God's Word was of great importance. He esteemed it at its proper worth. He counted it to be of grave importance and consulted God in prayer about it. He gathered together the dignitaries of his kingdom, so that they, together with himself, could be instructed out of God's Book concerning God's law.

When Ezra was seeking the reconstruction of his nation, the people assembled themselves together as one man before the water gate.

And they spake unto Ezra the scribe to bring the book of the law of Moses, which the LORD *had commanded to Israel. And Ezra the priest brought the law before the congregation both of men and women, and all that could hear with understanding....And he read therein before the street that was before the water gate from the morning until midday... and the ears of all the people were attentive unto the book of the law.* (Nehemiah 8:1–3)

This was Bible-reading day in Judah—a real revival of Scripture study. The leaders read the Law before the people. Their ears were keen to hear what God had to say to them out of the Book of the Law. But it was not only a Bible-reading day. It was a time when real preaching was done, as the following passage indicates: "*So they read in the book in the law of God distinctly, and gave the sense, and caused them to understand the reading*" (Nehemiah 8:8).

Here is the scriptural definition of preaching. No better definition can be given. To read the Word of God distinctly, so that the people could hear and understand the words presented boldly and clearly—that was the method followed in Jerusalem on this auspicious day. The sense of the words was made clear in the meeting held before the water gate. The people were treated to a high type of expository preaching. That was true preaching—preaching of a sort that is sorely needed today so that God's Word may have the same effect on the hearts of the people. This meeting in Jerusalem surely contains a lesson that all present-day preachers should learn and heed.

No one, having any knowledge of the existing facts, will deny the comparative lack of expository preaching in the pulpit today, and no one should do other than lament the lack. Topical, controversial, and historical preaching have, one supposes, their rightful place. But expository preaching, the prayerful expounding of the Word of God, is preaching that *is* preaching—pulpit effort *par excellence.*

For its successful accomplishment, however, a preacher must be a man of prayer. For every hour spent in study, he will have to spend two on his knees. For every hour devoted to wrestling with an obscure passage of Holy Scripture, he must have two hours in which he is found wrestling with God. Prayer and preaching! Preaching and prayer! They cannot be separated. The ancient cry was, *"To your tents, O Israel!"* (1 Kings 12:16). The modern cry should be, "To your knees, O preachers, to your knees!"

BOOK FIVE:

GUIDE TO SPIRITUAL WARFARE

FOREWORD[1]:

If you had lived during the early years of the twentieth century, you could have visited a small town and witnessed a most unusual sight. You could have seen Dr. Bounds walking the streets carrying his manuscripts. They would have been written on the backs of old, used envelopes and tied with twine string. He was looking for someone who would undertake to prepare them for publication. Dr. Bounds was continually asking his friends to pray that God would raise up a man who would put his writings into print.

Claudius Lysias Chilton, a scholarly friend of Dr. Bounds, said, "There is no man on earth today except the present editor who would have accepted this mass of matter and devoted the time to give it to the world—a world that will not begin to realize the magnitude and expanse of the work until editor, compiler, and reviewers have been in eternity many ages."

We take this occasion to offer our heartfelt thanks to the friends who have helped to compile, revise, rewrite, and edit the printed and unprinted works of Dr. Bounds. We thank the Reverend Robert O. Smith of Gainesville, Georgia, for introducing him to us in 1905 and insisting that we needed this apostolic man to teach us to pray and preach the Word.

---

1. This foreword is from the first edition of the book, published in 1922.

I here submit a few brief statements from Dr. Bounds' letters to me just before he died. These show his views of Satan before he was taken out of the Enemy's reach forever.

I am trying to give myself more and more to prayer. Our only hope is in God. I do sympathize with you and pray for you and hold you in loving affection. Rejoice that you are well situated. God save you from your buffeting devil. The Devil is a great help heavenward. The worse agents he has the better we will get on.

Pray more and more; keep at the 4:00 a.m. hour. God will be for it, the Devil against it. Press on; you can't pray too much; you may pray too little. The Devil will compromise with you to pray as the common standard, on going to bed, and a little prayer in the morning. Hell will be full if we don't do better for God than that. Pray, pray, pray, pray always, rejoice evermore, pray without ceasing, in everything give thanks.

I hope that many souls will be edified and made holier and more devout by the reading of this book. I pray that God will receive additional glory when Bounds' complete works have been given to a needy world.

Homer W. Hodge

Brooklyn, New York

ONE:

WHO IS THE INVISIBLE ENEMY?

How art thou fallen from heaven, O Lucifer, son of the morning! how art thou cut down to the ground, which didst weaken the nations! For thou hast said in thine heart, I will ascend into heaven, I will exalt my throne above the stars of God: I will sit also upon the mount of the congregation, in the sides of the north: I will ascend above the heights of the clouds; I will be like the most High. Yet thou shalt be brought down to hell, to the sides of the pit.
—Isaiah 14:12–15

The Bible does not give us any direct statements concerning the genesis of the Devil. It gives us no indication of his birth and no description of his creation. The Bible is concerned with the Devil only as he has part in the great crises of man's history. There are only occasional glimpses of him in his work of ruin and death. These glimpses put his acts in striking contrast and opposition to the works and aims of Christ. These inferences indicate an original purity, a high relationship to God, and a heavenly character and conduct. He was and is the head of the angels who left their first estate.

Peter presented the angels' fall as one of the events that illustrate God's justice, its certainty and fearfulness. He said, *"God spared not the angels that sinned, but cast them down to hell, and delivered them into chains of darkness, to be reserved unto judgment"* (2 Peter 2:4). Jude spoke about the same order of God's inflexible wrath when he told us that *"the angels which kept not their first estate, but left their own habitation, he hath reserved in everlasting chains under darkness unto the judgment of the great day"* (Jude 6).

The Revelation of John adds its testimony to this fact:

And there was war in heaven: Michael and his angels fought against the dragon; and the dragon fought and his angels, and prevailed not; neither was their place found any more in heaven. And the great dragon was cast out, that old serpent, called the Devil, and Satan, which deceiveth the whole world: he was cast out into the earth, and his angels were cast out with him. (Revelation 12:7–9)

UNVEILING THE ENEMY

We can approach the Word of God with the assurance that we will find traces of the Devil's steps and the unfolding of his conduct. God's Word tells us of his evil schemes that have eclipsed so much of earth's brightness and spoiled so much of its promise and hope.

We must have a childlike spirit of trust, and lay aside *"all filthiness and superfluity of naughtiness, and receive with meekness the engrafted word"* (James 1:21). Then we will find satisfaction and illumination of the truth. We will not satisfy our curiosity or find illumination in the fine points of philosophy, but we will find satisfaction and illumination in all things that pertain to the highest truth for the thoughtful, trustful, and prayerful mind.

In the Bible we have the facts and history of man's redemption. Other worlds and other beings are brought into prominence in light of redemption's purposes and plans. These revealed facts, whether incidental or essential, are to our faith what the facts of nature are to the biology student. They must shape theories and settle opinions. They must not be set aside. Reason must not ignore or reject them, but must lay them as the solid foundations of all investigation, the basis of every hypothesis. These

Bible facts demand our faith, though we may not be able to reach out into the unknown regions where harmony reigns.

The Word of God brings clearly to light the unseen world: its persons, places, facts, and history. These are revealed not in minute detail, but with enough information to provoke thought and inspire faith.

THE DEVIL REVEALED

The Bible does not enter into an argument to prove the being and person of God. It assumes His being and reveals His person and character. Without preface or introduction, the Bible brings God before us in all His majesty and omnipotence. God was at the world's beginning, and He created the beginning of all things. *"In the beginning God created the heaven and the earth"* (Genesis 1:1). How sublime and inspiring is our first glimpse of God! God is revealed not by argument but by work. We learn what He is from what He does.

The revelation of the Devil is the same. He is presented without introduction or ceremony as the Evil One, a graduate of the school of deception and evil. The curtain is drawn, and the chief actor is in full dress. A world is at stake; man is to be seduced; Eden is to be corrupted. No light is shed upon his past history. No knowledge is given of the school where he learned his evil trade. He was before earthly life. Eden does not date his birth. The temptation in the Garden is not the first chapter of his history or the first test of his hellish art.

We have no access to the archives of the past. Eden bounds our horizon, and the Devil is there. Since that time, his history has run parallel with the human race's. Man is the object of his schemes, his destructive devices, and his ambition. Earth is the favorite scene of his exploits. He is at the cradle of every baby, and he has much to do in shaping each person's character and determining his destiny.

The Bible is a revelation, not a philosophy or a poem, not a science. It reveals things and persons as they are, living and acting outside the range of earthly vision or natural discovery.

Biblical revelations are not against reason but above reason. They require the exercise of faith, man's highest faculty. The powers of reason are not able to discover these biblical facts. Yet these facts are for reason's use—its light, strength, and higher elevation. But most essentially, they are to form, nourish, and perfect faith.

THE DEVIL IS A REAL PERSON

The Bible reveals the Devil as a person—not a mere figure, not simply an influence. He is not only a personification, but also a real person. In the eighth chapter of John, Christ was accusing the Jews for their cruelty, falsehood, deceit, and hypocrisy. Jesus said, *"Ye are of your father the devil, and the lusts of your father ye will do. He was a murderer from the beginning, and abode not in the truth, because there is no truth in him"* (John 8:44).

Many myths have gathered around the person of the Devil throughout the ages. Much poetry, tradition, and even our fears have caricatured his person, exaggerated his character, and colored his conduct. But there is truth in regard to him, naked and simple truth.

There is much truth that needs to be learned about the Devil, and no age needs the plain, unvarnished truth about him more than this generation. We need the light of that truth as a warning, as an incentive to vigilance, and as an inspiration to effort. We need the knowledge about the Enemy—his character, presence, and power—in order to rouse men to action. This knowledge is vital to victory.

Many people deny the existence of Satan and his influence in our lives. Would Christ have used such plain and solemn words repeatedly before His disciples and the Jews to encourage a lying superstition? To deny the reality of demon possession as recorded in the Gospels is simply inconceivable.

THE DEVIL AND HIS ANGELS

When the Devil fell, others fell with him. This is what God's Word teaches us. We have no record of the number of these fallen spirits. In Ephesians these unseen foes are spoken of as *"spiritual hosts"* (Ephesians 6:12 RV), an uncounted, uncountable number.

How innumerable they are, we cannot tell. The demoniac of Gadara was named *"Legion: because many devils were entered into him"* (Luke 8:30).

Who Is the Invisible Enemy? 405

A legion was somewhat less than six thousand. The total number of fallen spirits must be great, because they were able to permit so many demons to possess one man, or to allow seven to control one woman, as was the case with Mary Magdalene.

> *The Bible clearly states that the Devil has a host of fallen angelic followers who are ready and eager in their efforts to hurt man and defeat God's kingdom on earth.*

There is a statement in Revelation that the *"great red dragon...[with] his tail drew the third part of the stars of heaven, and did cast them to the earth"* (Revelation 12:3–4). This may be a reference to the fall of the angels and their number.

The Bible clearly states that the Devil has a host of fallen angelic followers who are ready and eager in their efforts to hurt man and defeat God's kingdom on earth.

TWO:

IDENTIFYING THE DEVIL'S PERSONALITY

Ye are of your father the devil, and the lusts of your father ye will do.
He was a murderer from the beginning, and abode not in the truth,
because there is no truth in him. When he speaketh a lie, he speaketh
of his own: for he is a liar, and the father of it.
—John 8:44

The Devil is a personality with definite character. Character can give dignity and value to a person, or character can degrade a person. Character is the inner life of a person that forms action and shapes life. Character is a fountain—the head and stream of conduct.

However, a person's character is often opposed to his reputation. Character is what we are. Reputation is what people think we are. The real and the "think so" are often two different worlds. It would be marvelous if reputation were based on character, if the real and the reputed were one. A bad reputation can be coupled with good character. Conversely, a good reputation can cover up bad character. But the Devil has this characteristic about him: his reputation is based on his character. They are one. The Devil's reputation is bad, because his character is worse.

THE NATURE OF THE DEVIL

The Devil is a created being. He is therefore not selfexistent or eternal, but limited and finite. There was a time when he was not, when he began to be. His creation was after the order of the angels. The angels are not the offspring of the family relationship. All the tender emotions, training, sweetness, and growth of infancy are unknown to them. The pains and joys of childbirth are not theirs. Each angel is created, not born. Each is created directly and personally by God. As an angel, the Devil was created good—doubtless, very good. His purity as well as exaltation were sources of congratulation, wonderment, and praise in heaven.

The Devil is a positive character. That is to say, he wears disguises, but his objectives lie in only one direction. He is double faced but never double minded, never undecided, vague, or feeble in his purposes or ends. No irresolution, hesitancy, or aimless action ever spring from him.

The Devil has character if not horns, because character is often harder and sharper than horns. Character is felt. We feel the Devil. He orders and controls things. He is a great manager. He manages bad men and fallen angels. The Devil is an indirect, sinister, low, and worldly manager.

THE PERSONALITY OF THE DEVIL

Christ is a person, and He puts the Devil in contrast to Himself as a great, mighty, wicked person who is the sower of all evil—as Christ is the sower of all good.

> *The field is the world; the good seed are the children of the kingdom; but the tares are the children of the wicked one; the enemy that sowed them is the devil; the harvest is the end of the world; and the reapers are the angels.* (Matthew 13:38–39)

Is Christ impersonal? Are the children of the kingdom impersonal? Are the children of the Wicked One impersonal? Are not Christ and the children of the kingdom personal and persons? Are not the children of the Wicked One and the Devil himself personal and persons also?

In the Bible the personality of the Devil is established as a reality. He not only is the source of evil to others, but also is the embodiment of evil in a person. The Revised Version makes this clear. The petition in the Lord's prayer, *"Deliver us from evil,"* becomes personal, *"Deliver us from the evil one"* (Matthew 6:13 RV). So we find Christ praying not only that His disciples would be delivered from evil, all evil, impersonal and general, but also *"that thou shouldest keep them from the evil one"* (John 17:15 rv).

> *In the Bible the personality of the Devil is established as a reality. He not only is the source of evil to others, but also is the embodiment of evil in a person.*

The statement by John that *"the whole world lieth in wickedness"* also becomes personal in the Revised Version, where all wickedness concentrates in a person: *"The whole world lieth in the evil one"* (1 John 5:19). Here, too, the Devil is called the *"evil one."* Personality is attributed to him. We saw earlier that fatherhood also is attributed to him, because he is the father of all evil. He is the enemy of Jesus, destructive, active, crafty, cautious, and cowardly.

THE PRINCE OF EVIL

The Devil and his angels are of a higher order than the fallen sons of Adam, by rank, order, and intelligence. In the Bible the Devil is called a prince, a world ruler, *"prince of this world"* (John 12:31). He is designated as *"the devil and his angels"* (Matthew 25:41). He and they are held accountable for their sins. They are condemned for their revolt in leaving their *"first estate"* (Jude 6), the sphere for which they were created and in which they were originally placed by God.

This fact of their fall, and all the other scriptural statements concerning them, direct and incidental, emphasize that they are persons—living, acting, free, and accountable. That the fallen angels had a chief prince who organized all their movements, who was first in wisdom, leadership, and skill, is clear from all scriptural statements concerning the Devil and his angels.

In 2 Corinthians 11:13–15, Paul said,

For such are false apostles, deceitful workers, transforming themselves into the apostles of Christ. And no marvel; for Satan himself is transformed into an angel of light. Therefore it is no great thing if his ministers also be transformed as the ministers of righteousness; whose end shall be according to their works.

The statement *"Satan himself"* is an emphatic declaration of personality. He also has ministers. An influence does not have ministers. Paul was writing about persons who are fraudulent and alluring. He introduced this great leader as the Archimposter, the inspirer of all the fraud, hypocrisy, and error of his apostles, who are as false as he is.

In Jude there is a statement that brings into view many personalities:

Likewise also these filthy dreamers defile the flesh, despise dominion, and speak evil of dignities. Yet Michael the archangel, when contending with the devil he disputed about the body of Moses, durst not bring against him a railing accusation, but said, The Lord rebuke thee.

(Jude 8–9)

The *"filthy dreamers"* were persons. Moses was a great person. Michael, an archangel, is an actual being. What is the Devil, if not a living, active personality?

A HIGH DIGNITARY

During Moses's time, the Devil was contending with Michael, the highest angelic dignitary. Did the mighty archangel have to appeal for help against a mere influence, a shadowy, dreamy personification? This statement in Jude declares the Devil to be a high dignitary, whose person and presence are not to be treated with dishonor or frivolity.

The following statement in Peter gives further evidence of the fact that the Devil is a person of high nobility.

> The Lord knoweth how to deliver the godly out of temptations, and to reserve the unjust unto the day of judgment to be punished: but chiefly them that walk after the flesh in the lust of uncleanness, and despise government. Presumptuous are they, selfwilled, they are not afraid to speak evil of dignities. Whereas angels, which are greater in power and might, bring not railing accusation against them before the Lord. But these, as natural brute beasts, made to be taken and destroyed, speak evil of the things that they understand not; and shall utterly perish in their own corruption. (2 Peter 2:9–12)

Note how James put the mightiest beings in contrast and opposition: "*Submit yourselves therefore to God. Resist the devil, and he will flee from you. Draw nigh to God, and he will draw nigh to you*" (James 4:7–8). Why such a combination and contrast? Is God not a living personality? How can we then reduce the Devil to a mere influence? This passage teaches a personal Devil as surely as it does a personal God.

Why are God and the Devil spoken of in a similar manner in Peter's urgent exhortation?

> Humble yourselves therefore under the mighty hand of God, that he may exalt you in due time: casting all your care upon him; for he careth for you. Be sober, be vigilant; because your adversary the devil, as a roaring lion, walketh about, seeking whom he may devour. (1 Peter 5:6–8)

Why cast all care on Him? Why be sober and vigilant? "Your adversary" can be no less than an actual being against whom the Christian has to be armed with God's power.

"*Your adversary*"! Hate and destruction are his weapons. Can he be less than a person? The Devil is walking about like "*a roaring lion*," strong, full of passions and deadly hate! Can anything less than a being of fiery passion and infernal power fulfill this divine portrait?

To Peter, the existence and personality of this powerful adversary had had a sad demonstration in his own experience. These words were still on his conscience, heart, and memory: *"Simon, behold, Satan hath desired to have you, that he may sift you as wheat"* (Luke 22:31).

In the Revised Version, another reference to the personality of the Devil may be found in the instructions given in the Sermon on the Mount about swearing, affirmations, and conversation, where Jesus said, *"Let your speech be, Yea, yea; Nay, nay: and whatsoever is more than these is of the evil one"* (Matthew 5:37).

Under the powerful operations of the Cross and the Spirit, as well as the restraining influences of the Gospel, why has evil not been driven from the earth? It is because of the mighty personality and executive ability of the Devil.

JESUS AND THE DEVIL

We find many references, hints, and reminders of the power and personality of the Devil evident in the ministry of Christ. By calling him the *Devil*, Christ invested him with an infamous personality and clothed him with all the deceit, craft, and cruelty attached to that name. By using the name *Satan*, Christ put him as the adversary of God and man. By designating him as *"the prince of this world"* (John 12:31), Christ recognized Satan's royal power and ruling authority over evil in this world. The Devil's ability to affect the body with sickness is not merely hinted at but taken for granted in the Gospels.

The conflict between the Devil and Jesus is seen in the Lord's Prayer, that perfect and universal prayer that Jesus puts in the hearts and lips of His people. It contains, according to the Revised Version, this petition of conflict, peril, warning, and safety: *"Deliver us from the evil one"* (Matthew 6:13). Evil is comparatively harmless, feeble, and inert without the presence of its mighty inspirer. Deliverance from the Devil is deliverance from the many evils of which he is the source and inspiration.

WARNINGS ABOUT THE DEVIL

In the sixth chapter of Ephesians, the Christian is presented as a soldier in character, armor, conduct, and courage. Because of the Devil's power, and because the Christian's warfare is mainly against him, we are urged to:

> *Put on the whole armour of God, that ye may be able to stand against the wiles of the devil. For we wrestle not against flesh and blood, but against principalities, against powers, against the rulers of the darkness of this world, against spiritual wickedness in high places.*
>
> (Ephesians 6:11–12)

The Christian's comfort as administered by Paul in the sixteenth chapter of Romans is not only the impartation of, *"The grace of our Lord Jesus Christ be with you,"* but also, *"And the God of peace shall bruise Satan under your feet shortly"* (v. 20).

Peter's vital exhortation in his first epistle has a double imperative in it: he not only exhorted the casting of all our care upon God (1 Peter 5:7), but he also gave a loud and urgent call to watch and pray: *"Be sober, be vigilant; because your adversary the devil, as a roaring lion, walketh about, seeking whom he may devour"* (v. 8.)

Moreover, Peter recognized the hand of Satan in the deadly crime of Ananias and Sapphira, saying, *"Ananias, why hath Satan filled thine heart to lie to the Holy Ghost, and to keep back part of the price of the land?"* (Acts 5:3).

The warning that Christ sent to the church at Smyrna to prepare for tribulation recognized the personality and power of the Devil.

> *Fear none of those things which thou shalt suffer: behold, the devil shall cast some of you into prison, that ye may be tried; and ye shall have tribulation ten days: be thou faithful unto death, and I will give thee a crown of life.*
>
> (Revelation 2:10)

The explanation of the parable of the tares puts the wickedness, personality, and power of the Devil in contrast with Christ.

> *The field is the world; the good seed are the children of the kingdom; but the tares are the children of the wicked one; the enemy that sowed them is the devil; the harvest is the end of the world; and the reapers are the angels.*
>
> (Matthew 13:38–39)

THE DEVIL'S EVIL WORK

The defense of Christ against the Pharisees' charge that He had violated the Sabbath exposes the Devil in his work of evil: *"And ought not this woman, being a daughter of Abraham, whom Satan hath bound, lo, these eighteen years, be loosed from this bond on the sabbath day?"* (Luke 13:16).

The Bible says about Judas, *"And supper being ended, the devil having now put into the heart of Judas Iscariot, Simon's son, to betray him"* (John 13:2). This is a statement not of an influence or a personification, but of a personality outside of Judas, making suggestions to him and urging him on to his act of hypocrisy. This suggestion is strictly in keeping with the character of the Devil.

"And after the sop Satan entered into him. Then said Jesus unto him, That thou doest, do quickly" (John 13:27). This act is greatly advanced in power of action and influence compared to Satan's work in the Garden! There he used a serpent as his instrument. Here he uses a man, a chosen, trusted apostle.

Paul said,

> Lest I should be exalted above measure through the abundance of the revelations, there was given to me a thorn in the flesh, the messenger of Satan to buffet me, lest I should be exalted above measure.
>
> (2 Corinthians 12:7)

In this instance, the exalted revelation and experience of the person and power of Christ were closely followed by the revelation and experience of the person and power of the Devil.

Christ explained the fearful doom that awaits the wicked at the time of judgment: *"Then shall he say also unto them on the left hand, Depart from me, ye cursed, into everlasting fire, prepared for the devil and his angels"* (Matthew 25:41). The final doom of Satan is revealed in these words, *"And the devil that deceived them was cast into the lake of fire and brimstone, where the beast and the false prophet are, and shall be tormented day and night for ever and ever"* (Revelation 20:10).

These extracts are not simply arguments to prove the existence or personality of the Devil. Instead, they are logical, conclusive references to a being whose reality is taken for granted, universally accepted, and thoroughly believed by Christ and the early apostles.

Given this, a singular case would be the person who professed to accept God's Word and yet did not believe in the existence of the Devil. This would be a great breach both in logic and faith. It would be the same as if a person accepted the play *Macbeth* yet failed to recognize the person or existence of Lady Macbeth, whose character forms the plan and nature of the entire plot.

CHRIST'S VIEW OF THE DEVIL

Christ's encounters with those who were possessed by devils, or demons, illustrate His constant recognition of these fallen spirits as personal beings. He recognized their distinct individuality. He talked to them and commanded them as persons. They knew Christ, confessed His divinity, bowed to His authority, and obeyed, however unwillingly, His commands.

Jesus made a clear distinction between the human personality who was possessed by a demon, and the personality of the demon who held possession of the person. In His eyes, they were two distinct persons.

The exercising of this distinction gave a severe blow to Satan's kingdom. When the seventy disciples returned and reported about their mission, they said, *"Even the devils are subject unto us through thy name"* (Luke 10:17). Jesus exclaimed, *"I beheld Satan as lightning fall from heaven"* (v. 18), and then, amid their ecstasy and His joy, He renewed their commission:

> *Behold, I give unto you power to tread on serpents and scorpions, and over all the power of the enemy: and nothing shall by any means hurt you. Notwithstanding in this rejoice not, that the spirits are subject unto you; but rather rejoice, because your names are written in heaven.*
>
> (Luke 10:19–20)

"Over all the power of the enemy." The Devil is the enemy of Christ and of man. Jesus gave His disciples power over all the Devil's power. To Christ the Devil was a very real person. He recognized his personality, felt and acknowledged his power, abhorred his character, and warred against his kingdom.

THREE:

RECOGNIZING THE PRINCE OF THIS WORLD

Jesus answered and said, This voice came not because of me, but for your sakes. Now is the judgment of this world: now shall the prince of this world be cast out. And I, if I be lifted up from the earth, will draw all men unto me.
—John 12:30–32

The Holy Spirit is the substitute, representative, and successor of Jesus Christ. To the Holy Spirit was committed the work of breaking the deadly power of the world by breaking the power of its prince. Jesus reminded His disciples that the Devil, who occupied the royal position as the world's prince, was already judged, condemned, and sentenced.

Nevertheless I tell you the truth; it is expedient for you that I go away: for if I go not away, the Comforter will not come unto you; but if I depart, I will send him unto you. And when he is come, he will reprove the world of sin, and of righteousness, and of judgment: of sin, because they believe not on me; of righteousness, because I go to my Father, and ye see me no more; of judgment, because the prince of this world is judged. (John 16:7–11)

Satan may be the prince of this world, but there is an awful doom awaiting him, because he is the author of unbelief, sin, and unrighteousness.

WHAT IS SATAN'S POSITION?

In these declarations of Jesus Christ, we have the clear revelation of what the Devil is in his relationship to the world as a prince and ruler. We understand why the world is so alien to God, to God's Son, and to His cause. We understand how attachment to the world creates estrangement from and bitter enmity toward God. This happens because the world's beauty and charms reflect the opposition of the Devil to God. The world is the sensuous harlot with her snares of death and hell.

The Devil is recognized by Jesus Christ to be the prince of this world, not lawfully, but in the world's rebellion against God. The Devil is not to be submitted to, but to be renounced as a lawless criminal, dethroned as a usurper, and conquered as a rebel. The Son of God was given this mission: to dethrone and conquer the Devil.

We see how readily Jesus Christ acknowledged the position and power of the Devil. When He spoke of the Devil, He equated him with the world. The stroke of the Son of God falls on both: *"Now is the judgment of this world: now shall the prince of this world be cast out. And I, if I be lifted up from the earth, will draw all men unto me."* The world is condemned by the power of the Cross.

The Son of God was given this mission: to dethrone and conquer the Devil.

THE POWER OF THE CROSS

The sweet, attractive powers of the Cross dissolve the fatal fascinations of the world. The powers of that same Cross cast out the prince of this world from his ruling throne.

Christ affirmed the Devil's high position, but also signed and sealed his destiny and doom. *"God anointed Jesus of Nazareth with the Holy Ghost and with power: who went about doing good, and healing all that were oppressed of the devil; for God was with him"* (Acts 10:38).

Again the Son of God recognized the position that the Devil held as prince crowned by the world's powers. His presence quieted the Son of God. Man's words are not to be victors in this conflict. Jesus used God's words during the Temptation. (See Matthew 4:1–11.) With these He broke the power of Satan's assault and defeated his evil intentions. But Jesus left him still a sovereign with his kingly crown.

The Son of God remained silent at the Devil's approach. The Cross and its deep humiliation and bitter agony, its defeat and despair—it took all these to lift the crown from Satan's brow and bring his throne down to dust and ashes. The adorable Son of God saw *"the travail of his soul"* and was satisfied (Isaiah 53:11).

Jesus saw what it would cost Him and what it would cost every son of heaven to discrown that prince. Because of this, He lapsed into a solemn silence, the prestige of His victory. *"Hereafter I will not talk much with you: for the prince of this world cometh, and hath nothing in me"* (John 14:30).

FOUR:

WHAT IS THE DEVIL'S BUSINESS?

Then was Jesus led up of the Spirit into the wilderness to be tempted of the devil. And when he had fasted forty days and forty nights, he was afterward an hungered. And when the tempter came to him, he said, If thou be the Son of God, command that these stones be made bread. But he answered and said, It is written, Man shall not live by bread alone, but by every word that proceedeth out of the mouth of God. Then the devil taketh him up into the holy city, and setteth him on a pinnacle of the temple, and saith unto him, If thou be the Son of God, cast thyself down: for it is written, He shall give his angels charge concerning thee: and in their hands they shall bear thee up, lest at any time thou dash thy foot against a stone. Jesus said unto him, It is written again, Thou shalt not tempt the Lord thy God. Again, the devil taketh him up into an exceeding high mountain, and showeth him all the kingdoms of the world, and the glory of them; and saith unto him, All these things will I give thee, if thou wilt fall down and worship me. Then saith Jesus unto him, Get thee hence, Satan: for it is written, Thou shalt worship the Lord thy God, and him only shalt thou serve. Then the devil leaveth him, and, behold, angels came and ministered unto him.
—Matthew 4:1–11

What is the Devil's Business? 419

Iff there is any virtue in believing in God, the Devil may claim this virtue. If there is any praise for always being busy, the Devil may claim this praise, for he is always very busy. But his character does not spring from his faith. His faith makes him tremble (see James 2:19); his character makes him a devil.

The Devil is a very busy character. He does a big business, a very ugly business, but he does it well, that is, as well as an ugly business can be done. He has lots of experience, big brains, a black heart, great force, tireless energy, and is of great influence and great character. All his immense resources and powers are used for evil purposes.

Only evil inspires his activities and energies. He never moves to relieve or bless. He is a stranger to benevolent deeds and compassionate feeling.

Satan's history antedates the history of man. He and his angels are the only beings who have experienced heaven, earth, and hell. These three places are familiar to him. He has walked the streets of heaven side by side with its purest and best. He has felt the thrill of its purest joys. He also knows the bitterest anguish of hell and has felt its keenest flames.

THE DEVIL'S BIG BUSINESS

The Devil does a big business on earth. He is a prince and a leader. Men and devils are his agents. The elements of nature are often corrupted by him from their beneficial purposes and forced to destroy. He is busy tempting men to do evil. He has lots of experience in this business and is very adept at it. By his schemes, sin seems to lose its sinfulness, the world is clothed with double charms, and self is given twice the force. He turns faith into fanaticism and love into hate.

A spiritual character can work through other agencies or directly on the human spirit. Satan infuses thoughts and makes suggestions, and he does it so deftly that we do not know their origin. He tempted Eve to take the forbidden fruit. He put it into David's mind to number Israel, thereby provoking the wrath of God. (See 2 Samuel 24.) He influenced Ananias and Sapphira to lie to God. (See Acts 5:1–11.) Peter's yielding to presumption was instigated by Satan. Judas's betrayal was from the same poisonous source. The temptation of Christ was a typical masterpiece of Satan's craft. He tried to dissuade our Lord from God's purposes by showing Him his power to present alternatives with great persuasive logic.

Satan is blasphemous, arrogant, and presumptuous. He slanders God to men and infuses into their minds distorted thoughts about God. He intensifies their hatred and inflames their prejudice against Him. He leads them to deny God's existence and to misrepresent His character, thereby destroying the foundations of faith and all true worship.

Satan does all he can by insinuation and accusation to blacken saintly character and lower God's estimate of the good. He is the vilest of maligners, the most vicious and artful of slanderers. Goodness is the target of his constant attack. He says nothing good about the good, nothing bad about the bad.

> *Satan does all he can by insinuation and accusation to blacken saintly character and lower God's estimate of the good. He is the vilest of maligners, the most vicious and artful of slanderers.*

Satan is always at church before the preacher is in the pulpit or a member is in the pew. He comes to hinder the sower, to impoverish the soil, or to corrupt the seed. He uses these tactics only when courage and faith are in the pulpit, and zeal and prayer are in the pew; but if dead ritualism or live liberalism are in the pulpit, he does not attend, because they are no danger to him.

SATAN'S TOOLS OF THE TRADE

The Devil goes about to do evil and oppress men. Christ expressly declared that some sickness, at least, was directly inflicted by Satan. At every point the Devil is the antagonist of Him who *"went about doing good, and healing all that were oppressed of the devil"* (Acts 10:38). In some way he acquired the power of death and created in men a fearful bondage to it. Through death, Christ works to *destroy him that had the power of death, that is, the devil*" (Hebrews 2:14).

The Devil put a thorn in Paul's flesh and made a special effort to acquire Peter's loyalty. He directed the whirlwind, kindled the fire, and ordered the disease that devastated Job and his property. He armed the thieving Chaldeans and Sabines against Job, and got control of his wife. He directed the various offices of his empire to ruin this one saint. He will wreck an empire at any time to secure a soul.

Satan sows the tares in the wheat, the bad among the good, bad thoughts among good thoughts. All kinds of evil seed are sown by him in the harvest fields of earth. He is always trying to make the good bad and the bad worse. He filled the mind of Judas, and he inflamed and hurried him on to his infamous purpose. He filled Peter with an arrogant pride that tried to inject human views into the purpose of Christ instead of God's purpose.

The Devil goes about as fierce, as resolute, and as strong as a lion, intent only on destroying. He is restrained by no sentiments that soften and move human or divine hearts. He has no pity and no sympathy. He is great, but he is only great in evil. He has a great intellect, but he is driven and inspired by a vicious and cruel heart.

THE TEMPTATION OF CHRIST

At the threshold of Christ's ministry, He was met with temptation by the Devil. The historical account of the situation presents the Devil as a spiritual person. He is the head and embodiment of all evil, making a fierce and protracted assault on the Son of God. We are not informed as to what form he assumed in order to veil the treachery and wickedness of his attack.

The temptation of Christ is noted as one of the preliminary and pivotal facts of His ministry. It cannot be considered a vision any more than can His baptism, the descent of the Spirit, His wilderness trip, or His fasting. It was not an "influence" that tempted Christ. The whole transaction forbids such a conclusion. "*Then was Jesus led up of the Spirit into the wilderness to be tempted of the devil."* The Devil came to Him, and the Devil left Him, and then *"angels came and ministered unto him."*

In this temptation, the methods, hypocrisy, and craft of the Devil may be seen. He comes to the weak, exhausted Son of God with an air of concern. How innocent is Satan's suggestion that Jesus use His power to relieve His hunger! What could be more permissible than to use His spiritual power for physical purposes? How often is this done? Whenever faith is used to serve the natural, the source is always evil.

It is man living for bread alone that makes the temporal become priority. The secular and worldly take on supreme importance. Faith becomes secondary—subservient to money and business. The heavenly is used for the earthly, the spiritual for the natural. We become more intent on daily food than on daily grace, eyeing the seen more than the unseen.

That is the Devil's main business—to materialize religion, to get man to live for bread alone, to make earth bigger than heaven, to make time more intriguing than eternity. What a fearful conflict is being carried on in that quiet wilderness between the fainting Son of God and Satan! It is a struggle between the earthly and the heavenly, between God's religion and the Devil's religion.

THE POINTS OF THE CONFLICT

The conflict surges around three points: the fleshly, the presumptuous, and the worldly. This little circle holds all the shapes and forms of temptation—all the crafty devices, all the hidden depths, all the glittering seductions that Satan has devised to swerve men from the allegiance that faith demands.

The Devil's assault on Christ is in striking contrast to his temptation to beguile Eve. It is also in striking contrast to the fearful ordeal through which he tried Job's integrity. Satan cast no suspicion on God's goodness as he did with Eve. He caused no terrific, consuming sorrow as he did in Job's case. Instead, everything was friendly, sympathetic, and inviting.

The second temptation included the fanatical presumption of overheated zeal and brainless devotion. Satan used all the methods of sensational and abnormal religious practices. He tempted Jesus to take the shortcut by which the principles of genuine faith are set aside and superficial substitutes are brought in to make faith more attractive and popular. Presumption seeks to take man-devised methods, which are easy, sentimental, and material, instead of God's lowly way of godly sorrow, strict selfdenial, and prayerful surrender.

The last temptation involved the world with its kingdoms and its glory. These are the rewards for devotion to Satan and worship of the Devil—who is the world's god. How the Devil massed all his forces! Religion was invoked. The world and the flesh conspired, under Satan's power, to tempt the Son of God.

The reluctance with which the pure Son of God went into this close conflict with Satan is seen in Mark's statement: *"And immediately the Spirit driveth him into the wilderness"* (Mark 1:12). Nothing can warp this statement into saying that a mere influence tempted Jesus. The temptation of Jesus by the Devil is history—plain, simple, documented fact. Without a doubt or figure of speech, the Bible clearly stamps the whole transaction with personality.

In our text passage from Matthew 4, we read: *"Then was Jesus led up of the Spirit into the wilderness to be tempted of the devil,"* and *"Then the devil leaveth him, and, behold, angels came and ministered unto him."* In Mark 1:13, we read, *"And he was there in the wilderness forty days, tempted of Satan; and was with the wild beasts; and the angels ministered unto him."* These are not figures of speech, but narratives of a transaction and of persons engaged in the transaction. The wilderness and the fasting are literal. The beings are all literal: the wild beasts, the angels, Jesus, and the Devil.

The conflict of Jesus with Satan was not incidental, accidental, or casual, but was essential and vital. Satan held man and man's world in subjection. They had fallen into his hands and were held by him in bondage and ruled by him with desperate power.

The record has been made, *"And when the devil had ended all the temptation, he departed from him for a season"* (Luke 4:13).

THE AGONY IN THE GARDEN

In the Garden of Gethsemane, the season had ended, and Satan was back again as though he had brought seven other spirits more wicked than himself. (See Matthew 12:43–45.) Gethsemane was the sum of the Devil's most maddened and desperate methods. The disguises were off. He appeared there as he really is. It is a rare thing to get a clear, true light on the Devil. He assumes so many roles, acts so many parts, wears so many disguises.

In the Garden of Gethsemane, we see him in lifesize form. The air is heavier by his breath; the night is darker by his shadow; the ground is colder, and his chill is on it. Judas is falser still, and Peter is more cowardly, because Satan is there.

On the threshold of Gethsemane, Jesus exclaimed, "*My soul is exceeding sorrowful, even unto death*" (Matthew 26:38), and He "*began to be* [grieved] *and very heavy*" (v. 37). Why? It was because "*this is your hour, and the power of darkness*" (Luke 22:53). Why? "*Now is the judgment of this world: now shall the prince of this world be cast out*" (John 12:31). Everything was silent, and there was an air of dread and horror. Why? "*For the prince of this world cometh, and hath nothing in me*" (John 14:30).

In this situation, the Devil's method with Christ was much different than it was in the wilderness. Then there was an assumed sympathy, the spirit of an inquirer, one anxious to relieve. In the wilderness, Satan offered the most pleasant, attractive, and satisfying ministries to the flesh. There was something of the gentleness of a lamb, the interest and sympathy of a friend. But how that had changed in the Garden! The lamb was transformed into a lion, a roaring lion who was maddened and desperate.

In the wilderness, Jesus could not be seduced by the flesh or self or the world. He must be overwhelmed with dread and horror, thought Satan. His steadfastness must be overcome by weakness and fear. Satan comes to many saints in the fierceness and power of the lion when the gentle inducements fail.

FIVE:

SATAN'S MAIN TARGET

[Jesus] saith unto them, But whom say ye that I am? And Simon
Peter answered and said, Thou art the Christ, the Son of the living
God. And Jesus answered and said unto him, Blessed art thou, Simon
Barjona: for flesh and blood hath not revealed it unto thee, but my
Father which is in heaven. And I say also unto thee, That thou art
Peter, and upon this rock I will build my church; and the gates of hell
shall not prevail against it.
—Matthew 16:15–18

The Devil is too wise and too lordly in ambition to confine his aims to the individual. Instead, he seeks to direct the policies and sway the governments of nations. In his passion for success, he goes out *"to deceive the nations which are in the four quarters of the earth"* (Revelation 20:8).

Satan is an expert in all the arts of deceit. He is an archangel in execution, and he often succeeds in seducing the nations most loyal to Christ. He leads them into plans that pervert all scriptural principles. When the church itself, the bride of Christ, is seduced from her purity, she degenerates into worldly ritualism.

The *"gates of hell shall not prevail"* against the church. This promise of our Lord stands against every satanic device and assault. But this unchangeable word does not protect the church from the Devil's strategies, which often pervert the aims of the church and postpone the day of its final triumph.

THE PERVERTING OF THE CHURCH

The Devil is a hydraheaded monster who is multifaceted in plans and wisdom as well as in atrocities. His supreme effort is to gain control of the church, not to destroy its organization, but to pervert its divine purpose. He does this in the most insidious way, so that there is no startling change and nothing to shock or alarm those whom he is trying to undermine.

Sometimes revolutionary and destructive change is introduced under the disguise of a greater zeal for Christ's glory. It is often introduced by someone who is held in high esteem by the local church, but who is totally ignorant of the fact that the measure he is advocating is subversive.

One of Satan's most perverse schemes is to establish a wrong estimate of church strength. If he can create false assessments of local church power; if he can press the material things to the forefront; if he can make these forces powerful in commands and influence, he has accomplished his purpose.

Under the Law of Moses, the subversion of God's purposes and the substitution of material forces were guarded against. The kings of Israel were warned against accumulation of and reliance on material forces. King David was in violation of this law when he yielded to the temptation of Satan to number the people of Israel.

The third temptation of our Lord was intended to subvert the purposes of His kingdom. Satan planned to do this by substituting material elements of strength for spiritual ones.

This is one of the Devil's most insidious and successful methods to deceive, divert, and deprave. He parades the most attractive material results. He praises the power of human planning before church leaders until they are dazzled and ensnared. Then the church becomes thoroughly worldly while boasting of her spirituality. No deceiver is so artful in the diabolical trade of deception as Satan. As an *"angel of light"* (2 Corinthians 11:14), he leads souls to death.

To mistake the true power of the church's strength is to mistake the true character of the church. When its character is changed, then all its efforts and aims are also changed. The strength of the church lies in its devotion to God. All else is incidental and is not the source of its strength. But in worldly, popular language, a local church is called strong when its membership is large, and when it has social position and financial resources. A church is thought to be powerful when ability, learning, and eloquence fill the pulpit, and when the pews are filled by fashion, intelligence, money, and influence. An assumption of this kind is worldly to the fullest extent.

THE SOURCE OF TRUE POWER

The local church that defines its strength in this way is on the highway to apostasy. The strength of that church does not consist in any or all of these things. The faith, holiness, and zeal of the church are the elements of its power. The church's strength does not consist in its numbers and its money, but in the holiness of its members. The church's strength is not found in these worldly attachments or endowments, but in the endowment of the Holy Spirit on its members.

The most deadly symptom that can be seen in a church is the transference of its strength from spiritual to material forces, from the Holy Spirit to the world. The power of God in the church is the measure of its strength. This is the quality God looks for in a church. The power of the Holy Spirit gives the church the ability to accomplish the purposes for which it was designed.

On the contrary, show us a church that is poor, illiterate, obscure, and unknown, but composed of praying people. They may not be men of power, wealth, or influence. Their families may not know one week where they are to get their bread for the next. But with them is *"the hiding of [God's] power"* (Habakkuk 3:4), and their influence will be felt for eternity. Wherever they go there is a fountain of light, Christ in them is glorified, and His kingdom is advanced. They are His chosen vessels of salvation who reflect His light.

Within the church there are unmistakable signs that she has been blinded and caught by Satan's dazzling glare. The church is being seriously affected by the material progress of the age. We have heard so much about prosperity and gazed on it for so long that spiritual views no longer appeal to us. Everything must take on the rich quality, luxuriant growth, and magnificent appearance of the material, or else it seems beggarly. This is the most perilous condition the church has to face. It happens when the meek and lowly fruits of holiness are discounted by the showy and worldly charms with which material success crowds the church.

We must not yield to the flood. We must not for a moment, not with the hundredth part of an inch, give place to the world. Holiness and devotion to God must be stressed in every way and at every point. The church must be made to see this delusion and snare. This transference of strength from God to the world, this rejection of the Holy Spirit's endowment of might and power, must be recognized as yielding to Satan. The church, more and more, is inclined not only to disregard, but also to despise, the elements of spiritual strength and to set them aside for more impressive, worldly ideas.

THE MATERIAL DECEPTION

We have been taught to regard the principles of church prosperity as those items that can be seen only in a statistical column. We seek to impress an age geared to the objectivity of secular facts and figures. However, the most vital spiritual conditions and gains cannot be reduced to figures. For this reason, they are left out of the numerical column, and, after a while, they are neither noted nor observed.

If we do not change our methods, our ideas concerning the strength of the local church will become worldly. No matter how imposing our material results may be, or how magnificent and prosperous the secular arm of the church appears, we must go deeper than these for its strength. We must proclaim and reiterate with increased emphasis that the strength of the church does not lie in these things.

These are the gilded delusions that we mistake for the true riches. While we are vainly saying, "[We are] *rich, and increased with goods,*" God has written that we are *"wretched, and miserable, and poor, and blind, and naked"* (Revelation 3:17).

Wealth and prosperity may be the costly spices and splendid decorations that embalm and entomb our spirituality. True strength lies in the godliness of the people. The personal holiness of the members of each church is the only true measure of strength. Any other test offends God, dishonors Christ, grieves the Holy Spirit, and degrades religion.

A church can often make the best showing of material strength when death in its deadliest form is feeding on its vital organs. There is hardly a more damaging delusion than to judge the conditions of a church by its material prosperity or churchrelated activity. Spiritual barrenness and rottenness in a church are generally hidden by a pleasant exterior and unusual growth. However, a spiritual church converts people from sin soundly, clearly, and fully. Then it puts them on the road to holiness, where they strive to walk in a way that is pleasing to God.

This spirituality is not to be kept in a corner of the church, but is to be its primary and only business. God's church must continue to do this work of converting sinners and perfecting saints in holiness. Whenever this work becomes secondary, or other interests are held to be its equivalent, then the church becomes worldly. When material interests are emphasized, they come into prominence. Then the world comes to the throne and sways the scepter of Satan.

God's church must continue to do this work of converting sinners and perfecting saints in holiness. Whenever this work becomes secondary, or other interests are held to be its equivalent, then the church becomes worldly. When material interests are emphasized, they come into prominence. Then the world comes to the throne and sways the scepter of Satan.

There is no surer way to make the church worldly than to put its material prosperity in the forefront. This is the surest way to put Satan in charge.

It is easy for material assessments to become priority by emphasizing them until the opinion is created that these things are most important. When collecting money, building churches, and counting attendance become the evidence of church prosperity, then the world has a strong foothold, and Satan has achieved his purpose.

CREATING A HUMAN INSTITUTION

Another scheme of Satan is to eliminate from the church all the humble, selfdenying ordinances that are offensive to unsanctified tastes and unregenerate hearts. He seeks to reduce the church to a mere human institution—popular, natural, fleshly, and pleasing.

Satan has no scheme that can more thoroughly thwart God's high and holy purposes than transforming His church into a human institution according to man's views. God's right arm is thereby paralyzed, the body of Christ becomes the body of Satan, and light is turned into darkness and life into death.

Men who have religious leadership positions are often blinded by a false attachment to what they think is truth and what they consider honors Christ. They are found trying to eliminate from the teaching of Christ those painful, offensive, unpopular, and selfdenying features to which the Gospel owes all its saving beauty and power, and which stamp it as divine.

From the life of Peter we have a painful and most instructive warning:

From that time forth began Jesus to show unto his disciples, how that he must go unto Jerusalem, and suffer many things of the elders and chief priests and scribes, and be killed, and be raised again the third day. Then Peter took him, and began to rebuke him, saying, Be it far from thee, Lord: this shall not be unto thee. But he turned, and said unto Peter, Get thee behind me, Satan: thou art an offence unto me: for thou savourest not the things that be of God, but those that be of men. Then said Jesus unto his disciples, If any man will come after me, let him deny himself, and take up his cross, and follow me. For whosoever will save his life shall lose it: and whosoever will lose his life for my sake shall find it. For what is a man profited, if he shall gain the whole world, and lose his own soul? or what shall a man give in exchange for his soul?

For the Son of man shall come in the glory of his Father with his angels; and then he shall reward every man according to his works.

(Matthew 16:21–27)

Here is a lesson for all times and for all people. An apostle had become the mouthpiece of Satan! What an alarming, horrible, and revolting picture! An apostle, zealous for his Master's glory, advocated with fire and force a scheme that would forever destroy that glory! The apostle Peter became Satan's agent!

This is the same apostle who had just made the inspired confession, *"Thou art the Christ, the Son of the living God,"* that placed him in highest honor with Christ and the church! Before the words of that divine and marvelous confession had died from his lips, this same apostle became the advocate of plans that would nullify his confession and destroy the eternal foundations of the church.

THE EASY WAY

Peter, a chief apostle, advocated schemes that would have discrowned Christ of His messiahship and brought heaven's favorite plan to a disastrous and shameful end! What destructive impulse compelled Peter? Satan entered him and, for the time being, achieved his purposes. But Christ reproved Peter, and in the reproof struck a crushing blow at Satan.

"Get thee behind me, Satan" (Matthew 16:23) is a reminder and duplicate of Jesus's response to Satan during the wilderness temptation. *"Thou art an offence ["stumblingblock," RV] unto me"* (v. 23), He said. The temptation through Peter was the Devil's trigger to catch Christ in his trap, but Jesus saw through it. *"Thou savourest not the things which be of God, but those that be of men"* (v. 23). The Devil was not in sight. Man appeared, but Satan's views were pressed to the front.

The things that men savor in church planning and church life are against God's plan. The high and holy principles of selfdenial, godly living, and surrender to Christ are all against men's view of Christianity. The Devil seeks to destroy the church indirectly. Men's views eliminate all the unpopular principles of the Cross—selfdenial, life surrender, and separation from the world. When this is done, the Devil runs the church. Then the church becomes popular, selfsatisfying, modern, and progressive. But it is the Devil's church, founded on principles pleasing in every way to flesh and blood.

If this occurs, Christ is no longer in the church. There is no crucifixion of self, no crucifixion of the world, no second coming of Christ, no eternal judgment, no everlasting hell, no eternal heaven. Nothing is left that reminds us of God, because everything reeks of man. Man makes it the Devil's church by turning Christ's church over to human leaders. The world is sought and gained in the Devil's church, but the soul and heaven are lost to eternity.

The very heart of this disgraceful apostasy, this dethroning of Christ and enthroning of the Devil, is to remove the Holy Spirit from His leadership in the church. Satan's plan is to put unspiritual men in leadership to direct the church. Men of great ability and men with the powers of leadership have often displaced God's leadership. The ambition for leadership and the enthronement of human leaders is the doom and seal of apostasy. There is no leadership in God's church except the leadership of the Holy Spirit. The man who has the most of God's Spirit is God's chosen leader. He is zealous for the Spirit's sovereignty, ambitious to be the least, the slave of all.

SIX:

SATAN'S SUBVERSION OF THE CHURCH

Jesus answered, Verily, verily, I say unto thee, Except a man be born of water and of the Spirit, he cannot enter into the kingdom of God. That which is born of the flesh is flesh; and that which is born of the Spirit is spirit. Marvel not that I said unto thee, Ye must be born again.
—John 3:5–7

Ye worship ye know not what: we know what we worship: for salvation is of the Jews. But the hour cometh, and now is, when the true worshippers shall worship the Father in spirit and in truth: for the Father seeketh such to worship him. God is a Spirit: and they that worship him must worship him in spirit and in truth.
—John 4:22–24

There are two ways of directing the church: God's way and the Devil's way. God's way and man's way of running the church are entirely opposite. Man's wise plans, thoughtful resources, and easy solutions are Satan's devices. The Cross is retired and the world comes in. Selfdenial is eliminated, and all seems bright, cheerful, and prosperous. Satan's hand is on the controls, and men's schemes prevail. But the church fails under these devices of men, and the bankruptcy is so complete that the court of heaven will not even appoint a successor for the collapsed corporation.

All of God's plans have the mark of the Cross on them, and all His plans have death to self in them. All of God's plans have crucifixion to the world in them. But men's plans either ignore the offense of the Cross or despise it. Men's plans have no profound, stern, or sacrificial denial in them. Their gain is of the world. How many of these destructive elements does the Devil bring into the church, until all the holy aims and heavenly purposes of the church are retired and forgotten?

SOCIETY VERSUS SALVATION

One of these satanic devices is to pervert the aims of the church. He deludes church leaders into thinking that the main purpose of the church today is not so much to save individuals out of society as to save society, not so much to save souls as to save the bodies of men, not so much to save men out of a community as to save men and manhood in the community. The world, not the individual, is the subject of redemption.

This popular, seductive, and deadly fallacy entirely subverts the very foundation of Christ's church. This trend is so strong that it will sweep away every vestige of the spiritual and eternal. For this reason, we must watch, work, and speak with sleepless vigilance, tireless energy, and fearless boldness. The attitude and open declaration of much of the religious teaching we now hear are in the same strain and spirit that characterized the Unitarian, Jewish, and rationalistic thinking of the nineteenth century.

To save society is a kind of religious fad to which much enterprising church work is committed. Advanced thinkers have elaborated the same idea. They do not realize their true condition, which is one of going backward and not going forward. This backward step entombs religion in the grave where Judaism has been buried all these centuries. It may well be in agreement with the idle dreams of the worldly rabbis to think of regenerating the world and ignoring the individual.

The phrase "to save the world" has a pompous sound. It seems right for the church to apply itself to bettering the temporal surroundings of the individual and improving his sanitary conditions, to lessen the bad smells that greet his nose, to diminish the bacteria in his water, and to put granite in the pavement for him to walk on instead of wood or brick. All this sounds fine and agrees well with a material age. It becomes practical in operation and provides obvious, imposing results. But does this agree with the sublime dignity and essential aim of the church?

Do we need the church to accomplish these purposes? Concerned councilmen, an efficient street commissioner, and the ordinary vigilance of the average policeman will secure these results in the best way. They need no church, no Bible, no Christ, no personal holiness to accomplish these purposes. If the church concentrates its efforts on results that can be better accomplished by other agencies, it will soon be regarded as a nuisance and lose its influence in the world.

A UNIQUE INSTITUTION

The purpose of the church of God is far superior to these childish dreams and fruitless philosophies. Its purpose is to regenerate and sanctify the individual, to prepare him by purifying and training him for the high pursuits of eternal life.

The church is like a net cast into the sea. The purpose is not to change the sea but to catch the fish out of the sea. Let the sea roll on its essential nature while the net catches its fishes. What if fishermen spent all their energies trying by some chemical process to change the essential elements of the sea, vainly hoping to improve the stock of fish? They would never catch any fish! If the church used this method, personal holiness would be impossible, and heaven would be stricken from our creed, life, and hope.

To attempt to save the world while ignoring the individual is not only Utopian but also destructive in every way. To save the world sounds like a commendable goal, but it will result in making the church worldly and unfit for her holy and sublime mission. Christ said that gaining the world and saving the man are opposing objectives. (See Matthew 16:26.) Christ taught Peter that his satanic devices would gain the world to and for the church, but would lose the soul. Everything would seem to contribute to the cause of saving the world, when in reality all would be death.

The church is distinctly, preeminently, and absolutely a spiritual institution. It is an institution created, vitalized, possessed, and directed by the Spirit of God. Her ministers and doctrines have appeal, relevance, and power only when they are channels of the Holy Spirit. It is His indwelling and inspiration that give the church its divine character and accomplish its divine purposes.

THE SPIRITUAL SUBVERSION

If the Devil can by any methods shut the Holy Spirit out of the church, he has effectively prevented the church from being God's church on earth. He accomplishes this by retiring from the church the agencies or agents that the Holy Spirit uses. Satan displaces them with natural devices that are rarely if ever the channels used by the Holy Spirit. Christ announced this unchangeable, universal law when He said, "*That which is born of the flesh is flesh; and that which is born of the Spirit is spirit*" (John 3:6).

If a church has a holy preacher, a man of great prayerfulness, of great grace, filled with the Spirit, Satan will use any method to retire him and put in a man who does not pray, but who is eloquent and popular. The church may seem to have gained, but it has "gained" by the substitution of natural forces for spiritual ones, an exchange that has unknowingly revolutionized the church.

A church can be led by holy men who are not highly cultured, but are wellversed in the "*deep things of God*" (1 Corinthians 2:10); who are strong in devotion to Christ and His cause, but not wealthy or of high social position. A church may change these officers and put in men who are in every way decent and moral, but are not noted for prayer and piety. If you put in men of high social position who are capable administrators, the church will scarcely notice the change except for the marked improvement in finances. But an invisible and powerful change will have taken place in the church. It will have changed from a spiritual church to a worldly one. The change from noonday to midnight is not more extreme than that.

At this point, Satan is doing his deadliest and most damning work. It is deadliest and most damning because it is unnoticed, unseen; it produces no shock and excites no alarm.

It is not by the obvious works of evil that Satan perverts the church, but by quiet displacement and unnoticed substitution. The higher is retired, the spiritual gives place to the social, and the divine is eliminated because it is made secondary.

The perversion and subversion of the church are achieved by Satan when the spiritual forces are retired or made subordinate to the natural; when social entertainment, and not edification, becomes the desired goal. This process is intended to soften and modify the distinctly spiritual aims of the church and to broaden what is called the rigid exclusiveness of spiritual narrowness. But in the end it eliminates all that is distinctly spiritual.

> *The perversion and subversion of the church are achieved by Satan when the spiritual forces are retired or made subordinate to the natural; when social entertainment, and not edification, becomes the desired goal.*

That which is in any sense deeply religious will not survive the death of the spiritual. The church's leaders will lose sight of spiritual edification as the purpose of God's church. Instead, entertainment that is pleasing and pleasant will come to the forefront. The social forces not only will retire the spiritual forces, but also will effectually destroy them.

THE MODERN CHURCH

A modern church with its kitchen and parlor, with its club and gymnasium, and with its ministries to the flesh and to the world is both indicative and alarming. What a contrast there is between the principles that the early church originated and fostered and those that the modern and progressive church presents as substitutes.

The original churches were faithfully spiritual. Their only purpose was to strengthen and cultivate all the elements that combine to make a deep and clear experience of God. They were training schools for spiritual life. They never lingered in the regions of the moral, the aesthetic, and the mental. They fostered no desires or inclinations that were not spiritual and did not minister to the soul's progress.

The early church took it for granted that all who came to them really desired to *"flee from the wrath to come"* (Matthew 3:7) and were sincerely yearning after full redemption. They considered it their obligation to furnish these seekers with the most sacred and exacting assistance. It never occurred to them that entertainment and social gatherings were channels through which God's grace would flow and foster spiritual growth.

These social and fleshly forces are regarded in many denominations as the perfection of spiritual things. These events are arrayed as the mature fruit of spiritual piety, flavored and perfected by its culture and progress. They are ordained as the handmaidens of the prayer and testimony meeting. I object most seriously to the union of the worldly and the spiritual. What have they in common? *"Can two walk together, except they be agreed?"* (Amos 3:3).

What elements of piety are fostered by entertainment and social gatherings? What phases of spiritual life do they promote? What feature of the gymnasium produces faith? Where do you find any elements that are aids to piety? How do social parties produce a more prayerful and holy life? How do they bring the soul nearer to God? How do they form or strengthen the ties of Christian fellowship? Are social clubs not frivolous and worldly? Do parties not cater to and suit the tastes of the carnal and worldly? What unity of purpose and spirit is there between worldly entertainment and witnessing for Christ? The one is intensely spiritual; the other has in it no evidence of spiritual benefit.

We might as well add to the list of heavenly helpers the skating rink, calisthenics, and the gymnasium. If the young people desire to join a club, enjoy a social gathering, or play parlor games, let them do so. But do not deceive them and degrade holiness by calling these things holy institutions that feed the spiritual life.

CREATING A REVOLUTION

Disguise it as we may; reason about it as we will; apologize for it as we do; the truth is, we have lost the intensity of our personal spiritual experiences. We have lost the deep conviction about eternal things that is an evident feature of all great spiritual movements.

Many preachers and others have fallen so low in their spiritual experience that they do not cherish these distinct and strongly spiritual methods. Instead, they are devising plans and organizations to gratify their nonspiritual desires, which are midway between Christ and the world. While these desires are not essentially wrong, they do not possess one grain of spiritual power and can never be the channels of heavenly communication.

It is said that we cannot get church people to attend distinctly spiritual meetings. What is the problem? Are the institutions worn out and no longer of value to the humble, pious soul? Who will dare affirm this? It is said that the desires of the people are low and perverted. Should we then change the methods to suit unsanctified appetites? No, instead, let us tone up their appetites for spiritual things and elevate the tastes of our people.

Let the revolution begin with the preacher. Let him wrestle with God until his ordination vow becomes revitalized so that everyone can feel the pressure of his goal, the intensity of his zeal, the singleness of his purpose, and the holiness of his life. Let the people catch the fire and purpose of his heart until all press on to the regions of perfect love, panting for all the fullness of God. Under this united, divine inspiration, worldly entertainment will be forgotten and become stale. Then the spiritual meetings of the church will become attractive and delightful.

The church cannot become allied with nonspiritual agencies. By doing this, she breaks the tension of her faith and discards the Holy Spirit. She cannot be the supplier of unsanctified desires. Neither is it her business to fall down to the beggarly task of entertaining the people. This is her saddest mistake: when her evening services are surrendered to concerts and lectures; her praise is turned into worldly music; her classrooms become parlors; her social gatherings are more popular than her prayer meetings, and the house of God becomes a house of feasting instead of a house of prayer. The unity of the Spirit and the holy brotherhood are displaced and destroyed to make room for social affinities and worldly attractions.

It is the church's high and royal duty to maintain her spotless fidelity to her Lord, to stress holiness, and to use every means for its advancement and perfection. When this is done, spiritual character and holiness will order all the rest.

SEVEN:

OVERCOMING THE ENEMY OF GOD

I have written unto you, young men, because ye are strong, and the word of God abideth in you, and ye have overcome the wicked one. Love not the world, neither the things that are in the world. If any man love the world, the love of the Father is not in him. For all that is in the world, the lust of the flesh, and the lust of the eyes, and the pride of life, is not of the Father, but is of the world. And the world passeth away, and the lust thereof: but he that doeth the will of God abideth for ever.
—1 John 2:14–17

The world should be renounced by every true disciple of Christ. To love the world and the things of the world puts us in open enmity to God. If we have a relationship of love or friendship to the world, we are the enemies of God. We need commit no other sin except that of having an attachment to the world; by that alone, we are the enemies of God.

Christ Jesus said that between the world and His disciples there would be conflict, that the world would hate them. (See John 15:18–19.) Discipleship to both Himself and the world is impossible. The call, the touch, and the choice of Christ, when accepted and obeyed, become the secret and the source of the world's hatred.

Jesus declared the inevitable enmity of the world toward His followers: *"The world hath hated them, because they are not of the world, even as I am not of the world"* (John 17:14). Again, in His High Priestly Prayer, He declared this distinct and eternal separation and conflict: *"They are not of the world, even as I am not of the world."* By virtue of their relationship to Christ, they are separated from and are in conflict with the world.

SPIRITUAL ADULTERY

This conflict is represented by two persons in the Bible: Adam and Jesus, who is called the Second Adam. Their natures, affinities, and opposition are declared in the clearest language:

> *The first man is of the earth, earthy: the second man is the Lord from heaven. As is the earthy, such are they also that are earthy: and as is the heavenly, such are they also that are heavenly. And as we have borne the image of the earthy, we shall also bear the image of the heavenly.*
> (1 Corinthians 15:47–49)

Opposition to the world is strongly declared and demanded. The love of the world is hostile to and destructive of the love of God. The two cannot coexist.

"Ye adulterers and adulteresses, know ye not that the friendship of the world is enmity with God? whosoever therefore will be a friend of the world is the enemy of God" (James 4:4). Nothing is more explicit than this, nothing is more commanding, authoritative, and exacting.

"Love not the world." Nothing is more offensive to God, nothing is more criminal—more abominable—than love for the world. Loving the world violates the most sacred relationship of the soul with God. The purity of spiritual adulterers departs, and shame and illicit intercourse exist. Friendship with the world is heaven's greatest crime and God's greatest enemy.

The world is one of the enemies that must be fought and conquered on the way to heaven.

For this is the love of God, that we keep his commandments: and his commandments are not grievous. For whatsoever is born of God overcometh the world: and this is the victory that overcometh the world, even our faith. Who is he that overcometh the world, but he that believeth that Jesus is the Son of God? (1 John 5:3–5)

The Gospel is represented as a training school in which denying worldly desires is one part of its curriculum.

For the grace of God that bringeth salvation hath appeared to all men, teaching us that, denying ungodliness and worldly lusts, we should live soberly, righteously, and godly, in this present world; looking for that blessed hope, and the glorious appearing of the great God and our Saviour Jesus Christ; who gave himself for us, that he might redeem us from all iniquity, and purify unto himself a peculiar people, zealous of good works. (Titus 2:11–14)

There is something in the world that makes it a deadly enemy to the salvation of Christ and that poisons us against heaven.

Nothing is more offensive to God, nothing is more criminal— more abominable—than love for the world. Loving the world violates the most sacred relationship of the soul with God. The purity of spiritual adulterers departs, and shame and illicit intercourse exist. Friendship with the world is heaven's greatest crime and God's greatest enemy.

WHAT IS THE "WORLD"?

What is this "world" that so effectually alienates us from heaven and puts us in flagrant enmity with God? Why is it that our friendship with the world violates our wedding vow to God? Why is it that love of the world is enmity with God and criminal to the most abominable degree? What are *"the world, the lust of the flesh, and the lust of the eyes, and the pride of life"* (1 John 2:16)?

"The world" includes the mass of humanity that is alienated from God and therefore hostile to the cause of Christ. It involves worldly affairs, earthly things, riches, pleasures, and pursuits that are shallow, frail, and fleeting. These things stir desire, draw us away from God, and are obstacles to the cause of Christ. The divorced or torn relationship between heaven and earth, between God and His creatures, finds its expression in the term *"the world."*

Our English word *desire* expresses the meaning of the word *lust*. It includes the world of active lusts and desires that controls the seat of desire and the natural appetites.

Alford's Commentary says:

The world was constituted at first in Adam, well pleasing to God and obedient to Him. It was man's world, and in man it was summed up. In man the world fell into the darkness of selfish pursuits. Man became materialized in spirit and dragged down so as to become worldly and sensual. The world is man's world in his fall from God. "The lust of the flesh" is human nature in opposition to God. The "lust of the eyes" is that sense that takes note of physical things and is inflamed by them. The "pride of life" is the manner of worldly men whereby pride is displayed and pomp is cherished.

Bengel said,

The "lust of the flesh" means those things on which the sense of enjoyment, taste, and touch are fed. The "lust of the eyes" means those things by which the senses of investigation—the eye and sight, hearing, smelling, and feeling—are occupied. The "pride of life" means when anyone assumes too much about himself in words or actions. Even those who do not love arrogance of life may possibly pursue the lust of the eyes. Even those who have overpowered this fault still frequently retain the lust of the flesh. This problem prevails among the poor, the middle class, and the powerful. It is even found among those who appear to exercise selfdenial.

John Wesley said,

The "desire of the flesh" means the pleasures of the outward senses, whether of taste, smell, or touch. The "desire of the eye" refers to the pleasures of the imagination, to which the eye is chiefly subservient. It is that internal sense whereby we relish what is grand, new, or beautiful. The "pride of life" means everything that we use to generate respect from other people—fancy clothing, houses, furniture, and manner of living—anything that gratifies our pride and vanity. It therefore directly includes the desire for praise and involves a certain degree of covetousness. All these desires are not from God, but from the prince of this world.

THE ENEMY OF HEAVEN

This world arrays itself and all its forces against heaven. Worldliness is the epidemic foe of heaven. To live for this world is to lose heaven because of an opposite attraction. The Son of God declares of His disciples, "*Thou gavest me* [them] *out of the world*" (John 17:6), and reiterates the declaration to His Father as one of prime importance, "*They are not of the world, even as I am not of the world*" (v. 16). It remains true to this hour that all the genuine disciples of Jesus are not of the world, but are chosen out of the world, have renounced the world, and are crucified to the world.

What gives the world its fatal charms? What makes its charms so deadly? Sometimes its beauty is all withered, its brightness all night, its hope all despair, its joy the bitterest anguish, and all its prospects decay and desert. But still it holds and binds. We hate to leave it. What is the source of its deadly sorcery and its fatal snares? What is the source of its malignant hate, its hostility to God, and its alienation from heaven?

This world is the Devil's world. In that fatal hour when man fell from his allegiance and devotion to God, he carried the world with him in his rebellion against God. Man was the world's ruler, and the world fell with its master. This is the reason for its vicious rivalry with and intense opposition to heaven. The Devil has his kingdom here. It is his princedom. He clothes it with all beauty and seductive power as the rival of heaven.

Heaven's trinity of foes are the world, the flesh, and the Devil. The world is first, the most powerful and engaging. All three center in evil, because the Devil inspires and inflames them. The flesh wars against the spirit simply because the Devil inflames its desires. The world gets its deadly and fascinating snares from the Devil. The world is not simply the ally of Satan, but also is his instrument and agent. It represents him with the most servile and complete loyalty.

HOW TO OVERCOME THE WORLD

For a full understanding of the text from 1 John that was already quoted, *"Love not the world, neither the things that are in the world,"* we need to read what precedes it:

> *I write unto you, young men, because ye have overcome the wicked one. I write unto you, little children, because ye have known the Father. I have written unto you, fathers, because ye have known him that is from the beginning. I have written unto you, young men, because ye are strong, and the word of God abideth in you, and ye have overcome the wicked one.* (1 John 2:13–14)

In order to *"overcome the wicked one,"* the world, its love, and its things must be renounced. At the threshold of many church doors are written these words, which belong to every soul's true betrothal to Christ:

Dost thou renounce the Devil and all his works, the vain pomp and glory of the world, with all covetous desires of the same, and the carnal desires of the flesh, so that thou wilt not follow or be led by them?

"I renounce them all" was the answer solemnly given, and the preacher, the people, and our own hearts said, "Amen." And let it be amen now and forever. The world must be renounced, and that means renouncing Satan. This is the deadliest blow to his rule.

Friendship with the world violates our marriage vows to heaven. James, in his severe denunciations of the world, made friendship with the world criminal. He declared that to be the friend of the world is to be the enemy of God (James 4:4). We cannot understand this unless we realize he was declaring that the world's friendship is the Devil's religion, "*earthly, sensual, devilish*" (James 3:3). We can get back to God only by renouncing friendship with the world and by cleansing our hearts and hands of its soiling touch. We draw near to God by resisting the Devil. We resist the Devil by renouncing the world.

COUNTERFEIT RELIGION

The apostle James summed up the distinct characteristics of the Devil's worldcounterfeit religion. Passion, appetite, and pleasure reign and wage war. (See James 4:1–3.) How much of this passion, pleasure, and world religion has there been in the church? Too often its history is a history of passion, strife, ambition, and blood. Its ecumenical councils are the battlefield of passion in its unbridled, most destructive form. Earthly, sensual, and devilish is the divine stigma that marks and mars ecclesiastical history.

Many modern church members and churchgoers are friends of the world; they are its advocates and lovers. They only say prayers in order not to miss praying. There is no drawing near to God, no fighting against the Devil and driving him from the field of action. Their religion, its ceremonies, and its worship descend not from above, but are earthly, natural, and devilish.

"*Submit yourselves therefore to God*" and "*Resist the devil*" (James 4:7) are the keynotes of unworldly religion. A personal God and a personal Devil are among the primary articles of creed and experience in true religion. Surrender to God, draw near to Him, and live close to Him. Fight against the Devil, and get rid of him by denouncing and rejecting the world.

EIGHT:

SATAN'S MOBILIZING OF THE WORLD'S FORCES

And you hath he quickened, who were dead in trespasses and sins:
wherein in time past ye walked according to the course of this world,
according to the prince of the power of the air, the spirit
that now worketh in the children of disobedience: among whom also
we all had our conversation in times past in the lusts of our flesh,
fulfilling the desires of the flesh and of the mind; and were by nature
the children of wrath, even as others.
—Ephesians 2:1–3

The divine warning against the course of the world, against the fashion of the world, and against the spirit of the world is given because the Devil is directing the world's course. The Devil is creating the world's spirit, and the Devil is cutting the pattern of the world's fashion.

The touch of the world pollutes because Satan's fingers are in its touch. Its desires are deadly and heavenquenching because Satan kindles its desires. The world and its things are contraband in Christian warfare because Satan is the ruler of the world and the administrator of its affairs.

In Ephesians, Satan and his legions are called *"world-rulers"*:

Put on the whole armour of God, that ye may be able to stand against the wiles of the devil. For our wrestling is not against flesh and blood, but against the principalities, against the powers, against the world-rulers of this darkness, against the spiritual hosts of wickedness in the heavenly places. (Ephesians 6:11–12 RV)

The world rulers are principalities and powers that are under the direction of the Devil. They rule this world by ruling the things that rule this world.

THE FORCES OF THIS WORLD

Satan seizes and directs all the mighty forces of this world! War is seized by Satan, and it is no longer the patriot's struggle for freedom or the defense of home and native land. Instead, it becomes the tool of despotism; it crushes liberty and enslaves freedom. War carries on a campaign of lust, rape, cruelty, desolation, and death.

Money is another of the world's ruling forces that could be used to beautify the earth and to lay up a good foundation against the time to come. It should be used to ease the burdens of the poor, to banish poverty, and to brighten the homes of widows and orphans. Money is a mighty world-ruling power. The Devil rules it, and, instead of flowing at the command of compassionate love, it is diverted by Satan for selfish and unholy purposes. Satan excites men to covetousness and hardens them into callousness. Men become illustrious and esteemed by the world's standards when they are moneygetters and moneykeepers.

Education is another mighty worldruling force. Satan chains it, and it becomes the source of pride and ungodly power. Its mighty engineering is turned into "higher criticism." Under the guise of Christian learning, education becomes the most powerful ally to Satan by unsettling faith in God's Word and opening a wide door of skepticism in the temple of God.

In Ephesians 2:2, the Devil is called the *"prince of the power of the air."* The natural forces of the world are under his dangerous control. How many destructive storms and cyclones is he responsible for?

THE FLESH AND THE MIND

And you hath he quickened, who were dead in trespasses and sins: wherein in time past ye walked according to the course of this world, according to the prince of the power of the air, the spirit that now worketh in the children of disobedience: among whom also we all had our conversation in times past in the lusts of our flesh, fulfilling the desires of the flesh and of the mind; and were by nature the children of wrath, even as others.   (Ephesians 2:1–3)

In this passage, Paul spoke of himself and the saints. They had formerly lived in Satan's kingdom, and Satan had ruled them by the lusts of the flesh—he had fulfilled *"the desires of the flesh and of the mind."*

We see in these verses how Satan rules throughout the world. He is the *"god of this world"* (2 Corinthians 4:4), and he excites its desires, both low and high—low in the desires of the flesh and high in the desires of the mind. The world fills the passions and chains the mind in its high worldly pursuits and refined tastes. Yet it is all of Satan. The *"lust of the flesh, and the lust of the eyes, and the pride of life"* (1 John 2:16) are of the world, and Satan is the exciter of them: *"Then when lust hath conceived, it bringeth forth sin: and sin, when it is finished, bringeth forth death"* (James 1:15).

We know that whosoever is begotten of God sinneth not; but he that was begotten of God keepeth him, and the evil one toucheth him not. We know that we are of God, and the whole world lieth in the evil one.   (1 John 5:18–19 RV)

"The whole world lieth in the evil one" means that the world is in the power of the Devil, is held in subjection by him, and is fixed and established. The Devil is pictured not only as trying to kindle into a flame the desires that may remain in a good man's heart after conversion, but also as enfolding in his arms the whole world and making it subject to his power and submissive to his absolute control.

THE DEVIL'S HEAVEN

The world comes in through many doors, and it comes in many forms. Yet at whatever door and in whatever form it comes, the world is always the Devil's servant. It comes in to do his work as his most obedient and faithful slave. When the world comes in, dressed in its most seductive and beautiful garb, the Devil has fashioned its clothing and ordered its coming.

The world is the Devil's heaven. Its rest, crown, and reward are here. When the world comes in, God's heaven goes out. It fades from the eye and heart. The struggle for it ends, and God's heaven, with its fadeless and eternal glories, is lost.

In these statements from the Bible about the world and the Devil, we see why the world opposes heaven. We realize the enmity between the two. Heaven is Christ's place, the place where He is, and to which He wants men to come. The world is Satan's place. His power is here. To fix our hearts on the world is to be loyal to him. To fix our hearts on heaven is to be loyal to Christ.

Here we have the reason for the world's cruel hatred of Jesus, and why it has so bitterly persecuted His followers. We see why the *"flesh lusteth against the Spirit, and the Spirit against the flesh"* (Galatians 5:17). We see why these are not only contrary to one another, but also at war with one another. The Devil is in the flesh and rules it. Christ is in the Spirit. This world leads away from Christ. It is the invincible foe of Christ.

This great truth is illustrated and enforced by the fact that Christ's work is to get possession of the world and make its power accomplish His purposes. But He establishes a kingdom of heaven that is not of this world. A new power has come in; a new kingdom is established, and a new world made. It will take the fires of the judgment and the new creative power to make a new heaven and a new earth before the stains and ruin of the Devil's death-dealing hands can be removed, and this corrupted, yet beautiful, world can be prepared for God's holy purposes.

The Christian is called to renounce his allegiance to the world. By his very relationship to Jesus Christ, he is lifted out of the world's deadly embraces, and its polluting charms are broken. In this subserviency of the world to the Devil, we have the reason for the world's intense hatred of

Jesus Christ. We can see why the world has armed itself with all its forces under the power of the Devil to destroy the cause of Christ. The world's opposition and enmity have always been against true religion, but often its smiles are more fatal than its hate.

Christians are called to renounce their allegiance to the world. By their very relationship to Jesus Christ, they are lifted out of the world's deadly embraces, and its polluting charms are broken.

NINE:

HOW POWERFUL IS THE DEVIL?

Now there was a day when the sons of God came to present them-selves before the LORD, and Satan came also among them. And the LORD said unto Satan, Whence comest thou? Then Satan answered the LORD, and said, From going to and fro in the earth, and from walking up and down in it. And the LORD said unto Satan, Hast thou considered my servant Job, that there is none like him in the earth, a perfect and an upright man, one that feareth God, and escheweth evil? Then Satan answered the LORD, and said, Doth Job fear God for nought? Hast not thou made an hedge about him, and about his house, and about all that he hath on every side? thou hast blessed the work of his hands, and his substance is increased in the land. But put forth thine hand now, and touch all that he hath, and he will curse thee to thy face. And the LORD said unto Satan, Behold, all that he hath is in thy power; only upon himself put not forth thine hand. So Satan went forth from the presence of the LORD.
—Job 1:6–12

We have seen that, instead of minimizing the power of the Devil, Jesus exalted him to the pinnacle of power as the prince of this world. In the significant events of Christ's life, the Devil was the one evil agent whom Christ had in mind and to whose rule He was opposed. We have seen how soon the Devil followed in the wake of our Lord's baptism at the Jordan. Satan came to Jesus after He was anointed by the Holy Spirit and entered into His public ministry.

POWER OVER SATAN

When Jesus first commissioned His disciples, one of their assignments was to *"cast out devils"* (Matthew 10:8). Jesus appointed seventy more disciples to go forth to minister, and when they returned to report their work to Christ, they said, with evident surprise and gratification, *"Even the devils are subject unto us through thy name"* (Luke 10:17). He replied, *"I beheld Satan as lightning fall from heaven"* (v. 18). When He was opening His disciples' hearts to receive the great Comforter, He declared that the Holy Spirit was to *"reprove the world...of judgment, because the prince of this world is judged"* (John 16:8, 11).

In one of His impassioned outbreaks, as the pain of His great agony drew nearer, Jesus cried, *"Now is my soul troubled"* (John 12:27). However, the darkness is relieved by a gleam of light in which He sees the ruin of Satan's kingdom and the Devil spoiled, dethroned, and cast out by the power of His cross: *"Now is the judgment of this world: now shall the prince of this world be cast out. And I, if I be lifted up from the earth, will draw all men unto me"* (vv. 31–32).

SATAN'S POWER OVER MEN

But as the darkness grew deeper and the anguish more bitter, He saw the approaching form of him who controls the powers of darkness. Hushed into silence in the presence of this relentless and cruel Foe, the Son of God said to His sorrowing and awestruck disciples, *"Hereafter I will not talk much with you: for the prince of this world cometh, and hath nothing in me"* (John 14:30).

The Devil's sad and mighty influence is further seen within the circle of the chosen disciples. Peter staggered under the blow of the Devil. The shameful denial by Peter was referred to by Christ before it took place: *"Simon, Simon, behold, Satan hath desired to have you, that he may sift you as wheat: but I have prayed for thee, that thy faith fail not: and when thou art converted, strengthen thy brethren"* (Luke 22:31–32).

Jesus Christ acknowledged the great power and authority that the Devil has in the present deranged order of things. He declared, *"Now is the judgment of this world: now shall the prince of this world be cast out"* (John 12:31).

How defiant Satan is! He opposed Christ stubbornly with reckless and often successful courage. Into the chosen circle of the Twelve he entered, into the one who had been trusted as their treasurer, the receiver and the disburser of their money and their charity.

> *Jesus Christ acknowledged the great power and authority that the Devil has in the present deranged order of things. He declared, "Now is the judgment of this world: now shall the prince of this world be cast out" (John 12:31).*

One of the sacred Twelve was possessed and moved to carry out in the most hypocritical, false way Satan's infamous designs. He came very close to adding Peter to the black list of his disgraceful recruits. It is evident that the Devil had much to do with Peter's dastardly denial, his lying and blasphemy. The words of Christ make this plain:

> *And the Lord said, Simon, Simon, behold, Satan hath desired to have you, that he may sift you as wheat: but I have prayed for thee, that thy faith fail not: and when thou art converted, strengthen thy brethren. And he said unto him, Lord, I am ready to go with thee, both into prison, and to death. And he said, I tell thee, Peter, the cock shall not crow this day, before that thou shalt thrice deny that thou knowest me.*
>
> (Luke 22:31–34)

In the parable of the sower, Christ set forth the unseen but powerful influence that the Devil exerts to neutralize the Word of God. In the record of this parable by Matthew, the Devil is termed the *"wicked one"* (Matthew 13:19). This is a statement of his personality and of the concentration of his preeminent wickedness. He snatches away the seed of the Word with vigilant and diabolical hate. *"Then cometh the devil, and taketh away the word"* (Luke 8:12). He is the destroyer of the seeds of good. Satan is so powerful that the incorruptible and eternal Word of God is prevented from accomplishing its saving efforts because of his vigilance and influence over the mind.

POWER TO AFFLICT

In the story of Job and his trials, we see the Sabeans and Chaldeans ready to respond to Satan's suggestion to make their raids on Job's herds. Satan's power is not limited to outside influence, but is direct and powerful, getting on the inside. His suggestions of evil are almost godlike at times. They excite our passions or principles so we cannot see the wrong until it is too late. As we saw earlier, this was true in the case of Satan's suggestion to David to number Israel.

His power is so great that even the best men, who are able to resist his temptations, come under his power for a time. The Christians at Smyrna were so under his power that, while he could not alienate their affections or disturb their loyalty, he could put them in prison. All his life, Paul felt the buffeting inflicted by Satan's power.

When Peter denied Christ, he was in Satan's hands and was on the verge of giving in to his power. Job was for a while put under his power. He was driven and afflicted as if in a cruel tempest in which everything was wrecked and lost except his patience. How great was Satan's power to destroy fortune, family, friends, and reputation!

During the Temptation, the Son of God was led to the pinnacle of the temple and to a high mountain by the fearful spell of Satan.

Angels retired, and heaven hushed its music, was draped in silence, and trembled in awe while Satan's dread power was allowed to expend its dark forces on heaven's Anointed One.

The power of disease was also in the Devil's hands. He smote Job. Christ said of the woman with the spirit of infirmity: *"Ought not this woman, being a daughter of Abraham, whom Satan hath bound, lo, these eighteen years, be loosed from this bond on the sabbath day?"* (Luke 13:16).

Doubtless, much sickness is due to the power of the Devil. To this there is reference in the statements of Christ's work:

When the even was come, they brought unto him many that were possessed with devils: and he cast out the spirits with his word, and healed all that were sick: that it might be fulfilled which was spoken by Esaias [Isaiah] the prophet, saying, Himself took our infirmities, and bare our sicknesses. (Matthew 8:16–17)

God anointed Jesus of Nazareth with the Holy Ghost and with power: who went about doing good, and healing all that were oppressed of the devil; for God was with him. (Acts 10:38)

POWER OVER THE BODY

Satan's power did not extend to death in Job's case, but he did destroy the lives of his children. Satan was able to hold the Smyrna Christians in prison for only ten days, but thousands of others he held unto death. His own cruel, deadly hands weaved for them the martyr's crown of gold and glory.

The power of the Devil over the body is further seen and illustrated by a number of cases of demonic possession in the New Testament. The Devil had possession of the bodies of some people, using his demons to control them. Some of the people were fearfully tormented in body and almost wrecked in mind. Others had certain functions of their bodies suspended: some were made dumb by him, others were made deaf, and still others were made blind. These cases were many in number and of great variety. Among the most distressing cases were those who were not great sinners. Instead, the young, comparatively innocent ones were the victims of Satan's dread power. The whole person came under the power of this alien spirit. The power of Satan, his nearness and personality, had a constant and destructive manifestation in these cases.

It has been well said that the Gospel narratives are distinctly pledged to the historic truth of these occurrences of demon possession. Either they are true or the Gospels are false. They relate to us words spoken by the Lord Jesus in which the personality and presence of the Devil are distinctly stated. Either our Lord spoke these words or He did not. If He did not, then we must also set aside the concurrent testimony of the seventy disciples. In other words, we establish a principle that will overthrow every fact related in the Gospels.

TEN:

EXPOSING THE RULERS OF DARKNESS

And he showed me Joshua the high priest standing before the angel of the Lord, and Satan standing at his right hand to resist him. And the Lord said unto Satan, The Lord rebuke thee, O Satan; even the Lord that hath chosen Jerusalem rebuke thee: is not this a brand plucked out of the fire? Now Joshua was clothed with filthy garments, and stood before the angel. And he answered and spake unto those that stood before him, saying, Take away the filthy garments from him. And unto him he said, Behold, I have caused thine iniquity to pass from thee, and I will clothe thee with change of raiment.
—Zechariah 3:1–4

The power of Satan is far greater than that of God's highest and earthly saints. In the third chapter of Zechariah, we have the picture of his power with God's high official representatives. Joshua, the high priest, and the angel of the Lord are there. Standing at Joshua's right hand to resist all his righteous acts is Satan. Joshua and the angel realize their insufficiency when contending with Satan, and they send a cry to heaven, "The LORD rebuke thee."

Jude also gives us this interesting statement: "*Michael the archangel, when contending with the devil he disputed about the body of Moses, durst not bring against him a railing accusation, but said, The Lord rebuke thee*" (Jude 9).

This obscure text teaches us something regarding this contest between Michael and the Devil. It clearly shows that an archangel's strength is not sufficient to contend singlehandedly and alone with the Devil.

THE POWER OF THE UNSEEN

Daniel gives us a glimpse into the power and conflict that exist in the unseen and spiritual world that lies so near our own. This invisible world has much to do with how our spiritual battles are fought and our victories are won. Daniel had been praying for three weeks before the angel and the answer came.

> *Then said he unto me, Fear not, Daniel: for from the first day that thou didst set thine heart to understand, and to chasten thyself before thy God, thy words were heard, and I am come for thy words. But the prince of the kingdom of Persia withstood me one and twenty days: but, lo, Michael, one of the chief princes, came to help me.*
>
> (Daniel 10:12–13)

We see how Satan works. If he cannot keep people from praying, he can cause delay in the answer to prayer. In this way he tries to discourage and break down their faith. He wants Christians to minimize the power of urgent, persistent praying.

Satan's invisible influence is seen in his power to use people to cast others into prison. To the little church at Smyrna, Jesus Christ wrote in commendation, warning, and consolation,

> *Fear none of those things which thou shalt suffer: behold, the devil shall cast some of you into prison, that ye may be tried; and ye shall have tribulation ten days: be thou faithful unto death, and I will give thee a crown of life.*
>
> (Revelation 2:10)

> *We see how Satan works. If he cannot keep people from praying, he can cause delay in the answer to prayer. In this way he tries to discourage and break down their faith. He wants Christians to minimize the power of urgent, persistent praying.*

There are special seats or headquarters of his power, places where the Devil makes his home and rules with an absolute control. Christ referred to this in His letter to the church of Pergamos:

> *I know thy works and where thou dwellest, even where Satan's seat is: and thou holdest fast my name, and hast not denied my faith, even in those days wherein Antipas was my faithful martyr, who was slain among you, where Satan dwelleth.* (Revelation 2:13)

The book of Revelation speaks of some who *"say they are Jews...but are the synagogue of Satan"* (Revelation 2:9). Are there churches that are called Christian, but are really churches of Satan? In Christ's letters in Revelation to the seven churches in Asia, we see how the ascended and enthroned Son of God presented the same view of the Devil. The *"depths of Satan"* (Revelation 2:24) are referred to in the address to Thyatira. In this Revelation of Christ to John, the Devil is still declared to be *"the dragon, that old serpent, which is the Devil, and Satan"* (Revelation 20:2). He is declared to have "great wrath" (Revelation 12:12).

SATANIC WORSHIP

The Devil's power is greatly and strangely enhanced by his system of worship, which, while it degrades, fascinates many people. The system of pagan worship and devotion is very powerful. It holds its devotees by iron chains. It is not a work of chance, and it does not spring from native religious instincts. It is a system of rare power and skill constructed by a graduate in the craft of seduction and delusion. Satan's hand is at the root of all pagan worship—planning, ordering, and inspiring it. It is this fact that gives it strength and influence.

In the Old Testament, Jeroboam perverted the religious instinct and debased worship for sinister, worldly, and selfish purposes. It is said that he ordained priests for the devils. (See 1 Kings 12:32.) The psalmist declared that the Israelites sacrificed to devils (Psalm 106:37).

The New Testament declares that

the things which the Gentiles sacrifice, they sacrifice to devils, and not to God: and I would not that ye should have fellowship with devils. Ye cannot drink the cup of the Lord, and the cup of devils: ye cannot be partakers of the Lord's table, and of the table of devils.

(1 Corinthians 10:20–21)

Again it is declared, "*Now the Spirit speaketh expressly, that in the latter times some shall depart from the faith, giving heed to seducing spirits, and doctrines of devils*" (1 Timothy 4:1).

The intensity and power of the Devil's worship is illustrated in the last book of the New Testament. It shows how his worship will increase in intensity and war against the worship of the Lamb. Almost since the beginning of man, there have been rival altars and rival worship. The Devil is the author, inspirer, and protector of the counterfeit; and Christ is the author, inspirer, and protector of true and pure worship. There are martyrs in the false and devilish, as well as in the true and heavenly. There are also wonders and miracles in both.

SATAN'S RANK AND FILE

Revelation summarizes the situation:

And they had a king over them, which is the angel of the bottomless pit, whose name in the Hebrew tongue is Abaddon, but in the Greek tongue hath his name Apollyon. One woe is past; and, behold, there come two woes more hereafter. (Revelation 9:11–12)

These are not lawless "*woes,*" and their authors are not disorderly and reckless mobs. They are organized. Strictest obedience to the Devil prevails. They are "*principalities*" and "*powers*" (Ephesians 6:12) of the first order of creation and of great personal power and dignity. They are ordered and subordered, coordinated and subordinated.

They have the most perfect government—military in its discipline, absolute and orderly in its arrangement. They are under one supreme, dictatorial, powerful head, complete with rank and file and officers. *"For we wrestle not against flesh and blood, but against principalities, against powers, against the rulers of the darkness of this world, against spiritual wickedness in high places"* (Ephesians 6:12).

These high and wicked spirits are everywhere. They fill the air and are intent on evil. They follow the direction of their leader, carrying out his plans with ready obedience and implicit confidence. How loathsome is their nature! How marvelous and miracle-working is their power! How high and kingly is their influence! How military are their purposes!

All this is vividly and strongly set forth in the sixteenth chapter of Revelation:

> *And I saw three unclean spirits like frogs come out of the mouth of the dragon, and out of the mouth of the beast, and out of the mouth of the false prophet. For they are the spirits of devils, working miracles, which go forth unto the kings of the earth and of the whole world, to gather them to the battle of that great day of God Almighty.*
> (Revelation 16:13–14)

The power of Satan finds its great increase and expression in the efforts and operations of the unregenerate. They are under his power, subjects of his kingdom of darkness. More than that, they are intimate in their connection with Satan; they are so close in unity, purpose, and relationship that they belong to his family. His paternity gives birth and character to them; his fatherhood binds them in a strong embrace.

SATAN AND THE APOSTLES

How defiant, bold, sacrilegious, and presumptuous is the power of the Devil! He came so near the sacred person of Christ! He invaded the sacred circle of His chosen apostles. Judas fell from his high position—tempted, possessed by Satan, and filled with remorse. He committed suicide, and hell is his forever.

Peter acted as the spokesman for the Devil, becoming the advocate of a noncrossbearing, non-selfdenying worldly religion. He was so affected by the Devil's power that he cursed, swore, and lied. Peter found himself stained and defiled. He was saved only by the prayers of Christ.

John and James fell prey to the Devil when they wanted fire to come down from heaven and burn up the Samaritans. Christ sharply showed that they did not have His Spirit, but the other spirit—the spirit of the destroyer.

Paul had his apostolic plans interfered with and hindered by the Devil. To the Thessalonians, he wrote: *"Wherefore we would have come unto you, even I Paul, once and again; but Satan hindered us"* (1 Thessalonians 2:18). And he bore to his grave the marks on his body of the power of this ancient Foe of apostolic fidelity. (See Galatians 6:17.)

Yet the power of Satan is not supreme. It is limited. This was true in Job's case. Satan could go only so far in afflicting him. And ever since the Son of God came into the world, the Devil's power has been curtailed. The Cross gave a shock to Satan and his power. His realm of death has been abolished, and *"life and immortality* [have been brought] *to light through the gospel"* (2 Timothy 1:10). His kingdom received its death stroke on Calvary. The almighty forces of the Gospel are laying hold of the mighty forces of Satan.

ELEVEN:

THE DEVIL'S BATTLEGROUND

Now the serpent was more subtle than any beast of the field which the Lord God had made. And he said unto the woman, Yea, hath God said, Ye shall not eat of every tree of the garden? And the woman said unto the serpent, We may eat of the fruit of the trees of the garden: but of the fruit of the tree which is in the midst of the garden, God hath said, Ye shall not eat of it, neither shall ye touch it, lest ye die. And the serpent said unto the woman, Ye shall not surely die: for God doth know that in the day ye eat thereof, then your eyes shall be opened, and ye shall be as gods, knowing good and evil. And when the woman saw that the tree was good for food, and that it was pleasant to the eyes, and a tree to be desired to make one wise, she took of the fruit thereof, and did eat, and gave also unto her husband with her; and he did eat.
—Genesis 3:1–6

Both in the Old Testament and in the New, the Devil is represented as being persistent and tireless in his activities and efforts. In Job, in answer to God's inquiry, "*Whence comest thou?*" Satan replied, "*From going to and fro in the earth, and from walking up and down in it*" (Job 1:7). This statement reveals his rapid and extensive goings and his repeated and careful observations. He is said to be walking about "*as a roaring lion*" (1 Peter 5:8). Activity, scrutiny, power, and purpose are in his methods.

Thomas à Kempis said,

> Know that the ancient Enemy doth strive by all means to hinder thy desire to be good and to keep thee clear of all religious exercises. Many evil thoughts does he suggest to thee, that so he may cause a weariness and horror in thee, and to call thee back from prayer and holy reading.

The careless and halfhearted Christian knows nothing about the Devil or his devices. But those who serve God are the ones who demand Satan's attention, provoke his anger, and call forth his strategies.

Pastor Blumhart, a marvelous man of faith and power, said, "He who is ignorant of the wiles and artifices of the Enemy, only beats the air, and the Devil is not afraid of him." Blumhart himself is an illustration. "By concerning myself with a person who was possessed," he says, "I became involved in such a fearful conflict with the powers of darkness that it is not possible for me to describe."

> *The careless and halfhearted Christian knows nothing about the Devil or his devices. But those who serve God are the ones who demand Satan's attention, provoke his anger, and call forth his strategies.*

Christians may live and die completely unaware of the Devil's existence and hatred. At the same time, Satan is indifferent to their religion because they are not threatening to his kingdom. But a person like Blumhart causes a big commotion and fear in Satan's realm.

DECEPTIVE DISGUISES

Satan works by imitation. It is his policy to make something as close to the original as possible and, thereby, to break the force and value of the genuine. This is one of his favorite methods. As Jannes and Jambres withstood Moses by their false tricks, so Satan carries on his work by lying wonders. (See 2 Timothy 3:8.) As his apostles are transformed into angels of light (see 2 Corinthians 11:14–15), so his wonders are looked on as first-class miracles.

What about the revelations of his person? God and Christ have been revealed in bodily shape, by figure, and by representation. Majestic, visible manifestations have been seen by holy men of God. Does the Devil have the power to clothe himself in visible form to the human eye? Can he incarnate himself?

Satan seems to have clothed himself in some visible shape at the temptation of Christ. But the form he used is not recorded. Perhaps he appeared in the form of a man, doubtless a pious man. Or maybe he came as a religious hermit from the seclusion of the desert.

In the days of Christ, Satan revealed himself by taking absolute possession of a person, and he used other personalities through which to manifest his being and power. His manifestations are insidious and deceptive disguises. He sometimes appears as *"an angel of light"* (2 Corinthians 11:14), with the bloom, beauty, and spices of paradise on him. His appearance seems unearthly in splendor, his voice gentle, musical, persuasive, with no traces of the fall.

PHYSICAL ATTACKS

The Devil affects the body and, through the body, affects our loyalty to Christ. Job was tried by his sickness. So the Devil tries us by sickness. In the days of Christ, Satan was very active in affecting the body, not simply by ordinary diseases, but by what is termed *"possessed with a devil."* (See, for example, Matthew 9:32.) In those cases, he worked by breaking down some of the body's chief functions.

His method is to assume any shape that will suit his purposes at the time. Doubtless, there was something in the shape or character of the serpent that gave him easier access to Eve. Dressed as an *"angel of light"* (2 Corinthians 11:14), his appearance commends him to those who are pure and unsuspecting.

As a *"thorn"* (2 Corinthians 12:7), Satan desires to give only pain to those who, like Paul, cannot be seduced or swerved from the fixed course of fidelity. He put the Christians at Smyrna in prison and chained their bodies because he could not shackle their souls. With matchless cunning and unspeakable persistence, he applies his methods to seduce and damn.

THE BATTLEGROUND OF THE MIND

He has access to the minds of men from which he should forever be barred. But his tricks are so diabolical that he clothes the most sordid act with the fairest guise, and he conceals a world of iniquity with the beautiful colors of the rainbow. He deceived good David and provoked him to number Israel in opposition to God's will, bringing swift and fearful judgment on the nation.

In the parable of the sower, we are taught how the Devil is able to work on the mind and take away any good impressions that are made. *"Those by the way side are they that hear; then cometh the devil, and taketh away the word out of their hearts, lest they should believe and be saved"* (Luke 8:12).

We are also taught how the Devil influences the mind to do the most wicked things, as in the case of Judas. He was chosen as an apostle, into high and holy fellowship, a royal vocation, a select company. Satan had much to do in influencing Judas to the great crime that brought him to despair and suicide.

He readily snatches away from the mind any truth that is superficially received. He also blinds the minds of unbelievers and obstructs the light of saving truth. His processes of taking the Word out of the heart to prevent faith and of blinding the mind to the light of salvation are very common ones with him. He keeps working at it and eats no idle bread. He takes the Word of God out of the unprepared heart and sows tares among the wheat.

He makes people sick for the same reasons he made Job sick. He entices men to do wrong and urges them on to evil.

The Devil goes out into the wilderness and finds us in a fainting, discouraged condition, with our faith weak, the sky cloudy, and our vision obscured. Then he shows us the world from the loftiest peak of observation, clothed in its most attractive form, and tries to ensnare us with its enchanting wonders. He never gets tired of trying to ruin us until the coffin lid is sealed and our happy spirits are bathing in the land where *the wicked cease from troubling; and...the weary be at rest*" (Job 3:17).

Satan has the wisdom of an archangel and the experience of half an eternity as the captain of all the hosts of hell. He is an expert in the acts and arts of deception and trickery. He has almost inexhaustible resources at his command to serve his purposes. Other than God Himself, a wiser and more powerful spirit than Satan does not live. A more malicious power than he could not exist. There is no greater worker than he. His endless energy and tireless perseverance are the only things in him worthy of imitation. These are the things that make him so powerful and so dreadful.

Yet Satan's *"thorn in the flesh"* (2 Corinthians 12:7) changed Paul's sorrow into joy, his poverty into wealth, his weakness into strength, his reproaches into sweet, heavenly consolations. God must take measures to make Satan's evil deeds work together for good to those who love Him (Romans 8:28).

As an old saint says, "The Devil is but a whetstone to sharpen the faith and patience of the saints." Satan may keep God busy polishing the stones that he makes rough, but the Devil's dirt makes their luster brighter, and they become genuine diamonds of the highest quality.

THE DEVIL'S METHODS

Satan's methods are as varied as the people with whom he deals. The Devil knows each person's weaknesses and tendency to sin.

To Eve he came in the disguise of a wellwisher, subtle, serpentine, and deadly. He incited her to disobedience by pointing her to greater heights of godlikeness, along paths of sensual enjoyment. A false and selfish accusation was lodged in her mind against God. No danger was apparent, and he used no distressing tactics. Instead, he allured, deceived, and ensnared.

The method Satan used with Job was much different. He was a man of outstanding character, of whom the Lord said, *"There is none like him in the earth, a perfect and an upright man, one that feareth God and escheweth evil"* (Job 1:8). What methods could Satan devise for the saintliest of the saints?

Satan went to God and accused Job of being selfish in his motives, reducing his piety to the worldly and sinister. No alluring paths, no divergent flowery ways were pointed out to Job by Satan; not a word was said to him. Without a note of warning, tragedy and disaster came as an awful surprise and shock. With one desolating blow, his family of ten children were dead and his princely fortune was gone; one dark hour had robbed him of family and possessions. Stripped naked by the fearful rapidity and depth of his losses, he became homeless, childless, and friendless. His grief was inconsolable and the darkness impenetrable.

The integrity of Job is like a marble column blackened by smoke. He was unshaken by the fiery ordeal, but was still pursued by the Devil. Still Satan insinuated and maligned the genuineness of Job's piety.

He did not recognize Job's noble fidelity or lofty loyalty. Satan continued to attribute low motives as the reason for Job's integrity. With heartless cruelty and malicious lies, he pursued his deathdealing work.

Out of his arsenal of hellish weapons, he came with a loathsome disease. He concentrated on this one saint, adding affliction onto affliction, until his wife was alienated, his friends were estranged, and his enemies were triumphant. There was no relief for his hopeless, bitter grief. His pious reputation has been blackened, his body tortured, his mind put in agony. This is another of Satan's methods: to distress and defame those whom he cannot deceive.

THE DEADLIEST DISGUISE

To the Son of God in the wilderness, Satan did not come as he came to Job, in frustrating storms of distress, but in the form of apparent sympathy and friendliness. It may have been in the disguise of a saintly hermit in the wilderness. *"If thou be the Son of God"* (Matthew 4:3), he began. (In other words, "You want this matter of Your Sonship to God settled, and so do I. You are very hungry and faint.") He continued, *"Command that these stones be made bread"* (v. 3). This appears to be an innocent and proper way to quickly settle a great question and appease a great hunger.

Then Satan came to Christ and tempted Him with the sanctity of the temple. He gave Him an opportunity to attest His Messiahship before the wondering and awestruck worshippers assembled there. This seemed to be a shorter and better way to give credence to His mission than the slow and thankless process of daily teaching and ministering. It would appear to be easier than marching to the Cross with the dark shadows of its shame and heaviness darkening His way. Finally, Satan's desperate venture was to seduce Christ by the world's array of grandeur, power, and glory.

Satan plunged Job from a serene, cloudless, heavenly height down to a starless and stormy midnight. To the Son of God, Satan would be an available friend to save Him from pain, poverty, hunger, shame, toil, and death.

TWELVE:

SATAN'S CLEVER STRATEGIES

But if our gospel be hid, it is hid to them that are lost: in whom the god of this world hath blinded the minds of them which believe not, lest the light of the glorious gospel of Christ, who is the image of God, should shine unto them....For God, who commanded the light to shine out of darkness, hath shined in our hearts, to give the light of the knowledge of the glory of God in the face of Jesus Christ....We are troubled on every side, yet not distressed; we are perplexed, but not in despair; persecuted, but not forsaken; cast down, but not destroyed.
—2 Corinthians 4:3–4, 6, 8–9

The Devil is seldom seen in his movements and methods. He has the rare ability to get others to do his work and execute his plans.

BLINDED MINDS

His methods are to blind, to put a veil on the evil results and all the sad consequences of sin. He blinds people so that the evil cannot be seen. Even

Satan's Clever Strategies 473

David, who loved God, was blinded by Satan to the treachery, infamy, and murder in Uriah's case. (See 2 Samuel 11:2–12:10.)

This is how sinners are held in unbelief by Satan. He closes their eyes to all the light and glory of the shining Son of Righteousness. *"In whom the god of this world hath blinded the minds of them which believe not, lest the light of the glorious gospel of Christ, who is the image of God, should shine unto them"* (2 Corinthians 4:4).

The power of the Devil extends to the mind. He can influence the mind, insinuate thoughts, suggest purposes, and excite the imagination. Satan can inflame the passions, stir the appetites, awaken old habits, and fan dead flames or light new ones. He deceived the natural innocence of Eve. He entered into Judas, possessed him fully, and made his halfformed treason complete. Satan was involved in the private council of Ananias and Sapphira, a party to their fraud. He suggested their lying plan to deceive the apostles.

Satan's access to the mind is evident in that he snatches away the divine seed implanted in the soil of the heart, as taught in the parable of the sower. In Corinthians, the Devil is called the *"god of this world."* The Devil uses this world as a veil to shut out the truth of God and the light of His glorious Gospel. He closes the eyes of faith to all the discoveries in the unseen and eternal.

The antagonism between the children of the world who are possessed by Satan and the children of God who are possessed by God is set forth by John:

> *Ye are of God, little children, and have overcome them: because greater is he that is in you, than he that is in the world. They are of the world: therefore speak they of the world, and the world heareth them. We are of God: he that knoweth God heareth us; he that is not of God heareth not us. Hereby know we the spirit of truth, and the spirit of error.*
>
> (1 John 4:4–6)

Who is in us? God. Who is in the children of the world? The Devil. Our faith, our hope, and our final triumph are in the truth of the Word of God. *"Greater is he that is in* [us], *than he that is in the world."*

Satan perverts the things that are truly works of God and misemploys miracles to obscure God's glory.

FEAR AND DISCOURAGEMENT

The Devil often tries to break the soul down and reduce it to despair. In order to discourage us, he tells us that we will never succeed, that the way is too hard and the burden too heavy.

He takes advantage of weak, distracted nerves and suggests fears. Grace is hidden from sight, shortcomings are magnified, and weaknesses are classed as gross sins. Sometimes the fear of death is used by Satan to quench the fire of faith, and the grave becomes something awful.

He darkens the future. Heaven and God are hidden by a thick veil of tomorrow's cares, trials, and needs. The imaginary disasters, failures, and evils of the future are powerful weapons in Satan's hand. He suggests that the Lord is a hard master and that His promises will fail. He works on the corruption that remains in the heart and raises a great storm in the soul.

Samuel Rutherford said,

> Oh, if our faith could ride out against the high and proud waves and winds when our sea seemeth all on fire! Oh, how oft do I let my grips go. I am put to swimming and half sinking. I find the Devil hath the advantage in this battle, for he fighteth in known ground for our corruption. However matters go, it is our happiness to win new grounds daily in Christ's love and to add conquest to conquest until our Lord Jesus and we are so near each other that Satan cannot draw a straw or a thread between us.

TEMPTATIONS AND FEELINGS

He tempts us to lash out with evil tempers, to speak hasty words, and to be impatient. He tempts us to use carnal reasoning, which is his powerful ally in our minds. We must turn back to Christ. We need more of His Spiritrenewed commitment and thorough selfdedication. By sending prayers upward with uplifted eyes and hearts, we will be able to resist and conquer the great adversary of our souls.

One of the most intelligent and Godhonored among the saints wrote, "I have keen inward sufferings, what are termed the buffetings of Satan. Horror at times has taken hold of me. I felt much, but feared more."

The Devil may tempt us to think too little of ourselves as Moses did and too highly of ourselves as Peter did. In one sense, we cannot think too little of ourselves, but in another way we can. Satan persuades us that we are so poor and weak that we can do nothing. And so we are weakened in faith and broken in effort. But Satan's master method is to fill us with selfimportance and selfconfidence. Then faith is not only weakened but also destroyed. Our efforts and activities may increase in number and vain exhibition, but the seals of self and Satan are on them all.

John Wesley noted:

I preached on that delicate device of Satan to destroy the whole religion of the heart. Telling Christians not to regard feelings, but to live by naked faith, is, in plain terms, not to regard either love, joy, peace, or any other fruit of the Spirit; not to regard whether they feel them or the reverse; whether their souls be in a heavenly or hellish frame of mind. Satan's method with some is to make them rely too much on feelings. With others he deals the reverse and urges them to discard all feelings.

Naked faith is often nothing but fruitless, unconscious acceptance that brings fruitless, unconscious salvation with it, if it brings salvation at all.

POWER OVER THE ENEMY

Whatever Satan's methods or clever devices, the words of Jesus, his conqueror, to us are these: *"Behold, I give unto you power to tread on serpents and scorpions, and over all the power of the enemy: and nothing shall by any means hurt you"* (Luke 10:19).

Miss Havergal wrote concerning these verses,

Why, this is grand—power over all the power of the Enemy. Just where he is strongest there they shall prevail. Not over the very center of his power, not over his power here and there, nor now and then, but over all his power. And Jesus said, "Is not that enough to go into battle with?"

476 *E. M. Bounds on Prayer & Spiritual Warfare*

The Devil's brain is prolific with plans. He has many ways of doing many things. Perhaps he has many ways of doing each thing. With him nothing is stereotyped. He never runs in ruts. Fruitful, diverse, and ever fresh is his way of doing things. Indirect, cunning, and graceful are his plans. He acts by trickery, and always by guile.

According to the Bible, his plans are *"wiles"* (Ephesians 6:11). The original word means to "follow up or investigate by method and settled plan." It is not a bad word, but one of order, arrangement, and methods that are conceived and executed. But when the word gets into the Devil's hand, it is defined by his dictionary. It receives a strong stain, a deep coloring of cunning and trickery.

Sometimes Satan comes to us disrobed of his heavenly garments. He comes as a sharp, pointed, painful, poisoned thorn—a thorn that cannot be extracted by prayer. The saints who have seen most of heaven are often summoned to see most of hell. Saints who have the fullest and most transporting revelation of God often have the saddest experience with Satan.

Paul's thorn meant as much to Paul as his abundance of revelations. His thorn made him more a saint than his vision of the third heavens. Satan only lifted him higher by keeping him lower.

Satan may come to us in his own native character, the thorn-breeder and piercer. He may put thorns in us that no prayer power can extract— thorns that will poison and pain. But the thorn will enrich grace, increase humility, and make weakness strong and glorious. Satan's thorns will clothe necessities with richest attire, and change distresses and persecutions into the most divine pleasures.

> *Satan's thorns will make room for God's greatest power in us and on us.*

Satan's thorns will make room for God's greatest power in us and on us. The Enemy's thorns will make the lowest point of a spiritual depression the highest point of vision. His thorns will make strength out of weakness and wealth out of poverty.

THIRTEEN:

OUR MOST VULNERABLE AREAS

*To whom ye forgive any thing, I forgive also: for if I forgave any
thing, to whom I forgave it, for your sakes forgave I it in the person of
Christ; lest Satan should get an advantage of us: for we are not
ignorant of his devices.*
—2 Corinthians 2:10–11

There are positions and conditions that lie open to the attacks of Satan. These points must be guarded by sleepless vigilance. The Devil is a cruel and mighty foe. To watch him with unsleeping eye is not only a duty, but also essential to life. Deliverance from hell and the certainty of heaven are involved in overcoming the Devil. Stupidity, neglect, and being off guard in the conflict with Satan are much more than mistakes or indiscretions. They are fatal defeats—eternal and irreparable losses.

The apostle Paul placed his Corinthian brethren on the winning side in the war with the Devil when he declared, *"We are not ignorant of his devices."* Ignorance is always an exposed condition. Ignorance is open to attack and surprise by day and by night. To be ignorant of the existence, character, and ways of the Devil is the prelude to fatal results in the fight for heaven. If this is true, how hopeless is the case of one who not only is ignorant of temptations, but also denies or ignores the existence of the Tempter.

The Devil's great device, his masterpiece of temptation, is to destroy faith in his own existence. God's struggle is to establish faith in His own existence. The Devil's great work is to eradicate knowledge of all spiritual facts, principles, and persons. He who denies or ignores the existence of God, the Devil, good, and evil puts up a fatal barrier to ultimate salvation and paralyzes all efforts in that direction. This ignorance gives one over, chained hand and foot, to the merciless Foe whose existence has been denied and derided.

Nothing advances Satan's work with more skillful hands than to be ignorant of Satan and his ways. To escape his snare, we must have a strong faith in the fact that Satan exists. We must also have an intimate knowledge of him and his plans.

TAKING THE DEVIL LIGHTLY

Related to the foregoing vulnerable position is the one that makes light of Satan. Frivolous views of the Devil, his works, or his character, and light talk or jokes that dishonor him are detrimental to any serious views of life's great work and its serious conflicts. Presumption, selfwill, and foolishness are the characteristics of those who deal frivolously with these important concerns.

The existence and work of the Devil is a serious matter. It is to be considered and dealt with from the most serious standpoint, and only serious people can deal with it. For this reason, the New Testament gives the repeated note of warning, "Be sober." The point is emphatically made in the statement, "Be sober...because your adversary the devil, as a roaring lion, walketh about, seeking whom he may devour" (1 Peter 5:8).

Related to this attitude is Jude's incisive and almost rough handling of those who make light of sacred things and sacred persons:

Our Most Vulnerable Areas 479

Likewise also these filthy dreamers defile the flesh, despise dominion, and speak evil of dignities. Yet Michael the archangel, when contending with the devil he disputed about the body of Moses, durst not bring against him a railing accusation, but said, The Lord rebuke thee. But these speak evil of those things which they know not: but what they know naturally, as brute beasts, in those things they corrupt them-selves. (Jude 8–10)

Peter also had something to say about this same class of flippant, irreverent talkers:

Presumptuous are they, selfwilled, they are not afraid to speak evil of dignities. Whereas angels, which are greater in power and might, bring not railing accusation against them before the Lord. But these, as nat-ural brute beasts, made to be taken and destroyed, speak evil of the things that they understand not; and shall utterly perish in their own corruption; and shall receive the reward of unrighteous-ness, as they that count it pleasure to riot in the day time. Spots they are and blem-ishes, sporting themselves with their own deceivings while they feast with you. (2 Peter 2:10–13)

A paralyzing attitude in which we remain to listen to Satan's insinuations is fatal. This was Eve's mistake. His tongue is smooth as oil; his words circulate and inflame like poison. For this reason, our position must be one of bristling opposition, fortified for war, with no barriers down, no open gates, no low places. Fenced in and barricaded against the Devil is the only safe place.

AN UNFORGIVING SPIRIT

An unforgiving spirit invites satanic possession. His favorite realm is the spirit. To corrupt our spirits, to provoke us to retaliation, revenge, or unmercifulness—that is his chosen work and his most common and successful device. Paul brought this device out into the open so that we can thwart Satan's plans.

To whom ye forgive any thing, I forgive also: for if I forgave any thing, to whom I forgave it, for your sakes forgave I it in the person of Christ;

lest Satan should get an advantage of us: for we are not ignorant of his devices. (2 Corinthians 2:10–11)

When Satan generates an unforgiving spirit in us, then he has us, and we are on his ground. Then wicked men and good men, all kinds of people, are likely to do us harm, sometimes at vital and very sensitive points. Sometimes they unconsciously wrong us and sometimes they do it knowingly and willfully. As soon as a spirit of unkindness possesses us for the wrong done to us, Satan has the upper hand.

OATHS AND SWEARING

Let me quote the warning words of our Savior:

Again, ye have heard that it was said to them of old time, Thou shalt not forswear thyself, but shalt perform unto the Lord thine oaths: but I say unto you, Swear not at all; neither by the heaven, for it is the throne of God; nor by the earth, for it is the footstool of his feet; nor by Jerusalem, for it is the city of the great King. Neither shalt thou swear by thy head, for thou canst not make one hair white or black. But let your speech be, Yea, yea; Nay, nay: and whatsoever is more than these is of the evil one. (Matthew 5:33–37 RV)

The injunction is against using strong oaths in language. Expletives and appeals added to our words are wrong and expose us to the snare of Satan. *"In the multitude of words,"* says Proverbs, *"there wanteth not sin"* (Proverbs 10:19).

Satan tempts us to use assertions and declarations to confirm the truth of what we are saying. When we use additional words as a way of substantiating the truth of those already spoken, they expose us to Satan's power. *"But above all things, my brethren, swear not, neither by heaven, neither by the earth, neither by any other oath: but let your yea be yea; and your nay, nay; lest ye fall into condemnation"* (James 5:12). James sealed the words of Christ. The Devil lies concealed in many words. Simplicity, brevity, and seriousness of words will mightily hinder and thwart his ensnaring plans.

It is so easy for the Devil to stop us just short of a faith that will save, because of this type of wordiness. There are many speeches, prefaces, and introductions that are sometimes quite monotonous. They are often headed in the right direction, but they do not bring us to the heart of the matter. Like Sarah, they start with the full intent to go to Canaan, but stop at Haran and dwell there. (See Genesis 11:31.) Like Jacob, Shechem slows their steps and holds them instead of Bethel. (See Genesis 35:1–6.)

RELIGIOUS FANATICISM

Dangerous excessiveness takes other forms, as well. There are those who are earnestly striving after that *"holiness, without which no man shall see the Lord"* (Hebrews 12:14), but Satan tempts them to go a little too far, and their zeal degenerates into ungodly fervor that causes division in the church.

> *Satan watches and is always alert to try to hold us back from the final goal. Or he works in the opposite way to drive us on with an impetuous and obsessed spirit to go beyond the goal. It is Satan's purpose to uncover our strongest positions and turn them into vulnerable areas.*

Strengths are turned into weaknesses: Strict earnestness degenerates into severity, gentleness into weakness. Energetic activity turns into imprudent meddling and narrowness. Calm moderation soon becomes careless acquiesence. Bold convictions become intolerant, opinionated, and bigoted. Respect for the convictions of others degenerates into paralyzing indifference and skeptical laziness. Eager trust lapses into presumption and haughtiness. Cautious wisdom soon becomes cowardice and hesitating anxiety. Confession and profession evaporate into dry religious duty.

Satan watches and is always alert to try to hold us back from the final goal. Or he works in the opposite way to drive us on with an impetuous and obsessed spirit to go beyond the goal. It is Satan's purpose to uncover our strongest positions and turn them into vulnerable areas.

482 E. M. Bounds on Prayer & Spiritual Warfare

BEING UNEQUALLY YOKED

Becoming unequally yoked with unbelievers in intimate and confiding friendships creates exposed positions of which the Devil takes great advantage. Partnership in business or the more sacred union of marriage with unbelievers is perilous to the believer in Jesus Christ.

> *Be ye not unequally yoked together with unbelievers: for what fellowship hath righteousness with unrighteousness? and what communion hath light with darkness? And what concord hath Christ with Belial? or what part hath he that believeth with an infidel?*
>
> (2 Corinthians 6:14–15)

Satan is called *"Belial,"* which means someone who is worthless, contemptible, and wicked. He and Christ cannot be joined in agreement. No unequal yoking, no fellowship, no communion, no agreement can exist. The result is contamination and impurity. The fruit of these voluntary close yokings is a weakened spiritual condition. Under the law, an ox and an ass could not be yoked together. Under the Spirit, Christ and Satan can have no agreements.

Separation, cleansing, and perfected holiness are necessary to secure the vantage ground against Satan. The Bible gives strong, explicit, and comprehensive commands against union, communion, or intimate association with unbelievers. For those unequally yoked there can be no pulling together, no fellowship, no sharing, no communion, no intimacy, no agreement, no voting together.

Commentators have found in the above verses from 2 Corinthians, Paul's fine command of the Greek language. We find in them the fire of fervent and profound convictions. They demand selfdenying abstinence from forming intimate and voluntary associations with the unbelieving world in business, pleasure, or social pursuits.

Paul laid down this rule in his first epistle to the Corinthians:

> *I wrote unto you in an epistle not to company with fornicators: yet not altogether with the fornicators of this world, or with the covetous, or extortioners, or with idolaters; for then must ye needs go out of the world. But now I have written unto you not to keep company, if any*

man that is called a brother be a fornicator, or covetous, or an idolater, or a railer, or a drunkard, or an extortioner; with such an one no not to eat.   (1 Corinthians 5:9–11)

Paul is not objecting to casual, courteous Christian conversation but to more intimate and lasting relationships.

WORLDLY FRIENDSHIPS

James defined and opposed these worldly relationships and attachments as vulnerable positions that result in the most criminal violation of the holiest relationship. *"Ye adulterers and adulteresses, know ye not that the friendship of the world is enmity with God? whosoever therefore will be a friend of the world is the enemy of God"* (James 4:4). By such associations, the marriage vow of God is broken.

Dean Alford, commenting on this passage, said,

Of the world, it means men and men's interest, ambitions and employments, insofar as they are without God. The man who is taken out of the world by Christ cannot again become the friend and companion of worldly men and their schemes, without passing into enmity with God. God and the world stand opposed to one another, so that a man cannot join the one without deserting the other. He, therefore, who desires to be the friend of the world, and sets his mind and thought and wish that way, must make up his mind to be God's enemy.

We may ask, "But shouldn't I be friendly with my relatives, whether they fear God or not?" There is nothing we can do to change our family relationships, but there are some that are nearer to us than others. The nearest relatives are husbands and wives. They have taken each other for better or worse, and they must make the best of each other. God has joined them together, and no one can put them asunder.

Parents are also very closely connected with their children. You cannot part with your children while they are young, because it is your duty to "train them up in the way wherein they should go." (See Proverbs 22:6.) Once they are grown, your relationship with them changes, and you must use your own discretion to determine how close you will be to them.

Children must also determine how long it is expedient for them to remain with their parents. In general, if their parents do not fear God, they should leave them as soon as is convenient.

As for all other relatives, even brothers or sisters, if they are of the world, you are under no obligation to be closely associated with them. You may be courteous and friendly, but at a distance.

THE ONLY ESCAPE

Since *"friendship of the world is enmity with God"* (James 4:4), the only way to heaven is to avoid all intimacy with worldly people. Whatever the cost, flee spiritual adultery! Have no friendship with the world. No matter how tempted you are by profit or pleasure, do not become intimate with worldly-minded people. And if you are already involved with anyone who is of the world, break off the relationship without delay.

Your life is at stake—eternal life or eternal death. Is it not better to go into life having one eye or one hand, than having both, to be cast into hellfire? (See Matthew 5:29–30.) No matter how tempted you are to continue, have no friendship with the world. Look around and see the dreadful effects it has produced among your brethren! How many of the mighty have fallen because of this very thing! They would heed no warning. They conversed intimately with worldlyminded people until they themselves were back in the world again.

Oh, *"come out from among them"*! (2 Corinthians 6:17). Come out from all unholy men, however harmless they may appear, *"and be ye separate"* (v. 17)—at least have no intimacy with them. Your *"fellowship is with the Father, and with his Son Jesus Christ"* (1 John 1:3). So let your fellowship be with those, and those only, who at least seek the Lord Jesus Christ in sincerity. Then *"ye shall be,"* in a special sense, *"my sons and daughters, saith the Lord Almighty"* (2 Corinthians 6:18).

How Satan surrounds us! How strongly he holds us! How he entangles, chains, and binds us with worldly associations! We lie in the sweet friendship, the embraces, and the counsel of these worldly ones, while they lie in the arms of the Wicked One.

A SIMPLE ANSWER

If simplicity is removed from our faith, our defenses against Satan are weakened.

> *I am jealous over you with godly jealousy: for I have espoused you to one husband, that I may present you as a chaste virgin to Christ. But I fear, lest by any means, as the serpent beguiled Eve through his subtlety, so your minds should be corrupted from the simplicity that is in Christ.* (2 Corinthians 11:2–3)

Satan is recognized as the Serpent who is still busy at his old tricky trade. Satan has such a dexterous and successful hand at deception that Paul was uneasy. Lack of simplicity could be fatal to the purity and faith of the Corinthians, just as the taste of the forbidden fruit was fatal to Eve. It was the loss of a little thing, but, with it, all was lost.

THE IMPORTANCE OF DISCIPLINE

Finally, an undisciplined body readily exposes us to Satan's assaults. Even natural, innocent appetites and passions have to be held in with bit and bridle. Paul was aware of this: *"But I keep under my body, and bring it into subjection: lest that by any means, when I have preached to others, I myself should be a castaway"* (1 Corinthians 9:27). An undisciplined body could hurl Paul from the office of an apostle down to the fearful abyss of apostasy.

Two statements are made in reference to his body: *"keep under"* and *"bring it into subjection."* The first phrase refers to a blow to the face under the eyes. If something is restrained and suppressed by heavy blows, its power is broken. The second statement, *"bring it into subjection,"* means "to make a slave of, to treat with severity, to subject to stern and rigid discipline." The apostle saw the body as an important factor in the contest for heaven. He teaches us that if it is untrained, without the strong repressing hand of discipline, it becomes an easy prey to the assaults of Satan.

Peter gave the same directions:

> *Be sober, be vigilant; because your adversary the devil, as a roaring lion, walketh about, seeking whom he may devour: whom resist stedfast*

in the faith, knowing that the same afflictions are accomplished in your brethren that are in the world. (1 Peter 5:8–9)

A listless, drowsy, sleepy, stupid state can put us under Satan's power without a struggle or even the decency of a surrender.

Remember the strong injunction of Christ to the drowsy and fainting disciples: *"Watch and pray, that ye enter not into temptation: the spirit indeed is willing, but the flesh is weak"* (Matthew 26:41).

FOURTEEN:

WHERE DOES SATAN ATTACK?

This is a true saying, If a man desire the office of a bishop, he desireth a good work. A bishop then must be blameless, the husband of one wife, vigilant, sober, of good behaviour, given to hospitality, apt to teach; not given to wine, no striker, not greedy of filthy lucre; but patient, not a brawler, not covetous; one that ruleth well,...not a novice, lest being lifted up with pride he fall into the condemnation of the devil. Moreover he must have a good report of them which are without; lest he fall into reproach and the snare of the devil.
—1 Timothy 3:1–4, 6–7

We have two statements in 1 Timothy regarding the appointing of men to active and official leadership in the church. The first statement is against appointing novices to such leadership. *"Not a novice, lest being lifted up with pride he fall into the condemnation of the devil."*

To put immature believers in places of spiritual leadership causes them to become filled with pride. If the young convert is put into a highly visible position, he readily falls into the same condemnation into which the Devil fell because of pride. This text from 1 Timothy gives credence to the church's almost universally accepted opinion: the Devil fell through pride.

New converts must be matured by discipline before they are put to the front. Staying behind is often a greater cross, as well as a greater virtue, than pushing or being pushed to the front. The forefront is always an unsafe place for faith until faith has grown and matured.

Men of questionable reputation who are placed in church leadership or official positions bring reproach and help the Devil in his disgraceful business. *"Moreover he must have a good report of them which are without; lest he fall into reproach and the snare of the devil."* Having men of good character and spotless reputation in the leadership of church affairs closes Satan's mouth, cuts off his revenue, and slows down his business.

We must not violate these two rules of church government by putting novices and men whose reputations are not spotless into positions of leadership. It puts the novices in an uncomfortable position, and it increases the dangerous influence of leaders who have questionable reputations. The entire church is also put in an exposed condition, endangering the whole army.

Leaders are standard-bearers whose lives are clearly visible to everyone in the church. For this reason, they should be conspicuous in spotless piety. They should be mature in age; and sound and advanced in faith, love, and sobriety.

Gifted, wise, serious, and blameless leaders will make the church strong and victorious in the day of battle. Novices in positions of church leadership create conditions that cause them to be exposed to Satan's attacks. New converts should be sheltered and trained before they are given any responsibility in the local church.

THE DEVIL'S WORKSHOP

Young widowhood can also be a vulnerable condition for a believer in the church. Satan is always watching for any opportunity to invade the vulnerable position of the grieving widow. Paul knew the hidden traps that Satan often uses. He wrote tenderly, honestly, and with discrimination,

Honour widows that are widows indeed. But if any widow have children or nephews, let them learn first to show piety at home, and to requite their parents: for that is good and acceptable before God. Now she that is a widow indeed, and desolate, trusteth in God, and continueth in supplications and prayers night and day. But she that liveth in pleasure is dead while she liveth....But the younger widows refuse: for when they have begun to wax wanton against Christ, they will marry; having damnation, because they have cast off their first faith. And withal they learn to be idle, wandering about from house to house; and not only idle, but tattlers also and busybodies, speaking things which they ought not. I will therefore that the younger women marry, bear children, guide the house, give none occasion to the adversary to speak reproachfully. For some are already turned aside after Satan.

(1 Timothy 5:3–6; 11–15)

This advice helps relieve the sorrow of the young woman and puts her where her heart and hands are full of sweet and sacred responsibilities. Her time and heart are full of profitable activity. Satan has a hard job working on a person who is filled in heart and hands with the holy tasks of raising the home, state, and church of the future.

THE PROBLEM OF LUST

There are strong natural desires in man that the Scriptures term *lust.* They are called the *"lusts of the flesh"* (2 Peter 2:18; see 1 John 2:16), the *"lust of the eyes"* (1 John 2:16), *"worldly lusts"* (Titus 2:12), and the *"lusts of men"* (1 Peter 4:2). These are the cravings of the senses for which the heart naturally clamors.

These lusts form the basis of inner temptation. A cunning and powerful seducer may tempt and lead an innocent person astray even when that person is not normally tempted by such allurements, but inner lusts and desires generally form the basis and provide the groundwork for Satan's insidious temptations.

James described the whole process:

Let no man say when he is tempted, I am tempted of God: for God cannot be tempted with evil, neither tempteth he any man: but every man is tempted, when he is drawn away of his own lust, and enticed. Then when lust hath conceived, it bringeth forth sin: and sin, when it is finished, bringeth forth death. (James 1:13–15)

The term *"drawn away"* means "to lure forth." The metaphor is from hunting or fishing. As game is lured from the forests, so man by lust is allured from the safety of selfrestraint to sin. The word *"enticed"* means "to catch with bait."

The Scriptures demand that these lusts or desires be banned and denounced. We can see how Satan and the world are behind these lusts. The Gospel is a training school in which these lusts are to be denied.

For the grace of God that bringeth salvation hath appeared to all men, teaching us that, denying ungodliness and worldly lusts, we should live soberly, righteously, and godly, in this present world. (Titus 2:11–12)

This solemn declaration from Titus is made without qualification or deception. It is a declarative statement carrying the force of an imperative demand and also that of a condition: *"And they that are Christ's have crucified the flesh with the affections and lusts"* (Galatians 5:24).

The work of Christ is presented as a pattern for us to copy in destroying these lusts:

Forasmuch then as Christ hath suffered for us in the flesh, arm yourselves likewise with the same mind: for he that hath suffered in the flesh hath ceased from sin; that he no longer should live the rest of his time in the flesh to the lusts of men, but to the will of God. (1 Peter 4:1–2)

We are taught that these lusts are put in opposition to the will of God. We cannot yield to them and remain in obedience to God. No man can serve these two masters. These lusts are the foundations and sources of corruption. They war against the soul. We are to

put off concerning the former conversation the old man, which is corrupt according to the deceitful lusts; and be renewed in the spirit of your mind; and that ye put on the new man, which after God is created in righteousness and true holiness. (Ephesians 4:22–24)

A WEAKENED POSITION

The war with Satan is concerned with these lusts. This lusting after the pleasures of the senses is not completely destroyed when we are converted to Christ. It is broken in power and weakened, but the remains, the roots, are still there. Like a tree in life, cut down at its stump, it sends up many shoots. If we allow these shoots to remain, they will help Satan in his work.

Those who are content to leave the remains of these lusts inside them will be hampered by an internal struggle. To allow sin or the tendency to sin to remain in us is fatal. It is as fatal as leaving the original natives in the land of Canaan was to the piety, peace, and prosperity of Israel. God's command to Israel was that those nations were to be destroyed completely so as to leave neither root nor branch. Israel's failure to do this was the source of untold evil for them.

Any remaining lusts are exposed conditions just as the remains of a decayed tooth are the exposed conditions of a toothache. So we are challenged, *"For if ye live after the flesh, ye shall die: but if ye through the Spirit do mortify the deeds of the body, ye shall live"* (Romans 8:13).

In another text, we have these words: *"They that are Christ's have crucified the flesh with the affections and lusts"* (Galatians 5:24). *"Lust"* is the larger word in Scripture, including the whole world of active lusts and desires. The *"affections"* are not so much the soul's disease in its more active operations, but the diseased conditions out of which these spring.

The lusts spring from the passions and are nourished by them. They deserve the same punishment as the flesh. All of these—the flesh, the lusts, and the affections—are crucified. This puts the Christian in the best fortified condition to resist the attacks of the Devil. If these lusts remain, he is only half armed and wholly exposed.

LACK OF SPIRITUAL GROWTH

Low aims in the spiritual life and satisfaction with present circumstances also create an exposed condition. The Devil may visit the highlands and mountain ranges of spiritual elevation, but he makes his home in the lowlands. He will attack the strongest, most mature giant of piety, but he works his havoc and gains his spoils where the Christian slumbers in the cradle of spiritual babyhood. There is safety only in high aims, strenuous effort, and constant advance.

It is on the field of low aims and satisfied results that the Devil wins his chief victories. Spiritual growth, along with constant and sure spiritual development, are the surest safeguards against Satan's assaults and surprises. Constant growth keeps our eyes open and our hearts strong. Satan never finds growth asleep, drowsy, or weak. Onward and upward is the great battle cry. Constant advance is the steel armor in the fight with the Devil. Israel lost Canaan by not possessing Canaan. Satan has the vantage ground when we do not maintain an aggressive forward march.

> *Spiritual growth, along with constant and sure spiritual development, are the surest safeguards against Satan's assaults and surprises. Constant growth keeps our eyes open and our hearts strong.*

When the Bible sounded the clarion call, *"Let us go on unto perfection"* (Hebrews 6:1), it was seeking to arouse the church. The believers to whom the book of Hebrews was addressed had lost the vigor and fighting ability of Christian character by feeding on milk and indulging in the lazy luxury of being children. The Scriptures raised a standard and set a goal for them to attain. The goal line was far ahead, but it was a real point, as real as the point at which their steps were delayed. They were called out of the cradle and away from the nursery to the strength, conflict, and perfection of royal maturity.

A great writer said of Wesley that he was "the first of theological statesmen." This is no great compliment. But the spiritual perception of Wesley as a man of open, divine vision is his highest eulogy. This is evidenced by the fact that he reechoed the trumpet call of the Bible and sounded it on every key and in every refrain. He sought to stir the church into forward movement and to quicken its members to seek an advanced position. The yearning for spiritual growth had diminished in their experience and had been left out of their hopes and creeds.

God gives the beginnings of faith, and these beginnings are glorious. But for us to be content with the beginnings of faith is to forfeit its possibilities and leave us open and naked to Satan. Then we become a prey to his schemes.

Making additions to our spiritual treasury is the essential condition for stability in the Christian life. Retaining and maintaining this stability gives great victory over the Devil. To stand still in our faith is to lose it. To set up camp at the place of salvation is to forfeit regenerating grace. To stop at any station of progress is to go backward. The weakness of most people is their lack of determination to stick to their objective. We are willing to pay the personal cost for great temporal success, but the price for spiritual success is often too dear for us.

BABY CHRISTIANS

The tendency in religion is to be satisfied with spiritual birth and then to die in infancy. The teething phase is a perilous time for spiritual babes. The great sin of the Israelites was hugging the shores and not going up to possess the land. The marvelous glory of their entrance into Canaan was diminished by the lethargy and timidity of their advance.

Stopping and standing still in a nongrowing, nonfighting condition is a position fully exposed to Satan. Many run well and fight well, but at some point their running and fighting cease. When this happens, spiritual development is arrested, and the Devil moves at once to an easy victory.

This spiritual arrest may happen during the initial steps or stages of spiritual life. The excitement and triumphs of the first stages may arrest advance and cause a standstill. This may happen before the cradle is out of sight and while the first steps of the Christian toddler are still unsteady.

It is true that Paul called the Corinthian saints *"babes in Christ"* (1 Corinthians 3:1). But this was at the point where their saintship had turned back to carnality and lost its sanctity and strength. Their great sin and backslidings were found in their babyhood—not that they began as babes, but that they stayed babes. Baby Christianity is the popular Christianity of these days. To begin as babes is expected, but to remain babes for forty years is a fearful deformity.

Spiritual stagnation sometimes happens to those in the high echelons of spiritual prominence. It is true that a few of those who have received a great spiritual baptism after conversion have crystallized around this later point of advance. However, a far greater number of preachers and other believers have crystallized around the initial experience of salvation. There may be some specimens of Christian mummies who approached maturity, but the number who were petrified in the dwarfed and cradled state is countless.

SPIRITUAL STAGNATION

However, spiritual stagnation is not confined to the initial steps. Spiritual development's lifeblood may chill and its step halt at the point of highest advance. Many Christians are so enthusiastic over some marked advance, or some higher elevation gained, that they become enchanted with the beautiful and lofty regions. They are lulled to sleep and, like Bunyan's Pilgrim, lose their enthusiasm and are unconscious of their loss. Instead of pressing on with tireless steps, they cover the future with their imaginations. Then, while their minds are filled with fantasies of their advanced positions, they do not realize that their feet have slipped backward, and that they are in the valley again. They are so happy that it is almost impossible to bring them to their senses.

It is difficult to make them understand that there are many weary and toilsome steps between their Red Sea deliverance and the Promised Land. Even after the desert has been crossed, the Jordon has been divided, and their feet have touched the sanctified soil of Canaan, there are many battles to be fought. There are enemies to be destroyed before the good land is all possessed.

It is good to have singing and shouting sanctification. But if it is not joined by marching and fighting faith, it will sing and shout itself as thin as a ghost and as dry as a desert. *"Forgetting those things which are behind, and reaching forth unto those things which are before"* (Philippians 3:13). This is the divine process by which we hold onto what we have by getting more.

Paul's marvelous career was simple, not complex. He summed it up as fighting, running, watching—the three elements of continuous advance. Many great battles have been lost by the demoralizing effects of a halt caused by a partial victory in the earlier part of the conflict. It is not easy to keep in place and march in rank when the spoils of a halfgained victory cover the ground. There is no position this side of heaven that is free from the dangers of spiritual arrest and secure from the Devil's attacks. The conflict and vigilance of advance must mark every step until our feet are within the pearly gates.

Arrested spiritual development, either in the initial or the more advanced stages, is always an exposed position. Spiritual immaturity always leaves us vulnerable to Satan's attacks.

FIFTEEN:

USING OUR DEFENSES

*And unto the angel of the church in Sardis write; These things saith
he that hath the seven Spirits of God, and the seven stars; I know
thy works, that thou hast a name that thou livest, and art dead. Be
watchful, and strengthen the things which remain, that are ready to
die: for I have not found thy works perfect before God. Remember
therefore how thou hast received and heard, and hold fast, and repent.
If therefore thou shalt not watch, I will come on thee as a thief, and
thou shalt not know what hour I will come upon thee. Thou hast a few
names even in Sardis which have not defiled their garments; and they
shall walk with me in white: for they are worthy. He that overcometh,
the same shall be clothed in white raiment; and I will not blot out
his name out of the book of life, but I will confess his name before my
Father, and before his angels.*
—Revelation 3:1–5

Leave no room for the Devil. Be too busy for him. Have no time and no
place for him. Vacant places invite him. The Devil loves a vacuum. A very busy
person himself, he does his biggest business with those who have no business.

The apostle Paul, writing to the Ephesians, gave this direction: *"Neither give place to the devil"* (Ephesians 4:27). Leave no opening, no space for him. Keep him out by prepossession. Keep him out—nose, head, and all. Give him an inch, and he will take a mile.

"Give no place to the Devil." The apostle was writing about how anger can cause us to give full scope to the Devil. He comes into power and has full sway when we relinquish ourselves to the indulgence and continuance of evil passions. Our evil passions are the regions where Satan finds his favorite field and largest sphere of operation. Suppress evil and every tendency to indignation, bitterness, and wrath. Suppress and purge out every heated impulse, every unholy desire, every feeling that is not of God. The Devil's work is futile when gentleness and forgiveness reign in our spirits.

"Resist the devil, and he will flee from you" (James 4:7). This is James's curt directory for getting rid of the Devil. *"Resist"* means "to set one's self against, to withstand." Yield nothing to Satan at any point, but oppose him at every point. Always be against him, belonging to the party of the opposition as far as his plans, suggestions, and ways are concerned.

If we bravely and strongly resist what the Devil proposes, the victory is half won. To hesitate is to lose. To talk it over is to yield; to give an inch is to surrender the whole ground. The Devil cannot stand firmness, decision, and opposition. He is easily defeated if we are determined and uncompromising. Loyalty to God is ruin to Satan.

HOW TO RESIST THE DEVIL

We are taught this same simple, important lesson in Peter, along with an addition:

> *Be sober, be vigilant; because your adversary the devil, as a roaring lion, walketh about, seeking whom he may devour: whom resist stedfast in the faith, knowing that the same afflictions are accomplished in your brethren that are in the world.* (1 Peter 5:8–9)

The first part of this direction refers to the elements of personal character. What we are is of prime consideration in this conflict with the Devil. Strong, good character is fully armed. Character is revealed in all our relationships, duties, and trials. But nowhere is character more telling than in our encounters with Satan.

We must be sober, calm, and collected—free from passion or intemperance. We must always be aware of spiritual dangers and deceptions. If we are vigilant, cautious, and active, we will never be surprised or overcome because of inattention or laziness. We must remain awake because of the full apprehension of the presence of a powerful, dangerous, and cruel Foe. This is our strong defense.

As mentioned earlier, no sorrow is so pathetic as the sorrow of young widowhood. It is a sorrow exposed to Satan's attacks. Paul's direction puts widows on the defensive and guards them against the insidious attacks of the Enemy. *"I will therefore that the younger women marry, bear children, guide the house, give none occasion to the adversary to speak reproachfully. For some are already turned aside after Satan"* (1 Timothy 5:14–15). No defense is more secure against Satan than a life crowned and crowded with unselfish duties. When they are faithfully done, the Devil has no opportunity to speak reproachfully.

James directs us to "resist" (James 4:7)—to set ourselves against the Devil with will and thought, conscience and heart. We must hold the Word of God strictly, strongly, and rigidly. The truth of God inflexibly held will make one invincible to the Devil, unyielding to his assaults. Temptation, toil, and affliction have been put upon God's saints in all ages. But it is by this warfare with the Devil that we are perfected, established, strengthened, and settled.

"Be sober" (1 Peter 5:8), said the apostle, for your adversary, the Devil, walks about. This calm, selfcollected condition, free from passion, and with the full mastery of all our powers, is essential to successful resistance of Satan. A passionate man is a weak man. A cool head and a calm heart are the conditions of successful warfare with the Devil. The apostle added the condition of vigilance: "Be vigilant" (v. 8), he said. Watch, give strict attention, be cautious, be active. Vigilance awakens and sobriety arouses, giving us maximum strength.

The apostle James, in his frank, practical way, said, "Resist the devil, and he will flee from you" (James 4:7). "Resist" means to set yourself against and make no concession to the Enemy. We must meet the Devil only to fight him, and we must talk with him only to withstand him. "Whom resist," said Peter, "stedfast in the faith" (1 Peter 5:9). That is, be solid, firm, rigid in the faith. Be fixed in your beliefs, because the liberal person has no Devil—only a very friendly one, and it does not fight against him.

THE SUPREME DEFENSE

If the spirit of forgiveness is always maintained and constantly exercised, it is a supreme defense against the attacks of Satan. An unforgiving spirit is not only Satan's widest door into our hearts, but also his strongest invitation and warmest welcome.

Paul urged a spirit of forgiveness as a barrier against the Devil's entrance into our lives. Paul also hastened to close the door to him by his own readiness to forgive even in advance.

> *To whom ye forgive any thing, I forgive also: for if I forgave any thing, to whom I forgave it, for your sakes forgave I it in the person of Christ; lest Satan should get an advantage of us: for we are not ignorant of his devices.* (2 Corinthians 2:10–11)

A spirit of forgiveness that is free from all bitterness, revenge, or retaliation has freed itself from the conditions that invite Satan, and has effectually barred his entrance. The quickest way to keep Satan out is to keep the spirit of forgiveness in. The Devil is never deeper in hell nor farther removed from us than when we can pray, *"Father, forgive them; for they know not what they do"* (Luke 23:34).

> *A spirit of forgiveness that is free from all bitterness, revenge, or retaliation has freed itself from the conditions that invite Satan, and has effectually barred his entrance. The quickest way to keep Satan out is to keep the spirit of forgiveness in.*

The Devil's work is much helped or much hindered by the spirit of the servants of Christ. Gentleness is becoming to the servants of Christ not only as a beautiful adorning but also as the foundation stone. Meekness and gentleness win men, for they imitate Christ's character. Rudeness, impatience, and contention are not good recruiting officers for Christ.

> And the servant of the Lord must not strive; but be gentle unto all men, apt to teach, patient, in meekness instructing those that oppose themselves; if God peradventure will give them repentance to the acknowledging of the truth; and that they may recover themselves out of the snare of the devil, who are taken captive by him at his will.
>
> (2 Timothy 2:24–26)

YOUR CHIEF WEAPON

The Devil is to be overcome. He is not only a hypocrite, full of quiet, slippery, and artful ways, but he is also a man of war. He is a renowned warrior of many campaigns and many battlefields. His boldness and skill were tested in heaven. Angels were his enemies when heaven was the scene of his conflict and his defeat. Yet he still fights. It takes strong young blood with fire and valor to meet him and conquer.

The Devil must be defeated. Victory over him is victory all along the line. It takes strength and courage to overcome him. He is no coward, no disheartened enemy. The zeal and strength of mature faith is absolutely necessary in this battle.

The Word of God is the conquering sword in this warfare. The believer who has his quiver full of divine arrows is swift, strong, penetrating, and deadly to Satan and to sin. He will be more than a conqueror (Romans 8:37) over the Devil. The weapon used by the Son of God in His conflict with Satan was the Word of God, and by it, He conquered.

"I have written unto you, young men, because ye are strong, and the word of God abideth in you, and ye have overcome the wicked one" (1 John 2:14). John, the apostle of love who was nearest the heart of his Lord, was full of this victory. John's love was too genuine to shrink itself into sickly sentiment or evaporate the Devil into a mere influence. His experience was too profound and his memory too fresh to believe in an impersonal Devil or an impersonal Christ. John carried the scars of the battles with the adversary of his soul. He had witnessed the conflicts of many young soldiers. His soul had shared in their triumph and recorded their victories.

Fight the Devil and overcome him. This is John's method of becoming *"fathers"* (vv. 13–14) in spiritual power, rooted, grounded, and perfected. According to John, overcoming the Devil is prerequisite to overcoming the world.

THE SAFEST PLACE

The mighty newbirth experience makes a man watchful like a sentinel at his post. When the Enemy in power is massed in the front, the believer is like a watchman. He stands on the walls of the beleaguered city like a guard over a royal prisoner. This keeping and guarding himself is safety against Satan's inflaming touch.

The faithful, vigilant Christian keeps himself pure, and Satan comes and finds nothing in him. (See John 14:30.) Every vantage point is barred and sleeplessly watched.

> *We know that whosoever is born of God sinneth not; but he that is begotten of God keepeth himself, and that wicked one toucheth him not. And we know that we are of God, and the whole world lieth in wickedness ["the evil one," RV].* (1 John 5:18–19)

"Keeping ourselves" is the surest pledge that Satan will not keep us.

"Watch" is the keynote of safety. The Devil works on us with a thousand instruments, comes to us in a thousand ways, administers a thousand rebukes, and assaults by a thousand surprises. Watchfulness at all times is our only safety. We must not remain wide awake only when we see his form and fear his presence, but we must also remain wide awake to see him when he is not to be seen. We must repel him when he comes with any one of his ten thousand disguises—this is our wisest and safest course.

No cry of alarm is so frequent in the New Testament as the call to watch. No call hurts Satan so vitally or defeats him so readily as the call to watch. Being on the watchtower prevents all surprises and is essential to victory at all times.

The Son of God makes this call the keynote in many of His teachings. It is a call to be sleepless, to be vigilant, to be always ready. It is an image drawn from shepherds. In Jacob's indignant defense and protest against Laban, we see the image of the watchful shepherd: *"In the day the drought consumed me, and the frost by night; and my sleep departed from mine eyes"* (Genesis 31:40).

To watch is to be opposed to all listlessness. It implies a wakeful state as if in the presence of some great danger. It is a cautious state untouched by any slumbering influence. Drowsiness and bewilderment are gone. It quickens us against laziness and spiritual sloth.

Read how the church at Sardis was called to the exercise of watchfulness. She was put to sleep by the dulling effects of a fancy church exterior and a proper religious structure. (See Revelation 3:1–6.) The Ephesian church was advised to combine watching with persevering prayer (Ephesians 6:18). The Corinthian church was urged to watch and stand fast (1 Corinthians 16:13). The Colossians were exhorted to *"continue in prayer, and watch in the same"* (Colossians 4:2). The Thessalonians were to *"watch and be sober"* (1 Thessalonians 5:6).

Timothy, the young preacher, was to *"watch…in all things"* (2 Timothy 4:5). Peter's call was, *"Be ye therefore sober, and watch unto prayer,"* because the solemn end of all things is quickly approaching (1 Peter 4:7). Again he said, *"Be sober, be vigilant; because your adversary the devil, as a roaring lion, walketh about, seeking whom he might devour"* (1 Peter 5:8).

In Revelation we have the startling call, *"Behold, I come as a thief. Blessed is he that watcheth, and keepeth his garments, lest he walk naked, and they see his shame"* (Revelation 16:15).

The most frequent call to watchfulness was from our Lord. He said, *"Watch, therefore; for ye know not what hour your Lord doth come"* (Matthew 24:42). Again He called us to exercise this great grace: *"Watch therefore, for ye know neither the day nor the hour wherein the Son of man cometh"* (Matthew 25:13). Repeatedly, He calls us to *"watch ye therefore"* (Mark 13:35).

The herald cry and the trumpet call from Him to us is to be awake—to be fully awake, to be tremendously awake.

"Watch ye therefore, and pray always, that ye may be accounted worthy to escape all these things that shall come to pass, and to stand before the Son of

man" (Luke 21:36). "*Watch and pray*" (Matthew 26:41), He charged His disciples, and so He charges us to "*watch and pray, that ye enter not into temptation: the spirit indeed is willing, but the flesh is weak*" (v. 41). Still the flesh is weak, and watchfulness must always be united with prayer while we are in the flesh.

SATAN'S GREATEST FEAR

The martyrs who are faithful unto death, who love not their lives unto death, are victors in this warfare with the Devil:

And I heard a loud voice saying in heaven, Now is come salvation, and strength, and the kingdom of our God, and the power of his Christ: for the accuser of our brethren is cast down, which accused them before our God day and night. And they overcame him by the blood of the Lamb, and by the word of their testimony; and they loved not their lives unto the death. (Revelation 12:10–11)

"*The blood of the everlasting covenant*" (Hebrews 13:20) must be sprinkled on the warriors who are victors against Satan. They must have a clear, conscious experience of the saving power of that blood. They must have the ability to be martyrs and witness before any company at any cost. Their characteristics mark their devotion to Christ and their experience of His salvation. "[He] *is mine, and I am his*" (Song of Solomon 2:16).

Satan cannot stand against a display of the blood of Christ. He turns pale at every view of Calvary. The flowing wounds are the signals of Satan's retreat. A heart sprinkled with the blood is holy ground on which he dares not tread. Satan trembles and cowers in the presence of the blood-sprinkled warrior.

Satan fears the power of that blood more than the attack of a legion of archangels. The blood is like the charge of an irresistible military force that destroys everything in its path. It is the blood applied and the testimony of its application that Satan fears. The martyr who is a witness of the power of that blood is more a barrier against Satan than a wall of fire. An experience of the atoning blood is heaven's infallible protection against Satan. Those in heaven overcame the Devil in this way. We also overcome him by the blood of the Lamb and the word of our testimony.

SIXTEEN:

WEAPONS THAT WORK

Finally, my brethren, be strong in the Lord, and in the power of his might. Put on the whole armour of God, that ye may be able to stand against the wiles of the devil. For we wrestle not against flesh and blood, but against principalities, against powers, against the rulers of the darkness of this world, against spiritual wickedness in high places. Wherefore take unto you the whole armour of God, that ye may be able to withstand in the evil day, and having done all, to stand. Stand therefore, having your loins girt about with truth, and having on the breastplate of righteousness; and your feet shod with the preparation of the gospel of peace; above all, taking the shield of faith, wherewith ye shall be able to quench all the fiery darts of the wicked. And take the helmet of salvation, and the sword of the Spirit, which is the word of God: praying always with all prayer and supplication in the Spirit, and watching thereunto with all perseverance and supplication for all saints.
—Ephesians 6:10–18

Many prayers have missed the mark and been in vain because they were not combined with careful vigilance. There are many sad failures in the Christian life because watchfulness failed. The Devil's easiest target is a sleepy Christian. Many Christians have lost their souls because they failed to stay alert to Satan's attacks. Eternal vigilance is the price of political liberty. No less a price must be paid for our spiritual safety. The foolish virgins missed heaven because they failed in this virtue. Watchfulness would have brought them, along with the Bridegroom, into the high joys of heaven's most celebrated hour. (See Matthew 25:1–13.)

In the sixth chapter of Ephesians, as stated above, all the weapons of warfare with the Devil and his legions are described. The sources of defense and victory are also given. In this passage, we have a view of the strenuous conflict and the battlefield on which the issues of eternity are tossed.

SATAN'S ARMY

"For we wrestle not against flesh and blood, but against principalities, against powers, against the rulers of the darkness of this world, against spiritual wickedness in high places." The Christian's battle is with the Devil and his methods. Satan's struggle is arranged with order, wisdom, and skill.

Principalities and powers are under his management and subject to his orders. They are his lieutenants, his prime ministers, his captain generals who carry out his orders and represent him fully. They are the world rulers with worldwide control and power. They master and control all the evil forces of the world. The Devil and his high comrades are world rulers. Their might is as extensive as the world. Theirs is a fearful rule for evil, against the good and against man. Their subordinates, the rank and file, are innumerable and invincible, except to a Godequipped man.

What a vast and powerful array of aggressive, vicious, and cruel enemies. They are in heavenly places, the very place where Christ's power is located. These evil powers are over us, above us, and around us. They are too mighty for us. Against this invisible, innumerable, allpowerful, and vast array, we wrestle. Wrestling is a close conflict. It is an intense and difficult conflict that tests all strength and strains every fiber. It is handtohand, foottofoot, close contact.

This conflict is not with men, though men may give us much opposition in our Christian course. Our chief trouble and our great war is not with man but with all the mighty evil forces of the Devil. It is a life-and-death struggle—a war for heaven and hell, for time and eternity.

THE CHRISTIAN SOLDIER

The Christian must be a soldier by birth, by fortune, by trade. The most essential quality of a divine soldier is that he is not entangled *"with the affairs of this life"* (2 Timothy 2:4). The elements of selfdenial, courage, and endurance are the vital characteristics of this military training.

Strength is the fruit of these high qualities. But it is strength far beyond the Christian soldier's own strength. *"Strong in the Lord, and in the power of his might"* (Ephesians 6:10). In preparation for this war, the soldier must look beyond himself. The strength of God, the very strength of God's almightiness, must be his.

The ability to stand, to fight, to conquer, and to drive the Foe from the field will be found in God's armor. God's strength is imparted through God's armor. No power short of God can enable us to meet the Devil. No partial equipment will suffice.

In the passage from Ephesians, we are charged twice to make doubly sure to take the whole armor (Ephesians 6:11, 13). We take God by taking His armor. We must make His armor our own. We put on God by putting on His armor—not outside but inside, not objective but subjective, not physical but spiritual. Christ made the armor, and the Holy Spirit puts it on us and makes it ours.

> *The ability to stand, to fight, to conquer, and to drive the Foe from the field will be found in God's armor. God's strength is imparted through God's armor. No power short of God can enable us to meet the Devil. No partial equipment will suffice.*

We have to fight through to the end, *"and having done all, to stand."* We must first withstand and then stand. We gain and hold and then advance. Stand ready for the fight and stand in the fight.

TRUTH AND RIGHTEOUSNESS

We must be strong for the *"truth in the inward parts"* (Psalm 51:6). We are not imaginary soldiers fighting an imaginary war—all is real and true.

Because he is truthful, a girded soldier is strong, prepared, and intense in his fight. Truth is the ornament of a jeweled belt, a diamond set in gold. We must conquer the Devil by truth as the strength and support of our lives. We know the truth and have the truth because we have Christ who is the truth.

Heart righteousness makes head righteousness and life righteousness. We cannot fight without heart righteousness. The *"breastplate of righteousness"* protects the heart and makes us feel right. The old heart cannot be made right by the most skillful craftsman or by the most correct rituals. No tinkering on the old heart can make it right. It is as hard as a stone and as crooked as the Jordan. No melting can make it soft, and no human effort can make it straight. We need a new heart, soft as flesh and washed whiter than snow in the blood of Christ. A piece of Christ's heart—perfect, right, pure, and good—is what is needed.

PREPARATION AND FAITH

The feet must be shod with a preparation that is always ready to go, to do, and to suffer. This means no slow movements or reluctant doing of God's will. Being off guard creates a general unreadiness for life or death, for earth or heaven, for sacrifice or service, for doing or for suffering. It cuts the nerve of Christian valor and lays us open to surprises and crushing defeats. "Always ready" is the soldier's attitude of safety, and being ready to move precedes victory. Wakeful vigilance assures us of victory against the Devil.

The *"shield of faith"* is the allimportant and allcovering piece of armor. The Devil lets his fiery, poisoned darts fly, but faith catches them as they are directed at head or heart, and quenches them.

Do you believe all victories are possible to the soldier who is valiant and strong in faith? There has never been a battle planned by hell's most gifted strategist that can conquer faith. All his flaming and terrible darts fall harmless as they strike against the shield of faith. *"These all died in faith"* (Hebrews 11:13). Faith made their death the crowning point. Faith brought to their dying hour the spoils of their victories.

THE HELMET AND SWORD

"The helmet" protects the head. Bear in mind that headsalvation and heartsalvation, real and full, are stronger than brass to protect the head. A

heart fully saved holds the head firmly to truth and righteousness, as the anchor holds the ship in stormiest seas. *"The hope of salvation,"* said Paul in Thessalonians, is the helmet (1 Thessalonians 5:8).

The Christian soldier must put heaven strongly in his head and heart. He must see heaven, feel heaven, and keep heaven in the eye and in the heart all the time. He will stand with unsteady step if heaven seems far off. He will fight feebly if heaven is dimly seen. The full sight of heaven will give strength to his loins, zeal to his faith, glory to his future, and victory to the present.

The head will never be pierced while hope is its helmet. Nurture hope, strengthen hope, and brighten hope, for *"we are saved by hope"* (Romans 8:24). We must *"abound in hope, through the power of the Holy Ghost"* (Romans 15:13).

"The sword," the aggressive and powerful weapon, is the Word of God. The Spirit wields it and brings death to all our foes. The Word of God is our battlefield and victorious weapon. On it we stand and fight. With it we deal with and defeat and ruin every foe. The Christian soldier is *"not [to] live by bread alone, but by every word...of God"* (Matthew 4:4). We cannot make too much of the Word of God. Christ foiled Satan with it. If we are to be valiant, true, and invincible, we also must have the Word of God dwelling in us richly (Colossians 3:16).

The shield of our faith is the basis of our prayers and the essence of our girded truth. Head, hands, and hearts must be filled and saturated with God's Word; by it we live and by it we grow. It is our battle call and the sign by which we conquer. It is a glittering royal blade against all the assaults of Satan. "It is written" goes like steel to the heart of Satan.

As a weapon of defense and offense, God has magnified His Word above all His name. Those who are filled with God's Word are armed against all Satan's wiles and his devices. God's Word is *"quick, and powerful, and sharper than any twoedged sword, piercing even to the dividing asunder of soul and spirit, and of the joints and marrow"* (Hebrews 4:12). Satan feels it penetrating his joints and marrow, dissolving into weakness all his strength, and making foolish all his wisest plans.

THE WEAPON OF PRAYER

The soldiers in the warfare against the Devil must understand how to wear the armor of *"all prayer."* The demand is for *"all prayer"* at all seasons, in the intensest form, with a deep sense of personal need for God. Prayer must deepen and intensify into supplication. The Holy Spirit will help us into this kind of mighty praying and clothe us with this irresistible power of prayer.

This intense conflict with the Devil requires sleepless vigilance, midnight vigils, and a wakefulness that cannot be surprised. It also requires a perseverance that knows neither halting, fainting, nor depression. This kind of praying knows by clear spiritual intelligence what it needs. The prayer warrior knows the unlimited provisions that are available to supply all his needs. He knows the necessity of perseverance in prayer until the need is supplied and the provision is secured.

This kind of praying holds itself in loving sympathy with the entire family of God, making their conflicts, dangers, and needs its own. It is on the line of battle with the whole family of God. It takes on their enemies, their safety, and their dangers. *"Supplication for all saints"* gives victory to every saint. The line of battle is one. Defeat or victory must come to all. The soldier fully equipped in God's armor is a veteran against the Devil and invincible to all of his attacks.

It is not an easy thing to pray. Behind the praying there must lie the conditions of prayer. These conditions are possible, but they cannot be achieved in a moment by the prayerless person. They are always available to the faithful and holy, but cannot exist in a frivolous, negligent, and lazy spirit.

Prayer does not stand alone. It is not an isolated performance. Prayer is connected to all the duties of the Christian life. Prayer issues from a character that is made up of the elements of a vigorous and commanding faith. Prayer honors God, acknowledges His being, exalts His power, adores His providence, and secures His aid.

A skeptic would rationalize and cry out against devotion, charging that it does nothing but pray. But to pray well is to do all things well. If it is true that devotion does nothing but pray, then it really does do nothing at

510 *E. M. Bounds on Prayer & Spiritual Warfare*

all, for the conditions of prayer are the sum of *all* the energized forces and all the duties of practical working Christianity.

THE POWER OF PRAYER

Prayer brings God into the situation with commanding force. *"Ask me of things to come concerning my sons,"* says God, *"and concerning the work of my hands command ye me"* (Isaiah 45:11).

We are charged in God's Word: *"Pray without ceasing"* (1 Thessalonians 5:17). *"In every thing by prayer"* (Philippians 4:6). *"Continuing instant in prayer"* (Romans 12:12). *"Pray every where"* (1 Timothy 2:8). *"Praying always"* (Colossians 1:3).

The promise is as unlimited as the command is comprehensive. *"All things, whatsoever ye shall ask in prayer, believing, ye shall receive"* (Matthew 21:22). Jesus said, *"Whatsoever ye shall ask"* (John 14:13); *"if ye shall ask any thing"* (John 14:14); *"ye shall ask what ye will, and it shall be done unto you"* (John 15:7); and *"whatsoever ye shall ask the Father...he will give it you"* (John 16:23).

If there is anything not involved in *"all things whatsoever,"* or not found in the phrase, *"ask any thing,"* then these things can be left out of prayer. Language could not cover a wider range or involve more fully every detail of life. These statements are only samples of the allcomprehending possibilities of prayer under the promises of God to those who meet the conditions of right praying.

These passages, though, give only a general outline of the immense regions over which prayer extends its influence. The effect of prayer reaches and secures good things from regions that cannot be covered by language or thought. Paul exhausted his language and thought when he was praying. Still, he was conscious of necessities not covered, realms of good not reached, and of battles over enemies not conquered.

Paul covered these undiscovered regions by this general plea: *"Unto him that is able to do exceeding abundantly above all that we ask or think, according to the power that worketh in us"* (Ephesians 3:20). The promise is, *"Call unto me, and I will answer thee, and show thee great and mighty things, which thou knowest not"* (Jeremiah 33:3).

ABOUT THE AUTHOR

E. M. (Edward McKendree) Bounds (1835–1913) was born on August 15, 1835, in a small northeastern Missouri town. He attended a one-room school in Shelbyville, where his father served as a county clerk, and he was admitted to the bar shortly before he reached the age of nineteen. An avid reader of the Scriptures and an ardent admirer of John Wesley's sermons, Bounds practiced law until the age of twenty-four, when he suddenly felt called to preach the gospel.

His first pastorate was in the nearby town of Monticello, Missouri. Yet, in 1861, while he was pastor of a Methodist Episcopal church in Brunswick, the Civil War began, and Bounds was arrested by Union troops and charged for sympathizing with the Confederacy. He was made a prisoner of war and was held for a year and a half before being transferred to Memphis, Tennessee, and finally securing his release.

Armed only with an unquenchable desire to serve God, Bounds traveled nearly one hundred miles on foot to join General Pierce's command in Mississippi. Soon afterward he was made chaplain to the Confederate troops in Missouri. After the defeat of General John Hood's troops at Nashville, Tennessee, Bounds was again among those who were captured and held until swearing loyalty to the United States.

After the war, Bounds pastored churches in Nashville, Tennessee; Selma, Alabama; and St. Louis, Missouri. It was in Selma that he met Emma Barnett, whom he later married in 1876, and with whom he had three children, one of whom died at the age of six. After Emma's death, in 1887, bounds married Emma's cousin, Harriet Barnett, who survived him. The family included their five children, as well as two daughters from his first marriage.

While he was in St. Louis, Bounds accepted a position as associate editor for the regional Methodist journal, the *St. Louis Advocate*. Then, after only nineteen months, he moved to Nashville to become the editor of the *Christian Advocate*, the weekly paper for the entire Methodist Episcopal denomination in the South.

The final seventeen years of his life were spent with his family in Washington, Georgia, where both Emma and Harriet had grown up. Most of the time he spent reading, writing, and praying, but he often took an active part in revival ministry. Bounds was also in the habit of rising at four o'clock each morning in order to pray to God, for the great cares of the world were always upon his heart. He died on August 24, 1913, still relatively unknown to most of the Christian sphere.

Since the time of the apostles, no man besides Edward McKendree Bounds has left such a rich inheritance of research into the life of prayer. Prayer was as natural to him as breathing the air. He made prayer first and foremost in his life because he knew it as the strongest link between man and God. In the time of E. M. Bounds, human weakness, through prayer, could access the power of the overcoming Son of God, Jesus Christ. The same is true to this day.